KB236272

Total *iBT* TOEFL
Writing

Total *iBT* TOEFL
Writing

2006. 10. 17 / 1판 1쇄 인쇄
2006. 10. 25 / 1판 1쇄 발행

지은이_ 이을기 · 채미영
발행인_ 김용성

발행처_ **LNBpress**
등 록_ 2005년 12월09일 ㅣ 제6-772호

주 소_ 130-831 서울시 동대문구 이문2동 346-41호 영일B/D 202호
전 화_ 962-9154 ㅣ 팩 스_ 962-9156

정가_18,000원 ISBN 89-91999-07-7 13740

Total *iBT* TOEFL
Writing

이을기 · 채미영 박사
공저

LNBPRESS

Congratulation Message

Congratulation
Message

This book skillfully combines both the author's theoretical knowledge of English as a Foreign Language Education and practical expertise of an experienced EFL teacher. The systematic approach to test preparation found in this book should be extremely helpful to EFL learners preparing to take the new generation of iBT TOEFL test.

Maria Estela Brisk Ph.D Professor
Lynch School of Education Boston College

추천의 말

토탈 iBT TOEFL은 저자가 지닌 EFL 영어 교육에 대한 이론적 지식과 EFL 영어 교사로서 현장에서 얻은 전문성을 잘 연계해 만든 책이다. 이 책은 시험 준비에 대한 체계적인 접근을 통해 차세대 iBT TOEFL을 준비하는 EFL 영어 학습자들에게 커다란 도움을 줄 것이다.

보스턴 칼리지 린치 교육대학원
마리아 브리스크 박사

이중언어교육(Bilingual Education)이론의 세계적인 권위자인 마리아 브리스크 교수는 이 책의 저자인 채미영 박사가 보스턴 대학 박사 과정에 재학할 당시 지도교수였고, 현재는 보스턴 칼리지 린치 교육대학원 교수로 재직중이다.

대부분의 한국 학생들은 iBT 토플을 두려운 마음으로 맞이하고 있다. 말하기와 쓰기를 못하면 좋은 점수를 받을 수 없게 되었으니 학생들의 걱정도 이해가 된다. 하지만 조금 더 생각해 보면 iBT 토플은 영어 공부에 있어서 더할 나위 없는 축복이란 것을 알 수 있다. iBT 토플은 점수와 영어 실력이 함께 가는 정말 시험다운 시험이기 때문이다.

지금까지는 시험 공부와 영어 실력 키우기가 따로 놀았고, 시험 점수와 영어 실력이 따로 놀았다. 열심히 준비해서 토익 고득점을 받아도 영어로 이메일 한 통 못 쓰고, 죽어라 공부해서 토플 고득점을 받은 유학생이 수업을 못 따라가는 게 현실이었다. 그러나 영어의 4대 영역 전부를 통합적으로 평가하는 iBT 토플은 다르다. iBT 토플에서는 시험 준비 자체가 영어 실력을 높여 주는 의미 있는 과정이고, 시험 점수가 영어 실력을 말해 주는 의미 있는 결과인 것이다.

제작상의 어려움 때문에 실전 수준의 iBT 토플 교재를 구하기가 어려운 현실 속에 실전 수준의 문제로 구성된 Total iBT TOEFL 5종 시리즈가 실제 시험 대비에 큰 도움을 줄 것으로 기대한다. 또한 부록으로 제공되는 Total Note-taking System은 iBT 토플을 여는 열쇠 역할을 할 것이라 믿는다. Total iBT TOEFL 5종 시리즈를 장대 삼아 iBT 100점을 뛰어넘는 학생들이 많이 나오기를 바란다.

Total iBT TOEFL 5종 시리즈를 만들기 시작한 지 벌써 삼 년 가까운 시간이 지났다. 그동안 여러모로 도움을 주신 LNBPRESS의 김용성 사장님, 복잡한 교재 5권을 멋진 책으로 꾸며주신 한석희 실장님과 편집부 안은영 씨, 그리고 교재 5권 전체에 걸쳐 꼼꼼한 도움을 주면서도 통역대학원 수석을 놓치지 않은 이정은 선생님께 고마움을 전한다. 마지막으로 엄마 아빠가 토플 교재로 씨름하는 동안에도 맑고 밝게 자라 준 딸 지형에게 고마운 마음을 전한다.

2006년 8월
이을기/채미영

Total Note-taking의 장점

1. 청취력을 높여준다.
2. 들으면서 집중력을 유지하는 데 큰 도움이 된다.
3. 들은 내용을 체계적이고 논리적으로 복기할 수 있도록 해준다.
4. 영어 어순에 따라 정리되는 장점이 있어서 영어로 말하거나 쓰기를 할 때 유용하다.

왜 Total Note-taking인가?

iBT TOEFL의 시대가 도래하면서 새롭게 등장한 용어가 바로 Note-taking이다.

한국외대 동시통역대학원의 비밀병기 Note-taking의 혁신적 진화

통역사들이 익힌 Note-taking 기법을 iBT TOEFL에 적용하려면 다소의 개편이 필요하다. 영어에서 한국어로 혹은 한국어에서 영어로 나가는 통역과 달리, iBT TOEFL에서는 영어로 듣고 바로 영어로 말을 하고 글을 써야 하기 때문이다.

Total Note-taking은 이러한 차이를 염두에 두고 통역사용 Note-taking을 개편하여 개발된 최초의 iBT TOEFL 전용 Note-taking 훈련법인 것이다.

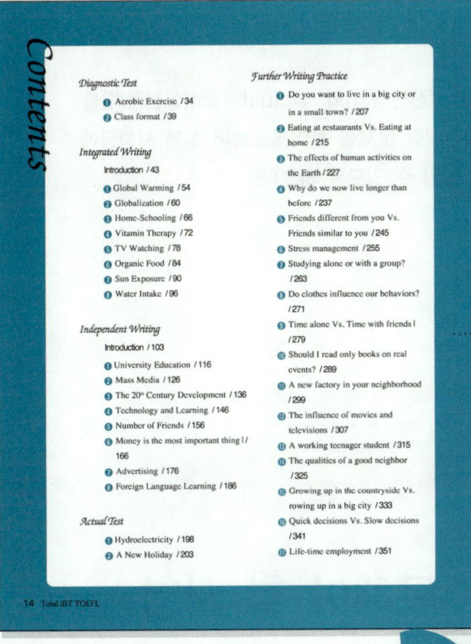

Contents

■ 2가지 Type의 Writing 유형 속에 8개의 기본강의와 진단평가, 실전평가 등 10가지로 구성되어 있으며, 이를 바탕으로 기본실력 배양과 함께 iBT TOEFL Writing의 경향을 한눈에 익힐 수 있도록 하였다.

■ Diagnostic과 Actual Test는 실제시험과 똑같이 구성한 것으로 본서와 함께 제공되는 CD를 통해 실전과 같은 환경에서 문제를 풀 수 있도록 했다.

■ ETS에서 출제하는 Writing 문제유형은 다음과 같이 두 가지로 나뉜다.

① Integrated Writing
② Independent Writing

■ 각 type마다 서로 다른 8개의 주제로 구성하여 다양한 주제로 type별 유형을 완벽하게 파악할 수 있도록 하였다.

Contents

Diagnostic Test

1 Aerobic Exercise /34
2 Class format /39

Integrated Writing

Introduction /43

1 Global Warming /54
2 Globalization /60
3 Home-Schooling /66
4 Vitamin Therapy /72
5 TV Watching /78
6 Organic Food /84
7 Sun Exposure /90
8 Water Intake /96

Diagnostic Test(진단평가)와 Actual Test(실전평가)를 CD에 담아, 실전처럼 문제를 풀어봄으로써 실제 시험장에서의 응용력을 높일 수 있도록 하였다.

2개의 type별 구성과 주목해야 할 사항

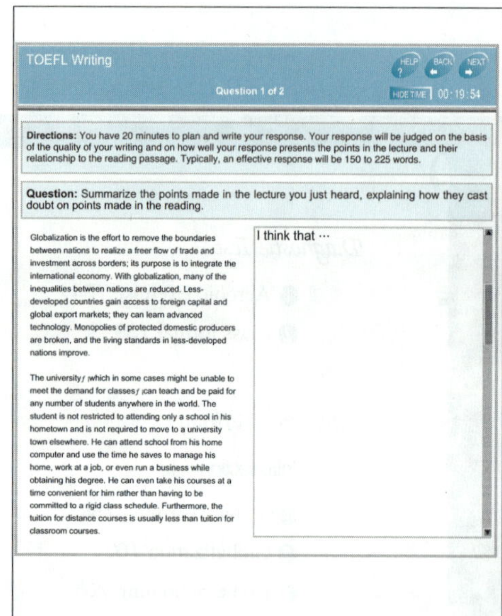

• *Integrated Writing*
- Reading -

Writing Task 1에 등장하는 Reading 자료는 학술적 주제에 관련된 약 230–300단어 길이의 지문으로 이를 3분 이내에 읽어야 한다. 지문의 주제는 Biology, Geology, US History, Astronomy, Sociology 등 다양한 학문 분야를 망라한다.

- **Integrated Writing**
  - Listening -

  Writing Task 1에 등장하는 Listening 자료도 학술적인 내용을 담고 있으며 교수의 일인 강의 형식이다. 길이는 약 2분 정도이며 강의 주제는 Reading 자료와 같지만 이와 대조되는 내용이 제시된다.

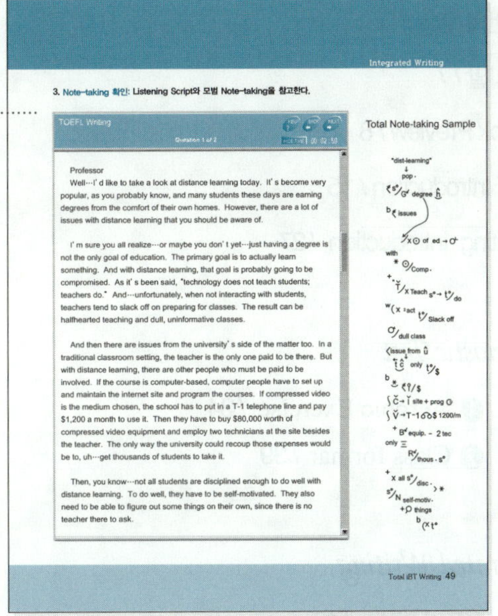

- **Independent Writing**

  Writing Task 2는 주어진 주제에 대해 30분 내에 최소 300단어 길이의 Essay를 써야 한다. 쓰기 능력만 평가하기 때문에 독립형 쓰기 (Independent Writing)라고 불린다.

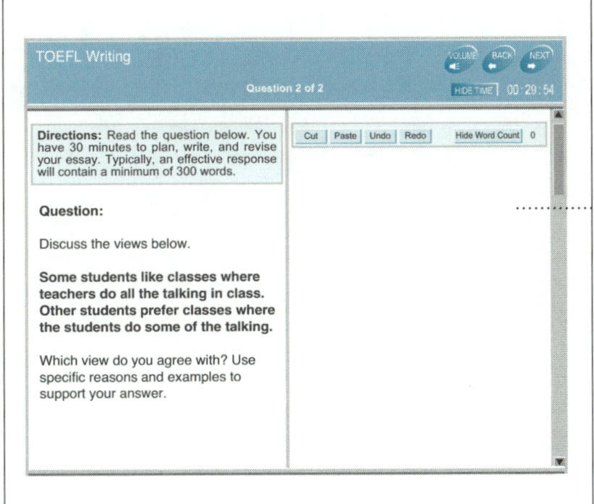

Contents

Total iBT TOEFL

Introduction

혁명적으로 달라진 iBT TOEFL의 개시

혁명적으로 달라진 iBT(internet-Based Test) 토플이 도입되었다. 차세대 iBT 토플은 제 3세대 토플 시험이다. 종이와 연필로 보던 PBT 토플이 1세대였고 이를 대체하며 2000년 10월 한국에 도입된 CBT 토플이 2세대였다. 6년 전 PBT에서 CBT 토플로 바뀔 때에도 Writing이 새로 추가되는 것에 대한 불안감이 컸다. 하지만 3세대 iBT 토플이 불러올 변화의 규모와 내용은 CBT 토플과는 비교가 안 될 정도로 혁명적이다. iBT 토플은 작게는 토플을 준비하는 학생들에게, 크게는 한국 영어 교육 전체에 엄청난 변화를 가져올 것이다.

Speaking / Writing이 총점의 절반을 차지한다.

토플 시험을 주관하는 미국의 ETS (Educational Testing Service)가 밝혔듯이 iBT 토플은 영어를 외국어로 사용하는 학생들의 영어 능력을 통합적으로 평가한다. 통합적인 평가를 위해 iBT 토플 시험의 출제 영역과 내용이 대폭 바뀌었다. 먼저 기존 토플에는 없던 Speaking 영역이 추가되었다. 더구나 Speaking은 보조적인 역할이 아닌 6개의 문제를 지닌 당당한 시험 영역으로 추가된 것이다. Writing 역시 작성해야 하는 Essay 숫자가 2개로 늘어나면서 독립적인 문제 영역으로 위상이 대폭 격상되었다. 이에 따라 iBT 토플에서는 주관식 문제 유형인 Speaking과 Writing이 전체 시험점수 120점의 절반인 60점을 차지하게 되었다.

진짜 영어 실력을 요구하는 통합형 문제

시험 영역의 변화 못지 않게 iBT 토플의 시험 내용에도 혁명적인 변화가 있다. 통합형 문제가 바로 그것이다. 기존 CBT 토플에서는 각 시험 영역이 별개의 문제로 출제되었다. 하지만 iBT 토플에서는 읽고-듣고-말하기, 듣고-말하기, 읽고-듣고-쓰기와 같이 2개 이상의 문제 영역을 연계해서 테스트하는 통합형 문제가 출제 된다. 지금까지는 읽기만 잘하거나 듣기만 잘해도 기본 점수는 받을 수 있었다. 하지만 이제는 Reading/Listening/Speaking/Writing을 고르게 잘 해야만 의미있는 토플 점수를 받을 수 있게 되었다. 적어도 토플 시험에 있어서는 문법만 달달 외고 있는 사람, 영어 청취만 잘 되는 사람은 더 이상 영어 고수라는 주장을 할 수 없게 되었다. 영어 능력의 전 영역을 통합적으로 평가하는

iBT 토플의 등장은 부분적인 영어 능력만을 파편적으로 측정하는 TOEIC이나 TEPS 같은 시험들을 초라한 시험으로 전락시킬 것이다.

iBT TOEFL의 구성과 출제 순서

출제 순서	시험 문제	시간	점수
1. Reading	3-5개의 지문 / 지문당 12-14개 문항	60-100분	30점
2. Listening	4-6개의 강의(Lecture) / 강의당 6개 문항	60-90분	30점
Break		10분	
3. Speaking	6개 문제: 2개의 독립형 말하기(Independent Speaking) 4개의 통합형 말하기(Integrated Speaking)	20분	30점
4. Writing	2개 문제: 1개의 통합형 쓰기 문제(Integrated Writing) 1개의 독립형 쓰기 문제(Independent Writing)	(총 50분) 20분 30분	30점

iBT TOEFL은 CBT와 어떻게 다른가?

시험 영역별 차이

Speaking

iBT에 새로 추가되는 영역으로 독립형 2문제와 통합형 4문제 등 총 6개의 문제가 출제된다. 통합형 문제 4개는 읽고-듣고-말하기 2문제와 듣고-말하기 2문제로 구성되어 있다. 미국에 있는 채점관에게 녹음파일이 보내져 채점되며 각 문제마다 최하 0점에서 최고 4점의 점수가 부여된다.

Writing

CBT에서는 보조적인 위치였지만 iBT에서는 4대 영역 중의 하나로 당당한 위치를 차지한다. 작성하는 Essay가 2개로 늘면서 CBT에서 출제되던 독립형 Essay에 더해 통합형 Essay (읽고-듣고-쓰기) 문제가 추가 되었다. Writing은 각 Essay마다 최하 0점에서 최고 5점의 점수가 부여된다

Structure (문법)

한국 학생들이 비교적 강세였던 문법 영역은 iBT에서는 사라진다. Speaking과 Writing 영역에서 통합적 영어 능력의 일부로 간접적으로만 평가된다. 하지만 문법을 위한 문법은 iBT에서는 사라진 것이다.

Reading

지문이 CBT 보다 2배 정도 길어졌고 난이도 또한 높아졌다. 지문의 핵심 내용을 차트로 분류하거나 요약하는 배점 높은 문제가 새로 추가되었다.

Listening

a. CBT 토플의 짧은 대화, 즉 Part A가 사라지고 긴 강의만 출제된다. 대학 생활과 관련된 대화(Conversations in an Academic Setting), 토론식 강의(Interactive Lectures), 일인 강의(Monologue Lectures)의 3가지 유형이 출제된다. 듣기 분량이 3분에서 5분 정도로 CBT보다 대폭 길어졌다.

b. 문제에 등장하는 대화자들의 발음도 미국 대학에서 실제 접하게 되는 다양한 영어 발음을 반영하는 방향으로 변경되었다. iBT Listening에서는 미국에서 실제로 사용되는 자연스러운 어투와 표현이 많이 등장하며 문제 Set 하나당 적어도 강의 한 개는 영국이나 호주 억양을 가진 원어민이 읽는다.

c. 어투나 대화 분위기를 통해 화자의 태도나 의도를 파악하는 문제가 iBT에 새로 추가되었다. 이미 들려준 강의의 일부를 다시 들려주고 문제를 푸는 Replay Question도 새로 추가되었다.

* iBT 각 영역에 대한 자세한 설명과 시험 전략은 5권의 Total iBT TOEFL 영역별 교재에 꼼꼼하게 제시되어 있다.

시험 운용 방식의 차이

토플 "후기"가 무용지물이 된다.

iBT TOEFL은 응시자의 실력에 따라 문제 난이도가 조절되는 Computer Adaptive 시험이 아니다. 또한 한 달을 주기로 몇 개의 문제 Set가 돌아가며 출제되지도 않는다. 전 세계 모든 응시자들이 같은 날 같은 문제 Set를 풀어야 한다. 이제는 소위 "후기"라는 편법이 무용지물이 되고 오직 실력으로 승부할 수 밖에 없게 되었다.

Note-taking이 허용된다.

시험을 보면서 내내 Note-taking을 할 수 있다. 따라서 체계적인 Note-taking 실력이 시험 성적에 결정적인 영향을 주게 된다. 시험이 끝난 뒤 필기한 종이는 수거되어 파기된다.

마이크에 대고 혼자서 말하는 Speaking

Speaking 영역에서 응시자는 화면에 나타나는 시간 막대를 보며 주어진 시간 안에 마이크에 대고 말을 해야 한다. 말한 내용은 컴퓨터 파일로 저장돼 ETS Online Scoring Network로 보내져 채점된다.

타자로만 작성해야 하는 Writing

Writing Essay 작성시 CBT 토플에서는 연필로 쓰거나 컴퓨터에 타자로 칠 수 있었다. 하지만 iBT에서는 컴퓨터에 타자로 치는 것만 허용된다. 따라서 기본적인 영타 실력을 미리 갖추어 놓아야 한다.

전세계에서 동시에 같은 시험을 본다.

iBT TOEFL은 거의 매일 실시되던 CBT와 달리 정해진 날에만 볼 수 있다. 일년에 약 30-40회 정도 실시될 예정이다. 한 달에 한 번 밖에 시험을 볼 수 없었던 CBT 토플과 달리 iBT 토플에서는 동일 응시자가 한 달에 여러 번 시험을 볼 수 있다. 또 전 세계에서 미리 정해진 시험일자에 동시에 시험이 실시된다. 이러한 변화가 가능한 것은 한 달을 주기로 몇 개의 문제 Set만 반복적으로 출제되던 기존의 CBT와 달리 iBT 토플은 매회 시험마다 다른 문제 Set가 출제되기 때문이다. 이에 따라 CBT에서 기승을 부리던 이른바 토플 "후기"라는 부정한 편법은 iBT에서는 설 자리를 잃게 된 것이다. 지금부터는 적어도 토플 시험에 있어서는 편법이나 요령이 아닌 영어 실력이 점수를 결정하게 된 것이다.

iBT와 CBT/PBT 점수 비교표

Score Comparison			Score Comparison, cont.		
New Internet-based TOEFL Total	Computer-based Total	Paper-based Total	New Internet-based TOEFL Total	Computer-based Total	Paper-based Total
120	300	677	62–63	177	503
120	297	673	61	173	500
119	293	670	59–60	170	497
118	290	667	58	167	493
117	287	660–663	57	163	487–490
116	283	657	56	160	483
114–115	280	650–653	54–55	157	480
113	277	647	53	153	477
111–112	273	640–643	52	150	470–473
110	270	637	51	147	467
109	267	630–633	49–50	143	463
106–108	263	623–627	48	140	460
105	260	617–620	47	137	457
103–104	257	613	45–46	133	450–453
101–102	253	607–610	44	130	447
100	250	600–603	43	127	443
98–99	247	597	41–42	123	437–440
96–97	243	590–593	40	120	433
94–95	240	587	39	117	430
92–93	237	580–583	38	113	423–427
90–91	233	577	36–37	110	420
88–89	230	570–573	35	107	417
86–87	227	567	34	103	410–413
84–85	223	563	33	100	407
83	220	557–560	32	97	400–403
81–82	217	553	30–31	93	397
79–80	213	550	29	90	390–393
77–78	210	547	28	87	387
76	207	540–543	26–27	83	380–383
74–75	203	537	25	80	377
72–73	200	533	24	77	370–373
71	197	527–530	23	73	363–367
69–70	193	523	22	70	357–360
68	190	520	21	67	353
66–67	187	517	19–20	63	347–350
65	183	513	18	60	340–343
64	180	507–510	17	57	333–337

iBT TOEFL 이렇게 준비해라!

iBT TOEFL은 어렵다. 특히 외국 경험이 없는 토종 국내파 학생들에게는 더욱 어렵게 느껴질 시험이다. 그렇다면 iBT TOEFL 고득점은 불가능한 미션인가? 절대 그렇지 않다. 기존의 어떤 영어 시험보다 어려운 건 사실이지만, 제대로만 준비한다면 높은 점수를 받는 것은 물론 진짜 영어 실력까지 갖출 수 있다. TOEIC 점수가 900이상인데도 영어 한 마디 못하는 웃지 못할 희극은 iBT에서는 없을 것이다. iBT 시험은 정복하기 어려운 산에 올라 기쁨도 누리고 등산 과정에서 체력도 좋아지는 일거양득의 등산에 비할 수 있다. iBT에서 좋은 점수와 실력을 동시에 얻기 위한 영역별 대비 방법은 다음과 같다.

1. Reading

다양한 주제의 지문을 두루 읽어라!

지문의 길이가 CBT에 비해 2배 정도나 길어졌고 지문 전체의 요지를 묻는 문제의 비중이 커진 만큼 평소에 다양한 주제의 영어 구문을 대상으로 폭넓은 독해 연습을 해야 한다. 처음부터 토플 책으로 시험 준비를 시작하기 보다는 자신의 독해 수준에 맞는 영어 책으로 시작하는 것이 좋다. 한 페이지에 모르는 단어가 10개 정도 나오는 지문이 적합하다. 요즘은 시중 대형 서점의 외국어 매장에 중고생 용으로 나온 영어 독해 책들이 아주 많다. 수준에 맞는 책을 골라 독해와 문제 풀기를 연습하며 영어 문장을 읽어내는 기본적인 글 눈을 먼저 길러야 한다.

어휘력은 문장을 통해서만 늘려라!

어휘력은 독해 지문에서 만나는 새 단어와 숙어를 철저히 자기 것으로 챙기면서 키워야 한다. 이와 함께 토플용 전문 Vocabulary 교재를 활용하는 것도 도움이 된다. 이 때 어휘책은 단순히 단어에만 치중하는 것보다는 예문을 읽으며 문맥에서 단어를 자연스럽게 익힐 수 있는 것이 좋다. 그런 점에서 Total 무한궤도 iBT TOEFL Vocabulary를 추천한다. 이 교재에는 전 날 공부한 35개의 단어들이 당일 공부하는 35개 단어들의 예문 안에 다시 한 번 등장하기 때문에 복습이 저절로 될 수 밖에 없다. 예문만 꼼꼼히 읽으면서 이 책을 한 번 공부하고 나면 다른 Vocabulary 책을 두 번 공부한 효과를 얻을 수 있는 것이다.

실전과 가장 유사한 교재로 마무리 하라!

일단 기본 독해력과 어휘력을 갖추고 난 다음 iBT TOEFL Reading 교재를 시작해야 한다. Total iBT TOEFL RC는 새로운 유형의 iBT 토플 RC 문제에 대한 상세한 분석과 함께 풍부한 유형별 문제까지 담고 있다. 이 교재에는 또 실제 문제와 가장 유사한 Actual Test도 들어 있어 iBT TOEFL에 가장 확실하게 대비할 수 있다.

2. Listening

Dictation으로 기초 청취력을 길러라!

iBT TOEFL Listening에서는 그나마 쉬웠던 짧은 대화 Part A가 없어지고 CBT보다 대폭 길어진 대화와 강의가 우리 학생들을 기다리고 있다. 기본 청취력이 약한 학생들은 받아쓰기(Dictation) 훈련을 많이 해야 한다. 눈으로 보면 아는 단어도 귀로 들으면 낯선 경우가 많다. 눈과 귀의 차이를 줄이는 데에는 Dictation이 가장 효과적이다.

점수를 결정하는 Note-taking 실력을 길러라!

기본적인 듣기가 되는 단계가 되면 듣는 내용을 효과적으로 정리해 기억하기 위한 Note-taking 훈련을 해야 한다. iBT TOEFL LC의 강의는 보통 3분에서 5분이나 되는 긴 분량이기 때문에, 내용을 이해하는 것 못지 않게 이해한 내용을 얼마나 잘 정리해 적을 수 있는지가 점수를 좌우할 것이다. 결국 iBT에서는 Note-taking 실력이 가장 결정적인 역할을 할 것이다. 바로 이 점 때문에 동시 통역 대학원에서 Note-taking 훈련을 받은 사람들은 iBT TOEFL 시험을 별도로 준비하지 않고서도 좋은 점수를 받을 수 있을 것이다.

Note-taking이 Speaking과 Writing 점수까지 올려준다.

Note-taking의 핵심은 최소의 기록으로 최대를 기억해 내는 것이다. 들리는 내용을 속기사처럼 전부 쓰는 것이 아니라 Idea Cluster 단위로 정리해서 적는 경제적인 Note-taking을 해야 한다. Total iBT TOEFL LC는 통역사들이 사용하는 전문 Note-taking 기법을 상세히 소개하고 있다. iBT 토플에서는 LC영역은 물론 Writing과 Speaking영역에서도 통합형 문제의 일부로 듣기 부분이 들어가 있는 만큼 Note-taking 기술을 익히지 않고서는 Writing과 Speaking에서도 좋은 점수를 받을 수 없다.

3. Speaking

5분 30초 동안 말을 할 수 있어야 한다.

기본적인 의사 표현 능력도 길러주지 못하는 우리 영어 교육의 현실때문에 iBT TOEFL Speaking은 우리 학생들에게는 가장 어려운 영역이다. 독립형 말하기 문제 2개, 읽기-듣기-말하기가 결합된 통합형 문제 2개, 듣기-말하기 통합형 문제 2개 등 총 6개의 문제가 출제된다. 독립형 말하기는 각 45초, 통합형은 각 1분씩 영어로 말을 해야 한다. Speaking 6문제를 다 합치면 총 5분 30초 동안 컴퓨터 마이크에 계속 말을 하는 것이다.

대화식 영어가 아닌 발표식 영어를 연습하라!

iBT TOEFL Speaking은 말 상대가 있는 양방향 대화가 아니다. 혼자서 자기 의견을 말하는 발표에 가깝다. 그래서 원어민과의 수업만으로는 좋은 점수를 얻기 어렵다. 주어진 주제에 대해 논리 정연하게 자신의 입장을 발표하는 연습을 해야 하고, 듣고 읽은 내용을 요약해서 짜임새 있게 말하는 훈련을 해야 한다. 결국 Presentation 방식으로 말하기 연습을 하는 것이 원어민 수업보다 훨씬 더 효과가 있을 것이다.

Shadowing과 실전 교재로 Fluency를 높여라!

Speaking의 주요 채점 기준 중 하나인 말 속도와 Fluency를 높이기 위해서는 초시계를 놓고 1분 안에 속도감 있게 말하는 연습을 해야 한다. 또 녹음된 영어 연설을 약 5초 간격을 두고 따라가며 말해보는 Shadowing 연습도 큰 도움이 된다. 기본적인 말하기가 되는 학생은 Total iBT TOEFL Speaking 교재에 들어 있는 말하기 문제들을 풀어볼 것을 권한다. 이들 문제들은 실제 문제 유형과 가장 가깝게 만들어져 있고 말하기에 자주 쓰이는 문장과 모범 답안까지도 친절하게 제시되어 있다. 또한 이 교재에 딸린 CD를 이용해 iBT 실제 시험과 꼭 같은 환경에서 Speaking 시험에 확실히 대비 할 수 있다.

4. Writing

통합형 Essay와 독립형 Essay

20분 동안 읽고 들은 내용에 대해 비판적으로 요약을 하는 통합형 쓰기 하나와 30분 동안 주어진 주제에 대해 논리적인 글을 쓰는 독립형 쓰기 하나를 해야 한다. 기본 문장을 영작할 수 있는 능력과 논리 정연한 Essay를 조직해내는 능력이 있어야 Writing에서 좋은 점수를 받을 수 있다.

기본 영작 훈련을 먼저 한 다음 Essay 작성법을 익혀라!

기본 문장 영작 능력이 부족한 학생에게는 "TOEFL 기초공사 Writing"이 많은 도움을 줄 것이다. 이 교재에 수록된 48개 독립형 주제에 대한 문장 단위의 기본 영작 연습이 Essay를 작성할 수 있도록 기초체력을 길러 줄 것이다. 기본 문장 영작 능력을 기른 뒤에는

Total iBT TOEFL Writing 교재를 이용해 실전 훈련을 하면 된다. 이 책에는 iBT Writing 문제에 대한 유형별 설명과 그에 대한 훈련 방법이 제시되어 있고 출제 가능성이 높은 글 주제에 대한 문장별 영작 연습과 Sample Essay까지 상세히 제시되어 있다. Essay에 주어지는 점수는 최저 0점이고 최고 5점이다. 기본 문장 영작과 Essay 훈련을 제대로 하고 나면 Writing에서 적어도 3점 이상의 점수는 받을 수 있을 것이다.

ETS가 추천하는 Writing에 유용한 연결어

6개 문제: 2개의 독립형 말하기	
Sequence 순서	Again, also, and, and then, finally, first, second, third, next, still, too, and so forth, afterward, subsequently, finally, consequently, previously, before this, simultaneously, concurrently
To add 추가	Besides, equally important, finally, further, furthermore, nor, lastly, what's more, moreover, in addition
To prove 입증, 근거	Because, for, since, for the same reason, obviously, evidently, furthermore, moreover, besides, indeed, in fact, in addition, in any case, that is
To compare and Contrast 비교 및 대비	Whereas, but, yet, on the other hand, however, nevertheless, on the other hand, on the contrary, by comparison, where, compared to, up against, balanced against, vis-a-vis, but, although, conversely, meanwhile, after all, in contrast, although this may be true, still, though, yet, despite, as opposed to
Time 시간	immediately, thereafter, soon, after a few hours, finally, then, later, previously, formerly, first (second, etc.), next, and then, as long as, as soon as
Cause-and-effect 인과관계	as a result, because, consequently, for this purpose, so, then, therefore, to this end
Emphasis 강조	Definitely, extremely, obviously, in fact, indeed, in any case, absolutely, positively, naturally, surprisingly, always, forever, perennially, eternally, never, emphatically, unquestionably, without a doubt, certainly, undeniably, without reservation
Exception 예외	Yet, still, however, nevertheless, in spite of, despite, of course, once in a while, sometimes
Examples 예시	For example, for instance, in this case, in another case, on this occasion, in this situation, for instance, in case of, to demonstrate, to illustrate, as an illustration, to illustrate, such as
To summarize and conclude 요약 및 결론	In brief, on the whole, summing up, to conclude, in conclusion, as I have shown, hence, therefore, accordingly, thus, as a result, consequently, as has been noted, as we have seen

미국 대학이 요구하는 iBT 점수

아직 미국 대학이 요구하는 점수 수준이 전부 확정되지는 않았다. 그러나, 일반 대학에서는 CBT 213점에 상응하는 iBT 80~85점 정도를, Ivy League 등 명문 대학들은 95~100점 대의 iBT 점수를 요구할 것으로 예상된다. 또한 기존의 CBT와는 달리 총점에 더해서 4대 영역별 최저 점수를 정하는 대학도 많을 것으로 예상된다. 영역별 점수를 요구하는 대학들은 Reading이나 Listening보다는 Speaking과 Writing 영역에서 상당히 높은 점수를 요구할 것으로 보인다.

이미 가지고 있는 CBT점수는 원칙적으로는 2년간 유효하다. 그러나 국내외 일부 대학과 중등 교육기관에서는 앞으로 iBT 점수만을 제출하도록 요구하거나 최근 1년간 받은 토플 점수만을 인정할 것으로 예상되는 만큼 진학을 희망하는 교육기관에 이에 대해 미리 확인을 해야 할 것이다.

iBT TOEFL 등록에서 성적 통지까지

▶ 시험 등록

- 등록비는 미화 170 달러 (2006년 현재). 등록비는 미국에서 결제 가능한 VISA, Master, American Express Card 중 하나로 지불할 수 있다. 미국에 개설한 은행 계좌가 있으면 전자 결제도 가능하다.
- 응시자가 몰리는 경우가 있으므로 원하는 응시일로부터 두 세달 여유를 두고 등록해야 한다.
- 등록시에 교부되는 등록확인번호를 잘 챙겨서 시험장에 가지고 간다. 이와 함께 응시자의 신분을 증명할 본인의 서명과 사진이 들어간 여권을 시험장에 반드시 가져 가야 한다.
- 시험 일자 변경과 취소 신청: 시험일자를 변경할 경우 미화 40달러를 지불해야 하고, 시험 취소 시 미화 65 달러만 환불된다. 시험 일자 변경과 취소는 지정된 시험일로부터 늦어도 근무일 기준 3일전까지만 가능하다.

▶ 3가지 등록 방법

1. 인터넷 등록 :　　www.prometric.com이나 www.ets.org에서 등록
2. 전화 등록 :　　한미 교육위원단 (02-3211-1233)에 전화로 등록.

전화 등록 시간: 오전 9시–오후 5시 (월–금요일)
희망 응시일로부터 늦어도 근무일 기준 3일전에 등록해야 한다.
3. 우편 등록 :   등록서식을 작성하여 ETS나 각 지역 등록센터로 보낸다.

▶ 시험 절차

- 예약된 시험 장소에 20분 정도 여유를 두고 도착
- 입실: 신원 확인 및 사진 촬영
- 안내 및 시험: 시험에 앞서 감독관이 컴퓨터 사용요령을 비롯한 시험 진행에 대한 설명을 하고 시험 개시

▶ 성적 통지

시험 성적표는 시험일로부터 근무일 기준 15일 이내에 우편을 통해 통지된다. 성적표에는 총점과 각 영역별 점수가 기재되며 응시자의 영어 실력에 대한 평가와 응시자가 영어로 수행할 수 있는 업무도 안내된다. iBT 토플 점수는 대부분의 미국 교육 기관에서 2년간 유효하게 사용할 수 있다. 하지만 Reading과 Listening에서 적어도 1개의 지문이나 강의, Writing에서 1개의 Essay, 그리고 Speaking에서 1개의 문제에 답을 하지 못한 경우 성적표가 발부되지 않는다.

Total *iBT* TOEFL

Writing

Introduction

iBT 토플에서 Writing의 점수 비중은 이전 CBT에 비해 크게 높아졌다. CBT에서는 Essay가 한 개만 있었고 그나마도 Structure의 일부로 포함되어 있어서 전체 점수에서 차지하는 비중이 크지 않았다. 하지만 iBT에서는 써야 하는 Essay도 두 개로 늘어난데다, 전체 120점 중에 30점을 차지하는 엄연한 독립 영역으로 자리잡았다. 총 50분이 주어지는 iBT Writing 시험은 Writing Task 1과 Writing Task 2로 구성되어 있다. 답안을 반드시 컴퓨터에 타이핑해야 하는 것도 CBT와의 또 다른 차이이다.

문제 유형

Task 종류	Task 안내
Task 1: 읽고–듣고–쓰기 통합형 (Integrated Writing)	읽기: 230–300단어 분량의 학술적인 내용의 지문이 화면에 제시되면 3분 이내에 읽는다. 듣기: 읽기 지문과 반대 입장을 펴는 약 2분 간의 강의를 듣는다. 쓰기 과제: 읽기와 듣기에 언급된 내용을 논리적으로 연결하는 Essay를 쓴다. Essay는 150–225단어 분량으로 20분 동안 작성해야 한다.
Task 2: 독립형 쓰기 (Independent Writing)	쓰기 과제: 특정 주제에 대한 자신의 입장을 Essay로 작성하되 구체적인 근거와 예를 들어야 한다. Essay는 최소 300단어 이상의 분량이어야 하고 주어지는 시간은 30분이다. 독립형 쓰기 과제는 대개 다음과 같이 주어진다. –다음 주장에 동의하는가 반대하는가? 구체적인 근거와 내용을 들어 자신의 입장을 뒷받침하라. –어떤 사람들은 X를 믿는다. 다른 이들은 Y를 믿는다. 당신은 어느 쪽 입장에 동의하는가? 구체적인 이유와 내용을 제시하라.

보다 자세한 Writing Task에 관한 설명과 대응 방안은 본 교재의 Task별 안내에 제시되어 있다.

채점 기준

Essay에는 최저 0점에서 최고 5점이 부여된다. 각 점수별 채점 기준은 다음과 같다.

통합형 쓰기(Integrated Writing) 채점 기준

지문을 읽고 그와 반대되는 입장을 제시하는 강의를 들은 다음 두 입장을 논리적으로 정리해야 하는 Integrated Writing에서는 다음과 같은 채점 기준이 적용된다.

점 수	채점 기준
5점	– 듣기 내용의 중요 부분을 정확하게 선별해 그에 해당되는 읽기 지문의 내용과 분명하게 연계한 글. – 글의 구조가 짜임새가 있다. – 미미한 표현이나 어법 상의 실수는 간혹 있으나 글 전체의 정확성에 지장을 주지는 않는다.
4점	– 듣기 자료와 읽기 자료의 중요 내용들을 연계하긴 했지만 생략이나 부정확함 또는 모호함이 다소 있는 글. – 표현이나 어법 상의 작은 실수들이 더 자주 눈에 띄어 글의 명확성이 떨어지는 경우가 간혹 있다. 그러나 전체적으로는 아이디어 전개가 제대로 이루어진 글이다.
3점	– 듣기 자료와 읽기 자료의 중요 내용들을 일부 연계하긴 했지만 다음의 항목 중 적어도 1개 이상에 해당된다. – 전체적으로는 글쓰기 기준에 충실하지만 글의 내용이 모호하고, 개괄적이며 불명확하거나 읽기와 듣기 자료의 내용을 잘못 연계했다. – 듣기 자료에 언급된 핵심 내용 하나를 놓쳤다. – 읽기와 듣기에 포함된 내용 그 자체나 이를 연결하는 내용 중 일부가 완성도가 떨어지거나 부정확하다. – 표현과 어법 상의 실수가 자주 있어 내용이 모호하거나 의미가 명확하지 않다.
2점	듣기 자료의 내용을 조금 언급하긴 하지만 표현과 어법 상의 실수가 두드러진다. 듣기 자료의 핵심 내용들이 빠져 있으며 듣기와 읽기 자료의 연계성도 눈에 띄게 떨어진다. 2점짜리 글은 다음과 같은 특징 중 1개 이상에 해당된다. – 듣기와 읽기 자료의 내용을 잘못 연결하거나 완전히 생략한다. – 듣기 자료의 핵심 내용을 빠뜨리거나 크게 잘못 전달한다. – 표현과 어법적인 실수로 인해 글 내용 전체가 분명하지 않아, 읽기와 듣기 자료의 내용을 모르는 사람은 이해하기 힘든 글.
1점	1점짜리 글은 다음과 같은 특징 중 1개 이상에 해당된다. – 듣기 자료에 포함된 주요 내용을 거의 언급하지 않는다. – 이해하기 힘들 정도로 표현 및 어법적 실수가 많다.
0점	– 화면에 제시되는 읽기 지문의 문장들을 그대로 베껴 쓴 글 – 쓰기 과제와 전혀 무관한 내용 – 영어가 아닌 다른 언어로 작성된 글 – 글자 대신 기호로 채우거나 아무 것도 쓰지 않은 경우

독립형 쓰기(Independent Writing) 채점 기준

주어진 주제에 대해 30분 동안 최소 300단어 이상 써야 하는 독립형 쓰기에서는 다음과 같은 채점 기준이 적용된다.

점 수	채점 기준
5점	5점 만점 글은 다음의 모든 특징들을 갖추고 있다. – 주제를 효과적으로 다룬다. – 글의 구조가 짜임새 있으며 적당한 설명과 예시 또는 세부 설명을 제시한다. – 글 전체에 일관성과 통일성이 있다. – 작은 표현이나 어법 상의 실수는 있지만 글의 전체 의미를 흐리지는 않는다. 영어를 편안하게 쓴다는 느낌을 주고 다양한 형식의 문장을 사용하며 적절한 어휘 및 관용구 선택이 돋보이는 글.
4점	4점짜리 글은 다음과 같은 모든 특징을 지니고 있다. – 일부 내용이 완전히 전개되지는 못했지만 전체적으로 주제를 잘 전개한다. – 전반적으로 글의 짜임새가 있으며 적절한 설명, 예시, 또는 세부 설명들을 충분히 제시한다. – 글의 일관성과 통일성이 보이나 지나친 부연 설명이나 주제에서 벗어난 내용이 일부 보인다. – 언어를 편안하게 사용하며 다양한 문장 구조 및 어휘를 구사한다. 미미한 어법, 어휘 또는 숙어 상의 실수가 있으나 글의 의미 전달에 방해가 되지는 않는 정도이다.
3점	3점짜리 글은 다음의 항목 중 적어도 1개 이상에 해당된다. – 주제를 설명, 예시, 세부 설명을 통해 전개한다. – 글의 일관성과 통일성이 보이나 아이디어 사이의 연관성이 분명하지 않은 경우가 있다. – 문장 작성에 어려움이 보이는 경우가 있으며 글의 의미를 흐리는 잘못된 어휘 선택이 가끔 보인다. – 어법에는 맞지만 제한적인 형식의 문장을 반복적으로 사용하고 어휘 사용 역시 제한적인 것이 눈에 띈다.
2점	2점짜리 글은 다음과 같은 항목 중 최소 1개 이상에 해당된다. – 주제를 제한적으로 전개한다. – 글의 구조가 흔들린다. – 설명, 예시, 세부 설명이 부적절하거나 충분하지 않다. – 잘못된 어휘 및 숙어 선택이 두드러진다. – 문장의 구조와 어법 상의 실수가 반복적으로 나타난다.

1점	1점짜리 글은 다음과 같은 항목 중 1개 이상에 해당되는 심각한 결함을 지니고 있다. – 글의 전개가 몹시 혼란스러우며 제대로 이루어지지 않는다. – 세부 설명이 전혀 없거나 주제와 무관한 예시 및 설명이 제시된다. – 심각한 어법 및 표현 상의 실수가 있다.
0점	다음에 해당되는 글은 0점을 받는다. – 문제 제시문을 베껴 쓰거나 주제와 무관한 내용을 쓴다. – 영어가 아닌 다른 언어로 작성된 글 – 글자 대신 기호로 채우거나 아무 것도 쓰지 않은 경우

Writing 점수 환산표

Writring Rubric Mean Average	Scaled Score
5.00	30
4.75	29
4.50	28
4.25	27
4.00	25
3.75	24
3.50	22
3.25	21
3.00	20
2.75	18
2.50	17
2.25	15
2.00	14
1.75	12
1.50	11
1.25	10
1.00	8
	7
	5
	4
	0

Narrator

Please listen carefully.

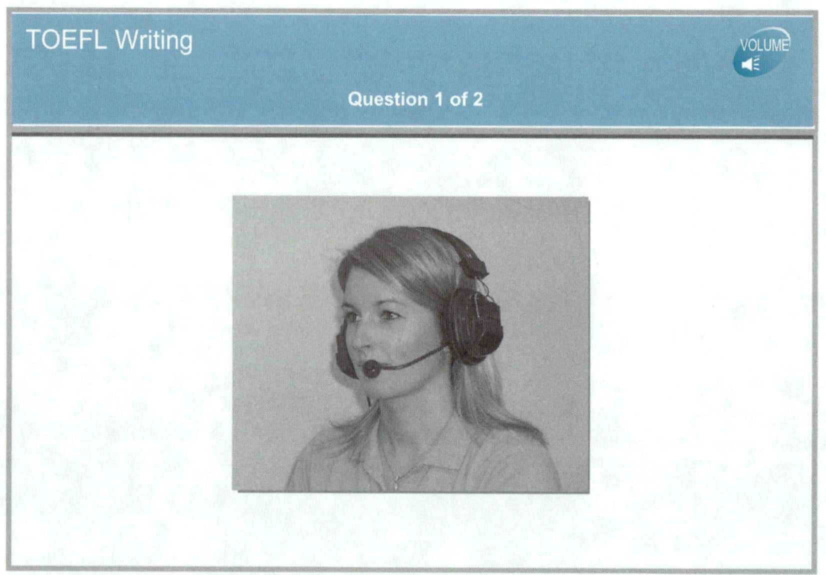

Narrator

You have 20 minutes to plan and write your response. Your response will be judged on the basis of the quality of your writing and on how well your response presents the points in the lecture and their relationship to the reading passage. Typically, an effective response will be 150 to 225 words.

Reading

Narrator

Now read a passage about an academic topic. You have 3 minutes to read the passage. Begin reading now.

Reading Time : 3 minutes

The benefits of aerobic exercise are well-known. Every women's magazine touts the benefits of it, and doctors, personal trainers, and diet programs add their endorsement as well. The benefits in terms of greater health and fitness are well documented, and there are probably few people in the civilized world who are not aware that it is beneficial.

Aerobic exercise is exercise that positively challenges the body's most important muscle, the heart, and stimulates it to become stronger and more efficient. However, the benefits of aerobic exercise are not confined to the heart but extend to the entire body. Acording to the Harvard Alumni Health Study, exercise increases the life span. People who exercise regularly are less vulnerable to colds and flu, and their immune systems are stronger. The risks of heart disease, high blood pressure, stroke, diabetes, and some forms of cancer are less in people who exercise. And weight-bearing exercise strengthens the bones, reducing the risk of osteoporosis.

Aerobic exercise burns more calories than other forms of exercise, so it is an excellent addition to a weight-loss or weight-maintenance program. People who engage in aerobic exercise can eat more food and still lose weight, and the calorie-burning effects last far beyond the actual exercise period. Not only does aerobic exercise improve the body, it also improves the mind. Aerobic exercise releases endorphins — the body's natural painkillers — which reduce stress, depression, and anxiety. Endorphins give the exerciser that "feel good" feeling that many people exercise to get. Some people may not have the time or money to go to a gym for their aerobic exercise, but they can still incorporate such exercise into their daily regimen. Aerobic dance is something that can be done at home, and so can other aerobic activities, such as walking and bicycling.

Note–taking

Listening

Narrator

Now listen to part of a lecture on the topic you just read about.

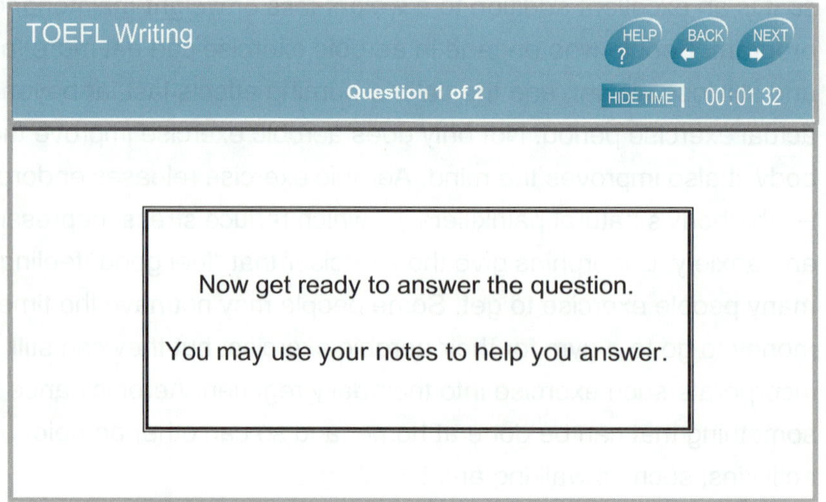

Narrator

Summarize the points made in the lecture you just heard, explaining how they cast doubt on points made in the reading.

TOEFL Writing

HELP ? | BACK ← | NEXT →

Question 1 of 2

HIDE TIME 00:19:54

Directions: You have 20 minutes to plan and write your response. Your response will be judged on the basis of the quality of your writing and on how well your response presents the points in the lecture and their relationship to the reading passage. Typically, an effective response will be 150 to 225 words.

Question: Summarize the points made in the lecture you just heard, explaining how they cast doubt on points made in the reading.

The benefits of aerobic exercise are well-known. Every women's magazine touts the benefits of it, and doctors, personal trainers, and diet programs add their endorsement as well. The benefits in terms of greater health and fitness are well documented, and there are probably few people in the civilized world who are not aware that it is beneficial.

Aerobic exercise is exercise that positively challenges the body's most important muscle, the heart, and stimulates it to become stronger and more efficient. However, the benefits of aerobic exercise are not confined to the heart but extend to the entire body. Acording to the Harvard Alumni Health Study, exercise increases the life span. People who exercise regularly are less vulnerable to colds and flu, and their immune systems are stronger. The risks of heart disease, high

I think that ⋯

Answer

Answer

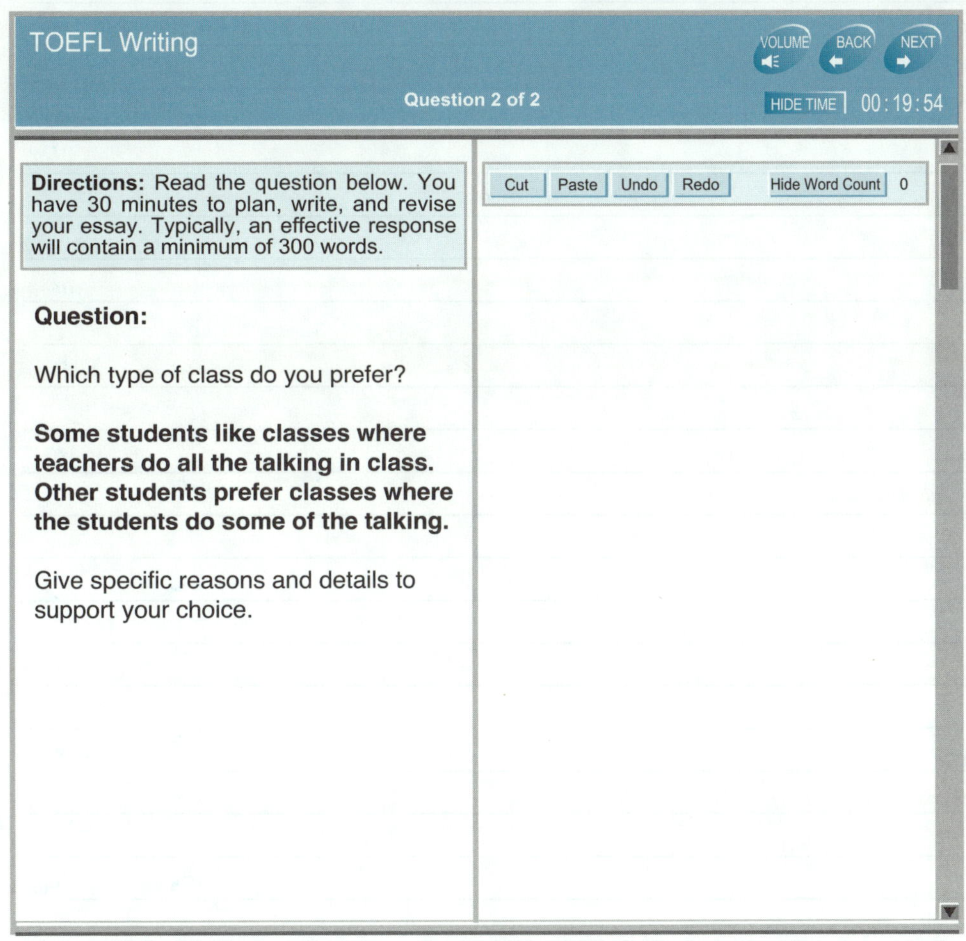

TOEFL Writing
VOLUME   BACK   NEXT
Question 2 of 2
HIDE TIME   00 : 19 : 54
Directions: Read the question below. You have 30 minutes to plan, write, and revise your essay. Typically, an effective response will contain a minimum of 300 words.
Question:
Which type of class do you prefer?
Some students like classes where teachers do all the talking in class. Other students prefer classes where the students do some of the talking.
Give specific reasons and details to support your choice.
Cut   Paste   Undo   Redo   Hide Word Count   0

Answer

Answer

Answer

통합형 쓰기인 Writing Task 1은 듣기 자료의 주요 내용을 읽기 자료의 내용과 연계하여 20분 동안 150에서 225단어 길이로 작성하는 Critical Summary-based Essay이다. 특정 주제를 주고 자유롭게 자신의 선택이나 입장을 전개해 나가는 독립형 쓰기인 Writing Task 2에 비해서 Essay에 담을 수 있는 내용이 제한된다. 주제에 대한 자신의 개인적인 생각을 써서는 안 된다. 화면에 제시된 지문의 내용과 들려 주는 강의 내용만을 바탕으로 논리적인 요약을 해야 좋은 점수를 기대할 수 있다. 또한 컴퓨터 화면에서 Essay 작성 공간 옆에 함께 제시되는 읽기 지문을 있는 그대로 Essay에 쓰면 감점을 받는다는 점도 잊지 말아야 한다. 읽기 지문의 일부 내용을 쓸 때에는 반드시 표현을 바꾸어(Paraphrasing) 사용해야 한다.

Writing Task 1에 등장하는 Reading 자료는 학술적 주제에 관련된 약 230-300단어 길이의 지문으로 이를 3분 이내에 읽어야 한다. 지문을 읽으면서 주요 내용을 메모해 두면 글을 쓸 때 고민하는 시간을 아낄 수 있다. 읽기 지문의 난이도는 iBT Reading 지문보다 조금 더 쉬운 편이다. 지문의 주제는 Biology, Geology, US History, Astronomy, Sociology 등 다양한 학문 분야를 망라한다.

Writing Task 1에 등장하는 Listening 자료도 학술적인 내용을 담고 있으며 교수의 일인 강의 형식이다. 길이는 약 2분 정도이며 난이도는 iBT Listening의 Lecture와 비슷하다. 강의 주제는 Reading 자료와 같지만 이와 대조되는 내용이 제시된다. 예를 들어 Reading 자료에서는 동물과 인간의 이타적 행동에 대해 설명한 다음 한 동물의 구체적인 이타적 행동에 대한 예를 든다. 듣기 자료에서는 이타적인 행동이 실제로는 이타적이지 않으며 Reading 지문에서 예로 든 동물도 이기적인 행동을 했다는 내용을 제시한다. 이렇듯 Reading 자료와 Listening 자료는 동일 주제에 대해 상반되는 입장을 피력한다. 따라서 듣기 자료를 들을 때에 읽기 지문에 반대되는 내용을 염두에 두면 강의 내용 파악에 크게 도움이 될 것이다. 물론 들을 때에는 반드시 본 교재 부록인 Total Note-taking에 소개된 Note-taking 기법을 활용해 최대한 많은 내용을 적어 두어야 한다.

Writing Task 1의 문제는 다음과 같이 제시된다.

Narrator

Summarize the points made in the lecture you just heard, explaining how they cast doubt on points made in the reading. (Writing Time: 20 minutes)

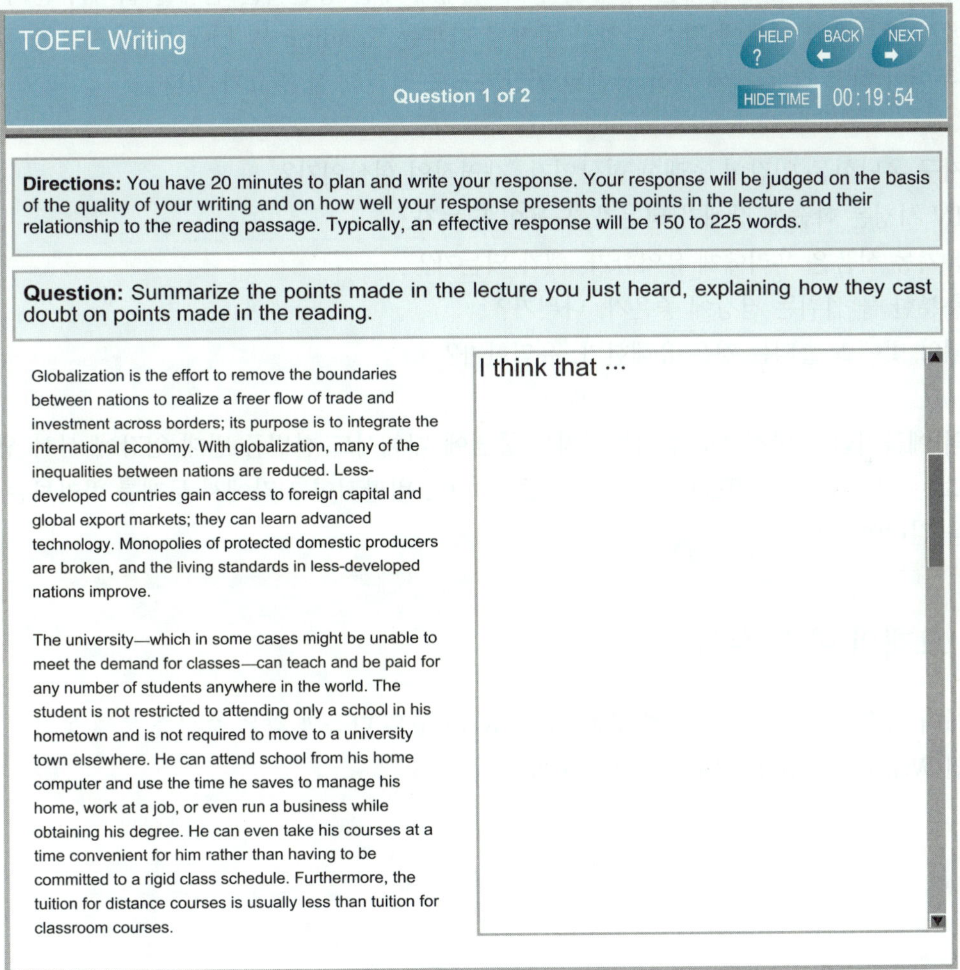

일단 듣기 자료의 핵심 포인트를 요약한 뒤 그것이 읽기 자료 내용을 어떻게 반박하고 있는지를 설명해야 한다. 듣기 자료만 요약해서는 좋은 점수를 기대할 수 없다. 꼭 읽기 자료와 연계해 어떻게 두 내용이 상반되는지를 지적해야 한다. 바로 이 점이 Writing Task 1을 Critical Summary-based Essay로 만든다.

출제 경향

다양한 학술적 주제가 출제된다. 그러나 각 주제에 대한 상반되는 견해를 읽기와 듣기 자료에서 제시하기 때문에 평소 다양한 주제를 다루는 Reading 및 Listening 자료를 공부해 두어야 하고 각 주제에 대한 상반된 입장까지도 정리해 볼 필요가 있다.

- 지구 온난화는 인간이 초래한 현상인가, 자연적인 현상인가?
- TV 시청은 학습에 장애가 되는가, 도움이 되는가?
- 유기농 식품은 우리에게 유익한가, 해가 되는가?
- 충분한 물 섭취는 건강에 좋은가, 나쁜가?
- 태양 빛에 노출되는 것은 유해한가, 유익한가?

위의 예들처럼 일반적으로 받아들여지는 통념에 대해서도 한번쯤 반대 입장에 서서 생각해 보는 것이 Writing Task 1에 도움을 줄 것이다. 비판적인 시각에서 문제를 바라보는 습관을 길러야 한다.

본 교재의 학습 순서

최대의 학습효과를 거두기 위해 Total iBT Writing은 다음과 같은 순서를 통해 통합형 쓰기인 Writing Task 1에 대비할 수 있도록 했다.

1. Reading 자료 읽기: 주어진 Reading 자료를 3분 동안 읽는다.

One of the technological developments of the modern age is distance learning—learning that takes place far from a classroom or a teacher, right in the student's own home. The popularity of this medium has been phenomenal. According to the American Council on Education, the number of students in distance learning doubled from 1995 to 1998, and totaled 1.6 million. With an increasing lack of physical classroom space for traditional classes, distance learning offers a solution that benefits both the university and the student.

The university—which in some cases might be unable to meet the demand for classes—can teach and be paid for any number of students anywhere in the world. The student is not restricted to attending only a school in his hometown and is not required to move to a university town elsewhere. He can attend school from his home computer and use the time he saves to manage his home, work at a job, or even run a business while obtaining his degree. He can even take his courses at a time convenient for him rather than having to be committed to a rigid class schedule. Furthermore, the tuition for distance courses is usually less than tuition for classroom courses.

There are various types of distance-learning technology. Many of the classes are available via the internet. In other cases, however, compressed video conferencing is utilized to reach remote students. Satellite campuses have recently opened at Arkansas State University and other campuses, and they hold promise for increasing enrollment tenfold.

All over the world, distance learning is helping universities control costs and respond to competitive pressures. Distance learning has enabled many people who could not otherwise obtain an education to complete their studies without disrupting their careers and family life.

이 Reading 지문은 Essay를 쓰는 20분 동안 컴퓨터 화면 오른쪽에 계속 표시되기 때문에 참고는 할 수 있다. 그러나 다시 읽는 데 드는 시간을 절약하려면 처음 읽을 때 지문의 중요 내용을 메모해 놓아야 한다.

2. **Listening 자료 듣기:** 강의 상황을 담은 사진을 지면으로 보면서 듣기 자료를 듣는다. 이때 교재에 주어진 Note-taking용 공란에 반드시 Note-taking을 한다. Note-taking을 체계적으로 하지 않으면 제대로 글을 쓰는 것이 불가능할 것이다.

Narrator

Now listen to part of a lecture on the topic you just read about.

Note-taking

3. Note-taking 확인: Listening Script와 모범 Note-taking을 참고한다.

TOEFL Writing | HELP ? | BACK ← | NEXT →

Question 1 of 2 | HIDE TIME | 00 : 02 : 59

Professor

Well···I'd like to take a look at distance learning today. It's become very popular, as you probably know, and many students these days are earning degrees from the comfort of their own homes. However, there are a lot of issues with distance learning that you should be aware of.

I'm sure you all realize···or maybe you don't yet···just having a degree is not the only goal of education. The primary goal is to actually learn something. And with distance learning, that goal is probably going to be compromised. As it's been said, "technology does not teach students; teachers do." And···unfortunately, when not interacting with students, teachers tend to slack off on preparing for classes. The result can be halfhearted teaching and dull, uninformative classes.

And then there are issues from the university's side of the matter too. In a traditional classroom setting, the teacher is the only one paid to be there. But with distance learning, there are other people who must be paid to be involved. If the course is computer-based, computer people have to set up and maintain the internet site and program the courses. If compressed video is the medium chosen, the school has to put in a T-1 telephone line and pay $1,200 a month to use it. Then they have to buy $80,000 worth of compressed video equipment and employ two technicians at the site besides the teacher. The only way the university could recoup those expenses would be to, uh···get thousands of students to take it.

Then, you know···not all students are disciplined enough to do well with distance learning. To do well, they have to be self-motivated. They also need to be able to figure out some things on their own, since there is no teacher there to ask.

Total Note-taking Sample

"dist-learning"
↓
pop.

s°/G degree ĥ

b issues

x⊙ of ed → O
with
⊙/Comp.

"T/x Teach s° → t°/do

w(x 2act t°/Slack off

O/dull class

⟨issue from û
t c only t°/$
b
* ?/$
∫C → ǐ site + prog G=
∫V → T-1 ∞$ 1200/m
+ B equip. – 2 tec
only Ξ
R/thous. s°

+ x all s°/disc. ⟩ *
s°/N self-motiv.
+O things
b
(x t°

듣기 대본을 눈으로 미리 읽으면 청취 훈련이 전혀 되지 않는다. 반드시 먼저 듣기를 한 뒤에 눈으로 대본을 확인해야 한다. Note-taking은 연습을 하면 할수록 발전해서 결국에는 모범 Total Note-taking과 닮은 꼴이 되어야 한다.

4. 문제 읽기: 대본을 확인 한 다음 Writing Task 1을 읽는다.

Question:

Summarize the points made in the lecture you just heard, explaining how they cast doubt on points made in the reading.

5. Essay 쓰기: 간결하게 글의 Outline을 작성한 다음, Note-taking 내용을 바탕으로 읽기와 듣기 자료의 대립적 입장이 부각되도록 20분 동안 약 20줄 정도로 쓴다.

6. Sample Writing과 비교하기: 답지에 있는 Sample Writing을 읽는다. 자신이 쓴 답안과 비교하면서 미흡한 부분을 비판적으로 정리한다. 항상 비판적인 정리를 해 두어야 다음에 좀 더 짜임새 있는 글을 쓸 수 있다.

Sample Writing

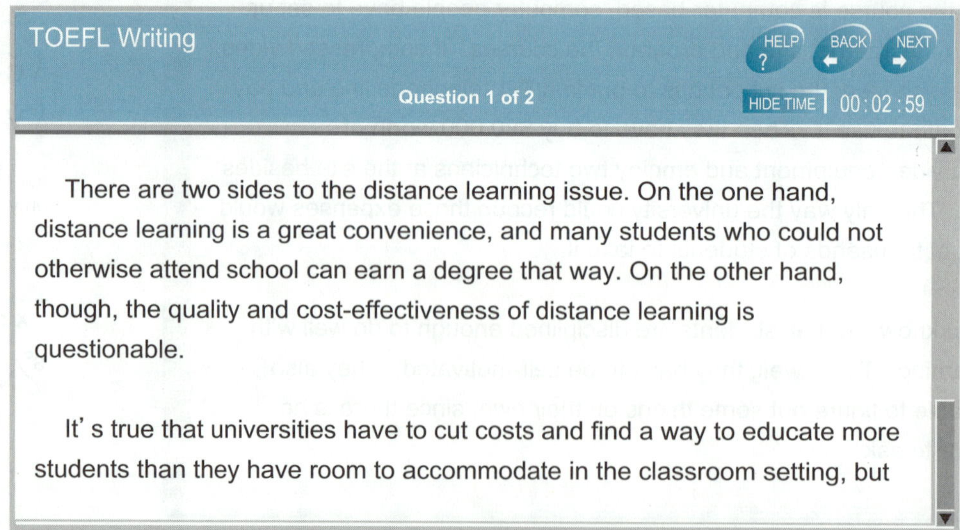

there are problems with distance learning. For one thing, the equipment and trained specialists needed to make it work are very expensive. And for another, not every student can adapt successfully to distance learning. Only students who are self-motivated and able to grasp most things on their own can do well at it.

The quality of the education is also an issue. Teachers do not think of distance teaching the same way they think of classroom teaching. They don't enjoy it as much either, because they do not have much or any interaction with their students. he result can be dull classes that have been poorly prepared and are lacking in information.

Anyone thinking of earning a degree by distance learning should thoroughly check out the university and the teachers, do a careful self-examination to be sure he or she can handle the ambiguity and unstructured environment, and try to contact others who have taken distance learning from that school.

원격교육에는 두 가지 측면이 있다. 한편으로, 원격교육은 매우 편리하며, 학교에 다닐 형편이 안 되는 많은 학생들은 원격교육을 통해 학위를 취득할 수 있다. 하지만 또 다른 한편으로는, 원격교육의 질과 비용 대비 효과가 불확실한 상태이다.

대학들이 비용을 줄이고, 교실에서 가르칠 수 있는 것보다 더 많은 학생들에게 교육을 제공할 수 있는 방법을 모색해야 하는 것은 사실이다. 하지만 원격교육에도 문제는 있다. 첫째, 원격교육에 필요한 장비와 훈련된 전문가들을 확보하는 데 많은 비용이 든다. 둘째, 모든 학생들이 원격교육환경에 성공적으로 적응할 수 있는 것이 아니다. 스스로 동기부여가 된 학생들과 대부분의 수업내용을 스스로 이해할 수 있는 학생들만이 원격학습에 성공할 수 있다. 교육의 질도 문제이다. 교사들은 원격교육과 교실수업을 똑같게 생각하지 않는다. 또한 학생들과의 상호작용이 적거나 거의 없기 때문에, 교사들이 원격교습을 즐기지도 못한다. 그 결과, 수업이 제대로 준비되지 않거나 배울 만한 내용이 부족해 지루해지기 쉽다.

원격교육을 통해 학위를 받으려고 생각하는 학생들은 대학교와 교사들을 꼼꼼히 확인해 보고, 애매하고 체계가 없는 환경에 자신이 잘 적응할 수 있을지 스스로를 신중하게 되돌아 봐야 한다. 그리고 그 대학에서 원격교습을 받은 다른 학생들과 연락을 취해 보도록 해야 할 것이다.

Narrator

Please listen carefully.

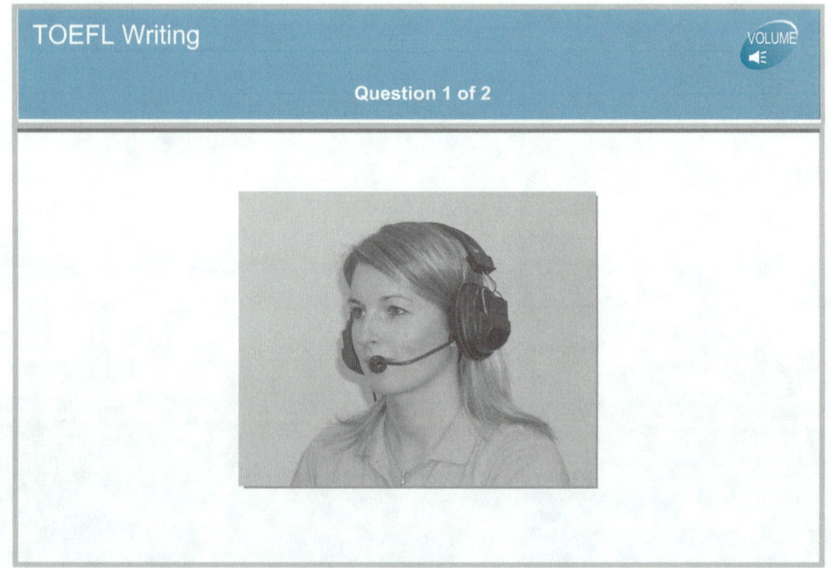

Narrator

You have 20 minutes to plan and write your response. Your response will be judged on the basis of the quality of your writing and on how well your response presents the points in the lecture and their relationship to the reading passage. Typically, an effective response will be 150 to 225 words.

Reading

Narrator

Now read a passage about an academic topic. You have 3 minutes to read the passage. Begin reading now.

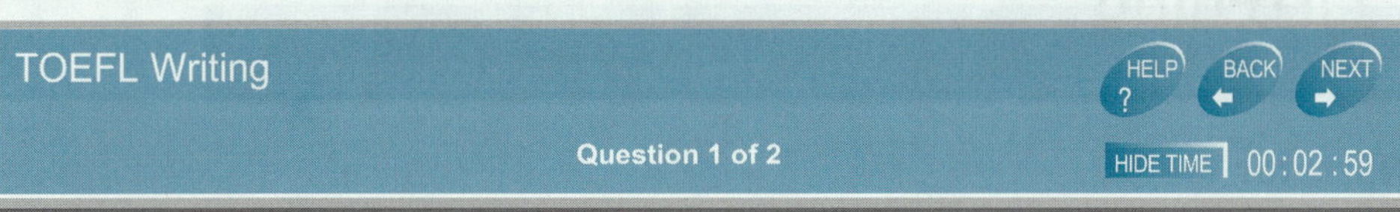

TOEFL Writing

HELP ?   BACK   NEXT

Question 1 of 2   HIDE TIME   00 : 02 : 59

Reading Time : 3 minutes

One of the gravest dangers posed to the future of planet Earth is the threat of global warming, also known as the greenhouse effect. Scientists have discovered that the earth is growing slightly warmer with passing time, and the worldwide effects of such warming are potentially devastating. Adaptations to even this slight temperature rise are already evident. A study of mountain plants in the Alps, for instance, shows that cold-area plants are responding to this temperature change by moving to higher and cooler climates.

However, much greater impacts are anticipated worldwide. Polar ice caps could melt, raising sea levels around the world and causing flooding. Hurricanes and tropical storms could intensify, increasing the damage that results from them. More extensive shoreline erosion would result, and wetlands would disappear as sea levels rose. A report issued in 1992 by the United Nations states that if carbon dioxide and other greenhouse gas emissions continued at the present rate, the coastal plains of Bangladesh and the Netherlands would flood by the year 2100 and the islands of the Maldives would completely disappear. It would only take a two-foot rise in sea level to cause devastation of that magnitude.

There are a number of causes of global warming; one is the destruction of forests. Trees are the largest land-based natural mechanism for removing carbon dioxide from the air, and with 5,500 acres of rain forest being destroyed daily, global carbon dioxide levels are rising at the rate of 0.4 percent each year to levels not experienced on this plant for millions of years. Population growth also contributes to global warming. There are several things we can all do to decrease global warming: reduce our electricity consumption, plant trees on the south side of our houses, and install energy-efficient thermostats with day and nighttime timers.

Note–taking

Listening

Narrator

Now listen to part of a lecture on the topic you just read about.

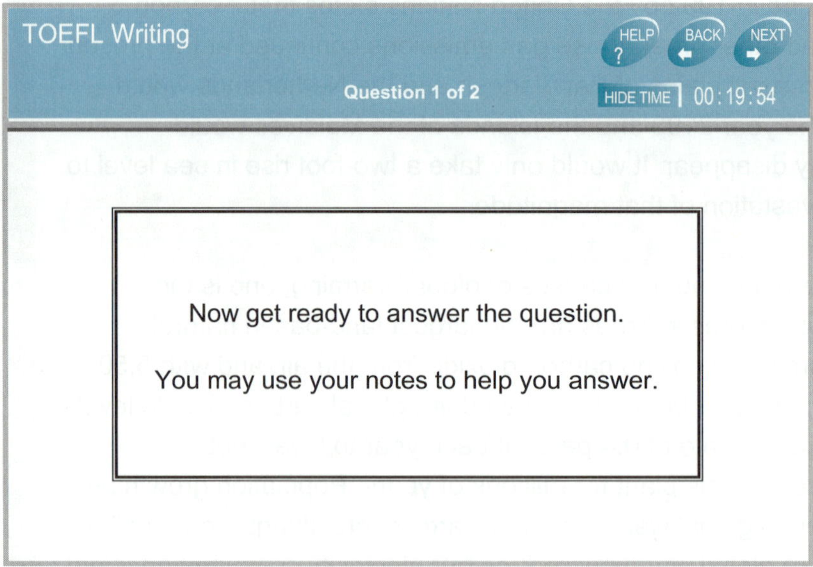

Narrator

Summarize the points made in the lecture you just heard, explaining how they cast doubt on points made in the reading.

TOEFL Writing

HELP ?   BACK ←   NEXT →

Question 1 of 2

HIDE TIME   00:19:54

Directions: You have 20 minutes to plan and write your response. Your response will be judged on the basis of the quality of your writing and on how well your response presents the points in the lecture and their relationship to the reading passage. Typically, an effective response will be 150 to 225 words.

Question: Summarize the points made in the lecture you just heard, explaining how they cast doubt on points made in the reading.

One of the gravest dangers posed to the future of planet Earth is the threat of global warming, also known as the greenhouse effect. Scientists have discovered that the earth is growing slightly warmer with passing time, and the worldwide effects of such warming are potentially devastating. Adaptations to even this slight temperature rise are already evident. A study of mountain plants in the Alps, for instance, shows that cold-area plants are responding to this temperature change by moving to higher and cooler climates.

However, much greater impacts are anticipated worldwide. Polar ice caps could melt, raising sea levels around the world and causing flooding. Hurricanes and tropical storms could intensify, increasing the damage that results from them. More extensive shoreline erosion would result, and wetlands would disappear as sea levels

I think that …

Answer

____

____

____

____

____

____

____

____

<table>
<tr><td>

Listening Script

Professor

Well, class, today we're on a hot topic — global warming. I'm sure you hear about this topic constantly in the media, just as I do, so you know that it's one of the biggest political hot buttons today. The claim is that the earth is warming up due to an increase in carbon dioxide in the atmosphere — which, by the way, is blamed on technology and the plundering of our forests — and that catastrophic environmental changes will result from this. As a matter of fact, though, global warming is really just a myth that millions of people have accepted as truth.

Although it is actually true that the amount of carbon dioxide in the atmosphere is rising, that rise does not correspond with the differences that come from humans burning coal, oil, and natural gas. So ⋯ it probably doesn't have anything to do with us. It's just something happening naturally in the environment ⋯ possibly due to fluctuations in the energy of the sun, and the rise is very slight.

There are also other factors that can counteract the global warming that does occur. For example, smoke from the burning of tropical forests and grasslands has a strong cooling effect on the climate. This cooling effect could nearly equal the warming power of greenhouse gases created by the fires.

Actually, scientists are now saying that the whole global-warming hypothesis is no longer valid. They have been able to test it carefully by making precise measurements of atmospheric temperature for the past 50 years. Those measurements definitely show that major atmospheric greenhouse warming is not occurring. And ⋯ it's not likely ever to occur. That catastrophic rise in temperatures doesn't fit with the statistics scientists have gathered. So the next time somebody brings up global warming to you, you can answer with just two words: "False alarm".

</td><td>

Note-taking

pol. issue
claim / b (↑ CO_2)
myth

true (CO_2 ↑
x Corr w/ ≠ ← c oil
n gas
≠ n :
sun

factors (Counteract
eg. s ← b of cool clim

sc hypoth / ⟶ x valid
Test atm t° 50y
meas / x + x
t°↑ / x =
→ false

</td></tr>
</table>

Narrator

Please listen carefully.

Narrator

You have 20 minutes to plan and write your response. Your response will be judged on the basis of the quality of your writing and on how well your response presents the points in the lecture and their relationship to the reading passage. Typically, an effective response will be 150 to 225 words.

Reading

Narrator

Now read a passage about an academic topic. You have 3 minutes to read the passage. Begin reading now.

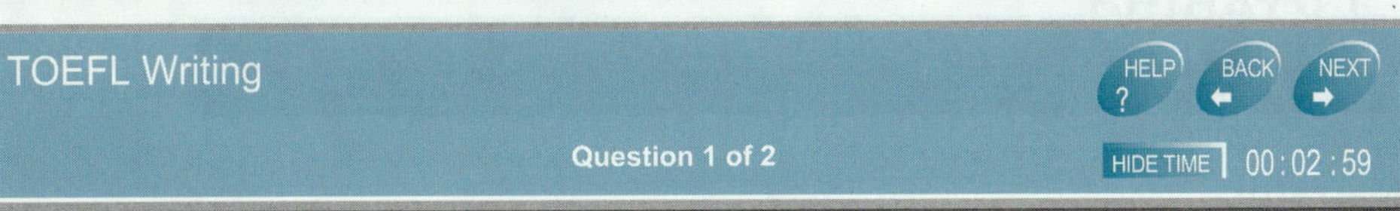

Reading Time : 3 minutes

Globalization is the effort to remove the boundaries between nations to realize a freer flow of trade and investment across borders; its purpose is to integrate the international economy. With globalization, many of the inequalities between nations are reduced. Less-developed countries gain access to foreign capital and global export markets; they can learn advanced technology. Monopolies of protected domestic producers are broken, and the living standards in less-developed nations improve. These upgrades lead to faster growth, ameliorating the effects of poverty, and higher living standards come into play.

One of the features of globalization is specialization. Specialization allows each country or region to grow crop or manufacture products which it is positioned most ideally to do. For example, if China can grow rice more efficiently than any other country because it has the perfect climate for it, and Oregon can grow timber better than any other region for the same reason, then China can trade rice to Oregon for timber. As a result of such trading, both will have more rice and more timber than before, so both will prosper.

Ugandan farmers used to live on the brink of starvation, trying to survive by subsistence farming. Then they began growing flowers for export to Europe and found that they can make more money that way. That money can be used to buy much more food than they could grow for themselves with subsistence farming. This is an example of the benefits of globalization. Poorer nations have the opportunity to find their niche and finally advance. Ultimately, globalization could wipe out poverty and even out the international playing field for everyone.

Listening

Narrator

Now listen to part of a lecture on the topic you just read about.

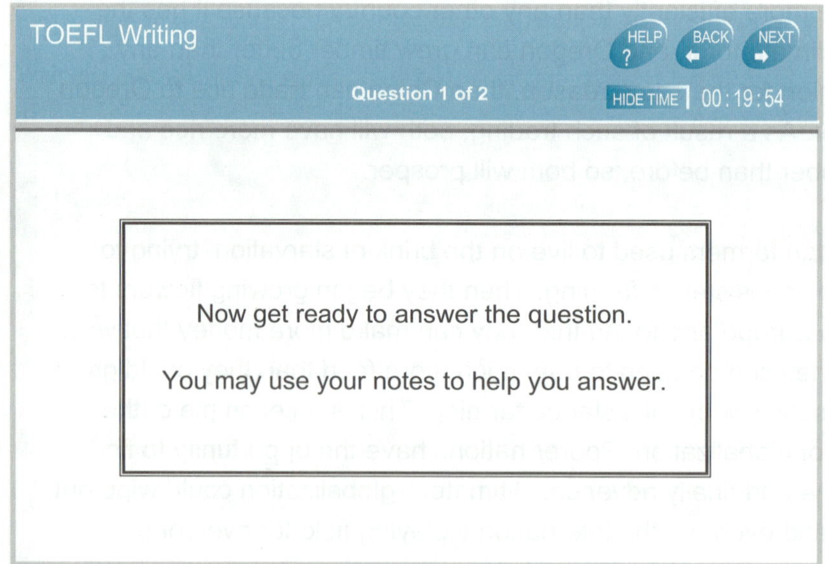

Narrator

Summarize the points made in the lecture you just heard, explaining how they cast doubt on points made in the reading.

TOEFL Writing

HELP ?   BACK ←   NEXT →

Question 1 of 2

HIDE TIME | 00 : 19 : 54

Directions: You have 20 minutes to plan and write your response. Your response will be judged on the basis of the quality of your writing and on how well your response presents the points in the lecture and their relationship to the reading passage. Typically, an effective response will be 150 to 225 words.

Question: Summarize the points made in the lecture you just heard, explaining how they cast doubt on points made in the reading.

Globalization is the effort to remove the boundaries between nations to realize a freer flow of trade and investment across borders; its purpose is to integrate the international economy. With globalization, many of the inequalities between nations are reduced. Less-developed countries gain access to foreign capital and global export markets; they can learn advanced technology. Monopolies of protected domestic producers are broken, and the living standards in less-developed nations improve. These upgrades lead to faster growth, ameliorating the effects of poverty, and higher living standards come into play.

One of the features of globalization is specialization. Specialization allows each country or region to grow or manufacture that which it is positioned most ideally to do. For example, if China can grow rice more efficiently than

I think that ⋯

Answer

Listening Script

Professor

Today I want to talk about the dangers of globalization. Now, you know ⋯ globalization is generally accepted as the answer to the world's poverty problem. And while globalization has some potential for improving that situation, it brings a lot of problems with it too.

One of the first things that gets sacrificed in globalization is individual differences. Whatever the advanced nations are doing ends up being what everyone does in order to compete successfully. So traditional ways of doing things in various regions become obsolete and cease to exist. Diversity just dies. Everything becomes "homogenized", so to speak; it all looks the same, and the individual qualities that used to characterize the goods of a particular country or region are no longer there.

And then you have to consider the little farmer in a developing country. Let's say he has a rice crop ready to go to market, but ⋯ don't forget, he's competing with all the big nations in the world ⋯ suddenly rice prices fall elsewhere in the world, and he can't sell his crop. If he were a big farmer in a big nation, he might be able to turn around and produce another crop. But this little farmer can't do that; he doesn't have the resources. So he's wiped out financially. So ⋯ that's a big drawback of globalization; it puts the little guy in the game with the big guys, and he's at a huge disadvantage.

Globalization could wreak havoc on the economies of nations and put local producers out of business. The opportunities for success in a globalized economy are unlimited, but so are the opportunities for failure. Developing nations need training and mentoring in order to compete successfully and not to be financially destroyed by competing in the world market. We need to make sure we have a lot of checks and balances in place before we open the doors completely to globalization.

Narrator

Please listen carefully.

Narrator

You have 20 minutes to plan and write your response. Your response will be judged on the basis of the quality of your writing and on how well your response presents the points in the lecture and their relationship to the reading passage. Typically, an effective response will be 150 to 225 words.

Reading

Narrator

Now read a passage about an academic topic. You have 3 minutes to read the passage. Begin reading now.

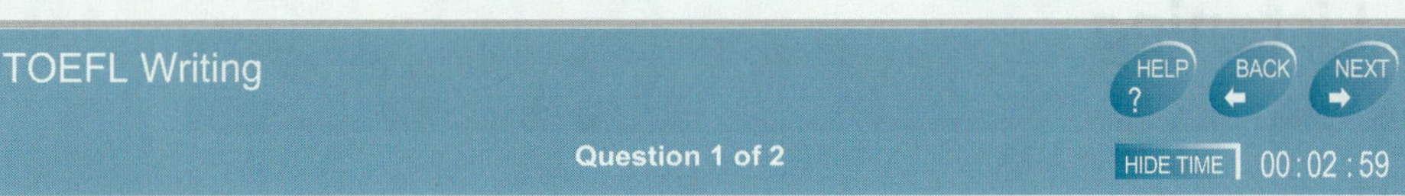

Reading Time : 3 minutes

Home schooling is a new trend in education that has found great favor with parents and their children. Children that are home schooled receive the most individual attention possible and are able to learn at their own pace. The ability to speed through easy sections prevents boredom, and the ability to slow down through difficult sections prevents confusion and incomplete comprehension. Students are not subjected to unfair teachers, harassment by other students, children that are a bad influence, or moral or religious ideas that their parents disapprove of.

Although critics of home schooling suggest that home-schooled children lack proper socialization, experience has not borne this out. Home-schooled children do not exhibit social dysfunction; rather, they seem actually better socialized than children who go to public school and less vulnerable to peer pressure.

Parents who home school their children recommend several precautions for success. First, they warn that the public school system is not generally in favor of home schooling. Some systems offer home school support programs that are merely a disguised means of controlling the child's education. Parents warn not to enroll in these programs. If so, the school will have the right to dictate what a child is taught. And second, they point out that home schooling should not be set up as an imitation of the classroom environment but should take advantage of the flexibility of being able to control the learning environment.

Although home schooling has its detractors, those who have experienced it are almost universal in their praise of its benefits. Not only does it provide a better learning environment than public schools, parents often prove to be better teachers than the tenured, disinterested teachers in lower-income school districts. Home schooling has been proven successful in the United States, Japan, and other countries around the world.

Note–taking

Listening

Narrator

Now listen to part of a lecture on the topic you just read about.

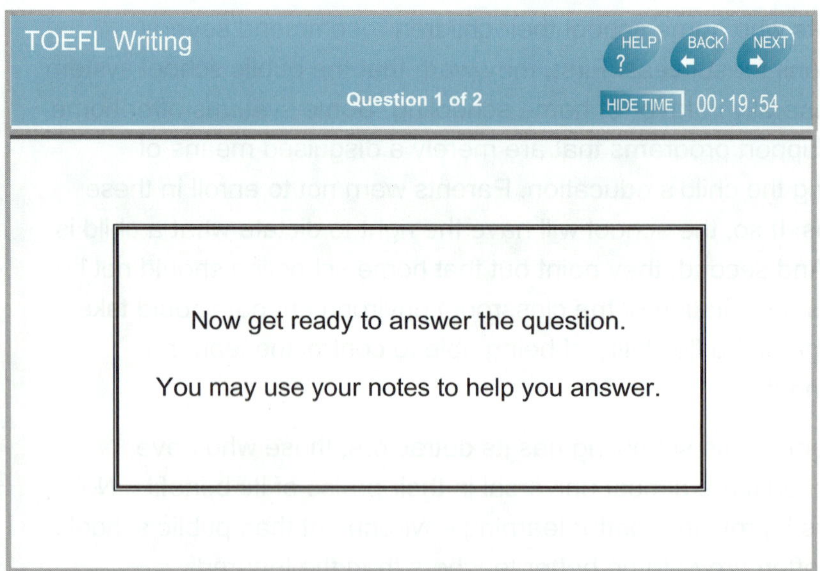

Narrator

Summarize the points made in the lecture you just heard, explaining how they cast doubt on points made in the reading.

TOEFL Writing

HELP ? | BACK ← | NEXT →

Question 1 of 2

HIDE TIME ⌐ 00 : 19 : 54

Directions: You have 20 minutes to plan and write your response. Your response will be judged on the basis of the quality of your writing and on how well your response presents the points in the lecture and their relationship to the reading passage. Typically, an effective response will be 150 to 225 words.

Question: Summarize the points made in the lecture you just heard, explaining how they cast doubt on points made in the reading.

Home schooling is a new trend in education that has found great favor with parents and their children. Children that are home schooled receive the most individual attention possible and are able to learn at their own pace. The ability to speed through easy sections prevents boredom, and the ability to slow down through difficult sections prevents confusion and incomplete comprehension. Students are not subjected to unfair teachers, harassment by other students, children that are a bad influence, or moral or religious ideas that their parents disapprove of.

Although critics of home schooling suggest that home-schooled children lack proper socialization, experience has not borne this out. Home-schooled children do not exhibit social dysfunction; rather, they seem actually better socialized than children who go to

I think that ⋯

Answer

Listening Script

Professor

With home schooling being the rage everywhere nowadays, I think we need to, um, take a look at some of the reasons it might be less than the perfect solution for education problems. For one thing, children schooled at home are isolated from the outside world and become socially handicapped as a result. The only people they learn to interact with are their parents and siblings. And of course ··· they are not exposed to the diversity of beliefs and backgrounds they would run into in public schools.

And then there is the question of academic training. In schools, teachers must meet government standards and have the appropriate certification in order to teach. But at home, parents lack teaching training as well as specific training for each content area. Parents may only teach students in the areas they themselves are skilled in, and you know what that can do ··· it can lead to more pronounced strengths and weaknesses in their child's abilities.

Parents can also have a problem with balancing teaching duties with other everyday tasks. If there is a lack of structure in the home, the learning environment suffers accordingly. The resources available to assist in learning are also obviously going to be limited. Parents aren't going to have chemistry labs or language labs in their homes. Nor are they probably going to have the money to provide educational experiences such as field trips, specialized tutors, and everyday school materials. And extracurricular activities such as drama club, band, and team sports are out of the question. Although many benefits are touted for home schooling, parents need to consider the option carefully and make sure they'll be able to provide a truly comprehensive and well-rounded education for their children.

Narrator

Please listen carefully.

Narrator

You have 20 minutes to plan and write your response. Your response
will be judged on the basis of the quality of your writing and on how
well your response presents the points in the lecture and their
relationship to the reading passage. Typically, an effective response
will be 150 to 225 words.

Reading

Narrator

Now read a passage about an academic topic. You have 3 minutes to
read the passage. Begin reading now.

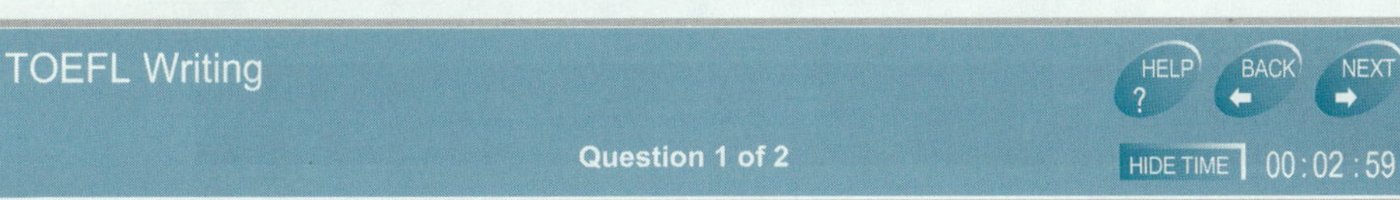

Reading Time : 3 minutes

Many people today are making a greater effort to eat healthfully, and doctors in general seem to have little appreciation for the benefits of vitamin therapy. However, many nutrition-oriented physicians and other medical practitioners believe that supplementing the diet with additional vitamins and minerals beyond those found naturally in food is advisable. Supplements are recommended not just to enhance overall health and well-being but also to treat specific ailments. Zinc, for example, is often prescribed for patients undergoing dialysis, for alcoholics suffering from cirrhosis who have vision problems, and for others who have zinc deficiencies. Likewise, iron is prescribed for iron-deficiency anemia, and vitamin A for severe acne.

One of the most noted pioneers in vitamin therapy, Nobel laureate Linus Pauling, advised taking megadoses — amounts that considerably exceed the established recommended daily allowance (RDA) — of certain vitamins and minerals. Pauling argued that while the RDAs were probably sufficient for preventing deficiency diseases like scurvy, they were completely inadequate for maintaining optimum health and that the body required considerably greater amounts of vitamins to achieve and maintain good health.

Pauling's primary research focus was on the use of vitamin C and its use in combating colds and preventing or treating a number of common diseases. Pauling pointed out that while the bodies of most mammals manufacture the vitamin C they need, human bodies do not have this capability; therefore, humans are dependent on external sources such as food and supplements for their vitamin C.

Megadoses of vitamins are contraindicated in pregnant women and certain other cases, and consumers must be careful not to develop exaggerated expectations of supplement therapy. For the most part, however, the larger doses Pauling prescribed are thought to be the body's true vitamin requirement for good health.

Listening

Narrator

Now listen to part of a lecture on the topic you just read about.

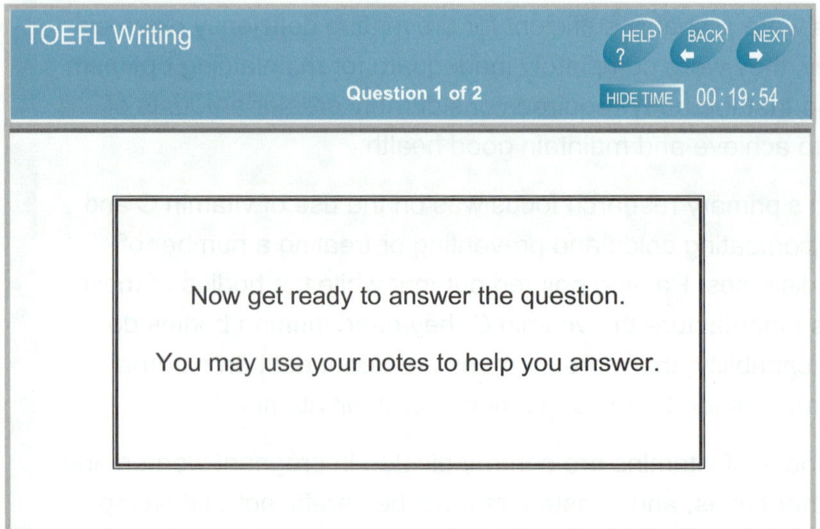

Narrator

Summarize the points made in the lecture you just heard, explaining how they cast doubt on points made in the reading.

TOEFL Writing

HELP ? | BACK ← | NEXT →

Question 1 of 2

HIDE TIME | 00:19:54

Directions: You have 20 minutes to plan and write your response. Your response will be judged on the basis of the quality of your writing and on how well your response presents the points in the lecture and their relationship to the reading passage. Typically, an effective response will be 150 to 225 words.

Question: Summarize the points made in the lecture you just heard, explaining how they cast doubt on points made in the reading.

Many people today are making a greater effort to eat healthfully, and doctors in general seem to have little appreciation for the benefits of vitamin therapy. However, many nutrition-oriented physicians and other medical practitioners believe that supplementing the diet with additional vitamins and minerals beyond those found naturally in food is advisable. Supplements are recommended not just to enhance overall health and well-being but also to treat specific ailments. Zinc, for example, is often prescribed for patients undergoing dialysis, for alcoholics suffering from cirrhosis who have vision problems, and for others who have zinc deficiencies. Likewise, iron is prescribed for iron-deficiency anemia, and vitamin A for severe acne.

One of the most noted pioneers in vitamin therapy, Nobel laureate Linus Pauling, advised taking megadoses

I think that ⋯

Answer

Listening Script

Professor

Now, I know that many of you are in the habit of taking megadoses of vitamins whenever you start to get a sniffle. And you've probably noticed some improvement when you take vitamin C for a cold ⋯ but you have to realize that not all doctors are in favor of megavitamin therapy. Most of them believe that, uh, although of course we all need vitamins in some amount, we can get what we need from our food as long as we eat a nice, well-balanced diet. If we want to be sure of getting enough of every vitamin and micronutrient, we can take an all-purpose multivitamin supplement that meets all the RDAs established by law.

Megavitamin therapy is discouraged by many doctors, you know. They claim that no scientific proof exists to indicate that vitamin therapy can improve or cure serious conditions like multiple sclerosis. Not only that, but it is possible that if you get too much of some vitamins, you may suffer from serious side effects as a result. Too much vitamin A, for example, can cause increased pressure within the skull and other unusual problems. Too much vitamin B6, on the other hand, can cause nerve damage similar to that caused by multiple sclerosis. Too much vitamin D can cause liver damage.

So you can see that, uh, it is not advisable to take megadoses of vitamins to treat medical conditions. To stay on the safe side, it's best to consult your healthcare provider before trying to treat any condition with megavitamins.

Narrator

Please listen carefully.

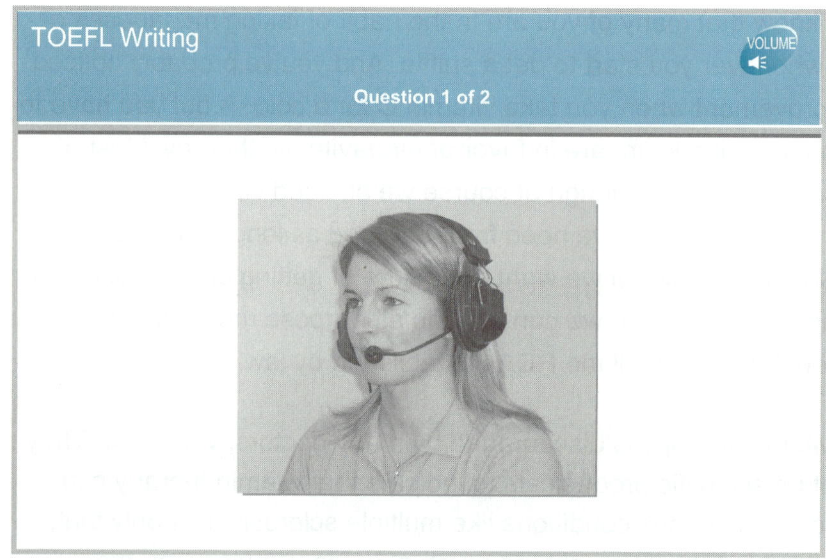

Narrator

You have 20 minutes to plan and write your response. Your response will be judged on the basis of the quality of your writing and on how well your response presents the points in the lecture and their relationship to the reading passage. Typically, an effective response will be 150 to 225 words.

Reading

Narrator

Now read a passage about an academic topic. You have 3 minutes to read the passage. Begin reading now.

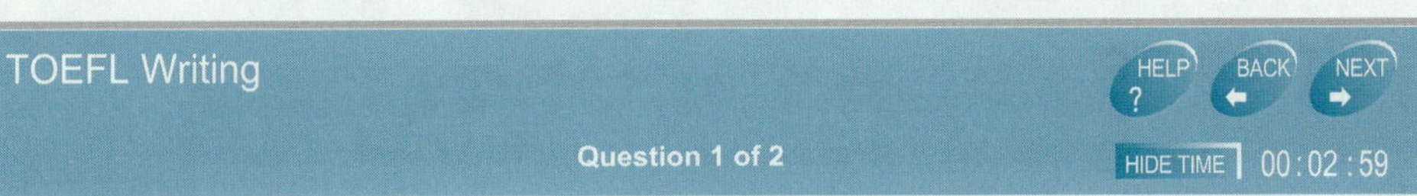

Reading Time : 3 minutes

We are only beginning to learn about all the negative effects that watching television can have on children. We have long understood that television is merely a passive experience. The viewer does little thinking or moving and just sits in front of the television, watching the screen. We have also understood that much of the content in television is inappropriate for children. Even cartoons can be violent or can introduce concepts that we would never intentionally expose our children to.

However, only recently has it been identified that television watching actually hampers a child's learning by demotivating him to read. Regardless of what a child watches on TV, there is something mesmerizing about watching. Parents describe the trancelike nature of their children's TV watching, and in the book *The Plug-In Drug*, author Marie Winn states, "There is certainly little indication that the child is active and alert". Winn asserts that there is a clear connection between TV watching and a decline in children's reading and writing abilities. Since reading requires the child to create pictures in his mind and use his imagination and points of reference to put the story together, watching TV provides a shortcut that eliminates all that effort. Children who watch a lot of TV, therefore, have a reduced ability to adjust to nonvisual experiences.

Most damning is the discovery detailed in the *Pediatrics Journal* that each hour in front of the TV increases a child's chances of developing attention deficit disorder by 10%. According to Dr. Dimitri Christakis, "The newborn brain develops very rapidly during the first two to three years of life. It's really being wired ⋯ TV can cause the developing mind to experience unnatural levels of stimulation". This effect is heightened by the way children's television uses rapid image changes to keep young children interested.

Listening

Narrator

Now listen to part of a lecture on the topic you just read about.

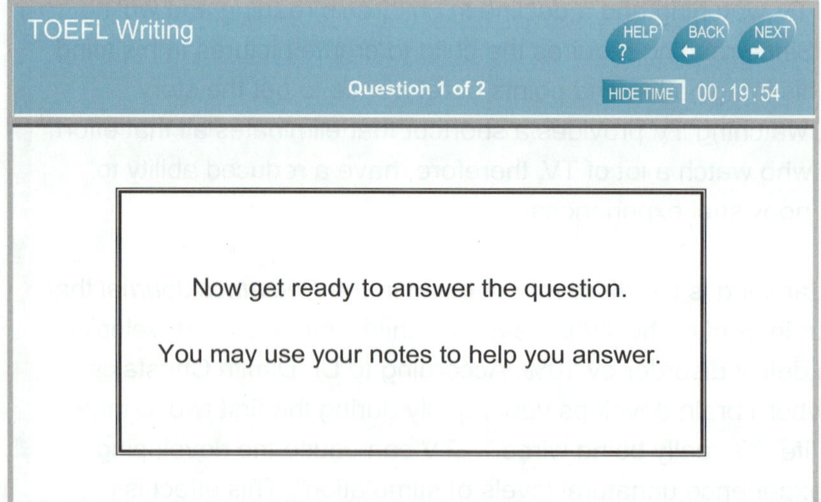

Narrator

Summarize the points made in the lecture you just heard, explaining how they cast doubt on points made in the reading.

TOEFL Writing

HELP ? BACK ← NEXT →

HIDE TIME 00 : 19 : 54

Directions: You have 20 minutes to plan and write your response. Your response will be judged on the basis of the quality of your writing and on how well your response presents the points in the lecture and their relationship to the reading passage. Typically, an effective response will be 150 to 225 words.

Question: Summarize the points made in the lecture you just heard, explaining how they cast doubt on points made in the reading.

We are only beginning to learn about all the negative effects that watching television can have on children. We have long understood that television is merely a passive experience. The viewer does little thinking or moving and just sits in front of the television, watching the screen. We have also understood that much of the content in television is inappropriate for children. Even cartoons can be violent or can introduce concepts that we would never intentionally expose our children to.

However, only recently has it been identified that television watching actually hampers a child's learning by demotivating him to read. Regardless of what a child watches on TV, there is something mesmerizing about watching. Parents describe the trancelike nature of their children's TV watching, and in the book *The Plug-In Drug*, author Marie Winn states, "There is certainly little

I think that ⋯

Answer

Listening Script

Professor

You know ··· parents these days have a lot of trouble figuring out how to interact with their kids. The kids are in one room watching TV, while the parents are in another balancing the checkbook or cooking dinner. Sometimes there doesn't seem to be any way to, uh ··· connect. And yet most families could be closer and spend more time together if they just made a point of watching TV together.

Yes, I know that not all TV programs are worth watching, but that's one of the advantages of watching TV with your kids. You can help them decide what to watch. And — this can be enlightening — you'll also find out what's actually in some of the shows they watch. So watching TV with your kids lets you monitor what they watch and help them interpret what they're seeing.

Another advantage of watching TV with your kids is that it gives you a great opportunity to cuddle with them. No matter what age your child is, he's probably had a tough day at school. Even nursery school has its bullies, and there can be tough teachers, rejecting classmates, and any number of experiences that erode your child's confidence and sense of well-being. When he snuggles with you on the couch, he feels restored and nurtured. And you get a chance to truly connect and communicate your love.

TV can also give you and your child a way of communicating indirectly about things that he isn't comfortable talking to you about straight out. He might, for example, be getting threatened at recess by older children who have told him not to tell anyone. If you watch a TV show about a child in a similar situation, you can ask your child how he feels about the character or the show.

Narrator

Please listen carefully.

Narrator

You have 20 minutes to plan and write your response. Your response will be judged on the basis of the quality of your writing and on how well your response presents the points in the lecture and their relationship to the reading passage. Typically, an effective response will be 150 to 225 words.

Reading

Narrator

Now read a passage about an academic topic. You have 3 minutes to read the passage. Begin reading now.

Reading Time : 3 minutes

Today's large-scale agriculture employs a vast array of pesticides that are extremely toxic to humans. Pesticides can cause cancers and other serious illnesses, so the government has set acceptable levels for each of the chemicals in them. However, surveys reveal that much of our food contains much higher levels of pesticide residues than government regulations allow. Furthermore, the long-term effects of the greater toxicity caused when the various pesticides are mixed together are unknown. As if toxic chemicals in our food weren't enough, high levels of pesticides and nitrates also filter through into our drinking water through water courses. The cost of reducing toxic levels in the water has to be paid for by the taxpayer.

One solution to the toxicity problem is organic farming. In organic farming, toxic pesticides are not used at all; instead, natural methods of increasing yield are used — manures instead of chemicals, maintaining the soil's quality with crop rotation instead of trying to remedy it with chemical fertilizers, and protecting the environment instead of depleting it. Organic farming brings with it a host of related benefits, such as less dependence on non-renewable resources like the fossil fuels used to produce fertilizers.

Studies show that organic farms support five times as many plants, 44 percent more in-field birds, 1.6 times as many arthropods (insects that birds feed on), and significantly fewer crop pests than conventional farms. Along with the safety and health benefits of uncontaminated food, organic farming offers greater biodiversity and protection for the environment. With the cost of other conservation approaches running very high, the actual cost of conventional farming, and the benefits of organic farming all considered, organic farming ends up being a cost-efficient agricultural method with much lower risk to the consumer.

Listening

Narrator

Now listen to part of a lecture on the topic you just read about.

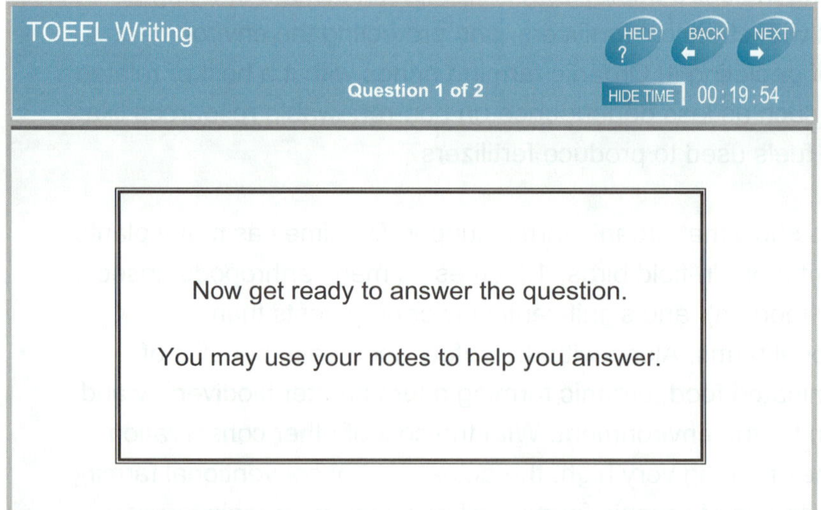

Narrator

Summarize the points made in the lecture you just heard, explaining how they cast doubt on points made in the reading.

TOEFL Writing

HELP ?   BACK ←   NEXT →

Question 1 of 2

HIDE TIME   00 : 19 : 54

Directions: You have 20 minutes to plan and write your response. Your response will be judged on the basis of the quality of your writing and on how well your response presents the points in the lecture and their relationship to the reading passage. Typically, an effective response will be 150 to 225 words.

Question: Summarize the points made in the lecture you just heard, explaining how they cast doubt on points made in the reading.

Today's large-scale agriculture employs a vast array of pesticides that are extremely toxic to humans. Pesticides can cause cancers and other serious illnesses, so the government has set acceptable levels for each of the chemicals in them. However, surveys reveal that much of our food contains much higher levels of pesticide residues than government regulations allow. Furthermore, the long-term effects of the greater toxicity caused when the various pesticides are mixed together are unknown. As if toxic chemicals in our food weren't enough, high levels of pesticides and nitrates also filter through into our drinking water through water courses. The cost of reducing toxic levels in the water has to be paid for by the taxpayer.

One solution to the toxicity problem is organic farming. In organic farming, toxic pesticides are not used

I think that …

Answer

Listening Script

Professor

I think we've all heard about the benefits of organic farming. And we probably all agree that we don't want to eat any more toxic chemicals with our food than we have to — right, class? But ··· let's not give organic farming too much credit. First of all, do we really want to throw away all the technological advances we've developed in the last 50 years? Those, uh, advances enable us to produce a lot more food in the same amount of time, whereas organic crops have much lower yields. In fact, organic farming could wipe out many of the starving people in the world because it will never be able to produce enough food fast enough to feed them.

It's also important to understand that even organic farming can cause problems if it is not done properly. While there are environmental benefits to avoiding the use of toxic chemicals, over-use of manure and other organic fertilizers can also lead to nitrogenous pollution. Besides that, the prices of organic products are about double those of conventionally grown products. That puts them out of the reach of many consumers. Not only is the cost to the consumer greater, the cost to the farmer is much greater too — and the higher price does not always make up for the lower yields. And then there's the issue of time. It takes several years to change land that was once used for conventional farming into organic farmland. I think we need to take a long look at organic farming and decide whether the so-called benefits are really worth everything we would have to give up for them.

Narrator

Please listen carefully.

Narrator

You have 20 minutes to plan and write your response. Your response will be judged on the basis of the quality of your writing and on how well your response presents the points in the lecture and their relationship to the reading passage. Typically, an effective response will be 150 to 225 words.

Reading

Narrator

Now read a passage about an academic topic. You have 3 minutes to read the passage. Begin reading now.

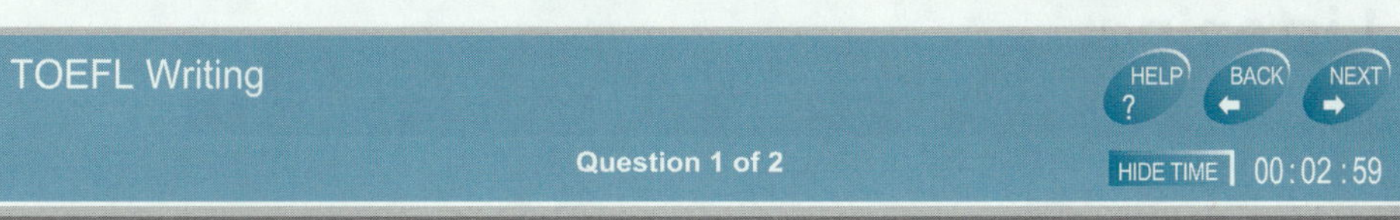

Reading Time : 3 minutes

A bronze tan is still a status symbol for many people in spite of findings that excessive sun exposure can be harmful. Sunlight gives off two types of ultraviolet (UV) rays — UVA and UVB — and the latter can damage skin as well as creating vision problems, allergic reactions, and depressed immune systems. UVB rays are known to cause sunburn, premature aging, and skin cancer. Unfortunately, the same process that causes the skin to tan can also cause the skin to burn and skin damage because overexposure to the sun is cumulative and cannot be reversed.

Skin cancer is not an ailment to be trifled with. Of the one million cases diagnosed in the United States each year, 7,300 are fatal. People who live in the sunbelt, where sun exposure is longer and hotter, have 2.5 times the cancer rate as those living in other areas. Caucasians have a higher fatality rate from skin cancer also, due to having less natural protection in their skin. Approximately 76% of skin cancer deaths involve melanoma, a form of skin cancer characterized by a dark patch that may resemble a mole.

Even those sun-worshippers who do not contract skin cancer still run the risk of premature aging. Increased sun exposure causes skin to lose its elasticity, wrinkle, and become leathery, in addition to developing spots and discolorations. Allergic reactions can also be troublesome, and these are increased by certain diseases and drugs.

And finally, extended sun exposure can even cause death due to sunstroke. The body has a limited tolerance for excessive heat, and other underlying conditions can reduce that tolerance. For this reason, it is important to drink plenty of water when sunbathing, to keep the head covered, and to come in out of the sun if starting to feel unwell.

Note–taking

Listening

Narrator

Now listen to part of a lecture on the topic you just read about.

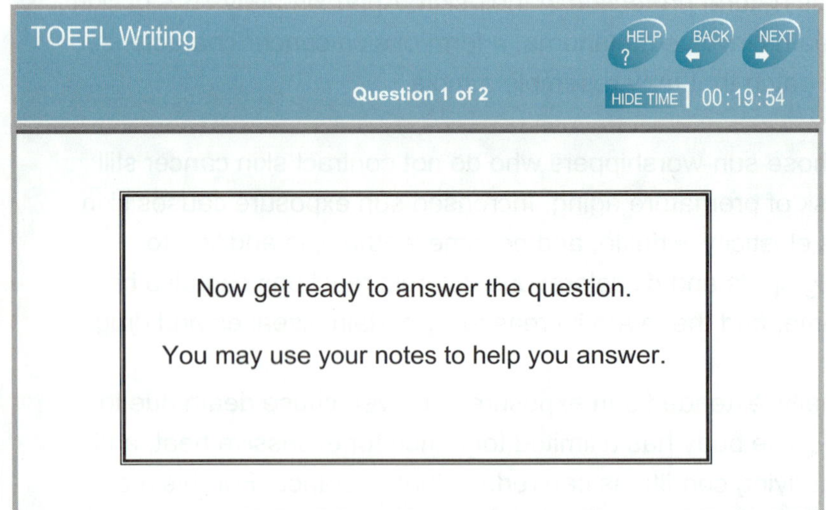

Narrator

Summarize the points made in the lecture you just heard, explaining how they cast doubt on points made in the reading.

TOEFL Writing

HELP ? BACK ← NEXT →

Question 1 of 2

HIDE TIME 00 : 19 : 54

Directions: You have 20 minutes to plan and write your response. Your response will be judged on the basis of the quality of your writing and on how well your response presents the points in the lecture and their relationship to the reading passage. Typically, an effective response will be 150 to 225 words.

Question: Summarize the points made in the lecture you just heard, explaining how they cast doubt on points made in the reading.

A bronze tan is still a status symbol for many people in spite of findings that excessive sun exposure can be harmful. Sunlight gives off two types of ultraviolet (UV) rays — UVA and UVB — and the latter can damage skin as well as creating vision problems, allergic reactions, and depressed immune systems. UVB rays are known to cause sunburn, premature aging, and skin cancer. Unfortunately, the same process that causes the skin to tan can also cause the skin to burn, and skin damage because overexposure to the sun is cumulative and cannot be reversed.

Skin cancer is not an ailment to be trifled with. Of the one million cases diagnosed in the United States each year, 7,300 are fatal. People who live in the sunbelt, where sun exposure is longer and hotter, have 2.5 times the cancer rate as those living in other areas. Caucasians

I think that ⋯

Answer

<table>
<tr><td>

Listening Script

Professor

You know, one of the most potent health-giving substances is available to everyone completely free ⋯ sunlight. The benefits of sunlight have been known for a long time, and doctors often prescribe that patients suffering from certain ailments move to a warmer climate.

Now, uh, one of the most basic benefits of sunlight is its warming infrared rays. The sun's heat can be used to treat neuralgia, arthritis ⋯ um ⋯ sinusitis, among other things. And warmth also brings healthful natural body oils to the surface of the skin, keeping it smooth and protected. We would not have much to eat if it weren't for sunlight, since most food depends on sunlight to grow.

The sun's ultraviolet rays also kill harmful organisms like bacteria and viruses. In fact ⋯ they can kill a host of things we don't want, even fungi, molds, and dust mites in the air and on the surfaces of things. The power of sunlight is so strong that even reflected sunlight from a north window can destroy bacteria in the dust on window sills and floors — and that's after the window glass has already filtered out about 95% of the ultraviolet rays. Ultraviolet rays kill germs directly on the skin, making it a great treatment for skin diseases like diaper rash, athlete's foot, and acne.

And we owe most of our vitamin D intake to sunlight; vitamin D lowers our cholesterol levels and helps our bodies process calcium correctly. A good rule of thumb for this is to expose at least six inches of our skin to direct sunlight for one hour per day to give us our minimum daily requirement of vitamin D.

Finally, sunlight helps regulate most bodily processes. It improves sleep, hormone levels, thyroid function, and blood sugar levels. It even increases the oxygen in the blood!

</td><td>

P~ health subs /fʳ → ☀s

d°/☻ p°(ill /M→ ☀w clim

1 bf / ☀w infrared ray

Treat dis
ⓝ body oil (↑ skin
◁ food / ☼ sun ⟩ ♂

UVR /kill ρ org° (bac / vir / fungi etc

*/〜 → ref */kill bac floor
glass/Filter 95% UVR

UVR /X germ on skin
cure skin dis (acne

vit D ← *
/↓ chol
◁ P= calc
6inch skin 1h/d
↓
daily req.

*/◁ Reg body P=
↑ sleep/horm/blood sug/oxygen

</td></tr>
</table>

Narrator

Please listen carefully.

Narrator

You have 20 minutes to plan and write your response. Your response will be judged on the basis of the quality of your writing and on how well your response presents the points in the lecture and their relationship to the reading passage. Typically, an effective response will be 150 to 225 words.

Reading

Narrator

Now read a passage about an academic topic. You have 3 minutes to read the passage. Begin reading now.

TOEFL Writing

HELP ?   BACK ←   NEXT →

Question 1 of 2

HIDE TIME ┃ 00 : 02 : 59

Reading Time : 3 minutes

The primary component of every living organism is water. In fact, after oxygen, water is the most important requirement for life. More than two-thirds of the human body is composed of water. The brain is nearly 85 percent water, and solid tissue is about 70 percent water. The body is made to utilize water for its processes. In fact, water is a universal solvent, capable of dissolving and carrying nearly any type of substance. Water is the basis for all bodily fluids, including digestive juices, blood, urine, lymph, and sweat. The body uses water to transport oxygen and nutrients to cells and to eliminate toxins and waste. Waste elimination reduces the burden on the lungs, kidneys, and liver. Water helps regulate body temperature and even lubricates the organs. A hydrated body keeps muscles and skin toned and aids in weight loss.

The body's water requirement is so critical to life that if it is not maintained, death will occur. Humans can live without food for more than two months but cannot live for more than a week without water. If the body is deficient in water, thirst and dehydration will occur. In order to maintain adequate hydration in the body, humans must take in approximately $1\frac{1}{2}$ quarts — six glasses — daily in the form of beverages or as a component in their food. Many experts recommend a minimum of eight glasses of water per day to obtain the full benefits of hydration in the body.

The effects of adequate water intake are obvious to the water-drinker. A person who goes from drinking too little water to drinking plenty will notice dramatic changes in his body; he will feel much better, have more energy, and will notice that his skin is much clearer. When you drink water, you are drinking a toast to your health.

Listening

Narrator

Now listen to part of a lecture on the topic you just read about.

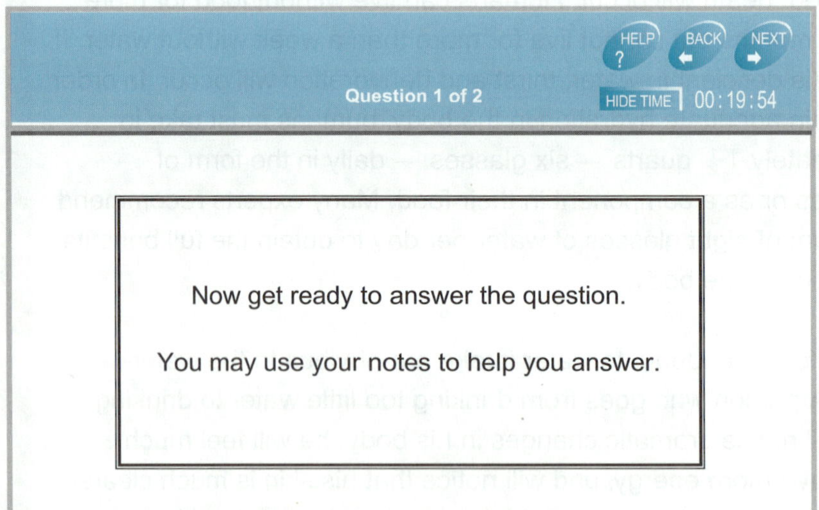

Narrator

Summarize the points made in the lecture you just heard, explaining how they cast doubt on points made in the reading.

TOEFL Writing

HELP ?   BACK ←   NEXT →

Question 1 of 2

HIDE TIME 00 : 19 : 54

Directions: You have 20 minutes to plan and write your response. Your response will be judged on the basis of the quality of your writing and on how well your response presents the points in the lecture and their relationship to the reading passage. Typically, an effective response will be 150 to 225 words.

Question: Summarize the points made in the lecture you just heard, explaining how they cast doubt on points made in the reading.

The primary component of every living organism is water. In fact, after oxygen, water is the most important requirement for life. More than two-thirds of the human body is composed of water. The brain is nearly 85 percent water, and solid tissue is about 70 percent water. The body is made to utilize water for its processes. In fact, water is a universal solvent, capable of dissolving and carrying nearly any type of substance. Water is the basis for all bodily fluids, including digestive juices, blood, urine, lymph, and sweat. The body uses water to transport oxygen and nutrients to cells and to eliminate toxins and waste. Waste elimination reduces the burden on the lungs, kidneys, and liver. Water helps regulate body temperature and even lubricates the organs. A hydrated body keeps muscles and skin toned and aids in weight loss.

I think that ⋯

Answer

Listening Script

Professor

Now, I know we've all heard that we should drink at least eight glasses of water every day. But Dartmouth Medical School physician Dr. Heinz Valtin now tells us that there is no scientific proof to back up this rule. Dr. Valtin is a kidney specialist and has written two books on the kidney and water balance. He believes that the traditional 8 x 8 rule (eight eight-ounce glasses of water per day) is just an obsession with people and does not need to be adhered to.

Valtin believes that the body is capable of maintaining proper water balance in healthy adults. He sees people carrying around bottles of water everywhere they go and feels that this is overkill. Large amounts of water are not needed, he says. And the old adage that you cannot count caffeinated drinks in part of your daily total is nonsense.

Now, uh ⋯ this does not apply to everyone. Valtin says it applies to healthy adults living in a temperate climate and leading a mostly sedentary lifestyle. Although he laughs at the 8 x 8 rule, he does admit that large intakes of fluid are advisable for the treatment or prevention of some conditions, such as kidney stones. And when engaging in strenuous physical activity, taking a long airplane flight, or exposed to hot weather, you will need more water. But aside from those considerations, he feels that most people are getting plenty of water.

In Valtin's opinion, too much water can actually be harmful. If a person drinks so much water that his kidneys cannot excrete enough, he can get "water intoxication", which can lead to confusion ⋯ or even death. Other disadvantages of a high water intake include intake of the pollutants in the water and frequent urination ⋯ that can be embarrassing as well as inconvenient.

Independent Writing

Introduction

Writing Task 2는 주어진 주제에 대해 30분 내에 최소 300단어 길이의 Essay를 써야 한다. 쓰기 능력만 평가하기 때문에 독립형 쓰기(Independent Writing)라고 불린다. 듣기 자료를 읽기와 연계해 요약하는 Writing Task 1과 달리, Writing Task 2는 자신의 선택이나 입장을 정연하게 전개하는 점에서 이전의 CBT 토플 Essay와 같다.

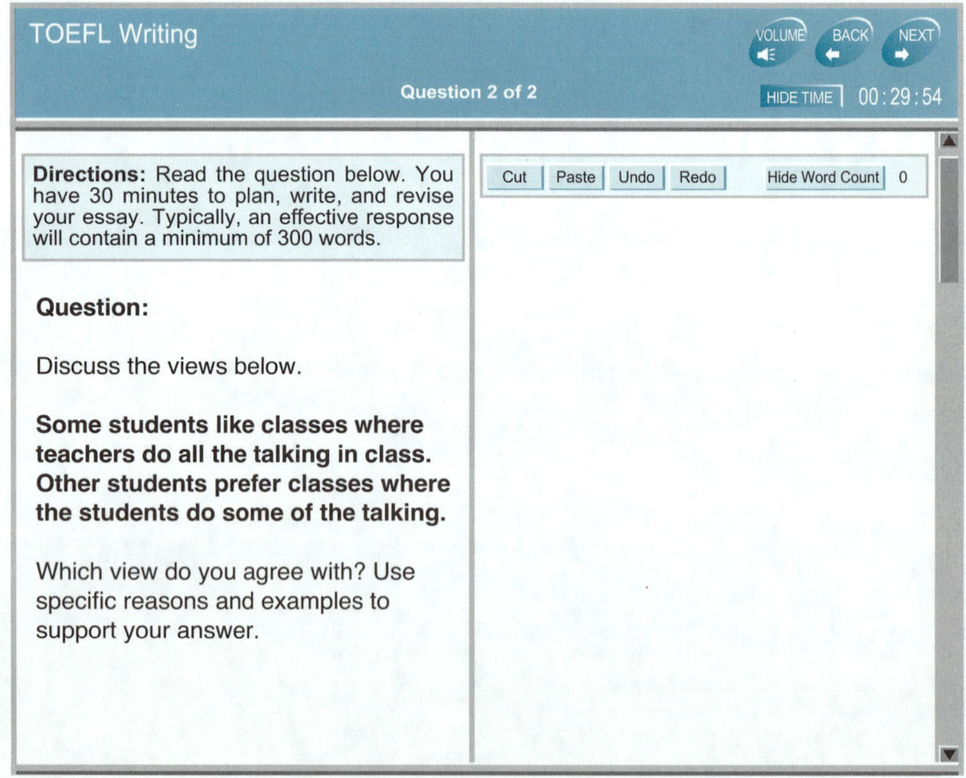

시험장에서 나누어 주는 메모 용지에 먼저 간단하게 Eassy의 Outline을 작성한 다음 Essay를 써야 짜임새 있는 글이 나온다.

문제 유형

기존 185개의 CBT Essay 주제와 유사한 것들이 출제될 것으로 전망된다. 그러나 문제 지시문은 CBT보다 더 간단하게 주어진다. iBT Writing 지시문은 크게 다음의 3가지 유형으로 구분된다.

1. 두 입장 중 한 가지를 선택해야 하는 유형

Some people believe A. Others believe B. Which view do you agree with?

2. 한 입장에 대해 찬성하는지 반대하는지를 묻는 유형

Do you agree or disagree with the following statement?

With the help of computer technology, students nowadays can learn more information and learn it more quickly.

3. 특정 주제에 대해 논리를 펴는 개방형 유형

Discuss the following statement.

Holidays honor people or event. If you could create a new holiday, what person or event would it honor and how would you want people to celebrate it?

Writing Task 2에 출제 가능성이 높은 주제들은 다음과 같다.

- 대학 교육은 누구나 받을 수 있어야 하는가? 다수의 학생인가 아니면 일부 재능있는 학생인가?
- 대중 매체가 유명인들의 사생활을 보도할 수 있는지에 관한 찬반
- 21세기의 가장 중요한 기술적 발전은 무엇인가?
- 컴퓨터 덕에 학습 환경이 더 쉬워졌는지에 관한 찬반
- 친구가 한두 명 있는 게 좋은가, 여러 명 있는 게 좋은가?
- 강의식 교육이 좋은가, 토론식 교육이 좋은가?
- 광고는 유익한가, 아니면 불필요한 소비만 조장하는가?

어떤 주제에 관한 지시문이 주어지더라도 구체적인 예와 이유를 들어 자신의 입장을 밝혀야 한다. 두루뭉실한 모호한 답변으로는 높은 점수를 기대할 수 없기 때문이다.

본 교재의 학습 순서

학습효과를 최대한 높이기 위해 Total iBT Writing은 다음과 같은 순서로 독립형 쓰기 Writing Task 2를 구성했다.

1. 문제 읽기: 먼저 지시문을 읽고 어떤 방향으로 써야 할지 정리한다.

Directions

Read the question below. You have 30 minutes to plan, write, and revise your essay. Typically, an effective response will contain a minimum of 300 words.

Question

Which type of class do you prefer?

Some students like classes where teachers do all the talking in class. Other students prefer classes where the students do some of the talking.

Give specific reasons and details to support your choice.

이 예제에서는 일부는 A를 주장하고, 다른 이들은 B를 주장하는데, 당신은 어느 쪽을 선택할지를 묻는 1번 문제유형이 제시되었다. 먼저 자신의 생각이 두 입장 중 어느 쪽에 가까운지를 정리해 본다.

2. Key Ideas 살피기: 양쪽 입장을 핵심 포인트로 정리해 놓은 Key Ideas를 읽으면서 자신의 입장과 일치하는 점이 있는지, 없다면 어떤 점을 추가하거나 바꿀 것인지 직접 종이에 쓰면서 고쳐 본다. 이렇듯 한 문제에 대해 포인트별로 생각을 정리하는 습관을 길러두면 실제 시험에서 많은 시간과 노력을 절약할 수 있다.

Key Ideas

교사 위주의 수업 방식

- 교사가 수업 내용을 가장 잘 안다.
- 수업 시간을 더 효율적으로 사용할 수 있다.

– 학생은 외우기만 하면 된다.

학생이 참여하는 수업 방식

– 정보화 시대에는 비판적 사고가 필요하다.
– 교사의 일방적인 수업은 수동적인 학생을 만든다.
– 토론과 발표를 통해 능동적인 학습을 유도해야 한다.

3. **Vocabulary Brainstorming**: 글 주제에 대한 생각을 구체적으로 정리한 다음에는 그 주제와 관련된 영어어휘들을 익혀두는 것이 필요하다.

대화: dialogue, conversation, exchange of ideas
교육: education, schooling
산업화: industrialization
수동적 학습: passive learning
일방적 지도: unilateral teaching
교사 위주의 수업: teacher-directed class
외우다: memorize
필기를 하다: take notes in class
정보화 시대: the Information Era
쌍방향 교육: interactive / two-way learning
능동적 학습: active learning
비판적, 창의적 사고: critical, creative mind / thinking
양성하다: foster
토론: discussion
발표: presentation

이렇게 주제별로 단어를 정리해 두면 Essay를 쓸 때 표현을 찾는 고민을 덜 해도 된다. 실제로 통역대학원에서도 주제별로 단어 정리를 많이 해 두는 훈련을 하는데, 이는 주제별 단어 정리가 통역이나 번역 시에 다채로운 영어 표현을 구사하는 데 큰 도움을 주기 때문이다. Independent Writing에서 주어진 30분 안에 300단어가 넘는 분량으로 논리 정연한 글을 쓰는 것은 결코 쉬운 일이 아니다. 시간을 벌기 위해서는 Key Ideas는 물론 Vocabulary Brainstorming처럼 관련 표현도 미리 챙겨 놓아야 한다. 이러한 표현 정리는 iBT Writing은 물론 Speaking에도 똑같이 큰 도움을 준다.

4. Basic Sentence 영작: 주제와 관련된 8개 정도의 기본 문장을 영작한다. 본격적인 Essay 작성에 앞서 꼭 거쳐야 하는 연습이다.

Basic Sentence Writing Practice

❶ 교사 주도의 수업은 가장 시간 효율적인 지도 방법이다.

____

____

연구 교사 주도의 teacher-centered, teacher-directed
가장 …하다: 최상급을 사용
시간 효율적인: time-efficient

❷ 그 어느 누구도 교사만큼 그 수업 내용을 잘 알지 못한다.

____

____

연구 부정문을 이용한 최상급 표현이다. Nobody … better than … 로 처리. 또는 The teacher is the one who … best 도 같은 의미.

❸ 학생들은 학우의 발표를 들음으로써 혼란스러워 할 것이다.

____

____

연구 혼란스러워 하다 get confused. 이때 confusing과 confused의 차이에 유의. '혼란스럽게 만드는' 은 confusing, '혼란스러워 하는' 은 confused.
…함으로써 by …ing

❹ 만약 교사가 모든 말을 다 하면, 학생들은 그저 수업 시간에 듣는 내용을 외우기만 하면 된다.

연구 모든 말을 다 하다 do all the talking
외우다 memorize

❺ 이러한 일방적 교육 방식의 주요 단점 중 하나는 그것이 수동적인 학습자를 만든다는 것이다.

연구 단점 shortcoming, disadvantage, drawback
일방적 unilateral
수동적 학습자 passive learner

❻ 창의적이고 비판적인 사고를 길러 주기 위해, 학생들이 수업 시간에 능동적인 역할을 할 수 있도록 해야 한다.

연구 …하기 위해 to + 부정사
기르다, 양성하다 foster
창의적인 creative   비판적인 critical
할 수 있도록 해야 한다 should be allowed + to 부정사
능동적 역할을 하다 take an active part, play an active role

❼ 우리가 대화에 참여할 때, 우리는 논리적인 주장을 제시하기 위해 우리의 생각을 날카롭게 하는 것을 배운다.

연구 …에 참여하다 be involved in, be engaged in, participate in, take part in
날카롭게 하다 sharpen up
논리적 주장 a logical argument

❽ 보다 능동적인 학습 방식을 설계하기 위해 소크라테스와 공자 같은 위대한 교사들이 사용한 양방향 교육 방식을 고려해야 한다.

⟨연구⟩ 소크라테스 Socrates   공자 Confucious
양방향 two-way, interactive
학습 방식 learning format

5. 모범답안 확인: Basic Sentence 영작에서 써 본 문장들을 답지에 있는 모범답안과 비교하면서 비판적으로 확인한다.

모범답안

1. The teacher-directed class is the most time-efficient teaching method.
2. Nobody knows the content of a class better than the teacher.
3. Students would get confused by listening to their classmates' presentations.
4. If the teacher does all the talking, the students just have to memorize what they hear in class.
5. One of the main drawbacks of this unilateral teaching method is that it creates passive learners.
6. To foster creative and critical minds, students should be allowed to take an active part in class.
7. When we are engaged in a conversation, we learn to sharpen up our ideas to present a logical argument.
8. The two-way educational methods used by great teachers like Socrates and Confucious should be considered to design a more active learning format.

6. Essay 쓰기

주제문을 다시 한 번 읽어 본 다음 교재에 주어진 공란에 최소 300단어 길이의 글을 속도감 있게 써 본다. 연습할 때에는 쓰기 시간이 30분을 초과해도 괜찮다. 점점 쓰는 시간을 줄여나가다가 시험 날짜가 임박하면 25분 내에 쓰는 훈련을 해야 한다. 시험장에서 실제로 느끼게 될 긴장감까지 고려하면 25분에 쓰는 연습을 해 두는 것이 도움이 많이 된다. 300단어 이상을 써야 한다고 해서 단어의 수를 일일이 셀 시간은 없다. 약 4줄 길이의 단락을 5개 쓴다고 생각하면 된다. 단락 구분은 반드시 해야 글의 짜임새가 있어 잘 읽힌다.

채점자는 친절한 독자가 아니라는 점을 기억해야 한다. 최대한 친절하게, 자세하게 글을 전개해야 좋은 점수를 받을 수 있다.

7. Sample Essay 확인

답지에 있는 Sample Essay를 읽어 보면서 자신의 Essay와 비교·분석한다. 문장의 길이, 단락의 길이, 아이디어 전개 방법, 사용된 표현들을 꼼꼼히 살피면서 앞으로 보완해 나갈 부분을 정리한다.

이상과 같은 7단계를 따라 Total iBT Writing을 공부하면 영작은 물론 논리력까지 함께 좋아진다는 것을 스스로 느끼게 될 것이다. 기본 영작에 어려움이 많은 학생들은 자매서 "TOEFL 기초공사 Writing"을 공부하면 많은 도움이 될 것이다.

Sample Essay

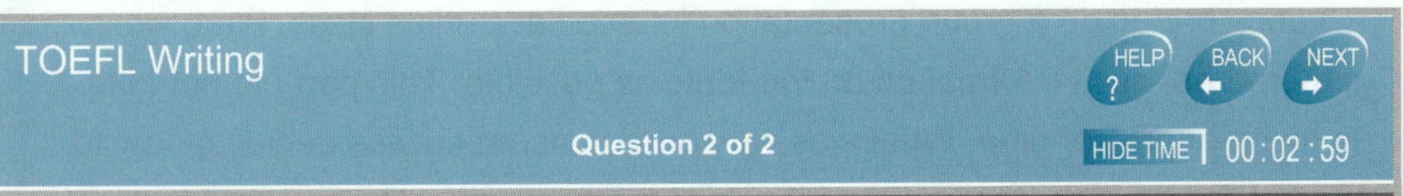

The most primitive format of education was based on dialogues between a teacher and his students. The exchange of ideas between Socrates and his followers is a good case in point. With industrialization, however, school became a training center for propective workers in factories. Teacher-directed class became the norm because it was considered the most time-efficient way to foster passive workers. Now in the Information Era, such a passive learning method cannot meet the intellectual requirements of the modern society.

Most of us are used to teacher-directed class format. While the teacher does all the talking, we have to just take notes and do the assigned homework. A high test score served as proof that we digested well what we had learned in class. One of the main drawbacks of this unilateral teaching method is that it creates passive learners. Since the basic task of a student is to just memorize what's being told, he or she does not use his critical thinking. Regurgitating what one heard in class is not evidence of his or her intelligence. Today's society needs people who can think critically and creatively. To foster creative, critical minds, students should be allowed to take an active part in class.

Both Confucious and Socrates, the two major scholars of the East and the West, are known to have taught their students through dialogues. That means they did not do all the talking. Instead, they let their students participate in the learning by exchanging ideas. When one is engaged in a conversation, he learns to sharpen up his ideas to present a logical argument. In modern schools, I think students can learn to arrange their ideas in a more logical manner through presentations or discussions in class.

I once had to do a group presentation in a social studies class. First, we gathered as much information on the topic as possible. This part did not take up much energy or time. What was very time-consuming was deciding how to present the topic. It was very perplexing in the beginning. We did not know how to arrange all the information we collected. Fortunately, after much discussion, we found a good focus on which to base our presentation. From that experience, I learned that knowing details of a topic is not enough. Facts can be easily retrieved from diverse sources including the Internet. What really matters is how logically we arrange the facts we have collected. I would not have learned this if I had not had an opportunity to take an active role in class.

In the Information Era, critical and creative thinking is more important than ever. Given this, I believe interactive learning, in which students actively participate in class, should be encouraged. Presentations and discussions are good ways to make students get involved in the learning process. The two-way educational methods used by such great teachers as Socrates and Confucious should be considered to design a more active learning format.

가장 원시적인 형태의 교육은 교사와 학생 간의 대화를 위주로 이루어졌다. 소크라테스와 그의 추종자들 사이의 의견교환이 좋은 사례이다. 하지만 산업화로 인해 학교는 공장에서 일하게 될 노동자들을 훈련하는 곳이 되었다. 교사위주의 수업이 수동적인 노동자 양성을 위해 가장 시간 효율적인 방법이라고 여겨졌기 때문에, 이러한 방식의 수업이 주를 이루게 되었다. 오늘날의 정보시대에서는 그러한 수동적 학습 방법은 복잡한 현대사회의 지적 요구수준을 충족시키지 못한다.

우리의 대부분은 교사위주의 수업 형태에 익숙해 있다. 교사 혼자서 말을 하는 동안 우리는 그저 필기를 하고, 숙제를 해야 한다. 높은 시험점수는 우리가 수업시간에 배운 내용을 잘 이해했다는 증거였다. 이러한 일방적 교습 방식의 주요 단점 중 하나는 학생을 수동적으로 만든다는 것이다. 학생은 그저 들은 것을 외우기만 하면 되기 때문에, 비판적인 사고를 하지 못한다. 수업시간에 들은 내용을 그대로 되뇌는 것으로 그 학생의 지능을 알 수는 없다. 오늘날의 사회는 비판적 그리고 창의적 사고를 가진 사람들을 필요로 하고 있다. 창의적이고 비판적인 사고를 기르기 위해서는 학생들이 수업에 적극 참여할 수 있도록 해야 한다.

각각 동양과 서양의 주요 학자인 공자와 소크라테스는 대화를 통해 학생을 가르쳤던 것으로 알려졌다. 이는 그들만이 말을 하지는 않았다는 뜻이다. 그 대신, 의견을 주고받음으로써 학생들이 학습과정에 참여할 수 있도록 해 주었다. 대화를 하는 사람은 논리적인 주장을 발표하기 위해 좀더 예리하게 생각하게 된다. 나는 현대 학교에서는 학생들이 수업시간에 발표와 토론을 함으로써 자신의 생각을 좀더 논리적으로 정리할 수 있다고 생각한다.

한번은 사회학 수업시간에 그룹 발표를 해야 했었다. 먼저 우리는 발표 주제에 대한 정보를 최대한 많이 모았다. 이 부분은 그다지 많이 힘들거나 시간이 오래 걸리지 않았다. 시간이 정말 많이 걸린 부분은 그 주제를 어떻게 발표할지 결정하는 일이었다. 처음에는 정말 어떻게 해야 할지몰랐다. 우리는 그 동안 모은 정보를 어떻게 정리해야 할지 몰랐다. 다행히도 오랜 토론 끝에, 어떤 관점에서 주제를 발표해야 할지 알아냈다. 그 때의 경험을 통해 나는 한 주제를 자세하게 아는 것으로는 충분하지 않다는 것을 배웠다. 정보는 인터넷을 포함해 다양한 출처에서 쉽게 찾을 수 있다. 정말 중요한 것은 그렇게 찾은 정보를 얼마나 논리 정연하게 정리하느냐이다. 만일 수업에 적극적으로 참여할 기회가 없었다면 이러한 사실을 알지 못했을 것이다.

정보시대에는 비판적, 창의적 사고가 그 어느 때보다 중요하다. 이 점을 감안할 때, 나는 학생들이 수업에 적극 참여하는 쌍방향 교육이 장려되어야 한다고 생각한다. 발표와 토론은 학생이 학습과정에 참여할 수 있도록 하는 좋은 방법들이다. 보다 역동적인 학습방법을 만들기 위해서는 과거 소크라테스와 공자 같은 학자들이 사용했던 양방향 교육 방법이 고려되어야 한다.

Independent Writing

Practice **1** University Education

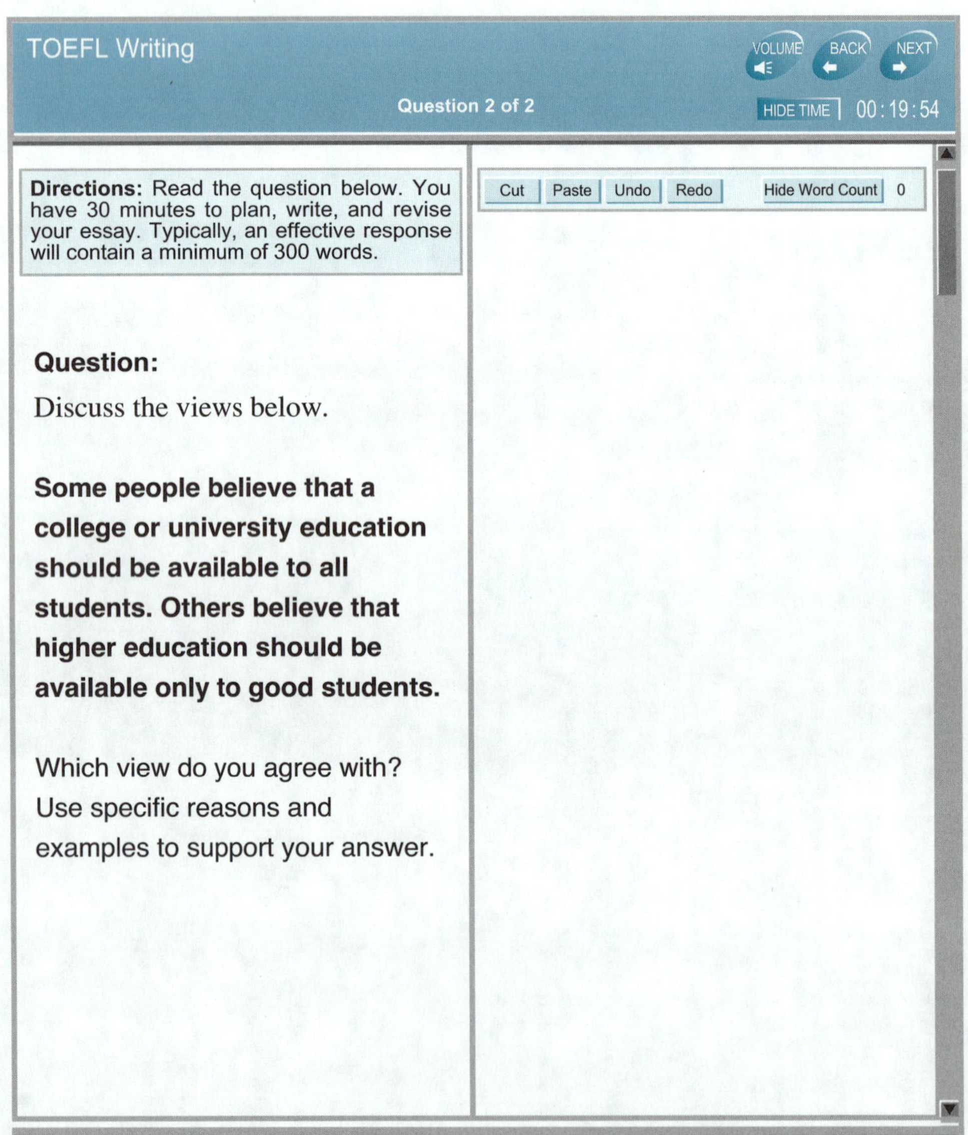

Key Ideas

University education for all students

−뒤늦게 공부하고 싶은 분야를 발견하는 학생들이 있다.
−공부의 기회는 누구에게나 동등하게 주어져야 한다.
−중고등학교 때 공부를 잘 한 학생이 대학교에서도 잘 한다는 법은 없다.

University education only for good students

−대학 말고도 고등학교 졸업 후 다양한 진로 선택이 있다.
−고등 교육은 공부에 소질과 관심이 있는 학생만을 대상으로 이루어져야 한다.
−모든 학생에게 대학을 개방하면 대학교육의 수준이 떨어진다.

Vocabulary Brainstorming

- 학사 학위: college degree, bachelor's degree
- 중고등 교육: secondary education
- 고등 교육: higher education, univesity education, advanced education
- 성적: grades
- 대학 입학: college admission
- 대학에 들어가다: enter a university
- 입학 조건: entrance requirement
- 대학 입학 시험: college entrance exam
- 졸업하다: graduate from
- 대학 졸업생: college graduate
- 대학생: undergraduate student
- 대학원생: graduate student
- 대학원: graduate school

Basic Sentence Writing Practice

❶ 나는 모든 학생들이 대학에 들어갈 수 있는 기회를 가져야 한다고 생각한다.

____

____

____

🔵 ⋯할 기회를 갖다 have the chance + to 부정사
⋯에 들어가다 enter + 장소. '~에 들어가다' 는 의미의 enter 뒤에는 in이 안 온다!

❷ 나의 믿음은 대학 입학 시험 과정이 공정하지 않다는 사실에 그 바탕을 두고 있다.

____

____

____

🔵 ⋯에 토대 · 바탕을 두고 있다 be based on ⋯
⋯라는 사실 the fact that + 절

❸ 입학 시험은 한 학생이 전공 공부를 얼마나 잘 할지를 측정하지 못한다.

____

____

____

🔵 측정하다 measure, assess, evaluate
누가 어떻게 할지 ⋯ how + 주어 + 동사
전공 major

❹ 일부 학생들은 공부의 중요성을 고등학교 졸업 후 깨닫는다.

연구 **깨닫다** realize, learn
~한 뒤 after + ~ing
졸업하다 graduate from

❺ 대학에 들어가는 것이 고등학교 졸업생들에게 주어지는 유일한 선택은 아니다.

연구 **대학에 들어가다** enter a university, college

❻ 그들은 졸업 후 무엇을 할지를 선택하기 전에 자신들의 재능과 소질을 평가해야 한다.

연구 **평가하다** assess, judge, evaluate, measure
재능과 소질 talents and tendencies, abilities and aptitutes

❼ 대학은 학문적으로 소질이 있는 이들만이 잘 할 수 있는 학문의 장이다.

연구 **학문의 장** an academic place, academia
학문적으로 소질이 있는 academically talented
잘 하다 do / perform well

❽ 어려운 대학 입학 시험과 높은 평균 성적을 요구하는 것은 선발하는 과정
의 중요한 부분들이다.

연구 **대학 입학 시험** university entrance exam
평균 성적 grade point average
…의 중요한 부분이다 an important part of …
선발하는 과정 screening / selecting process

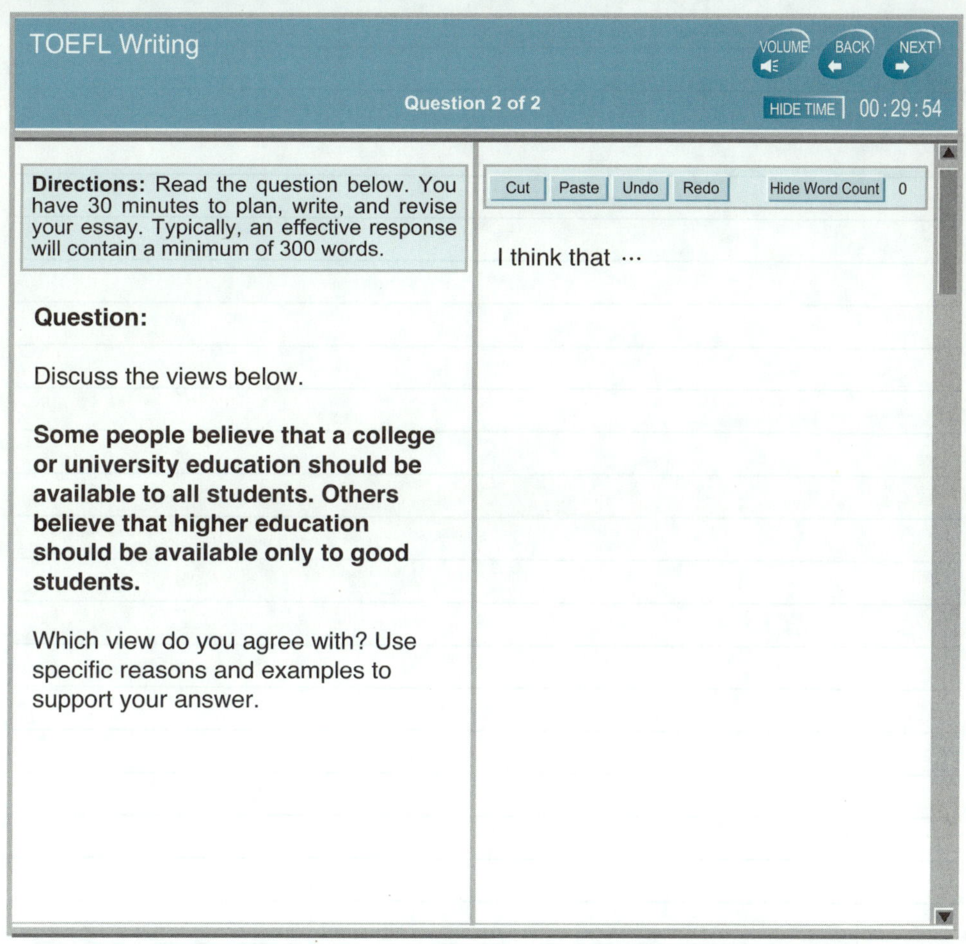

TOEFL Writing
VOLUME   BACK   NEXT
Question 2 of 2
HIDE TIME   00 : 29 : 54
Directions: Read the question below. You have 30 minutes to plan, write, and revise your essay. Typically, an effective response will contain a minimum of 300 words.
Question:
Discuss the views below.
Some people believe that a college or university education should be available to all students. Others believe that higher education should be available only to good students.
Which view do you agree with? Use specific reasons and examples to support your answer.
Cut   Paste   Undo   Redo   Hide Word Count   0
I think that ⋯

Answer

Sample Answer

After graduating from high school, one is faced with many choices. Some decide to continue studying, while others enter the world of work. It is true that in our society people regard going to university a much better choice than holding a job right after finishing high school. However, I believe higher education is only for those students who are good at and enjoy studying for the following set of reasons.

Firstly, entering a college is not the only option available to high school graduates. There are many career choices awaiting them when they finish secondary education. Some may decide to start working for a company, others may pursue their dreams which are not related to academic studying. One of my friends, for instance, wanted to be a singer and complained throughout high school that she did not have enough time to practice singing. She went to a music institute right after graduation and is now working as a singer for a musical band. Higher education is a good choice but not the only one for high school students. They have to assess their talents and tendencies before choosing what to do after graduation.

After all, university is an academic place that offers higher education. Not everyone can perform well in college. Only those who are academically minded and talented can enjoy the benefits of higher education. If a student did not do well in middle and high school, he is very unlikely to do well in universtiy. In a sense, secondary education is a preparatory course for higher education. Without good preparation, university education will be just a waste of time and money. This is one of the most important reasons why I believe that higher education should be available only to good students.

Lastly, if universities are open to all students without any screening process, the level of higher education will drop dramatically. Tough college entrance examinations and high grade point average requirements are important parts of the screening process. Without them, it would be difficult for universities to choose good candidates. I deplore the present reality in which all high school students have to spend too many hours studying to meet the college admission requirements. However, I believe a strict screening process is very important to maintain the quality of higher education.

My position on this statement is primarily based on the belief that college is basically an academic place where only academically talented ones can perform well. A university degree is important, but it is not the only tool to be successful in life. Those who are not good at studying may pursue other careers where they can realize their full potential. Higher education is a good choice, but not the best or the only one for every student.

Practice ❷ Mass Media

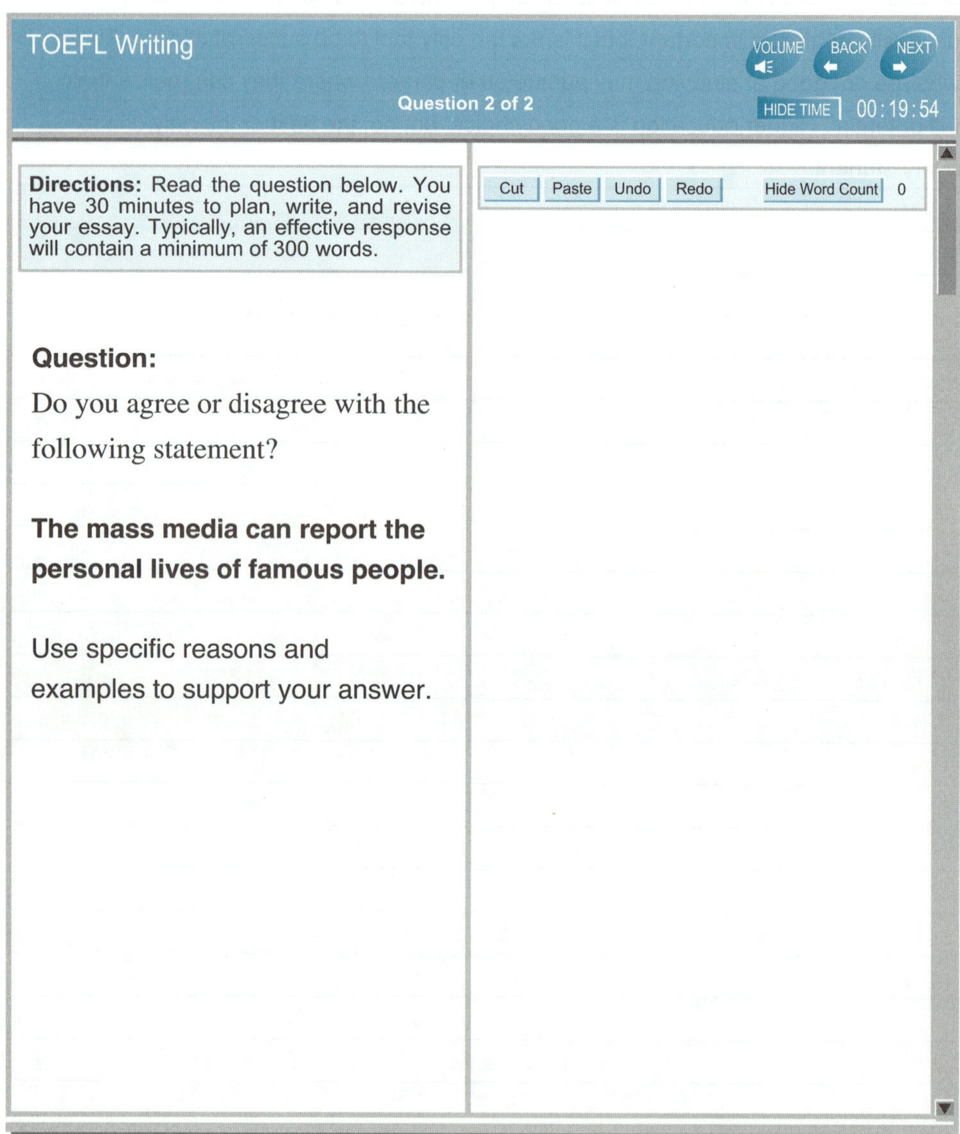

Key Ideas

Agree

-공적인 인물이기 때문에 사생활도 보도되어야 한다.
-공적인 직업을 선택했가 때문에 감수해야 하는 부분이다.
-때로는 사적인 부분에 대한 보도를 통해 그 사람의 됨됨이를 알 수 있다.

Disagree

-사생활은 보호되어야 한다.
-사생활 침해를 상품화 하고 있다.
-다른 정말 중요한 사건들을 보도해야 한다.

Vocabulary Brainstorming

- 사생활을 침해하다 invade one's privacy
- 사생활 침해 invasion / infringement / violation of privacy
- 공적인 인물, 공인 public figures
- 유명 인사 celebrities
- 조명을 받는 사람들 people in the spotlight
- 사진 기자들을 피하다 escape photographers
- 미디어의 관심을 끌다 attract media attention
- 경력을 망가트리다 damage one's career
- 사생활에 대한 지나친 초점 excessive focus on the private lives
- 방송인 broadcaster

Basic Sentence Writing Practice

❶ 유명한 사람들의 사생활에 대한 권리는 존중되어야 한다.

연구 ~에 대한 권리 rights to

❷ 유명인사들은 공적인 생활과 사적인 생활을 분리할 수 있어야 한다.

연구 ⋯할 수 있어야 한다 should be able + to 부정사
공적인 public
사적인 private
A를 어떤 상태로 유지하다 keep A + 형용사

❸ 그들의 일이 그들을 관심의 대상으로 만든다.

연구 관심의 대상, 관심을 받는 in the spotlight, the object of people's attention
무생물 주어를 과감하게 써본다!

❹ TV 카메라는 종종 유명한 스타들의 모든 움직임을 따라다닌다.

연구 **따라다니다** follow
모든 움직임 every move, all the moves

❺ 지나친 미디어의 관심이 유명한 사람들의 생명을 위험하게 만들 수 있다.

연구 **지나친** excessive, too much
위험하게 하다 endanger

❻ 방송인들은 공적인 정보에 매달려야 한다.

연구 ··· **매달리다** stick to, focus on, concentrate on

❼ 미디어는 유명인사와 공인들의 사생활을 존중할 필요가 있다.

연구 **존중하다** respect **공인** public figures

❽ 미디어는 이러한 사실들을 신중한 고려 없이 들추어내는 것 같다.

<hr>

연구 ~인 것 같다 it seems that …
들추어내다 dig up, uncover, unveil, report
신중한 고려 thorough / careful consideration

❾ 사생활의 세부사항을 노출시킴으로써, 미디어는 공인들의 경력을 부당하게 망가뜨릴 수 있다.

<hr>

연구 부당하게 unjustly, unfairly
경력, 직업 career
노출시키다 expose
~함으로써 by ~ing

❿ 미디어가 한 사람의 사생활을 조사하면서 시간을 보낼 때, 이것이 다른 중요한 이슈를 위한 시간을 빼앗는다.

<hr>

연구 …하면서 시간을 보내다 spend time ~ing
조사하다 investigate, look into, scrutinize
시간을 빼앗다 take time away from

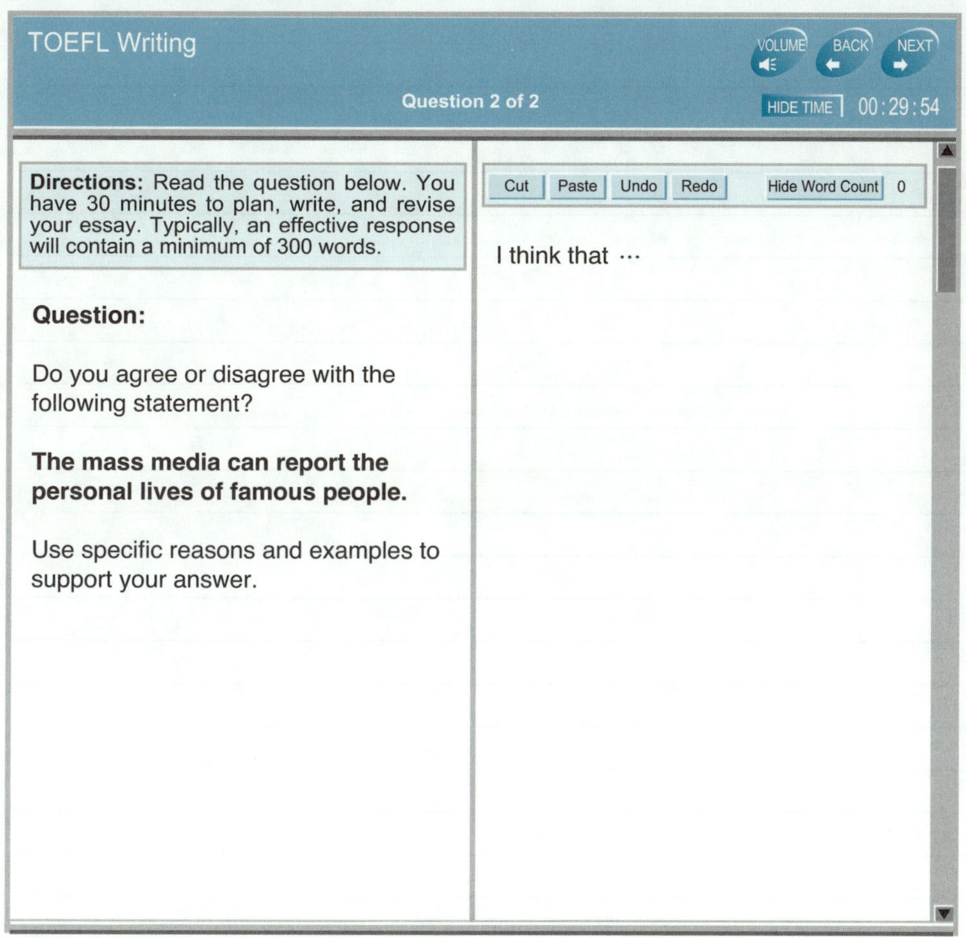

TOEFL Writing
VOLUME
BACK
NEXT
Question 2 of 2
HIDE TIME 00:29:54
Directions: Read the question below. You have 30 minutes to plan, write, and revise your essay. Typically, an effective response will contain a minimum of 300 words.
Question:
Do you agree or disagree with the following statement?
The mass media can report the personal lives of famous people.
Use specific reasons and examples to support your answer.
Cut Paste Undo Redo Hide Word Count 0
I think that …

Answer

Sample Answer

It is true that the names of renowned actresses on the front page of a newspaper are more eye-catching than any economic or political news. Taking full advantage of such tendency, the media reports every move of public figures and celebrities. This often infringes upon their privacy, and can even damage their public careers. Then, one may wonder whether the media has such authority to expose someone's personal life to the public. I disagree that the mass media can report the personal lives of famous people for the following set of reasons.

First, although public figures and celebrities have chosen careers that attract media attention, they are still entitled to have their private lives. Therefore, the media should respect their rights to privacy by only reporting the public aspect of the celebrities' actions. Then, the famous people can keep their public and private lives separate. After all, the judgement of public figures should be based on what they do professionally, not on the irrelevant gossip of their private lives.

Another reason why I disagree with the statement is that the mass media can be classified as a form of commercial activities. They report news in exchange for money. Paparazzi are a good case in point. They relentlessly follow stars with their camera to get bits of their candid personal lives. Then they sell the photos for hundreds of dollars. To a different degree, the mass media also profits by digging up the private sides of public figures' lives.

Lastly, when the media spends time investigating a person's private life, it takes time away from other important issues. I do not want to hear about the extramarrital affairs of an actress. Rather, I want to know what's happening in the real world. There are numerous important political, economic, and social developments that should be focused on. The main function of the mass media is to report meaningful news that matters to the general public's lives.

Although I admit that the gossip about famous people's lives attract my attention, I disagree that the mass media has the rights to invade their privacy. They have rights to privacy just like any other citizen, and the media should respect it. Taking profits by violating a person's privacy is just immoral. Besides, there are many other important news items that should be covered by the media.

Practice ❸ The 20ᵗʰ Century Development

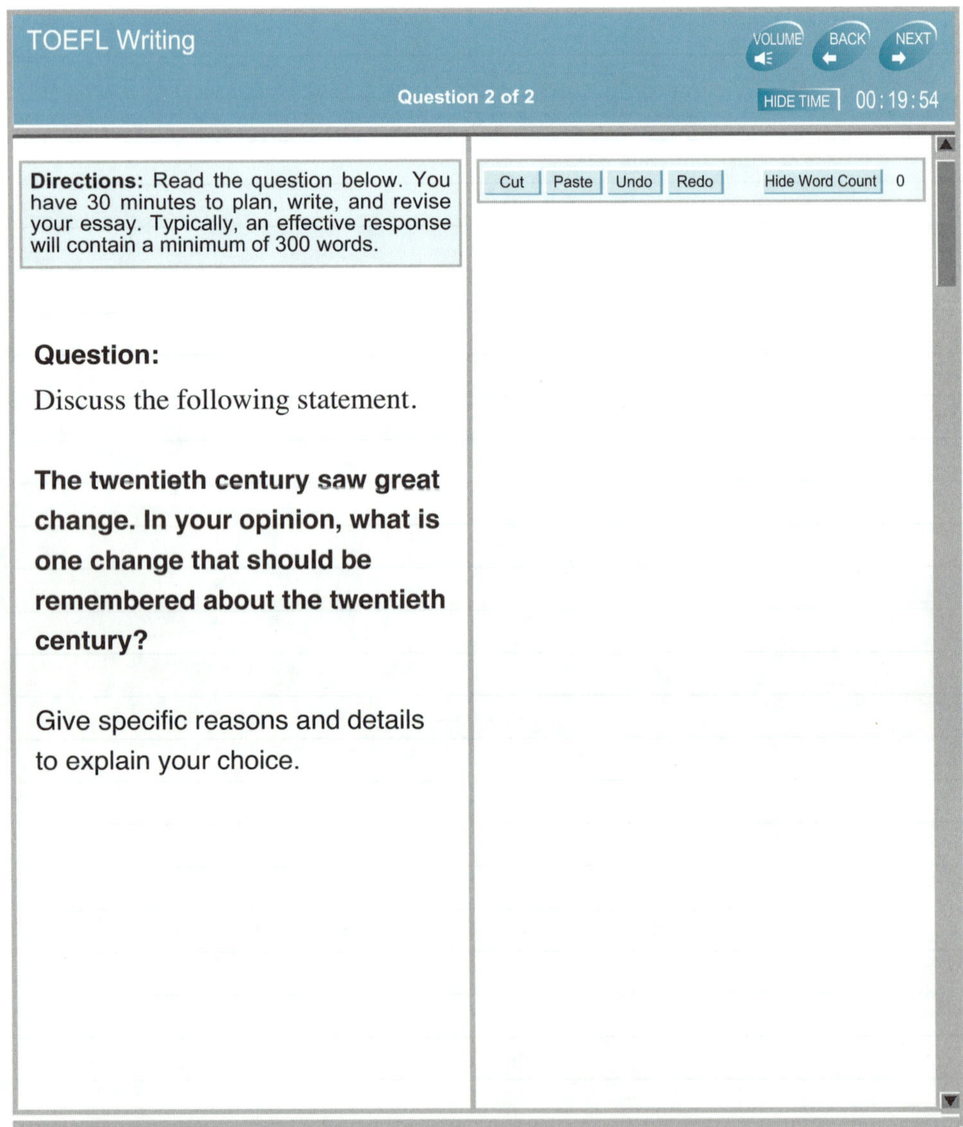

Key Ideas

–정보 통신 기술의 발달이 가장 인상적이다.
–인터넷은 지리적, 시간적 제약을 제거했다.
–이동 전화는 언제 어디서나 정보 교류를 할 수 있게 만들었다.
–정보 통신 혁명으로 우리는 시간 효율적인 편리한 삶을 누릴 수 있게 되
 었다.

Vocabulary Brainstorming

- 기술적 technological
- 발전 development, advancement, improvement
- 인터넷 the Internet, the worldwide web
- 이동 전화, 핸드폰 mobile, cellular phone
- 혁신 innovation, breakthrough
- 혁명적으로 바꾸다 revolutionize
- 정보 통신 telecommunication
- 통신 채널 communication channel
- 채팅하다 chat with
- 양방향 통신 interactive, two-way communication
- 문자를 전송하다 transmit / send text messages
- 시청각 자료 audio-visual materials
- 정보를 찾아내다 search, retrieve information
- 시간 효율적인 time-efficient

Basic Sentence Writing Practice

❶ 20세기는 기술적인 측면과 사회적 측면에서 많은 변화를 목격했다.

____

____

____

🔵 **기술적 측면** technological aspect, front. 단 front를 사용하면 앞에 전치사는 on을 쓴다.
목격하다 witness

❷ 특히 인터넷의 출현이 우리 삶의 질을 향상시키는 데 크게 기여했다.

____

____

____

🔵 **…의 출현, 등장** the advent of
크게 기여하다 greatly contribute to (이때 to는 전치사여서 뒤에 오는 ~동사는 ing로 처리).

❸ 대부분의 사람들은 인터넷이 가장 뛰어난 금세기의 발전 중 하나라는 사실에 동의할 것이다.

____

____

____

🔵 **대부분의 사람들** most people, the majority of people
가장… 것 중 하나 one of the most …
뛰어난 outstanding, important, significant, meaningful, crucial 등 다양한 동의어는 함께 정리.

❹ 이러한 전 세계 네트워크가 양방향 통신 채널을 열었다.

🔵 **전세계 네트워크** global / worldwide network
양방향 interactive, two-way

❺ 인터넷 덕분에 우리는 심지어는 책상을 떠나지 않고도 전 세계 사람들과 채팅할 수 있다.

🔵 **…덕분에** thanks to …
채팅하다 chat with
전 세계 사람들 people across the world / around the world

❻ 이러한 실시간 양방향 통신은 인터넷의 위대한 혜택 중 하나이다.

🔵 **실시간** real time
혜택 benefit

❼ 오늘날의 핸드폰은 최첨단 기능을 갖추고 있다.

(연구) **최첨단** cutting-edge, latest, sophisticated
갖추고 있다 be equipped with

❽ 핸드폰이 있으면 당신은 언제 어디서나 인터넷에 접속할 수 있다.

(연구) **핸드폰이 있으면** with a cell phone
인터넷에 접속하다 hook up to the Internet, log onto the Internet
언제 어디서나 wherever you are and whenever you want

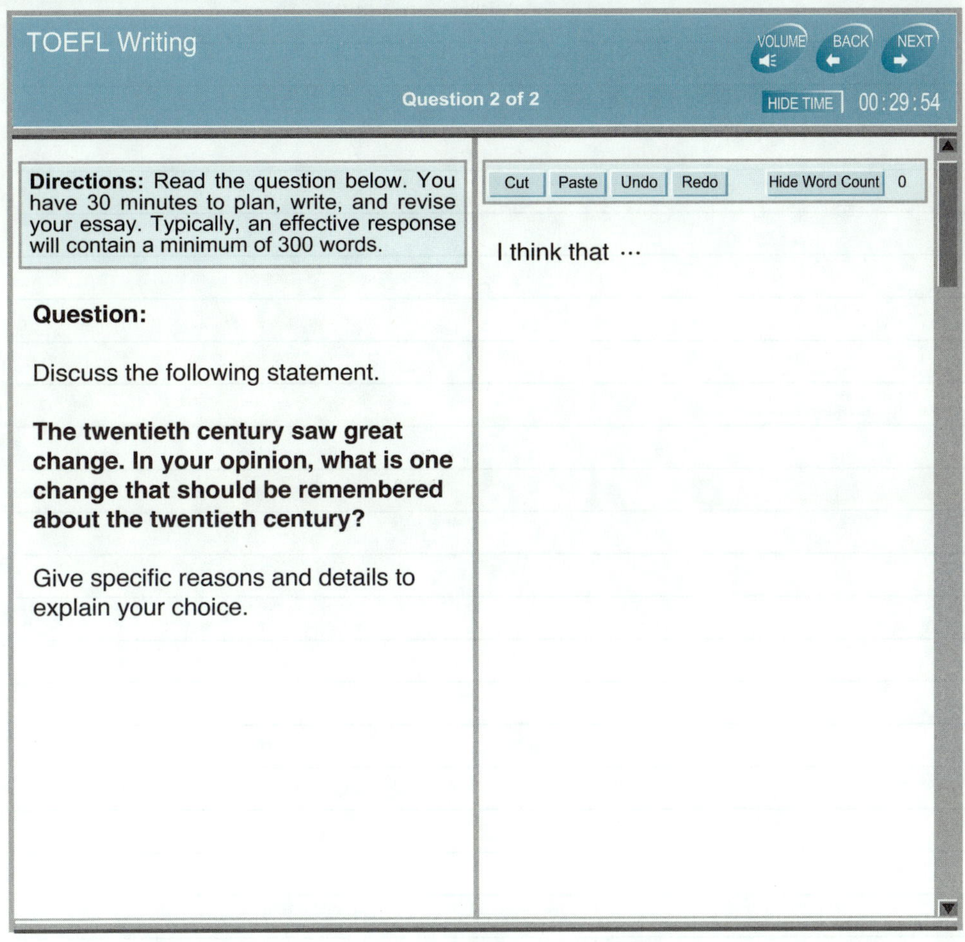
TOEFL Writing
VOLUME   BACK   NEXT
Question 2 of 2
HIDE TIME   00 : 29 : 54
Directions: Read the question below. You have 30 minutes to plan, write, and revise your essay. Typically, an effective response will contain a minimum of 300 words.
Question:
Discuss the following statement.
The twentieth century saw great change. In your opinion, what is one change that should be remembered about the twentieth century?
Give specific reasons and details to explain your choice.
Cut   Paste   Undo   Redo   Hide Word Count   0
I think that …

Answer

Sample Answer

The 20th century has witnessed many changes both on technological and social fronts. If I had to choose one change that should be remembered, I would definitely opt for the dramatic development in telecommunication. The advent of the Internet and cellular phones, in particular, has significantly contributed to improving the quality of our lives. Thanks to these two innovations, we can lead our social and business lives beyond limitations of time and geographical distances.

Most people would agree that computers and the Internet were two of the most outstanding developments of this century. Computers alone brought out meaningful changes to our lives. Producing and keeping records of information became much easier than when we had to resort only to typewriters. The contribution of the computers, however, has increased dramatically as they became linked to each other through a worldwide web, known as the Internet. This global network opened an interactive communication channel, thus connecting people beyond national boundaries. Thanks to the Internet, we can chat with people from around the world without even leaving our desks. The exchange of information and opinions became much smoother and swifter. Something that has happened on the other side of the globe is known to us almost instantly. We not only passively get the news but also actively participate by providing real time feedbacks on the event. This instant two-way communication is one of the great benefits of the Internet.

Another breakthrough in telecommunication is the development of cellular phones. Computers are not the only terminal through which one can access the Internet. Today's cellular phones are equipped with functions to transmit text and audio-visual materials through the Internet. In countries like Korea, the use of cell phones is so widespread that this new gadget has already become an essential part of one's life. This portable terminal allows people not only talk to each other but also to instantly retrieve information from the Internet. One no longer has to look for a payphone to call someone or a PC room to log onto the Internet. The cell phones provide all these functions wherever you are and whenever you want.

In conclusion, although there have been many important changes in the 20th century, I believe the advancement in telecommunications, represented mostly by the development of the Internet and cellular phones, is the most noteworthy change. The Internet almost eliminated the geographical limitations in pursuing effective social and business lives. Cellular phones also greatly contributed to saving our time and efforts by opening an instant channel for communication and information exchanges. Thanks to these innovations, we can lead much more comfortable and time-efficient lives.

Practice 4 Technology and Learning

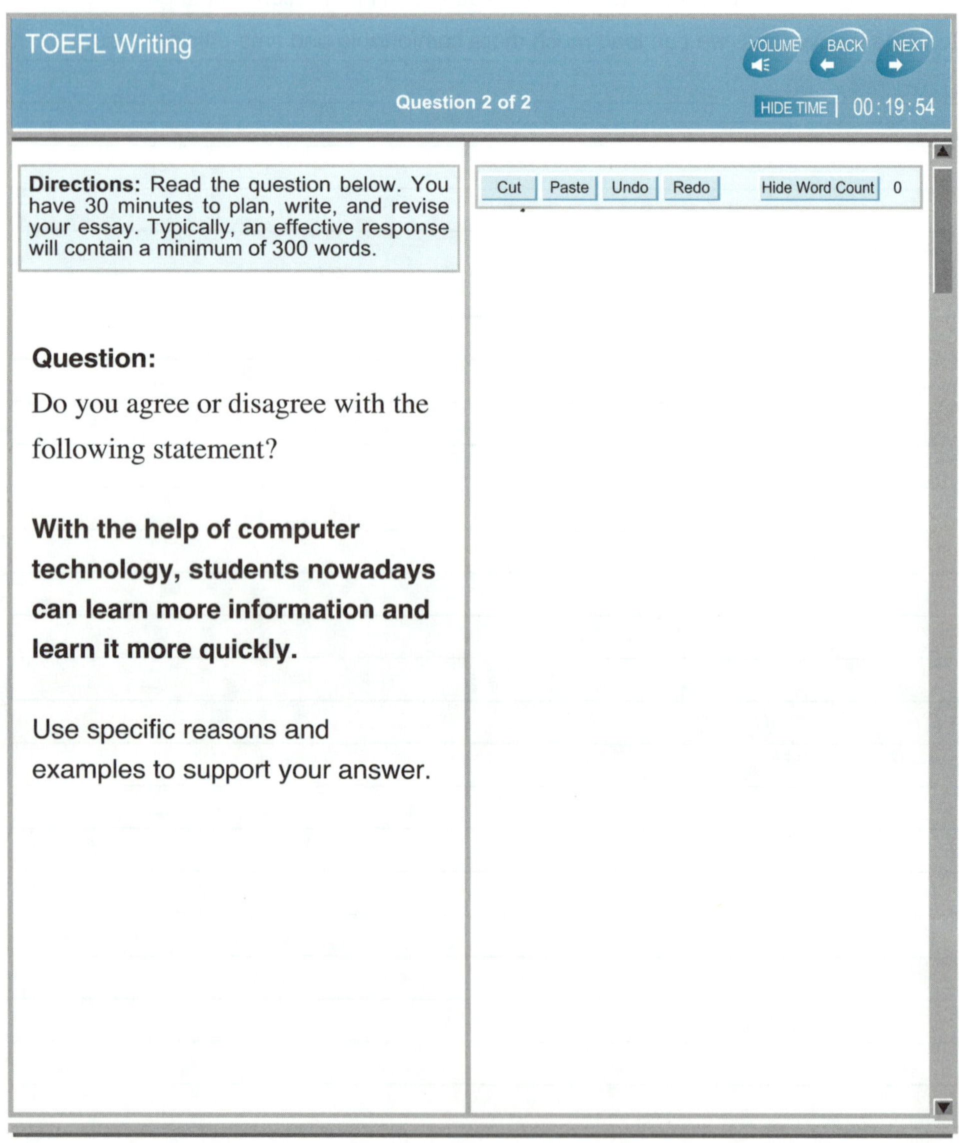

Key Ideas

Agree

–움직이지 않아도 다양한 곳에서 필요한 정보를 얻을 수 있다.
–인터넷 덕분에 양방향 교육이 가능하다.
–문자뿐 아니라 시청각 교육도 가능하다. (외국어 공부에 특히 도움)

Disagree

–컴퓨터는 공부보다 오락을 위해 사용되는 경우가 더 많다.
–유해 정보를 여과 없이 받아들일 수 있다.
–정보 홍수로 오히려 산만해지고 시간 낭비하기 쉽다.

Vocabulary Brainstorming

- 정보를 구하는 방법: the way we get information
- 검색어를 입력하다: type in search words
- 검색 엔진: search engine
- 마우스를 클릭해서: with a click of the mouse
- 원거리 교육: distance learning
- 많은 정보: a wealth of information
- 기술의 혜택을 보다: benefit from technology
- 전산화된 학습 프로그램: computerized learning program
- 산만하게 하다: distract
- 오락: entertainment
- 학습적 / 학술적 용도: academic purposes
- 연구/ 조사: research
- 보고서를 작성하다: write papers
- 양방향 교육: interactive / two-way education
- 시청각: audio visual

Basic Sentence Writing Practice

❶ 컴퓨터 기술은 우리가 정보를 얻는 방법을 크게 개선해 주었다.

____

____

____

연구 **크게** greatly, significantly등은 "변화하다, 영향 주다, 좋아지다, 나빠지다" 등의 의미를 지닌 동사 앞에 써 그 동사의 강도를 보여준다. *e.g.* His comments *greatly* influeced the outcome of the election.
개선하다 improve, enhance, *make something better*

❷ 인터넷을 통해 학생들은 마우스를 클릭해서 정보를 수집할 수 있다.

____

____

____

연구 **수집하다** collect, gather, obtain
마우스를 클릭해서 with a click of the mouse

❸ 집에 앉아서 컴퓨터를 이용해서 조사하는 것이 당연히 더 편리하다.

____

____

____

연구 '~ 하는 것이 어떠하다' 는 'It is + 형용사 + to 부정사' 의 구조로 영작하자!
당연히 certainly, surely, for sure, there is no doubt that …
편리하다 convenient, comfortable, less troublesome (이렇게 반대말을 부정으로 처리해 표현 하는 것도 편리)

❹ 학생들은 이제 이용 가능한 많은 정보를 인터넷을 통해서 얻을 수 있다.

많은 정보 a lot of information / a wealth of information
이용 가능한 available

❺ 그들은 전 세계 도서관의 데이터 베이스에 접근할 수 있다.

…에 접근하다, 들어가다 have access to …
전 세계의 around the globe, across the world

❻ 요즘 학생들은 원거리 학습을 통해 혜택을 볼 수 있다.

원거리 학습 distance learning
혜택을 보다 benefit from

❼ 컴퓨터 기술은 단지 학생들을 한층 더 학습에서 한눈팔게 한다.

한층 더 further (farther는 거리가 '더 먼'을 의미, 반면 further는 '정도'의 의미)
A를 B에서 한눈팔게 하다/ 산만하게 만들다. distract A from B

❽ 대부분의 학생들은 컴퓨터를 인터넷 게임을 하고 친구들과 채팅하는 데
사용한다.

____

____

____

🔵연구 A를 B하는 데 사용하다 use A to do B
채팅하다 chat with …

❾ 컴퓨터는 또 하나의 오락이 되었다.

____

____

____

🔵연구 …되다 become, get, turn
오락 entertainment, pastime

❿ 컴퓨터 기술은 학생들의 진정한 학습에 방해가 되는 경우가 많다.

____

____

____

🔵연구 방해하다 hinder, be in the way, retard
경우가 많다 in many cases / instances …

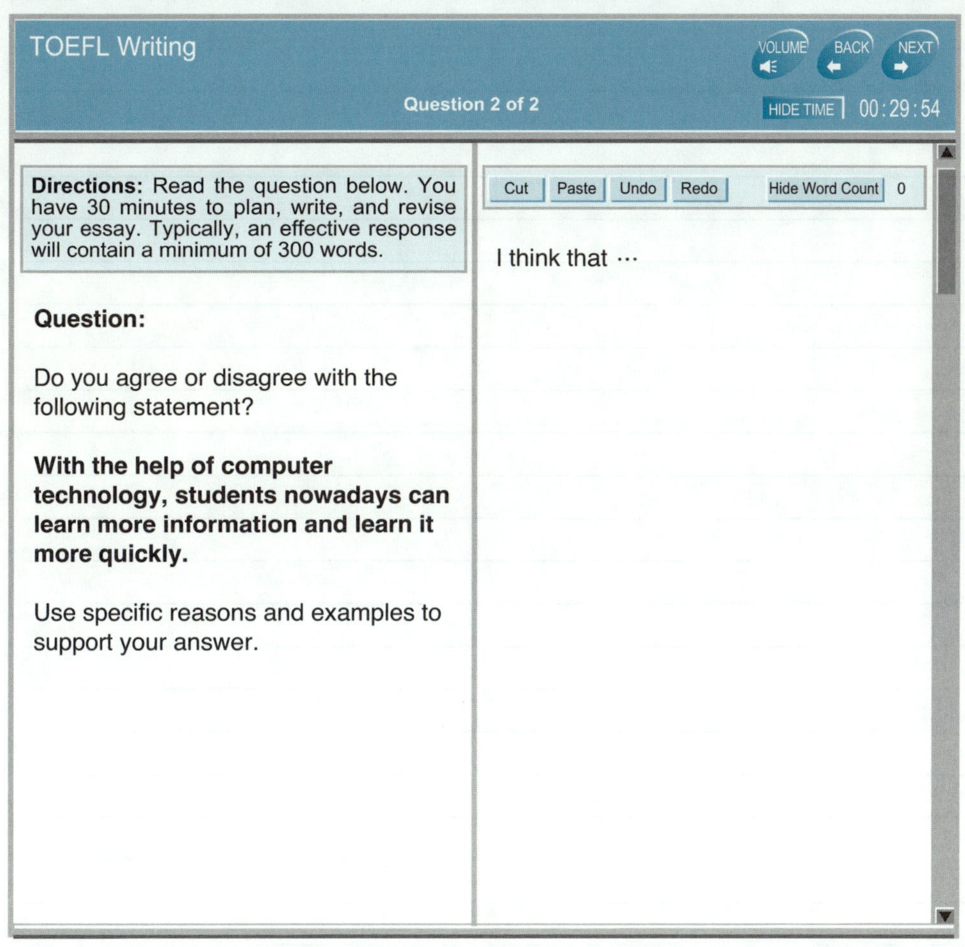

TOEFL Writing
VOLUME   BACK   NEXT
Question 2 of 2
HIDE TIME   00:29:54
Directions: Read the question below. You have 30 minutes to plan, write, and revise your essay. Typically, an effective response will contain a minimum of 300 words.

Question:

Do you agree or disagree with the following statement?

With the help of computer technology, students nowadays can learn more information and learn it more quickly.

Use specific reasons and examples to support your answer.
Cut   Paste   Undo   Redo   Hide Word Count   0
I think that …

Answer

Sample Answer

The 20th century has brought about many technological developments in every aspect of our lives. Sophisticated machines have made our work much easier than before. This is also the case with our learning activities. Thanks to the invention of computers, in particular, we can learn new information much quicker and easier. Although some people may disagree with this, I personally think that computer technology has significantly contributed to our learning in both its quantity and quality for the following reasons.

Firstly, the Internet and the World Wide Web have opened every major library and database to students around the world. In the past, we had to resort only to local libraries to look for needed information. But now the Internet, which is open 24 hours a day and seven days a week, has given us access to resources beyond the geographical and time limitations. This unlimited, easy access allows students to get more information and learn it more quickly.

Another beauty of computer technology is that it has created an interactive learning environment. Unlike books, where the learners only passively receive the information, the computer and the Internet make it possible for learners to exchange opinions not only with the author of the book but also with other readers. This "dialogue" is, in fact, the most effective form of acquiring knowledge. The massive exchanges of e-mails between college students and professors testify such effectiveness.

Lastly, the computer technology diversified the types of information that students can use to learn. While books give us only written messages, the computer and its related equipment are offering audio-visual materials as well. In foreign language education, for example, audio materials play an important role in providing accurate pronunciation. Nowadays, with the help of the Internet websites based on audio-visual materials, many students are learning English-as-a-foreign-language more quickly and easily than before.

In sum, technology, especially computer-related technology, has made our lives more convenient than ever. Despite its unintended drawbacks, I believe that the computer and the Internet are making learning easier and quicker. As long as we are aware of the problems and willing to solve them, I think we have a lot to gain from this ever-developing technology.

Practice ⑤ Number of Friends

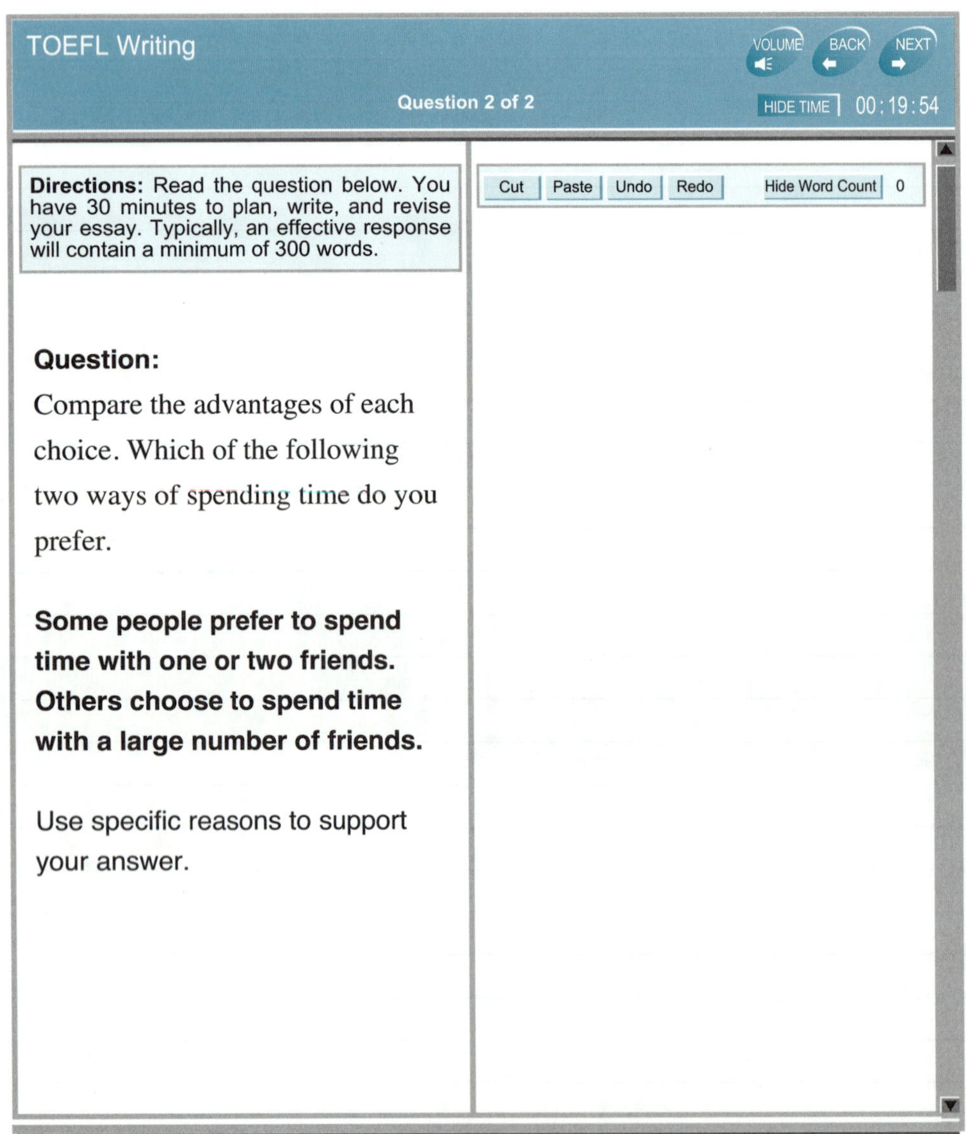

Key Ideas

A small group of friends

－깊은 대화를 할 수 있다.
－의미 있는 시간을 보낼 수 있다.
－모임을 정하는 시간을 절약할 수 있다.

A large group of friends

－다양한 사람들을 통해 세상 돌아가는 것을 알 수 있다.
－지루하지 않다.
－대인 관계가 좋아진다.

Vocabulary Brainstorming

- 시간을 같이 보내다: spend time with, be around, enjoy the company of
- 아는 사람: acquaintance
- 소수의 선택된 사람들: a few selected people
- 개인 성격: an individual's personality
- 외향적인 사람: an outgoing person
- 내향적인 사람: an introvert, a shy person
- 친구 그룹: a group of friends, a bunch of friends
- 깊은 대화: in-depth talk / conversation
- 대인 관계: interpersonal relationship

Basic Sentence Writing Practice

❶ 우리는 모두 문제가 있을 때나 행복할 때 다 친구가 필요하다.

____

____

____

🔵 **연구** **문제가있을때** in times of trouble
행복할때 in times of happiness

❷ 많은 친구와 있음으로써 다양한 경험을 얻을 수 있다.

____

____

____

🔵 **연구** **~함으로써** by ~ing로 처리하면 편리.
친구와있다 be with friends, surround oneself with friends, spend time with friends

❸ 나는 주변에 친구를 많이 두고 싶다. 그래야 새로운 것을 다른 사람들로부터 배울 수 있으니까.

____

____

____

🔵 **연구** **친구를많이두다** have a large number of friends, establish a large circle of friends, have many friends around.
…할수있으니까 so I can … 또는 because로 처리해도 된다.

❹ 외향적인 사람들은 많은 친구들과 시간 보내는 것을 선호하는 경향이 있다.

> **연구** 외향적인 outgoing, active
> 선호하다 prefer
> …하는 경향이 있다 tend + to 부정사

❺ 한 두 명의 친구와는 보다 돈독하고 깊은 관계를 갖을 수 있다.

> **연구** 돈독한 solid
> 관계를 맺다, 갖다 establish / build a relationship

❻ 개인적인 문제를 공유하고 심리적 위안을 얻을 수 있다.

> **연구** 개인적인 문제 personal problems
> 공유하다 share
> 심리적 위안 pychological comfort

❼ 그러한 깊은 관계의 또 다른 혜택은 친구들과 무엇을 할지를 결정하는 데 있어서 시간을 절약할 수 있다는 것이다.

🔵 **또 다른혜택** another benefit of
시간을 절약하다 save time
뭘 할지 what to do 이렇듯 의문사와 to 부정사를 함께 쓰면 편리.

❽ 한 개인의 성격과 선호가 그가 함께 있고 싶은 친구의 숫자에 분명히 영향을 준다.

🔵 **성격과 선호** personality and preferences 같은 알파벳으로 시작하는 두 단어를 짝으로 하면 좋다. *e.g.* tastes and tendencies
분명… definitely, certainly, surely 등을 동사 앞에 넣는다.
영향을 주다 affect, influence, give some influece onto

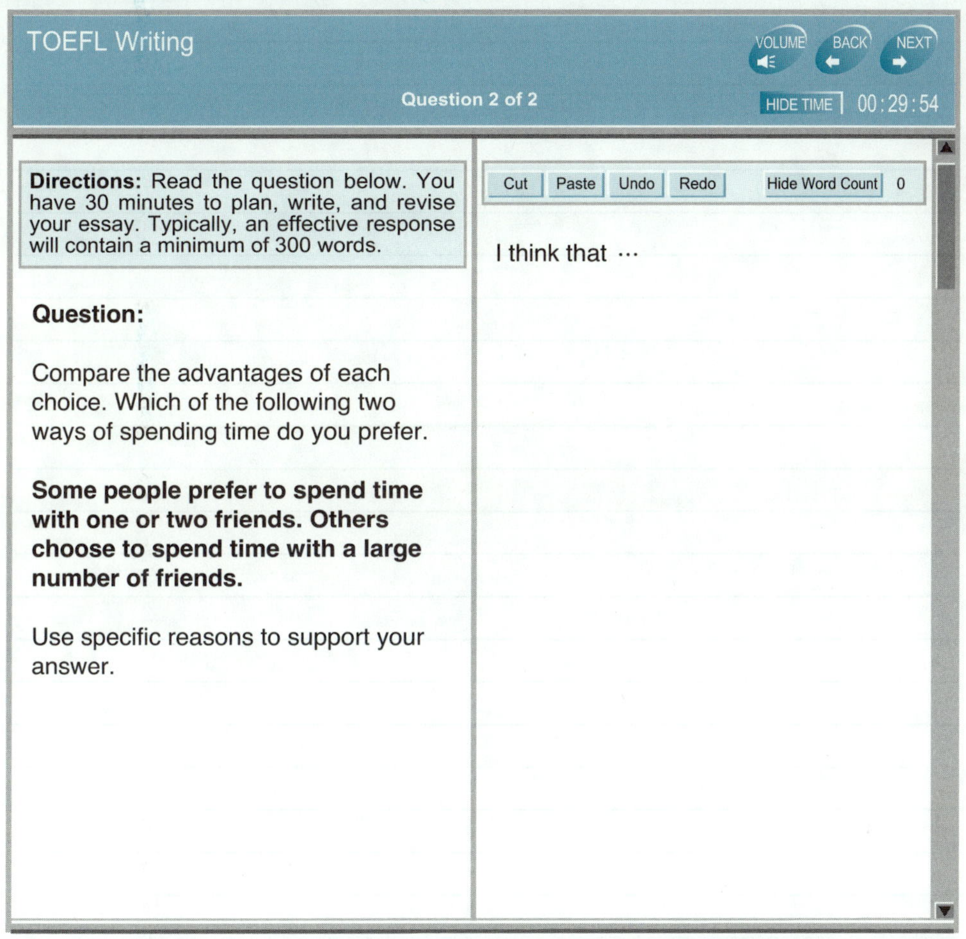

TOEFL Writing
VOLUME   BACK   NEXT
Question 2 of 2
HIDE TIME   00 : 29 : 54
Directions: Read the question below. You have 30 minutes to plan, write, and revise your essay. Typically, an effective response will contain a minimum of 300 words.
Question:
Compare the advantages of each choice. Which of the following two ways of spending time do you prefer.
Some people prefer to spend time with one or two friends. Others choose to spend time with a large number of friends.
Use specific reasons to support your answer.
Cut   Paste   Undo   Redo   Hide Word Count   0
I think that ···

Answer

Sample Answer

Some people prefer to be around a large number of friends, while others want to be with only one or two close friends. It is difficult to say which is a better way of spending time because the choice depends on one's personality and preferences. As for me, though at times I like being with many people, I prefer a smaller group.

Spending time with a large number of friends can be a lot of fun and helpful. To some people, more company equals more fun. Since you are with many different kinds of people, you can learn new things from them. This way you can catch up on more varieties of social issues. The diverse experiences that you can get from your large pool of acquaintances may enrich your relationship. Usually outgoing people tend to prefer this type of friendship. They find diverse experience more important than deeper relationships with one or two friends.

Surrounding oneself with just a couple of friends, on the other hand, has its own advantages as well. First of all, one can establish a more solid, deeper friendship. Though having a bunch of friends around may be entertaining, it does not create a setting for private, intimate conversations. With one or two friends, you can share your personal problems and get some psychological comfort. Although some people may say that such a small circle of friends may be boring, I prefer to have quality time with my friends. Shy, quiet people often prefer this kind of friendship.

Another benefit of such deep relationship is that one can save time in deciding what to do with friends. In a large group, it usually takes much more time and trouble to reach an agreement on what to do together. Different people mean different opinions and tastes. With just one or two friends, however, the decision can be made more easily and quickly. It's certainly much easier to go places, for example, with only a couple of friends. The trip would be much more enjoyable and time-efficient.

An individual's personality and preferences definitely influence the type of group in which he or she wants to be. Though there may be some exceptions, usually outgoing people prefer to be around a large number of people, while quiet ones spend time with a couple of friends. Given the quality time I can have with a small circle of close friends, I personally prefer the latter type of friendship. I value the in-depth conversation with a close friend much more than the excitement of being in a large group.

Practice ❻ Money is the most important thing

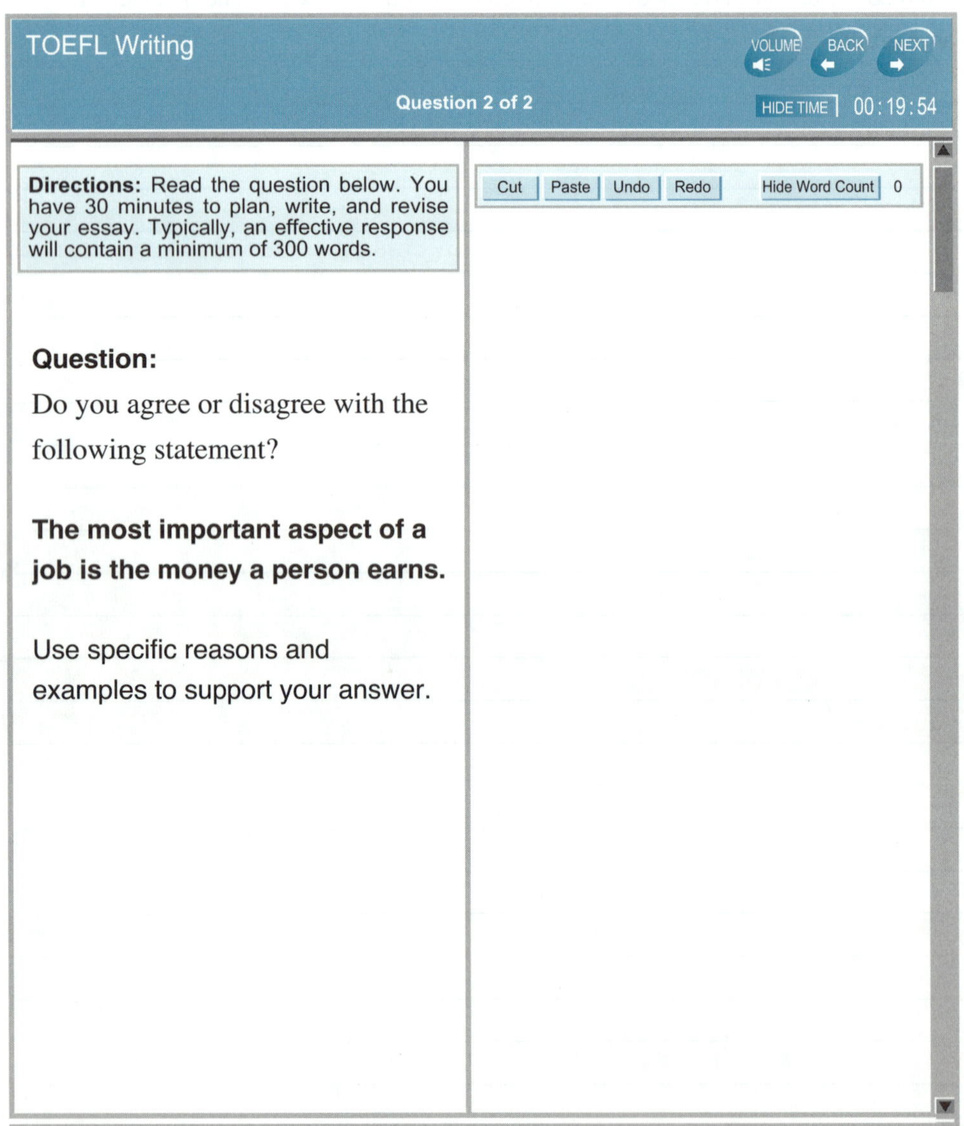

Key Ideas

Agree

-돈은 생존 수단이다.
-일은 돈을 받는다는 전제로 한다.
-아무리 좋아하는 일도 보수가 나쁘면 오래 할 수 없다.

Disagree

-급여는 직업 선택의 중요한 요건 중 하나에 불과하다.
-돈 외에도 직업에서 다른 보람을 느낄 수 있다.
-일은 인생의 많은 시간을 차지하기 때문에 자신의 취향과 능력에 맞는지
　가 더 중요하다.

Vocabulary Brainstorming:

- 돈을 벌다: make / earn money
- 직업을 갖다: hold a job/ profession
- 직업 선택: career choice
- 급여: wage, salary, pay
- 급여가 높은 직업: a high-paying job
- 직장: workplace, work
- 취향: tastes, tendencies, preferance
- 능력: competence, capacity
- 보람: reward
- 만족감: sense of satisfaction

Basic Sentence Writing Practice

❶ 돈은 중요한 생존 수단이다.

____

____

____

🔵연구 **수단** means 이땐 꼭 s가 붙지만 단수로 여겨진다!

❷ 대부분 개인의 직업 선택은 급여를 바탕으로 내려진다.

____

____

____

🔵연구 **대부분의 경우, 주로** : in most cases, usually, in general, often
 선택하다 make a choice란 기본 골격을 이용한다.
  …를 바탕으로, …를 기본으로 based on … / hinged on …

❸ 일에서 버는 돈의 양은 직업 선택을 하는 데 가장 중요한 역할을 한다.

____

____

____

🔵연구 **…하는 데 중요한 역할을 한다** play an important / crucial / vital role in 물론 be 동사를 써서 작
  문할 수 있겠지만 'play a role' 이란 표현을 사용하면 글에 박진감을 줄 수 있다.
  직업 career, job, profession, work

❹ 아무리 멋진 직업이라도 괜찮은 급여 없이는 오랫동안 그 일을 할 수 없다.

___

___

___

> **[연구]** 아무리 … 한다 할지라도 no matter how + 형용사
>   *e.g.* No matter how beautiful she may be,
> **직장을 갖다** hold a job
> **일정기간동안** for … time 이때 전치사 for를 빠트리지 말도록!
> **괜찮은 급여** a decent pay

❺ 나는 직업을 선택하는 데에 가장 중요한 요인이 우리가 버는 돈이라는 것에 강하게 반대한다.

___

___

___

> **[연구]** **강하게 반대한다** strongly disagree 뒤에는 that절이나 with + 명사구가 온다.
>   *e.g.* I strongly disagee *that* she is the most inteligent.
>   I strongly disagree *with* the idea.
> **요인** factor

❻ 우리는 종종 높은 급여를 주는 직업이 낮은 급여를 주는 것보다 더 보람차다고 생각하는 경향이 있다.

___

___

___

> **[연구]** … 하는 경향이 있다 tend + to 부정사
> **급여가 높은 직업** higher-paying jobs
> **보람 있는** rewarding, satisfactory

❼ 직업을 고를 때 개인의 취향과 성향을 진지하게 고려해야 한다.

연구 **취향** tastes, preferances, tendencies
고려되다 be considered
~할때 when ~ing

❽ 우리가 급여만 생각한다면, 그 일을 오래 하기가 어려울 것이다.

연구 **우리가…하는것이…것이다** : It will be + 형용사 + for us + to 부정사.

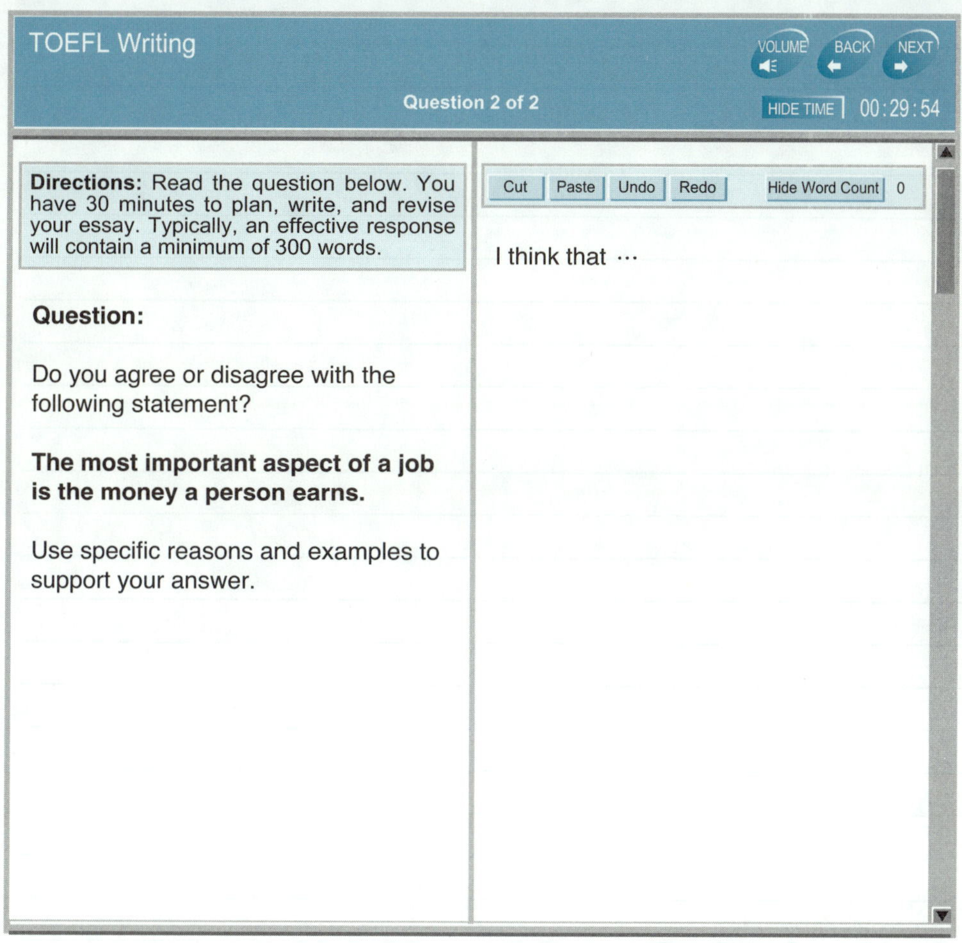

TOEFL Writing
VOLUME   BACK   NEXT
Question 2 of 2
HIDE TIME   00:29:54
Directions: Read the question below. You have 30 minutes to plan, write, and revise your essay. Typically, an effective response will contain a minimum of 300 words.
Question:
Do you agree or disagree with the following statement?
The most important aspect of a job is the money a person earns.
Use specific reasons and examples to support your answer.
Cut   Paste   Undo   Redo   Hide Word Count   0
I think that …

Answer

Sample Answer

Holding a job is an important part of our lives. Some people start working right after finishing high school, while others after graduating from university. Regardless of the educational level, we all have to choose a career when we step into the adult life. The pay one can get from a job definitely plays a crucial role in the choice, but I disagree that it is the most important aspect of a job.

First of all, money is one of the many aspects that we have to consider but not the single most important one. One of my teachers, for example, once told us that he was reluctant to get into the teaching profession because of the low pay. In terms of money, it was much more profitable for him to become an office worker than a high school teacher. Now after 20 years of teaching, he says that he was wise enough to consider aspects other than the pay. Although he might have made some more money, he can't imagine himself working stuck in an office for his entire life. He is very happy with his career choice.

The wage is just one kind of reward we get from work. We often tend to think that higher-paying jobs are better and more rewarding than lower-paying ones. But that's not always the case. Sense of satisfaction, achievement, and worthiness are other forms of reward that we can get from a job. I love teaching and have no doubt that I'll become a teacher when I have to choose a career. As my high school teacher said, this profession is not the most attractive one in terms of pay. However, I know I will get greater satisfaction and happiness by doing something that I consider meaningful not only for me but also for society.

Lastly, a career-choice should be made based on our tastes and tendencies, since we spend most of our time working. If we spend only a small fraction of our time and effort on work, our preference will not matter much. But the truth is that many of us have to spend most of our time at a workplace. Therefore, it is important for us to consider what we can do and would like to do best. If we consider only the pay of a job, it will be hard for us to bear the work for a long time. If I hold a profession that I can do best while enjoying it, I will be able to withstand the hardship involved in the work.

In sum, I clearly disagree with the statement that money is the most important aspect of a job. Money is one of the many critical factors to consider when choosing a profession but not the single most important one. Sense of satisfaction and worthiness are also meaningful reward we get from a job. Besides, our competence and preference should be considered when making a career choice as well.

Practice **7** Advertising

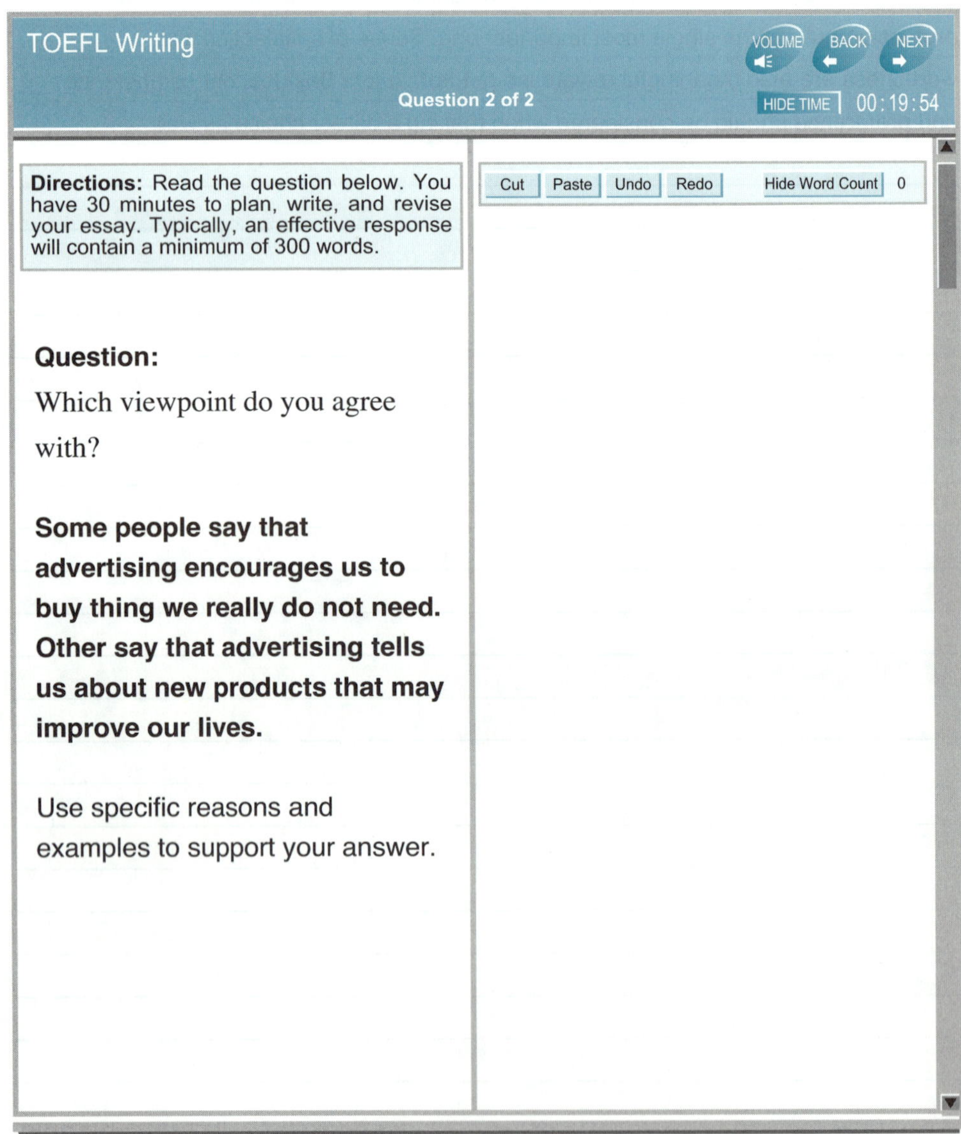

Key Ideas

필요 없는 물건만 사게 만든다

-광고는 기본적으로 물건을 팔기 위한 것이다.
-불필요한 유행을 만들어 소비를 부추긴다.
-지출 예산을 초과해서 돈을 쓰게 만든다.

도움이 되는 제품 정보를 제공한다

-수없이 많은 제품과 서비스에 대한 정보를 제공한다.
-오늘날의 소비자는 거짓 광고를 알아볼 수 있다.
-제품의 질이 뒷받침 되지 않는 광고는 성공적인 판매로 이어지지 않는
 다.

Vocabulary Brainstorming

- 광고: advertisement, commercial, ad, advertising
- 광고하다: advertise
- 홍보하다: promote
- 광고하는 사람, 광고주: advertiser
- 시장에 출시되다: hit the market, be released in the market
- 소비자 신뢰: consumer trust
- 환불: refund
- 삶을 개선하다: improve one's life, enhance the quality of life

Basic Sentence Writing Practice

❶ 요즘 우리는 지속적인 광고의 폭격을 받고 있다.

____

____

____

🔵 **요즘** these days, nowadays
…**의 폭격을 받다** be bombarded with, be constantly surrounded with
지속적인 constant

❷ 광고를 하는 전적인 이유는 우리로 하여금 필요하지 않은 물건들을 사게 부추기기 위한 것이다.

____

____

____

🔵 **~하는 전적인 이유** the whole point of ~ing, the main reason for ~ing, the primary purpose of ~ing
…**하게 부추기다** encourage A to do B

❸ 우리는 이웃에 뒤지지 않기 위해 많은 돈을 쓴다.

____

____

____

🔵 **~하는 데 돈을 쓰다** spend money ~ing
따라 가다, 뒤지지 않다 to keep up with, not to be left behind

❹ 광고는 우리 예산을 초과하는 삶을 살도록 강요하는 필요악이다.

____
____
____

> 연구 **필요악** a necessary evil
> **…하도록 강요하다** force A to do B
> **예산을 초과하는** beyond one's budget

❺ 광고는 사람들에게 그들의 삶을 좋게 할 수 있는 새로운 제품에 대해 말해 주는 최고의 방법이다.

____
____
____

> 연구 **…하는 최고의 방법이다** the best way + to 부정사
> **개선하다, 좋게 하다** improve, enhance

❻ 오늘날의 소비자는 거짓 광고인지 아닌지 구분하기에 충분할 정도로 똑똑하다.

____
____
____

> 연구 **소비자** consumer
> **…하기에 충분하게 …하다** 형용사+enough + to 부정사
> **구분하다** tell, discern

❼ 기업은 오늘날의 소비자들이 쓸데 없는 광고에 속지 않는다는 사실을 언제나 유념해야 한다.

____

____

____

연구 **유념하다** be aware of, keep in mind
속다 be fooled by

❽ 대다수의 광고는 우리 삶의 질을 높여줄 수 있는 새 제품과 서비스에 대해 우리에게 알려준다.

____

____

____

연구 **대다수** the majority of
…에게 …에 관해 알려주다 inform A about B
삶의 질을 높이다 improve the quality of one's life

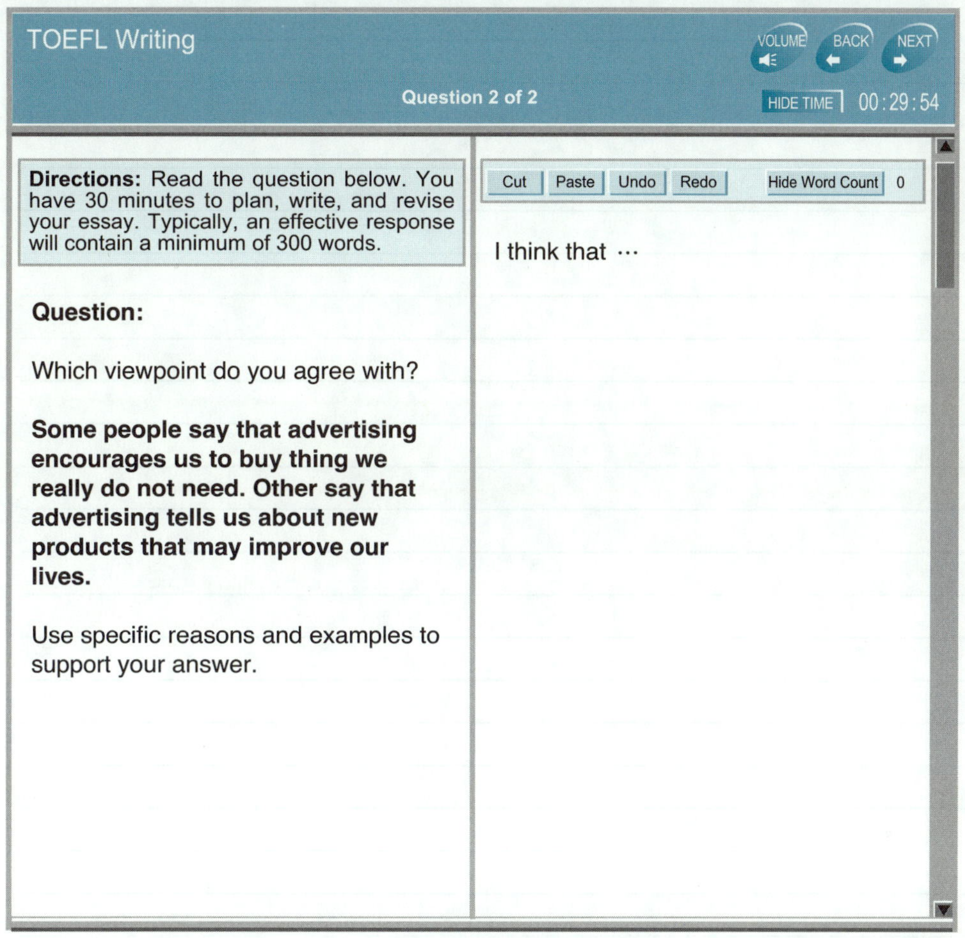

TOEFL Writing
VOLUME   BACK   NEXT
Question 2 of 2
HIDE TIME   00 : 29 : 54
Directions: Read the question below. You have 30 minutes to plan, write, and revise your essay. Typically, an effective response will contain a minimum of 300 words.
Question:
Which viewpoint do you agree with?
Some people say that advertising encourages us to buy thing we really do not need. Other say that advertising tells us about new products that may improve our lives.
Use specific reasons and examples to support your answer.
Cut   Paste   Undo   Redo   Hide Word Count   0
I think that …

Answer

Sample Answer

Compared to the past, these days we are surrounded by constant commercials coming from different media. Television, radio, newspapers, and the Internet are all full of advertisements promoting new products and services. You may want to run away from all these messages trying to sell you things. But the truth is that they actually make our complicated modern lives easier. Without the help of the information we get from the ads, it would be much more difficult and confusing for us to decide what to buy. Therefore, I personally think that in general commercials play a positive role in improving our lives.

First, advertising is the best way to tell us about new products that can enhance our lives. Everyday tons of new products and services hit the market. Some of them can make our lives more comfortable and convenient. Yet, since there are so many new things being released at the same time that it is difficult for ordinary consumers to tell the difference among them. Advertising helps us discern which product and service will really improve the quality of our lives. Recently, I saw an advertisement for an air purifier on a cable channel. The ad was very detailed and showed me all the benefits of having the air purifier in an apartment. I bought the product and am happy with my purchase. Thanks to the clean air coming from the purifier, I have had headaches less frequently.

Successful advertising does not always mean successful products. Today's consumers are smart enough to tell whether a commercial is a false ad or not. Businesses cannot sell the products simply by posting a fancy advertisement. They have to provide quality products that match the message of their advertising. Otherwise, they will lose their consumers' trust. If the air purifier had not been as good as the advertisement claimed, I would have returned the product and never bought that company's product again. However, since I liked the quality of the air purifier, I know that the company is trustworthy. This consumer's trust is one of the keys to success in the business world. Companies and advertisers should always keep in mind that today's consumers cannot be fooled by useless, ungrounded advertising.

It is true that some advertisements may try to sell us things that we really do not need. However, the majority of them inform us about new products and services that could improve the quality of our lives. As long as we have an eye to tell which ones are false ads, I think we can get some handy information about things that can be useful to us. Besides, such marketing policies as free refund service make our decision based on advertisement much easier than before. If you don't like what you've purchased, you can just return it. Since companies are aware of this, they are very unlikely to promote false ads.

Practice 8 Foreign Language Learning

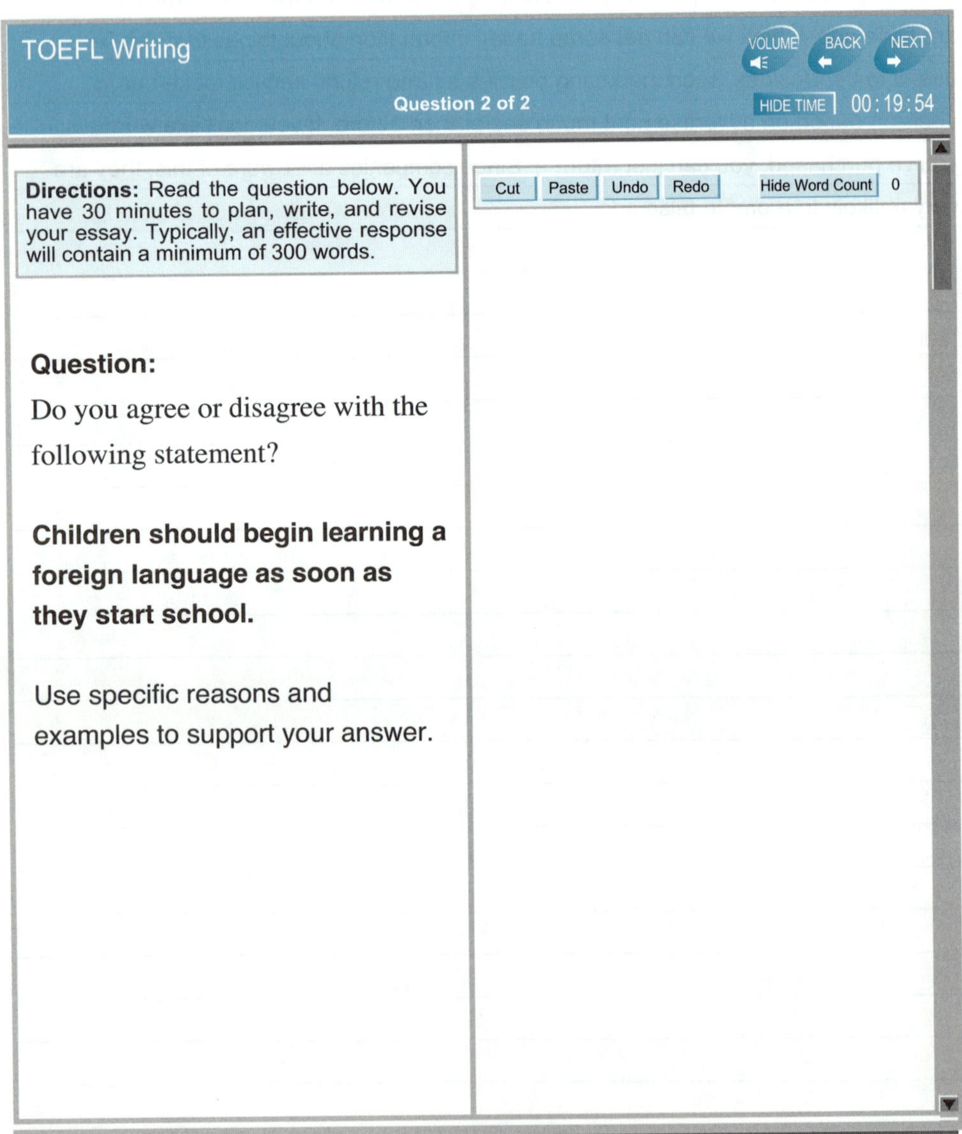

Key Ideas

Agree

- 어릴 때 배워야 쉽게 습득한다.
- 한 아이는 여러 개의 언어를 동시에 배울 수 있다.
- 외국어 학습을 통해 모국어와 자국 문화에 대한 이해를 높일 수 있다.

Disagree

- 아이가 혼란스러워 한다.
- 모국어 먼저 확실하게 다져야 한다.
- 외국어는 나중에 배워도 된다.

Vocabulary Brainstorming

- 어린 나이에 at an early age
- 외국어에 대한 노출 exposure to a foreign language
- 외국어 학습 foreign-language instruction
- 외국어 습득 acquisition of a foreign language
- 모국어 one's native language, first language, mother tongue
- 지평을 넓히다 broaden one's horizon world

Basic Sentence Writing Practice

❶ 아이들은 어린 나이에 외국어를 공부함으로써 혜택을 볼 수 있다.

연구 …에서 혜택을 보다 benefit from …
어린 나이에 at an early age, when they are young

❷ 학교를 시작하자마자 외국어 학습을 시작해야 할 좋은 이유는 없다.

연구 외국어 학습 foreign-language instruction
…하자마자 the moment / as soon as …

❸ 두 개의 언어를 동시에 배우려고 하는 것은 아이에게 너무 어려울 수 있다.

연구 동명사를 주어로 쓰면 문장 만들기가 쉬워진다 Trying to …
할 수 있다 may + 동사 원형
동시에 at once

❹ 아이가 혼란스러워 할 수 있고 결국엔 두 언어 다 제대로 못 배울 수 있다.

___

___

연구 **혼란스러워 하다** get / become / turn confused / mixed up
결국에는 ~되다 end up + ~ing
둘 다 아니다 neither

❺ 외국어 교육을 어린 나이부터 시작하는 데는 장단점이 다 있다.

___

___

연구 **장점** advantage **단점** disadvantage 장단점을 동시에 언급할 땐 대칭이 되도록 한다 : good
and bad sides / postive and negatives aspects / merits and drawbacks 등
둘 다 있다 both A and B

❻ 오늘날 외국어로서의 영어 수요가 매우 높다.

___

___

연구 **오늘날** nowadays, these days, recently, lately, today
수요가 높다 be in great demand
cf. **수요가 없다 / 적다** be in poor demand

❼ 조기 외국어 교육은 외국어 습득을 쉽게 만든다.

연구 **조기 외국어 교육** early foreign language education / instruction
A는 B를 쉽게 만든다 A makes B easier / A facilitates B / Thanks to A, B becomes easier. 한 가지 내용을 여러 영어 표현으로 쓸 수 있는 사고의 융통성이 중요하다!

❽ 모국어 습득을 방해하지 않으면서 아이는 여러 개의 외국어를 동시에 배울 수 있다.

연구 **동시에** at the same time, at once
~하지 않으면서 without ~ing

❾ 여러 연구가 이와 같은 사실들을 뒷받침한다.

연구 **여러 연구** many studies / study after study / a number of studies
뒷받침하다 support / validate / serve as evidence for / confirm

❿ 지평을 넓힐 수 있기 때문에 외국어 학습을 통해 다른 나라에 대해 배우는 것은 아이들에게 이롭다.

연구 **…에게 이롭다** be beneficial for …
지평을 넓히다 broaden / widen one's horizon / world.

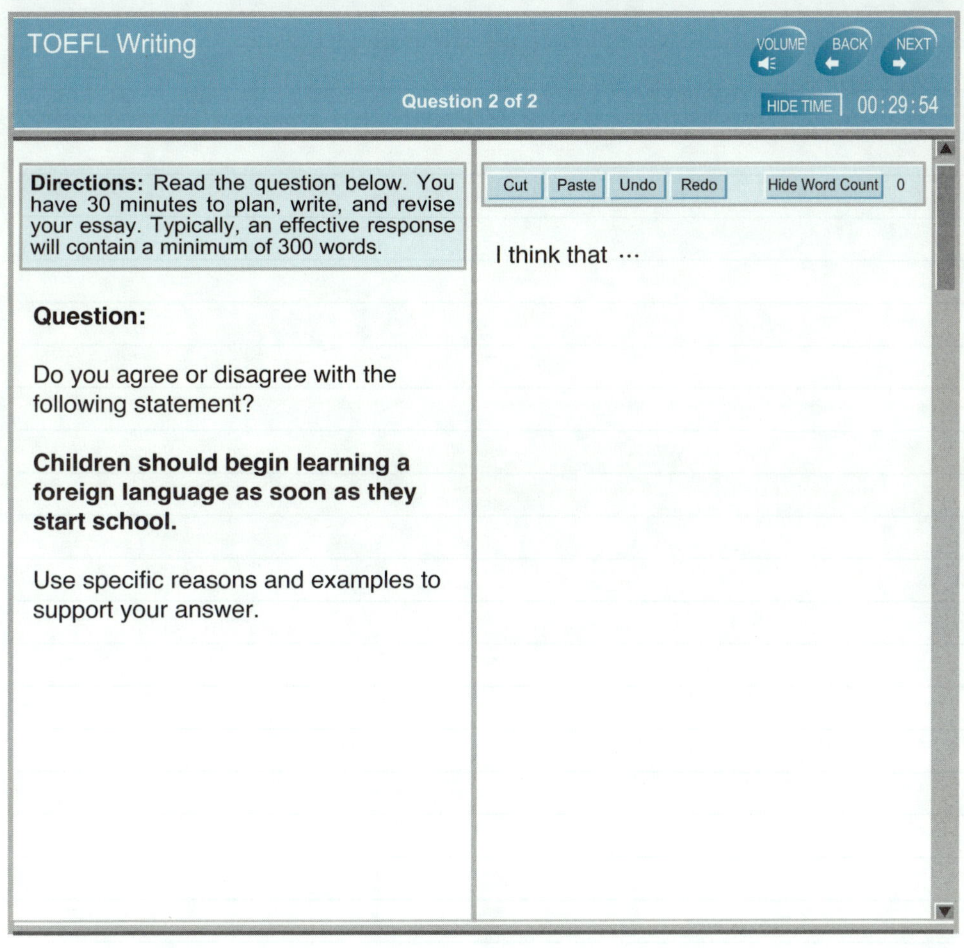

TOEFL Writing
VOLUME   BACK   NEXT
Question 2 of 2
HIDE TIME   00:29:54
Directions: Read the question below. You have 30 minutes to plan, write, and revise your essay. Typically, an effective response will contain a minimum of 300 words.
Question:
Do you agree or disagree with the following statement?
Children should begin learning a foreign language as soon as they start school.
Use specific reasons and examples to support your answer.
Cut   Paste   Undo   Redo   Hide Word Count   0
I think that …

Answer

Sample Answer

In general, people agree that at least one foreign language, especially English, is necessary to be successful in today's society. However, they do not show such a solid consensus as to when to start learning English. Some argue that the sooner we start learning it, the better off we will be. Others, however, oppose English language learning at an early age saying that it will hamper their native language acquisition. I, personally, believe that early foreign language education is beneficial for the following reasons.

First of all, a young child can learn a foreign language much easier and quicker than an adult. They do not take it as something that they have to analyze and memorize. Rather, they approach the language the way they do their mother tongue. They learn it naturally without being bothered by complicated grammar rules. Some linguists scanned the brains of a child and an adult while they were speaking a foreign language. To our surprise, they were found to be using different parts of their brain for the same activity. The adult used the section of the brain that specializes in analysis, while the child used the part that is utilized for one's native language processing.

Those who oppose early foreign language learning often argue that it will damage a child's first language acquisition. However, study after study has shown that a child can learn many languages at the same time as long as the "one-person one-language" principle is respected. When the consistency is maintained, a child can learn up to nine languages at once without losing his or her native language. Although nine is too many, I believe one foreign language won't disturb the child's first language development.

Lastly, early exposure to a foreign language will help a child to have a broader perspective. We live in a globalized world, where the social and economic exchanges across national boundaries have become a part of our lives. By learning a foreing language from an early age, a child can learn about different cultures and lifestyles as well. This will help him develop a more cosmopolitan view. Besides, by learning others' language and culture, one can understand and appreciate one's own language and culture better.

In conclusion, given the above benefits, I agree with the statement that children should start learning a foreign language as soon as they start school. I even believe that they should be exposed to a foreign language much earlier than that. Not only is the acquisition of the language easier at an early age, but it also provides the child with a wider world perspective.

Narrator
Please listen carefully.

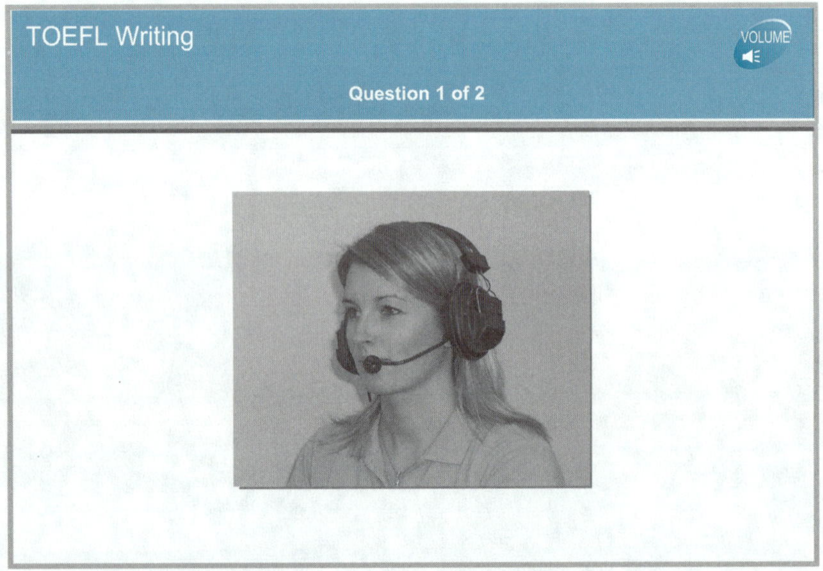

Narrator
You have 20 minutes to plan and write your response. Your response will be judged on the basis of the quality of your writing and on how well your response presents the points in the lecture and their relationship to the reading passage. Typically, an effective response will be 150 to 225 words.

Reading

Narrator
Now read a passage about an academic topic. You have 3 minutes to read the passage. Begin reading now.

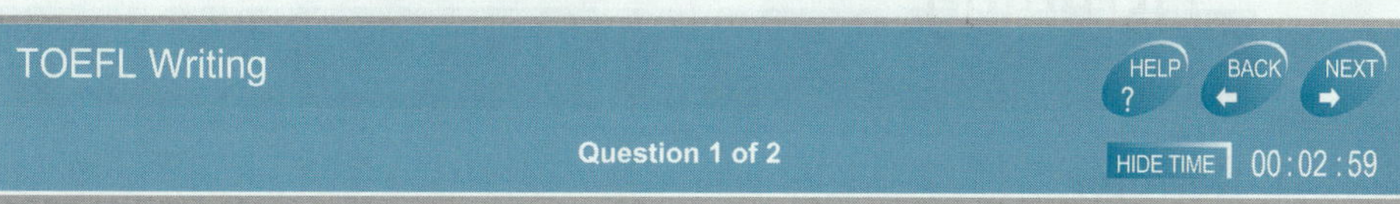

Reading Time : 3 minutes

Hydroelectricity is one of the best energy resources available. It is clean, renewable, and reliable and meets environmental policy objectives. Hydropower uses falling water to convert kinetic energy into electricity. A large river that falls down a steep slope is suitable for generating hydroelectric power. The river is dammed at the top, and the valley is flooded, creating a large reservoir — or lake — of water. A water gate is opened on the upper side of the dam, causing water to course through a tunnel that leads to turbines. The water turns the turbines, which in turn spin the generators; the generators generate electricity. That electricity is then carried through cables to its destination. Then, as the sun evaporates water from the sea and lakes, the water forms clouds and falls as rain in the mountains, keeping the dam supplied with water.

Hydroelectricity is extremely efficient because it neither requires nor gives off any heat in spinning the turbines. This makes hydroelectric power very inexpensive. The consumer price is about 3 cents per kilowatt hour, a price that is possible because of the relatively low cost of operating hydroelectric facilities. Since water is a fuel that can never be depleted, hydroelectric power is renewable and enduring. Only minimal maintenance is needed to generate hydroelectric power. Once the dam and its works are built, only a supervisional staff is usually required to man it. The dam provides excellent flood control and can also control the rate that water flows downstream. Electricity can be generated constantly and is much more reliable than wind, solar, or wave power.

Hydroelectricity does not involve any radiation or pollution, so the environmental impact is very low. Since it also incurs low operating costs and increases tourism and recreational activities, hydroelectricity is an outstanding energy resource.

Listening

Narrator

Now listen to part of a lecture on the topic you just read about.

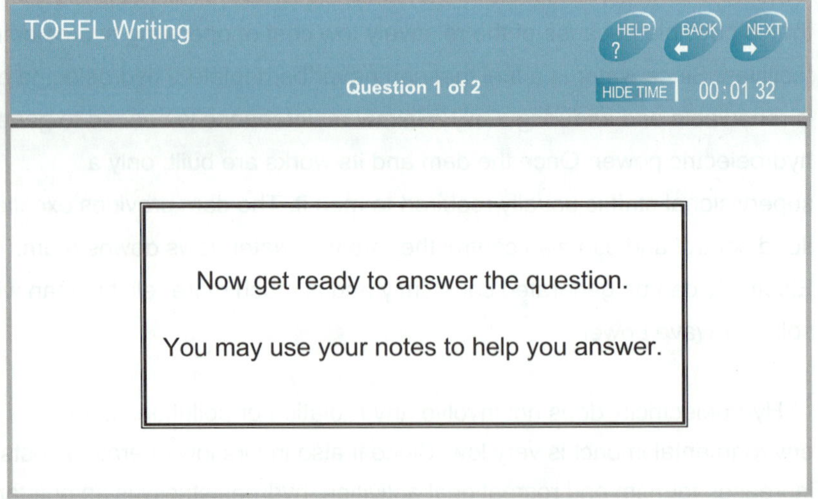

Narrator

Summarize the points made in the lecture you just heard, explaining how they cast doubt on points made in the reading.

TOEFL Writing

HELP ?   BACK ←   NEXT →

Question 1 of 2

HIDE TIME   00:19:54

Directions: You have 20 minutes to plan and write your response. Your response will be judged on the basis of the quality of your writing and on how well your response presents the points in the lecture and their relationship to the reading passage. Typically, an effective response will be 150 to 225 words.

Question: Summarize the points made in the lecture you just heard, explaining how they cast doubt on points made in the reading.

Hydroelectricity is one of the best energy resources available. It is clean, renewable, and reliable and meets environmental policy objectives. Hydropower uses falling water to convert kinetic energy into electricity. A large river that falls down a steep slope is suitable for generating hydroelectric power. The river is dammed at the top, and the valley is flooded, creating a large reservoir — or lake — of water. A water gate is opened on the upper side of the dam, causing water to course through a tunnel that leads to turbines. The water turns the turbines, which in turn spin the generators; the generators generate electricity. That electricity is then carried through cables to its destination. Then, as the sun evaporates water from the sea and lakes, the water forms clouds and falls as rain in the mountains, keeping the dam supplied with water.

I think that …

Answer

Answer

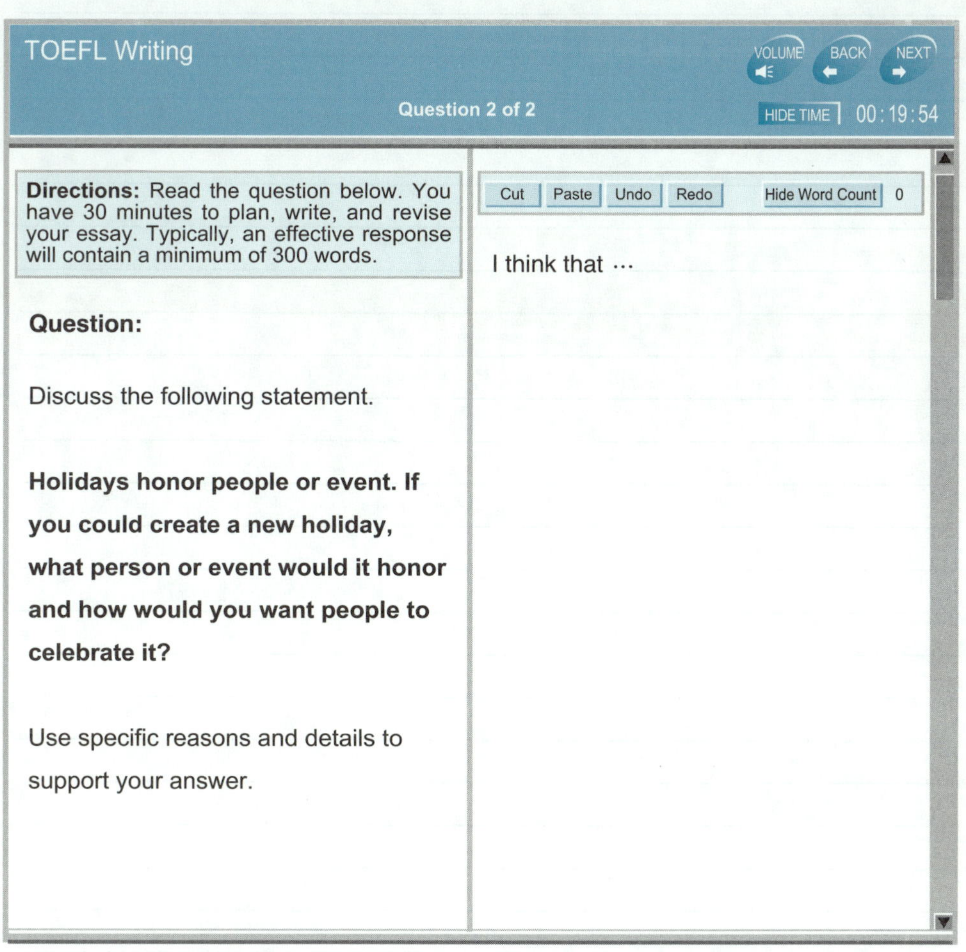

TOEFL Writing
VOLUME
BACK
NEXT
Question 2 of 2
HIDE TIME　00 : 19 : 54
Directions: Read the question below. You have 30 minutes to plan, write, and revise your essay. Typically, an effective response will contain a minimum of 300 words.
Question:
Discuss the following statement.
Holidays honor people or event. If you could create a new holiday, what person or event would it honor and how would you want people to celebrate it?
Use specific reasons and details to support your answer.
Cut　Paste　Undo　Redo　Hide Word Count　0
I think that …

Answer

Answer

Answer

Independent Writing
Further Writing Practice 1

1

Do you want to live in a big city or in a small town?

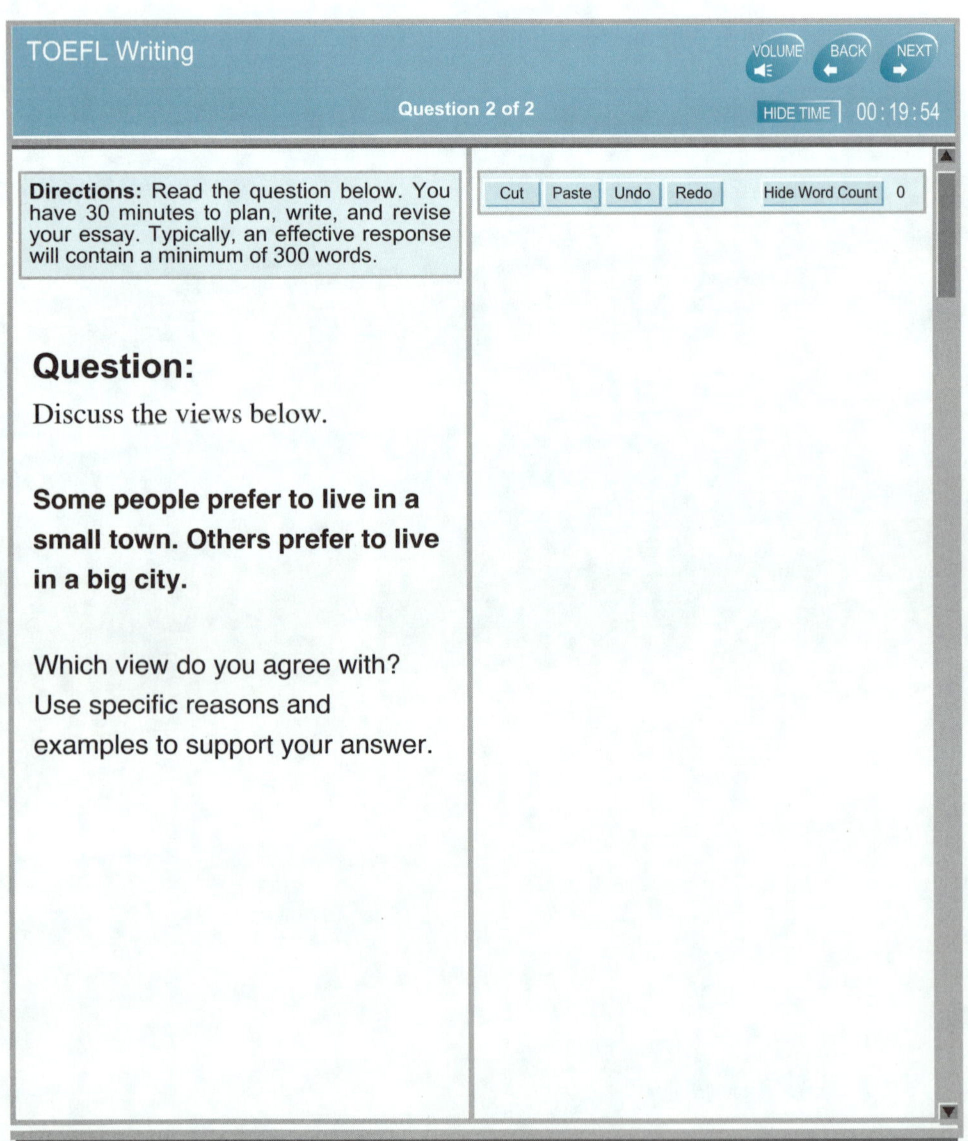

Key Ideas

작은마을

❋ 서로 다 알고 지내기 때문에 가족적이다.

❋ 아이들이 자연과 가까이서 자랄 수 있다.

❋ 아이들이 건강하게 자랄 수 있다.

큰도시

❖ 서로 인사를 안 해도 되는 익명성이 있어 자유롭다.

❖ 다양한 시설이 있어 편리하다.

❖ 문화 생활이 가능하다.

❖ 대중 교통이 발달되어 있어 차가 없어도 좋다.

Vocabulary Brainstorming

- 차량이 많은 → heavy traffic

- 대도시의 짜릿함 → the excitement of big cities

- 작은 마을의 느린 페이스 → the slow pace of a small town

- 사생활 → privacy

- 익명성 → anonymity

- 도시 사람 → city dwellers

- 다양한 문화 활동 → diverse cultural activities

- 지역 사회 → community

01.

내가 작은 타운과 대도시에 모두 살아 보았기 때문에, 나는 양쪽의 좋은 면과 나쁜 면을 모두 경험했다.

연구
- since ~ : ~했기 때문에
- experience A : A를 경험하다, 겪다 (know도 ok.)
- the good and bad sides of A : A의 좋은 면과 나쁜 면

02.

개인적으로, 나는 작은 타운보다는 큰 도시에 사는 것을 선호한다.

연구
- 개인적인 입장을 밝힐 때 personally, in my opinion 등으로 시작하면 좋다.
- A rather than B~ : B보다는 A

03.

큰 도시에 10년 동안 살았기 때문에, 나는 작은 타운에 사는 내 자신을 상상할 수 없다.

연구
- '10년 동안' 할 땐 전치사 for+기간. '언제 이후로'는 since+기점을 적는다. since childhood/ 1990 : 어린 시절 이후로/1990년 이후로
- can't imagine oneself ~ing : ~ 하는 자신을 상상할 수 없다

04. 대도시에서는, 당신은 많은 일들을 낮이나 밤이나 할 수 있다.

(연구) • day or night 낮이나 밤이나 *cf.* day and night 밤낮, 계속해서

05. 나는 대도시에서 이용할 수 있는 여러 즐길 거리에 익숙해졌다.

(연구) • grow accustomed to A : A에 익숙해지다 (=become used to, get accustomed to)
• available in A : A에서 이용할 수 있는, 찾을 수 있는 (entertainments one can find in big cities로 처리해도 된다.)

06. 대도시에서는, 대중 교통이 아주 편리하기 때문에 당신은 자동차가 없어도 살 수 있다.

(연구) • '대도시에서는'을 강조하기 위해 문장의 맨 앞으로 놓은 다음, 뒤에 쉼표를 찍는다.

07. 수퍼마켓들이 24시간 열려 있기 때문에, 당신은 당신이 편리할 때 쇼핑을 할 수 있다.

연구 • be open 24 hours : 24시간 열려 있다 (=be open around the clock, all day long)
• at A's convenience 편할 때, 편리에 따라 (=whenever it is convenient for A)

08. 대도시에서 사는 또 다른 좋은 점은 이용할 수 있는 문화 활동이 다양하다는 것이다.

연구 • good thing about A : A의 좋은 점
• the variety of A : A의 다양함
• cultural activities 문화생활, 활동 (도시 생활에 관한 글을 쓸 때 필요할 법한 표현이다.)

09. 도시 사람들은 같은 아파트 건물에서 20년 동안을 살고도 그들의 이웃들과 결코 친해지지 않는다.

____

____

____

연구 • get to know A : A를 알게 되다, 친해지다 (=make friends with, build a relationship or friendship with A)

10. 모든 것을 고려할 때, 대도시는 작은 타운보다 더 많은 기회와 짜릿함을 준다.

____

____

____

연구 • all in all 모든 걸 고려할 때 (=all things considered)
• 일반적으로 '대도시, 작은 타운'을 표현할 땐 big cities, small towns처럼 복수 처리한다.

Independent Writing
Further Writing Practice 2

2

Eating at restaurants Vs. Eating at home

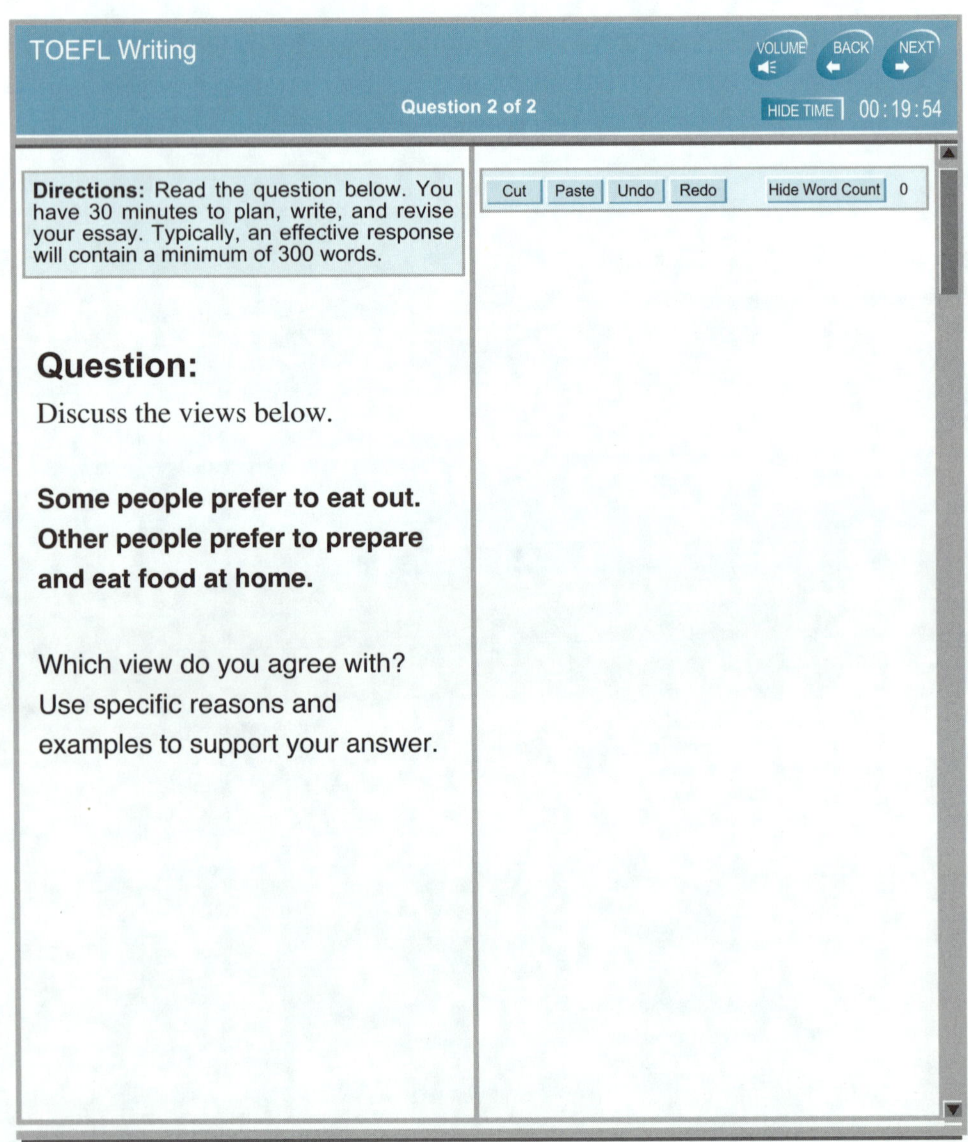

Key Ideas

집에서 먹다

❖ 경제적이다.
❖ 청결하다.
❖ 먹는 음식의 양과 질을 조절할 수 있다.

외식하다

❖ 시간이 절약된다.
❖ 기분 전환이 된다.
❖ 편하다.

Vocabulary Brainstorming

- 외식하다   → eat out

- 간이 음식점   → food stand

- 음식재료   → ingredients

- 집에서 먹다   → eat at home

- 집에서 만든 음식   → home-made food

- 건강한 음식   → healthy food

- 일인분   → one portion

- 음식을 주문하다   → order food

- 음식을 요리하다   → cook food

Eating at home

01. 나는 아래에 언급된 여러 이유 때문에 집에서 식사하는 것을 선호한다.

- the reason for A : A에 대한 이유 / the reason why+절 : ~하는 이유
- 때로는 why나 for를 생략하고 바로 절이 오기도 한다. *e.g.* The reason he left the meeting earlier is still unclear to me. 그가 회의에서 일찍 나간 이유가 내겐 여전히 분명치 않다.
- 언급하다 mention, state, present

02. 대체로, 집에서 식사하는 것이 외식하는 것보다 덜 비싸다.

- overall 대체로, 전반적으로 (=all in all, generally speaking)

03. 식당이 당신에게 시간을 절약하게 해 줄 수는 있지만, 식당은 분명 당신에게 돈을 절약하게 해 주지는 않는다.

- save someone something 누구에게 ~을 절약하게 하다, 덜어주다 (주로 돈, 시간, 노고, 문제 등을 덜어주다. *e.g.* This machine will save you a lot money. 이 기계는 당신에게 많은 돈을 절약하게 해 줄 것이다.)

0 4. 심지어 패스트 푸드 점심식사도 집에서 만든 점심보다 비용이 더 든다.

연구 • cost 비용, 돈이 들다 *e.g.* The plan will cost us a lot of money. 그 계획은 우리에게 많은 돈이 들 것이다.

0 5. 집에서 음식을 요리하면 구체적인 요리재료에 대해서 더 조절을 할 수 있다.

연구 • provide 제공하다, 주다의 의미지만, '~하면 ~할 수 있다'는 용법으로 사용해 깔끔하고 간단한 문장을 만들 수 있다.

0 6. 집에서는 과식을 막기 위해 일인분 양을 조절할 수 있다.

연구 • control one's portion size 먹는 양을 조절하다
  cf. one portion, two portions 1인분, 2인분
• prevent A (명사 or ~ing) : A를 막다, 예방하다
• ~ so as to do A : A할 수 있도록

07. 사실, 집에서 식사하는 것이 밖에서 먹는 것보다 시간을 더 많이 절약해 준다. 식당으로 운전하고 가서, 주차하고, 식사 기다리고, 집으로 운전해 다시 돌아오는 데 드는 시간을 고려하면.

연구 • 동사에 ing를 붙여 동명사로 만들어 주어로 사용하면 전체 문장 만들기가 훨씬 수월해진다.
e.g. Studying overseas is not an easy job. 외국에서 공부하기가 쉬운 일이 아니다.
• ~한다는 것은 …이다 : ~ing is …

08. 나는 자주 페스트 푸드를 먹으면 흔히 병이 난다.

연구 • get sick 병이 나다

09. 나는 신선한 음식을 먹기를 좋아하는데 페스트 푸드 식당은 대개 음식을 미리 조리한다.

연구 • pre-cook the food 음식을 미리 익히다, 조리하다

10.

비록 내가 멋진 식당에서 식사하는 것을 즐기긴 하지만, 내가 매일 그렇게 할 만한 형편이 되지는 못할 것이다.

연구
- 여기서 while은 '~하지만', '비록 ~하지만'을 의미할 때 쓴다.
- afford to do something ~하는 것을 감당하다, ~할 수 있는 형편이 된다.
  e.g. I cannot affort this car. 나는 이 차를 살 형편이 못 된다.

11.

집에서 요리하는 것은 외식하는 것보다 돈도 덜 들고 건강에도 더 좋다.

연구
- healthy 건강에 좋은
- eat out 외식하다

Eating out

01.
어떤 사람들은 정기적으로 외식하는 것을 즐긴다.

- 주로 some people이 들어간 문장 뒤에는 others로 시작하는 문장이 온다. 한 문장에 다 담으려면 While some, others 로 처리하면 좋다.
- Some people like mathematics. Others prefer history.
- While some people like mathematics, others prefer history. 또는 Some people like mathematics, while others prefer history.

02.
나로서는 식당에 가는 것이 많은 이유로 최선의 선택이다.

- for me 나로서는, 내게는
- the best option/choice 최선의 선택

03.
밖에서 아주 바쁜 일을 하는 사람들은 요리할 시간이 없다.

- Those+who/whose+with : ~하는 이들은
- Those whose job is correcting college entrance exams are busy in December. 대입 시험을 채점하는 직업을 가진 이들은 12월에 바쁘다.

04. 그들은 외식의 편리함을 좋아한다.

- the inconvenience/convenience of ~ : ~의 불편함/편리함
- People flock into cities because of the convenience of living in a metropolis.
  사람들은 대도시에 사는 편리함 때문에 도시로 몰린다.

05. 비록 내가 요리하는 것을 즐기지만, 나는 가능한 자주 식당에서 먹는다.

- Though 비록 (although와 같다.)
- as+부사+as possible : 가능한 ~하게
  e.g. I'll let you know about it as fast as possible. 가능한 빨리 그것에 대해 알려줄게.

06. 많은 사람들이 외식이 비싸다고 생각하는데, 반드시 그런 것만은 아니다.

- that's not necessarily ~ : 꼭, 반드시 그런 것 만은 아니다
- affordable 감당할 만한, 지불할 수 있는 (cheap 대신 사용하면 좋다.)

07. 어떤 식당들은 가격이 저렴해서 상당히 감당할 만 하다.

연구 • another benefit to ~ : ~의 또 다른 혜택, 좋은 점 (=advantage to, good thing of, merit of)

08. 음식 판매대나 식당에서 먹는 또 다른 좋은 점이 있다.

09. 외식할 때는, 당신이 손가락 하나 까딱하지 않아도 음식이 준비되어 식탁으로 배달된다.

연구 • without your lifting a finger 손 하나 까딱 안 하고 (~ 할 수 있다)
• deliver 배달하다

10. 식당에서는, 식사 후에 치울 걱정이 없다.

연구 • there is no worry about A : A에 대한 걱정이 없다 (=there is no need to worry about A)

11.

식당에서 먹는 것은 집에서 음식을 요리하는 것보다 시간이 훨씬 덜 든다.

연구
- 동명사를 주어로 잡는다.
- take up time 시간이 든다, 걸린다

12.

만약 내가 감당만 할 수 있다면, 나는 매일 외식을 할 것이다.

연구
- afford to do something ~하는 것을 감당하다, 할 수 있다

13.

결론적으로, 외식이 시간을 절약해 주고 아주 편리하기 때문에 나는 외식을 선호한다.

연구
- In conclusion 결론적으로

Independent Writing
Further Writing Practice 3

3

The effects of human activities on the Earth

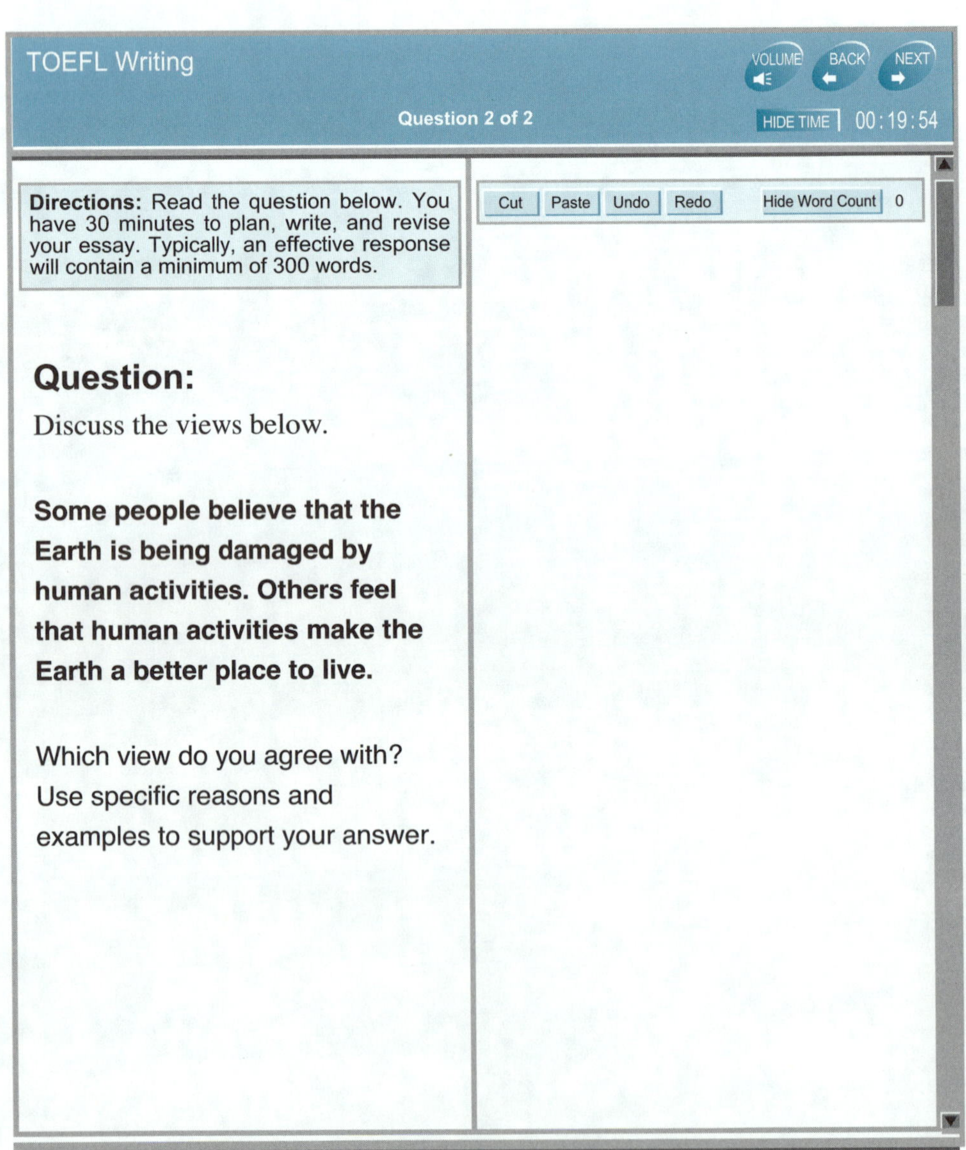

Key Ideas

❖ 경제 발전과 환경 보존은 나란히 달성할 수 있다.
❖ 무분별한 개발보다는 지속 가능한 개발이 필요하다.
❖ 이를 위해 우선 청정 에너지를 개발해야 한다.

Vocabulary Brainstorming

• 인간 삶의 질 → the quality of human life

• 오염된 → polluted, contaminated

• 천연 자원 → natural resources

• 자원을 고갈하다 → deplete resources

• 공장에서 나오는 배기 → emissions from factories

• 유해 화학 물질 → harmful/hazardous chemicals

• 산업 쓰레기 → industrial waste

• 매립지 → landfill

• 에너지 절약형 → energy-saving

• 대체 에너지 → alternative energy

• 청정 에너지 → clean/green/environmentally-friendly energy

• 대중 교통 → public transportation

• 카풀 → carpool, ridesharing

• 지속 가능한 경제 발전 → sustainable economic development

• 불매운동을 벌이다 → boycott

01. 인간의 관점에서 볼 때, 지구는 과거보다 훨씬 더 살기에 편리한 곳이다.

연구
- from the human perspective 인간의 관점에서 볼 때 (=from the point of view of human beings)
- the Earth 지구 (이때 꼭 정관사 the가 들어가야 한다.)
- a convenient place to live in은 기본 문장 구조인 we live in a convenient place의 변형 구조이기 때문에 뒤에 있는 전치사 in은 살려두도록 한다.
- '과거, 현재, 미래에는' 은 영어로는 'in the past, in the present, in the future'로 하며 the 를 꼭 넣는다.

02. 환경적인 관점에서 볼 때는, 그렇지만, 지구는 인간 활동을 통해 오염되었다.

연구
- from the environmental point of view 환경의 측면에서 볼 때 (If one considers the situation from the environmental perspective로 풀어 써도 좋다.)
- became polluted through human activities 인간의 활동을 통해, 때문에 오염됐다 (through 대신에 because of, due to, with를 넣어도 된다.)

03. 강과 하천은, 예를 들어, 통제되지 않은 공장 배출물들에 의해 오염되었다.

- for example을 문장 맨 앞에 넣어도 되지만, 주어 뒤 쉼표 사이에 써도 멋스럽다. for instance도 '예를 들어'란 의미로 쓰인다.
- contaminated 오염된 (polluted, degraded, spoiled까지도 정리해 두자.)
- unchecked 통제되지 않은, 관리, 검사 받지 않은 (=uncontrolled)
- emission 배출/배출물 (동사로는 emit)

04. 대도시들에서는, 환경 문제가 공기와 수질 오염을 포함한다.

- '대도시에서는'이라고 막연하게 말할 땐 복수(cities)로 하든지, in a large city처럼 부정관사 a를 넣어 단수 처리한다.
- environmental concerns 환경에 대한 우려, 걱정, 문제
  (problems about/concerning/related to the environment로 해도 좋다.)

05. 기업들과 지역사회들이 그들의 수원에 쓰레기를 쏟아 붓는다.

- dump waste 쓰레기를 버리다 (=throw away garbage)

06. 또 다른 문제는 우리들이 우리의 천연 자원을 아주 빨리 고갈시키고 있다는 점이다.

연구
- another problem or reason is that이란 표현을 통해 두 번째 이유나 주장을 전개하면, 단락의 도입에 secondly/second/next란 말을 쓰지 않고도 글 전체의 논리적 흐름을 전개해 나갈 수 있다.
- deplete natural resources '자원을 고갈시키다'란 표현은 환경에 관련된 글을 쓸 때 단골로 등장한다.

07. 환경오염을 막는 한가지 방법은 환경 파괴를 일으키는 회사들의 제품들에 대해 불매 운동을 하는 것이다.

연구
- one way to do A is by ~ing B : A를 하는 방법 중 하나는 B를 하는 것이다 (알아두면 여러 상황에서 쓸 수 있는 문장 구조이다.)
- that cause environmental damage 환경 파괴를 일으키는 (damage를 동사로 사용해 that damage the environment로 써도 된다.)
- boycott 불매운동을 하다

08. 우리는 환경 친화적인 대안들을 추구함으로써 지구를 보다 살기 좋은 곳으로 만들 수 있다.

 • environmentally friendly+명사 : 친환경적 ~ (에너지를 얘기할 땐 green을 형용사로 써도
  좋다. 청정 에너지 green energy)
 • alternative 대안, 대체 (alternative energy 대체 에너지)

09.

자동차에 의한 대기 오염은 대도시들이 직면하고 있는 가장 심각한
문제들 중의 하나이다.

____

____

____

 • air pollution 대기 오염 (=air contamination), water pollution 수질 오염
 • one of the+최상급 형용사+명사 복수 : 최고로 ~한 것 중 하나
 • the gravest 가장 심각한 (=the most serious)
 • facing 당면하고 있는
   e.g. Energy shortage is the most serious problem facing our nation.
   에너지 부족이 우리 나라가 당면한 가장 심각한 문제이다.
   이때 주어를 our nation으로 잡으면 facing 대신에 be faced with로 처리해야 한다.
   Our nation is faced with the problem of energy shortage.

10.

서울에서는, 예를 들어, 대중 교통과 카풀의 이용을 장려하는 캠페인
이 있다.

____

____

____

 • 일반 명사 주어 대신 장소/시간 부사절이나 구가 올 경우 뒤에 쉼표를 넣어주어야 좋다.
 • for instance 예를 들어 (for example과 섞어 사용하면 반복을 피할 수 있다.)
 • encourage 장려하다 (encourage someone to do something, encourage something)

11. 매립지에 그냥 쓰레기를 묻는 것보다 우리가 만들어 내는 쓰레기를 제거하는 더 효과적인 방법들이 있어야 한다.

연구
- there is/are의 기본 형태에서 there should be, there must be 등 조동사를 사용해 '있어야 한다, 있을 것이 분명하다' 등의 표현을 만드는 연습도 해두는 것이 좋다.
- a way of ~ing 하는 방법 (a way to do도 ok.)
- get rid of something 제거하다, 없애다 (=eliminate)
- landfill 매립지

12. 기업들은 새로운 대체 청정 에너지를 개발해야 한다.

13. 소비자로서, 우리는 에너지 절약형 제품들을 구입해야 한다.

연구
- as consumers 소비자로서 (이때 as는 ~자격으로.)
- energy-saving 에너지 절약형

14. 인간 삶의 전반적인 질이 과거 수 십년에 걸쳐 크게 개선된 것은 사실이다.

 • it is true that ~ : ~인 것은 사실이다

• 토플 에세이를 쓸 때 자신의 입장과 상반되는 입장을 잠시 언급할 땐 it is true that ~나 of course ~로 시작하는 것이 좋다. 그 뒤의 문장은 however로 시작해 원래 주장하는 입장으로 다시 돌아가는 게 일반적인 논리 전개이다.

e.g. I believe human activities caused a lot of harm to the Earth. It is true that (대신 Of course를 넣어도 좋다) we are now living in a more convenient world. However, we will have to pay a high price for the convenience we obtained at the expense of the environment.

나는 인간의 활동이 지구에 많은 피해를 입혔다고 믿는다. 우리가 (예전보다는) 더 편리한 세상에 살고 있는 건 사실이다. 그러나 우리는 환경을 희생하며 얻은 편리함에 대한 비싼 대가를 지불하게 될 것이다.

15. 그러나, 인간이 산업 쓰레기와 유해 화학물질과 같은 환경 문제들을 해결할 수 있으려면 먼 길을 가야 한다.

 • still 그러나, 여전히 (=however, yet, nevertheless)

• there is a long way to go before+절 : ~를 하려면 먼 길을 가야 한다/아직 멀었다

• such as는 붙여서 쓰는 경우도 있고 떨어뜨려 사용하기도 한다.

Independent Writing
Further Writing Practice 4

4

Why do we now live longer than before?

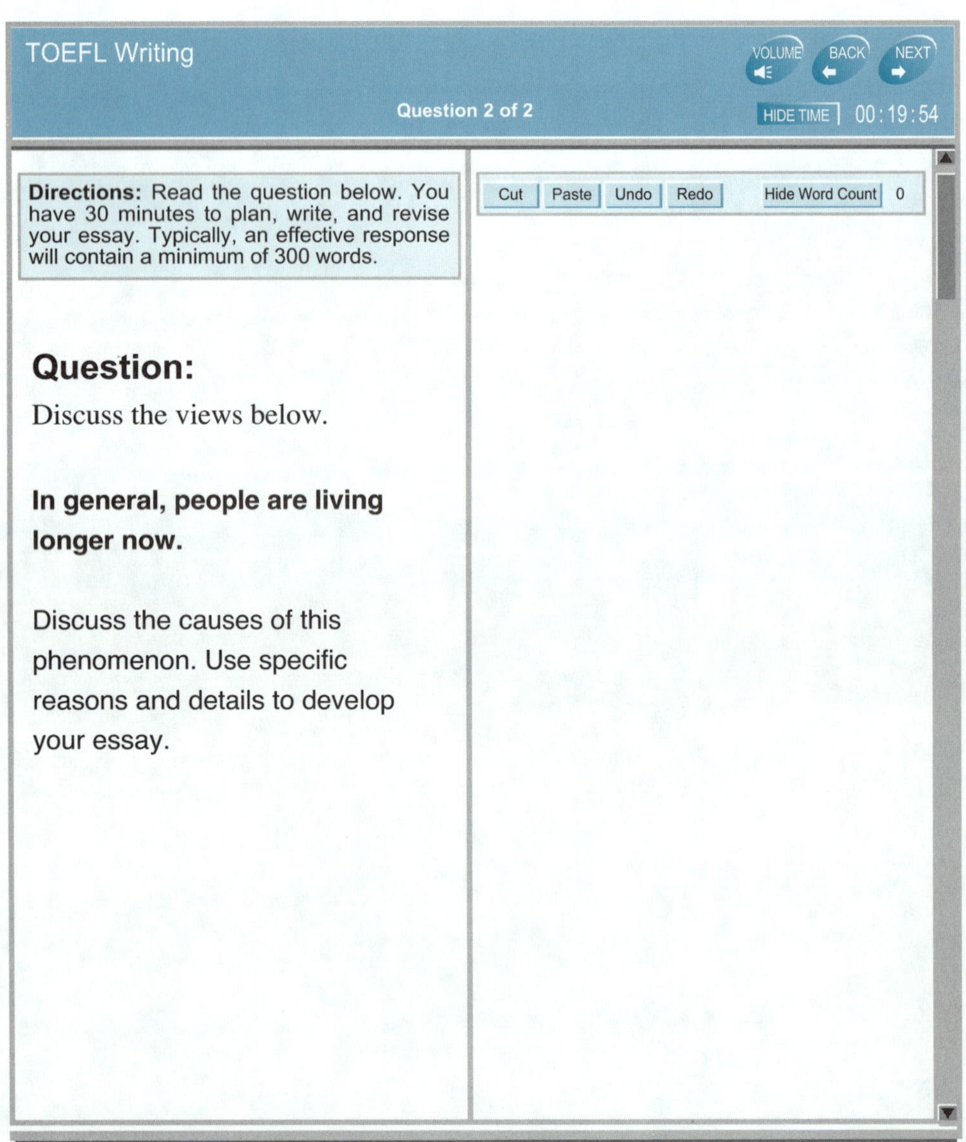

Key Ideas

❖ 전보다 더 위생적인 생활을 한다.
❖ 의학기술의 발달이 생명을 연장하는 데 크게 기여했다.
❖ 전보다 더 균형이 잡힌 식생활도 수명을 연장하는 데 도움이 됐다.
❖ 건강에 대한 인식이 높아져서 더 건강하게 오래 살 수 있게 되었다.

Vocabulary Brainstorming

• 개선된 의료 서비스
  → improved health care

• 영양
  → nutrition

• 균형 잡힌 영양
  → balanced nutrition

• 수명
  → life span, longevity

• 평균수명
  → life expectancy

• 수명을 연장한다
  → extend our life span

• 저지방 식단
  → low-fat diet

01.
왜 사람들이 지금 더 오래 살고 있는지에 대한 여러 가지 이유가 있다고 나는 생각한다.

___

(연구) • there are several or many reasons why+절 : ~하는 데는 여러 가지 이유가 있다

02.
장수의 두 가지 주된 이유는 누구나 이용할 수 있는 개선된 의료 서비스와 보다 나은 영양이다.

___

(연구) • the main reason for A : A의 주된 이유는 (=the most important reason for A)
• longevity 장수, 수명
• improved health care 개선된 의료 서비스
• be available to everyone 누구나 이용 가능한, 모두에게 제공되는
  (=be offered to everyone)

03.
교육, 의료 서비스, 그리고 작업장 안전 모두가 수명을 늘리는 데 주된 역할을 했다.

___

(연구) • workplace safety 작업장 안전
• play a major role in ~ing or 명사 : ~하는 데 주된 역할을 하다, 한 몫을 톡톡히 하다

04.

비록 모두가 최고의 의료 서비스를 얻는 것은 아니지만, 모두가 기본적인 의료 서비스를 받을 수 있다.

• not everyone can ~ : 누구나 ~할 수 있는 건 아니다

05.

한 사람이 자기 건강을 어떻게 돌볼지를 알게 될 때, 그 사람은 종종 더 오래, 더 행복하게 산다.

• be informed about A : A에 대해서 알게 되다, 통보를 받다, 교육을 받다
• take care of A : A를 돌보다 (=look after)

06.

오늘날 우리의 수명을 연장한 주된 요소는 의과학에서 이루어진 진보에서 그 원인을 찾을 수 있다.

• the major factor ~ing : ~하는 주된 요소는
• be attributed to A : A에 기인한다, A에 있다고 생각한다
• advancement in A : A의 발전 (=development, improvement)

07.

오래 전, 의료 서비스가 모두에게 이용 가능하지 않았기 때문에, 많은 사람들이 민간 요법에 의존했다.

연구
- since ~ : ~했음으로, 했기 때문에
- resort to A : A에 의존하다 (=depend, rely on)
- folk remedies 민간요법

08.

보다 나은 약과 의료 서비스가 이용 가능할 때는, 어린 나이에 죽는 사람 수가 감소하는 것이 사실이다.

연구
- the truth is that+절 : ~라는 게 사실이다
- die at an early age 어린 나이에 죽다 (=die young)
- the number of A gets reduced : A의 숫자가 줄다 (=there is less A)

09.

오늘날, 의사들은 무엇이 질병을 일으키고 어떻게 그들을 치료할지에 대해 더 많이 안다.

연구
- what causes diseases 무엇이 질병을 일으키는지 (=the causes of diseases or illnesses)
- how to cure them 어떻게 그것들을 치료해야 하는지
  (=the cure or treatment of diseases)

10. 양질의 의료 서비스에 접근할 수 있는 것이 수명에 크게 영향을 줄 수 있다.

- have access to A : A에게 접근 할 수 있다
- quality+명사 : 양질의 ~

11. 이제 우리는 감염을 치료하는 것을 돕는 항생제와 다른 약품들을 가지고 있다.

- antibiotics 항생제
- infections 감염

12. 균형 잡힌 영양 또한 우리의 수명을 연장하는 데 크게 기여했다.

- balanced nutrition 균형 잡힌 영양
- greatly contributed to A : A에 크게 기여하다
  (to 뒤에 오는 동사는 ~ing 형태를 띄어야 한다.)
- extend one's life span 수명을 연장하다 (=make a person live longer)

13.

사람들은 저지방 식품과 더 많은 야채와 과일을 먹으려고 노력하는데, 이들 음식들은 이제 일 년 내내 구할 수 있다.

연구
- low-fat food 저지방 음식
  cf. food rich in vitamin C : 비타민 C가 풍부한, 다량 함유된 음식
- available year-round 일년 내내 제공되는, 구할 수 있는

14.

저지방 식단과 소금이 덜 들어간 음식이 사람들의 수명을 늘리는 데 기여했다.

연구
- foods with less salt 소금이 적은 음식

15.

간단히 말해서, 늘어난 건강 교육, 개선된 의료 서비스, 그리고 균형 잡힌 영양 덕분에, 사람들은 전보다 훨씬 더 오래 살 수 있다.

연구
- in summary 간단히 말해서
- thanks to A : A 덕분에 (because of A도 '때문에' 혹은 '덕분에'의 의미.)
- much+비교급 형용사 : 훨씬 더 ~한 (much대신에 far도 쓰인다. : far longer than before)

Independent Writing
Further Writing Practice 5

5
Friends different from you
Vs. Friends similar to you

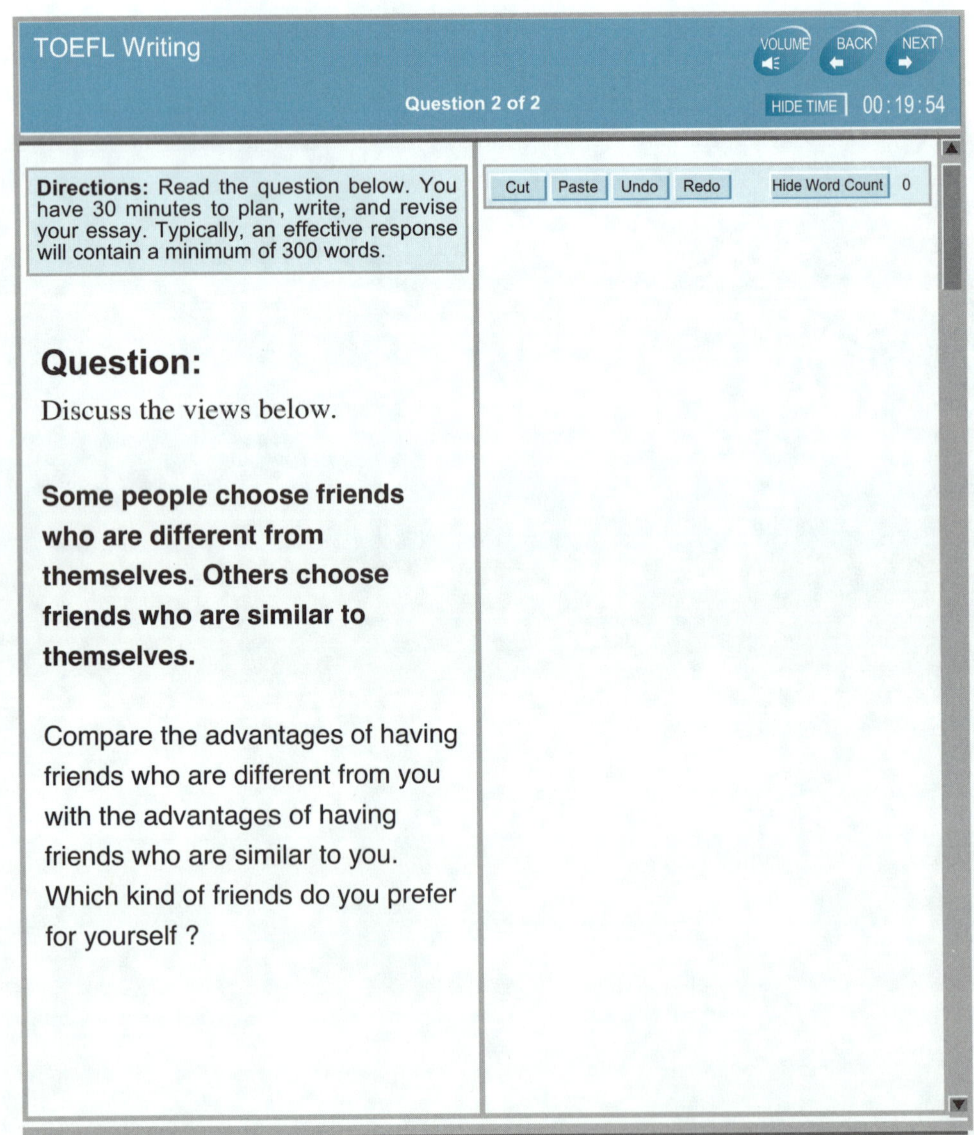

Key Ideas

나와 다른 친구

❋ 새로운 것을 배울 수 있어 재미 있다.

❋ 세상을 다른 관점에서 보는 기회를 가질 수 있다.

❋ 혼자라면 하지 않을 색다른 경험들을 할 수 있다.

나와 비슷한 친구

❖ 언제나 의견 일치를 볼 수 있어 편하다.

❖ 뭘 해도 같이 즐길 수 있어 우정이 더 깊어진다.

❖ 성격 문제로 다툴 필요가 없다.

Vocabulary Brainstorming

- 경험

  → experience

- 상황

  → situation

- 가치관

  → values

- 공통 관심사를 가진 친구

  → friends with common interests

- 신뢰

  → trust

- 취향

  → tastes

- 생각을 나누다

  → share views on something

01.

당신과 비슷하거나 아니면 다른 사람과 친구가 되는 것은 장점과 단점을 다 가지고 있다.

연구
- similar to A : A와 유사한 *cf.* the same as A : A와 똑 같은
- different from A : A와 다른 (언제나 뒤에 따라 붙는 전치사를 눈 여겨 봐 두어야 한다.)
- 이 문장은 being friends with people whose tastes differ from yours has ～로 처리해도 된다. 이때 'differ from A : A와 다르다'는 동사구를 사용하면 편리하다.

02.

나로서는, 나와 다른 사람을 친구로 사귀는 것을 나는 좋아한다.

연구
- make friends with ～와 친구가 되다 (=build friendship with)
- as for me 나로서는

03.

일단, 그들은 종종 우리의 삶에 새로운 관점을 가져다 준다.

연구
- for one thing 일단, 하나는
- A brings B to C : A는 C에게 B를 가져다 준다, 선사한다, 준다 (=A offers C B.)
- It brings more opportunities to you. If offers you more opportunities.
- a new point of view 새로운 관점 (=a fresh perspective)

04.

당신은 또한 당신의 친구와 많은 것을 공유하지 않는 데서 오는 다양한 경험을 즐길 수 있다.

연구
- various 다양한 (=diverse, a variety or diversity of)
- have much in common with A : A와 비슷한 점, 공통점이 많다
  (=be similar to A, have almost the same tastes as A does)

05.

다른 한편, 우리와 다른 친구들은 우리가 새로운 것들을 시도해 보고 새로운 경험을 갖도록 돕는다.

연구
- on the other hand 반면에, 한편
- help A (to) do B : A가 B하게 돕다, 할 수 있도록 한다

06.

다른 취향을 가진 친구가 있는 사람들은 입장의 차이를 고맙게 여기는 경향이 있다.

연구
- tend to do A : A를 하는 경향이 있다
- appreciate 고맙게 생각하다, 가치롭게 여기다 (=value somebody or something highly)
- differences of opinion 입장의 차이

07.

당신과 다른 어떤 사람은 일반적으로 주어진 상황에 대해 당신과 같은 대응을 하지 않을 것이다.

• someone who+절 : ~하는 누군가 (=a person who ~)
• the same ~ as A : A와 같은~
• reaction to A : A에 대한 반응 (전치사 to를 기억해 두자.)

08.

우리와 크게 다른 사람들과 우리의 의견과 취향을 나누는 것은 흥미롭고 유익할 수 있다.

• interesting and informative 재미있으면서도 유익한 정보를 주는, 배울게 있는 (다르게 표현해도 되지만, 이렇듯 같은 글자로 시작하는 두 단어로 묶으면 글이 한결 잘 읽힌다.)
• share A with B : A를 B와 나누다
• differ from A : A와 다르다 (=be different or dissimilar from A)
• it's + 형용사 + to부정사 형식으로 문장의 구조를 잡는다.

09.

다른 한편, 공통 관심이 없는 우정을 유지하는 것은 어려울 수 있다.

• 'it is + 형용사 + to부정사'의 변형. it can be ~일 수 있다, it will be ~일 것이다 등.
• have common interests 공통 관심을 갖다 (=have similar interests)
• 뒷부분을 friendships without much in common으로 처리해도 된다.

10.

먼저, 공통 관심을 가진 친구들은 그들이 대개 같은 일을 하는 것을 즐기기 때문에 무엇을 할지에 대해 논쟁하지 않는 경향이 있다.

연구
- tend to 동사원형 : ~하는 경향이 있다
  / tend not to 동사원형 : ~ 안 하는 경향이 있다 (이때 not의 위치를 잘 기억해두자.)
- argue with A about B : A와 B에 대해 논의하다, 논쟁하다
- what to do 무엇을 할지

11.

그리고 그들이 비슷하기 때문에, 그들은 아마도 서로 많은 것을 공유할 것이다.

연구
- 'since+절, ~ : ~하니까, ~하다'의 문장 구조.
- likely 아마 (=probably)
- one another, each other 서로

12.

게다가, 우리가 보는 것과 같은 관점에서 인생을 보는 사람들과 시간을 보내는 것은 즐거운 일이다.

연구
- besides 게다가, 더군다나 (=in addition, moreover)
- 이 문장 역시 'it is + 형용사 + to부정사'의 구조이다.
- those who+절 : ~하는 이들
- from the same vantage points as A : A와 동일한 관점 (=point of view, perspective)

13. 더구나, 비슷한 취향을 가진 것이 두 사람 사이에 가능한 신뢰와 우정의 수준을 깊게 하는 것을 도와 준다.

___

연구
- 동사를 ~ing로 처리해 주어로 잡으면 편리하다.
- deepen A : A를 깊게 하다, 공고히 하다 (=strengthen, solidify, cement)
- the level of A : A의 수준, 정도 (=the degree of A)

14. 그들이 비슷하게 생각할 가능성이 아주 높기 때문에, 비슷한 취향을 가진 친구들은 거의 성격 충돌이 없다.

___

연구
- likely 앞에 most, very를 넣어 가능성이 높다는 것을 표현할 수 있다.
- alike 같은, 비슷한 (=in the same way)
- seldom 거의 ~한 적이 없다, 하는 경우가 없다 (=hardly, barely, scarcely)
- personality conflict 성격 충돌

15. 모든 것을 고려할 때, 나와 비슷한 친구를 갖는 것이 더 좋다고 나는 생각한다.

___

연구
- all things considered 모든 걸 고려했을 때 (=all in all)
- 'it is preferable to+동사원형'의 구조도 좋고, 'personally, I prefer A : 개인적으로 난 A를 더 좋아한다, 선호한다'로 표현해도 좋다.

16. 내 경우에는, 두 종류의 친구를 갖는 것이 만족스럽다고 나는 느낀다. 그 두 종류의 친구는 나와 다른 친구와 나와 비슷한 친구이다.

- in my case 내 경우엔 (=as for me, personally)
- I find it+형용사+동사원형 : 나는 ~하는 것이 ~하다고 생각한다, 느낀다
  (이 문장 구조도 알아두면 편리하다.)

17. 마지막으로, 나와 다른 친구를 많이 갖는 것은 나로 하여금 다른 인생관을 가진 사람들과 내 인생관을 나눌 수 있도록 해준다.

- A enables B to do C : A는 B로 하여금 C를 가능케 한다
  (이때 A가 무생물 주어일 경우엔, 'A 덕분에 B는 C를 할 수 있다'는 뜻.)
- view on A : A에 대한 입장, 견해, 생각

Independent Writing
Further Writing Practice 6

6

Stress management

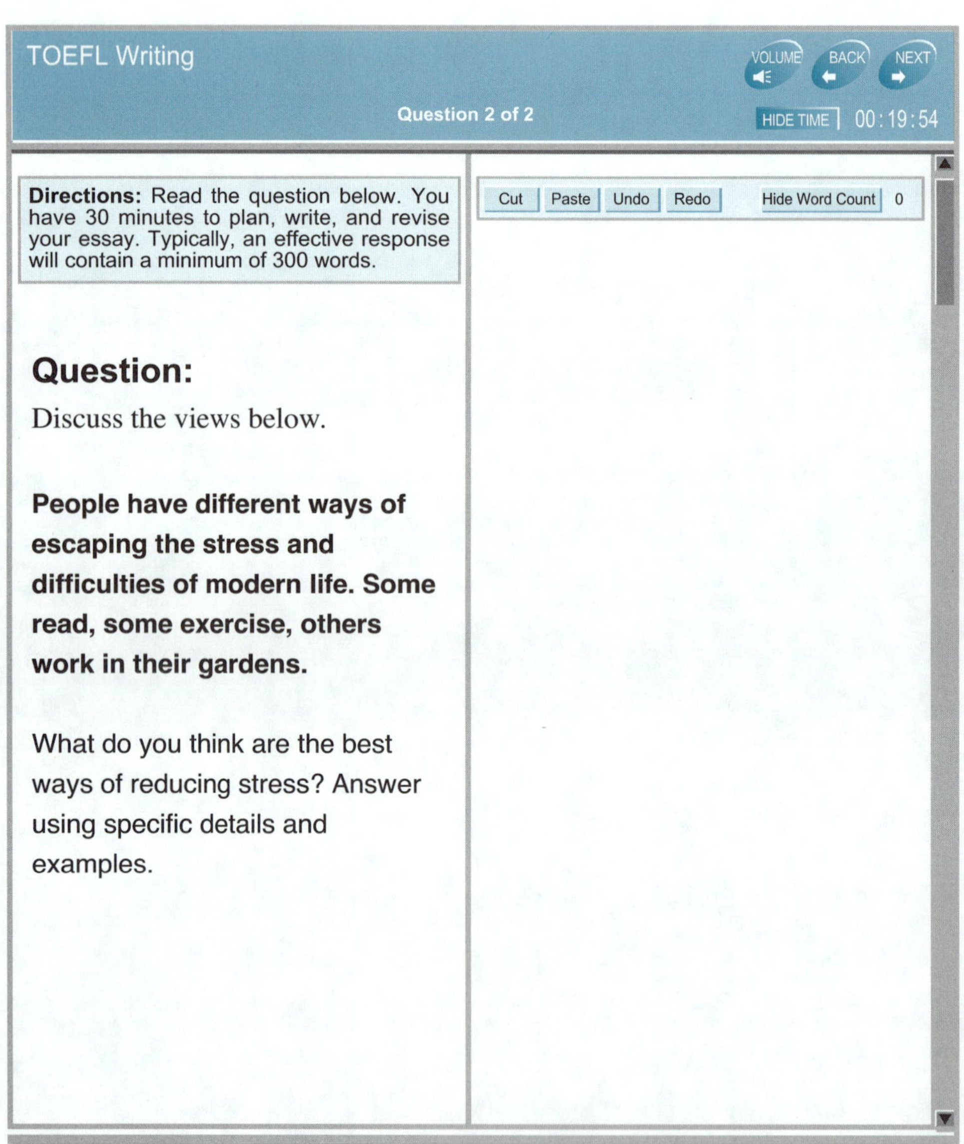

Key Ideas

❖ 충분한 휴식을 취하는 것이 중요하다.
❖ 좋아하는 운동을 규칙적으로 해주는 것이 필요하다.
❖ 가능하면 자주 자연을 접하는 것이 도움이 된다.
❖ 친구들과 충분한 대화를 하면 스트레스가 해소된다.

Vocabulary Brainstorming

- 스트레스를 없애다, 해소하다
    → get rid of/eliminate/cure/cope with stress
- 스트레스를 줄이다
    → reduce stress or lower stress level
- 일에서 오는 스트레스
    → work-related stress
- 초조함
    → anxiety, feel anxious
- 긴장하다
    → feel nervous
- 스트레스를 많이 받은 사람
    → a stressed-out person
- 격렬한 운동
    → strenuous exercise, to work out strenuously/vigorously
- 스트레스 없는 생활
    → a stress-free life

01. 스트레스는 사람의 건강에 큰 문제이다.

____

____

____

🔵 연구 • a major enemy of ～ : ～의 주적, 큰 문제

02. 현대 생활에는 높은 수준의 스트레스가 있게 마련이다.

____

____

____

🔵 연구 • tend to+동사 원형 : ～하는 경향이 있다, ～하게 마련이다 이렇게 쓰면 표현이 한결 부드러워진다. 여기서는 원래 there is/are 대신 사이에 tend를 넣어, '～있는 경우가 있다, ～하기 마련이다'로 만든다.

03. 전 세계에 걸쳐 사람들이 점점 더 바빠지고 있다.

____

____

____

🔵 연구 • 점점 더 ～되다 : 비교급+and+비교급 (이때 앞에는 become이나 get 동사가 자주 사용된다. *e.g.* She's getting fatter and fatter. 그녀는 점점 뚱뚱해 지고 있다.)

04.
그 결과, 사람의 매일의 일상이 엄청난 양의 스트레스의 원인이 될 수 있다.

- as a result 그 결과, 결과적으로 (=consequently)
- routine 일상
- ~의 원인 : the cause of ~

05.
스트레스를 없애는 데 있어 첫번째 단계는 원인을 확인하는 것이다.

- the first step in ~ing : ~하는 데 첫번째로 해야할 일은, 첫 단계는 (the first step to do something 역시 같은 내용을 담을 수 있는 표현이다.)
- 원인을 확인하다 : identify the cause

06.
건강한 생활습관을 유지함으로써 사람들은 자기 생활에서 스트레스를 줄일 수 있다.

- you can do A by ~ing : ~함으로써 A를 할 수 있다 '~를 함으로써'란 표현을 자주 쓰게 되는데, by ~ing가 이를 잘 담아 낸다. '~를 통해'라고 할 땐 through/with+명사를 써도 좋다. People can *reduce* stress in their lives *through/with* daily *exercises*.

07. 운동을 하고 명상을 하는 것은 사람의 스트레스 수준을 줄이는 최선의 방법들이다.

연구 • 앞 vocabulary brainstorming에서 지적했듯이, '스트레스를 없애다'에 대한 영어 표현은 eliminate, get rid of, reduce, relieve [stress] 혹은 free oneself from stress, lower one's stress level 등 다양하게 알아 둘 필요가 있다.

08. 걷기와 같은 운동들은 사람에게 자연에 가까워지는 기회를 준다.

연구 • 명사 복수+such as+명사 : ~와 같은 ~것들, 앞에 복수로 나오는 명사의 구체적인 예를 들 때 such as가 안성맞춤이다.
• *e.g.* Terrible kids such as my niece 내 조카와 같은 극성인 아이들

09. 일과 관련된 스트레스는 다른 유형의 스트레스보다 맞서 싸우기 더 쉽다.

연구 • A명사−related+B명사 : A에 관련된 B (related 앞에 하이픈을 넣어 '~에 관련된'이라는 형용사를 만들어 쓰면 표현이 간결해 진다.)
• *e.g.* computer−related jobs, IT−related businesses

10. 다른 때에는, 나는 반시간 동안 트레드밀(운동기구)에서 달린다.

연구 • Sometimes, I do A. Other times, I do B : 때로는 A를 하고 다른 때는 B를 한다. A를 할 때도 있는가하면 B를 할 때도 있다. (이렇듯 Some 뒤에는 other가 따라와 논리적 흐름을 만들어 주는 경우가 많다. *e.g.* Some people agree with the statement. Other people, however, don't. Some support the ideas, while others do not. 토플 에세이를 쓸 때 한 번은 쓰게 될 표현인 만큼 눈여겨 봐두어야 한다.)

11. 밤에 잠을 잘 자는 것은 스트레스를 줄이는 데 있어 또 다른 효과적인 방법이다.

연구 • a good night's sleep 밤에 잠을 잘 자는 것, 숙면 (good rest도 비슷한 의미이다.)
• a way/method of 또는 in ~ing : ~하는 방법

12. 업무와 관련된 스트레스는 잠시 업무로부터 휴식을 취함으로써 줄어들 수 있다.

연구 • take a break from ~로부터 휴식을 취하다
• for a while 잠시, 잠깐 동안 (for some time도 좋은 표현이다.)

13. 어떤 사람들에게, 긍정적인 태도는 여러 상황과 인생 경험에 있어서 나쁜 측면보다는 좋은 측면을 찾아내는 것을 의미한다.

연구
- positive attitude 긍정적 태도
- the good and the bad 좋은 측면과 나쁜 측면, 즉 긍정적인 면과 부정적인 면 (형용사 앞에 the를 붙여 그 형용사의 의미를 지닌 명사로 만들 수 있다.)
- 앞에서 지적했듯이, for some people이 왔으니까, 이 문장 뒤에 for others라고 온다면 글이 잘 읽힐 것이다.

14. 다른 이들에게는, 인간관계 때문에 생기는 스트레스가 덜어내기에 가장 어려운 유형의 스트레스로 여겨진다.

연구
- 역시 for others가 등장했군!
- stress stemming from A : A에서 비롯되는, A 때문에 생기는, A가 유발하는 (stress caused by, stress resulting from도 같이 알아 두면 마음이 든든해 진다.)

15. 결론적으로, 스트레스는 삶의 한 부분이지만 사람은 심리적 육체적 건강을 유지함으로써 스트레스를 줄일 수 있다.

- a part of A : A의 일부, 일원
- psychological and physical 심리적 그리고 육체적

Independent Writing
Further Writing Practice 7

7

Studying alone or with a group?

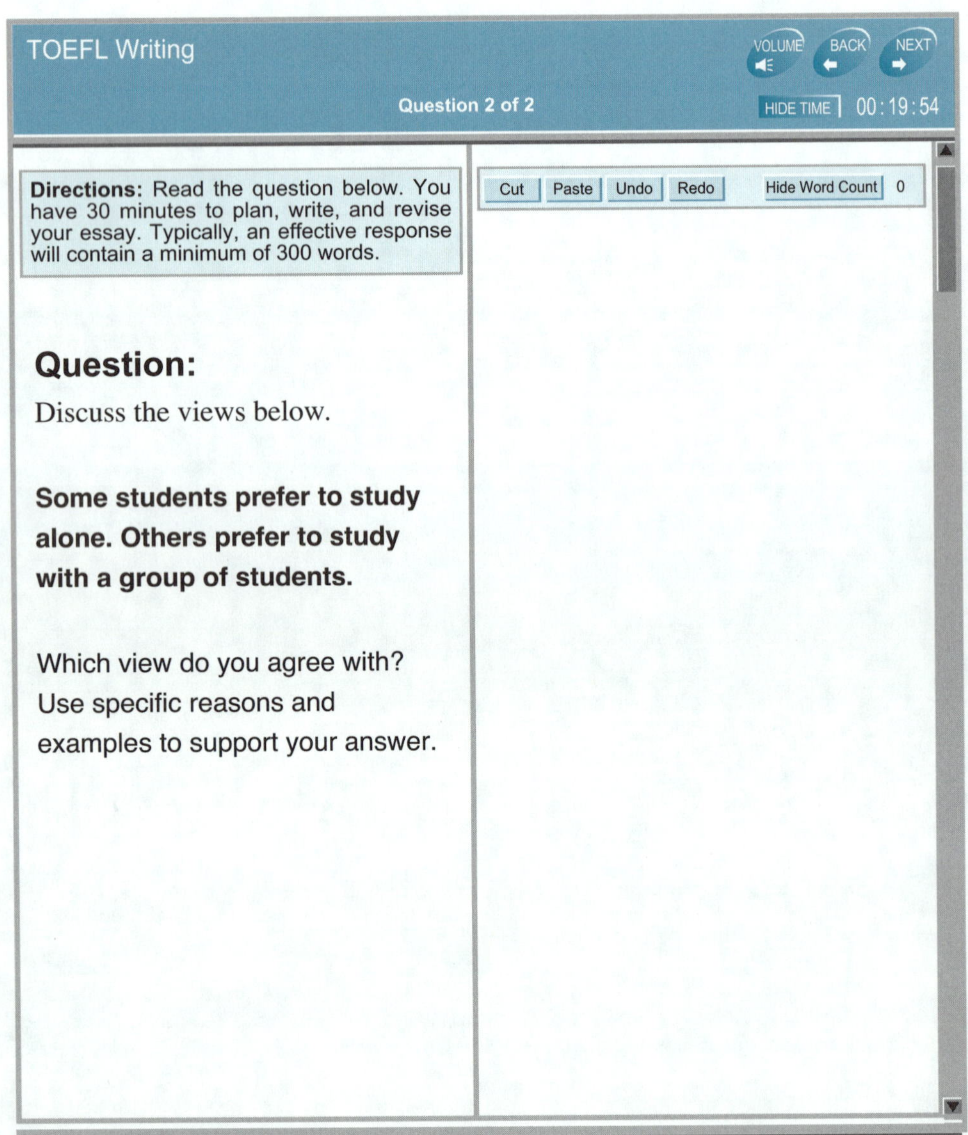

Key Ideas

- **혼자서 공부한다**
❖ 시간 낭비가 적다.
❖ 다른 사람의 공부 스타일에 맞출 필요가 없다.
❖ 혼자 조용히 공부할 수 있어 내용을 깊이 있게 이해 할 수 있다.

- **그룹으로 공부한다**
❖ 토론을 통해 서로에게 배울 수 있다.
❖ 집에서 혼자 공부하면 효율이 떨어진다.
❖ 집중해서 공부할 수 있다.
❖ 다른 사람의 입장을 배울 수 있다.
❖ 필기 내용을 비교할 수 있다.
❖ 경쟁을 통해 학습 효과를 높일 수 있다.

Vocabulary Brainstorming

- 쉬다/휴식 시간을 갖다
    → take a break

- 그룹 토론
    → group discussions

- 지적인, 학구적인 주제
    → an intellectual/academic topic

- 공부 습관
    → study habits

- 학습 방법
    → learning methods

01.

어떤 사람들은 혼자서 공부하길 좋아하고, 반면 다른 사람들은 그룹으로 공부하길 좋아한다.

____

- like to do or doing : ∼하는 것을 좋아하다
- some ∼, while others … : 어떤 이들은 ∼ 반면에, 다른 이들은 …
  (알아두면 쓸모가 많은 기본 문장 구조이다.)

02.

나에 대해 말하자면, 나는 다른 학생들과 그룹으로 공부하길 선호한다.

____

- as for me 나에 관해 말하자면, 나로서는
- prefer 뒤에 to do나 doing 모두 올 수 있다.

03.

나는 혼자 공부하는 것이 나에게 더 효과적이라는 것을 깨달았다.

____

- realize that+절 : ∼하다는 것을 깨닫다, 알게 되다

04. 개인적으로, 나는 두 가지 방법이 모두 장점과 단점을 가지고 있다고 믿는다.

____

____

____

 • I personally believe that ~로 써도 되지만, '개인적으로는'을 강조하려면 personally를 문장의 맨 앞으로 빼는 것이 좋다.
 • both methods 앞에 두개의 방법이 이미 제시된 경우 이를 반복하지 않고 지칭할 때 쓰면 편리하다. (=the two methods)

05. 나로서는, 집에서 혼자 공부할 때 아주 쉽게 딴 곳에 정신을 팔게 된다.

____

____

____

 • do by oneself 혼자서, 스스로 하다
 • get distracted 한눈을 팔다, 딴 생각을 하게 되다
  (=cannot focus well, fail to concentrate on)

06. 내가 집에서 혼자 공부하면 원하면 언제든지 쉴 수 있기 때문에 나는 진도를 거의 나가지 못한다.

____

____

____

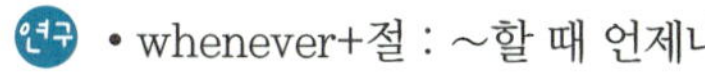 • whenever+절 : ~할 때 언제나
 • make little progress 진전이 거의 없다, 거의 공부를 못하다
  (a 없이 little은 '거의 없다'의 의미이기 때문에 문장 전체가 부정의 뜻을 갖게 된다.)

07. 그룹으로 공부하는 것의 한 가지 장점은 당신이 당신의 노트를 다른 사람 것과 비교할 수 있다는 것이다.

• one advantage to ~ing : ~하는 것의 한 가지 장점은

08. 당신은 그룹 토론을 통해 주제에 대한 다른 사람들의 관점을 또한 배울 수 있다.

• one's perspective on A : A에 대한 생각, 견해, 관점

09. 일단 우리가 언제 어디서 공부할지를 정하고 나면, 우리는 딴 데 정신 팔리지 않고 우리 공부에 쉽게 집중할 수 있다.

• once+절 : 일단 ~하고 나면
• concentrate on A : A에 집중하다 (=focus on)

1o.

물론, 만약 당신이 공부를 심각하게 생각하지 않는 그룹 안에 있다면 그것은 도움이 되지 않는다.

연구
- it doesn't help if+절 : 만약 ～한다면 도움이 안 된다
- take A seriously or lightly : A를 진지하게/가볍게 받아들이다

11.

더구나, 함께 공부할 때, 당신은 다른 사람들이 무엇을 생각하는지를 알아 낼 수 있다.

연구
- in addition 게다가, 더군다나
  (=besides, moreover) ('～에 덧붙여' 할 땐 in addition to A로 처리한다.)
- find out 알아내다, 이해하다 (=get to know)

12.

마지막으로, 나는 지적인 주제에 관해 내 친구들과 이야기하는 것을 무엇보다 즐긴다.

연구
- there is nothing I enjoy more than A : 내가 A보다 즐기는 건 없다 / 난 A를 가장 좋아한다. I enjoy A most.
- talk with A about B : A와 B에 대해 말하다
  (참고로 tell A about B할 땐 with가 필요 없고 'discuss B with A : B 에 대해 A와 말하다, 논의하다' 할 땐 about이 생략된다.)

13. 간단히 말해서, 내가 그룹으로 공부를 더 잘 한다는 것을 마침내 깨닫는 데 여러 해가 걸렸다.

연구
- it takes A+기간+to 동사원형 : A가 ~하는 데 ~라는 시간이 걸리다
  (쉬운 듯 하면서도 영작할 때 잘 틀리는 문장 구조이다.)

14. 요약하자면, 여러 다른 공부 방법이 있기 때문에, 각자 자기에게 가장 잘 맞는 방법을 찾는 것이 중요하다.

연구
- in sum 요약하자면 (=in summary, in short, in a nutshell)
- it is important for A to do B : A가 B하는 것은 중요하다 (자주 쓰는 문장 구조이다.)
- fit A : A에게 어울리다, 맞다 (=suit A)

15. 결론적으로, 당신이 혼자 공부하든 아니면 그룹으로 공부하든 그것은 당신의 공부 습관과 성격에 크게 달려있다.

연구
- whether A or B : A를 하든 B를 하든
- A depends a lot on B : A는 B에 크게 달려있다, B에 의해 상당 부분 좌지우지 된다, 결정된다 (=A largely depends on B, A is mostly determined by B)

Independent Writing
Further Writing Practice 8

8

Do clothes influence our behaviors?

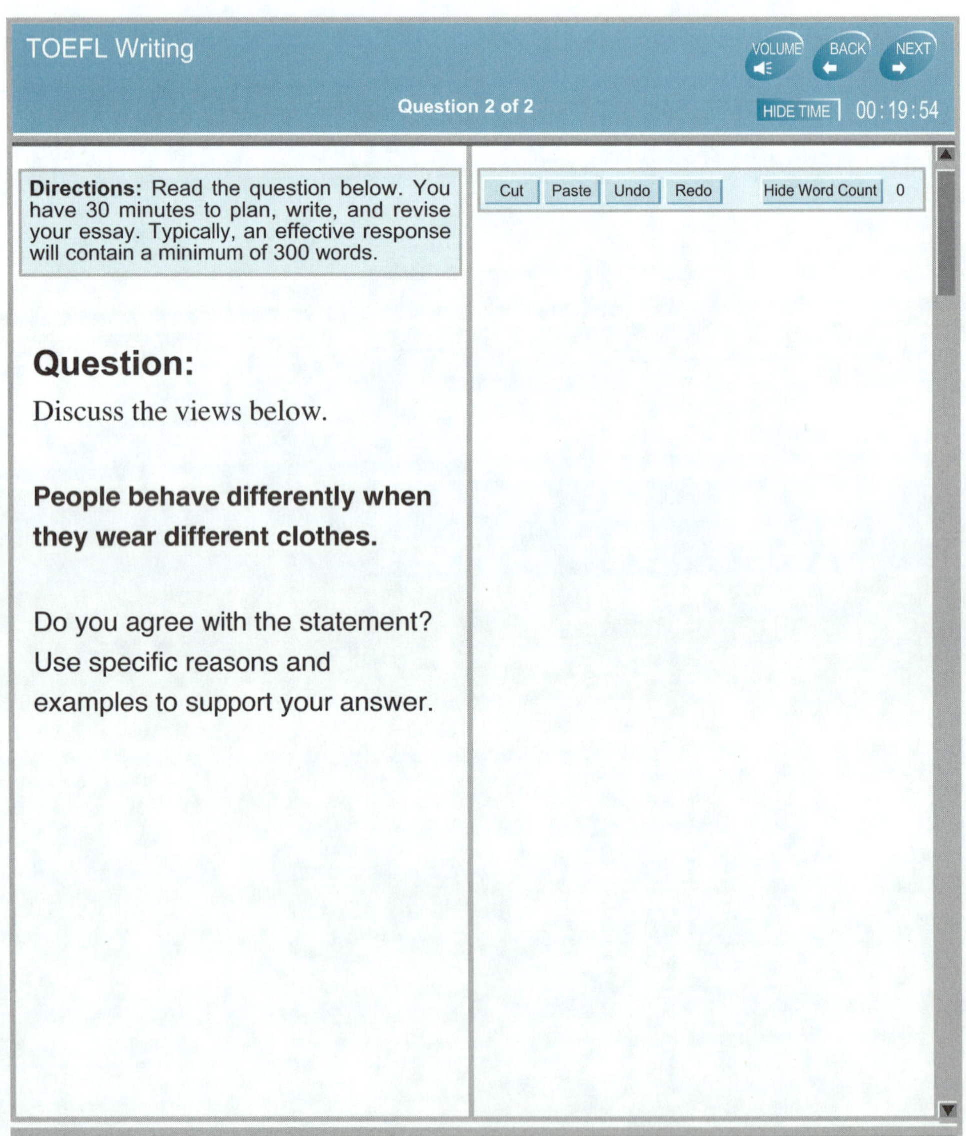

Key Ideas

찬성

❖ 사람들은 다른 사람들이 기대하는 대로 행동하는 경우가 많다.

❖ 옷은 그 사람의 취향을 보여주고 또한 그 사람의 행동에도 영향을 준다.

❖ 정장을 입게 되면 그에 맞게 행동을 더 의젓하게 한다.

반대

❖ 사람의 본질은 변하지 않기 때문에 옷이 영향을 주지 못한다.

❖ 옷을 고를 때 그 옷이 자신의 행동에 어떤 영향을 주는지 생각하지 않는다.

❖ 다른 옷을 입는다고 사람의 행동이나 성격이 그 때마다 변하는 것은 아니다.

Vocabulary Brainstorming

- 입다
    - → wear/dress/put on a cloth
- 바지
    - → pants
- 정장
    - → suit
- 옷을 잘 못 입다
    - → dress poorly, wear inappropriate clothes.
- 거지처럼 입다
    - → be dressed like a bum
- 옷
    - → clothes, clothing, what we've wearing, garment, attire
- 영향을 주다
    - → influence/affect/have an impact on

01. 사람들은 그들이 무엇을 입고 있는지에 따라 다르게 행동한다.

연구
- depending on ~ : ~에 따라 (=according to) (원래 depend on은 '~에 의지하다, 의존하다'의 의미이다. 비슷한 표현을 정리하자면, rely on, resort to, count on.)
- what은 평서문에서는 뒤에 오는 절을 받는다.
  e.g. I can't understand what you mean.
  여기서 what you mean은 '네가 무슨 뜻으로 말하는지'의 의미이다. 이렇듯 what+절은 '~하는 것'을 표현하는 데 편리한 구조다.

02. 나는 옷이 행동에 영향을 준다는 데 동의한다.

연구
- affect 영향을 주다 (influence도 가능하다.)

03. 우리가 입는 옷들이 우리의 자기 인식과 태도에 영향을 준다.

연구
- The clothes that we wear 해도 되지만 목적관계사 that은 생략해도 된다.
- A as well as B : B는 물론 A도 (not only B but also A도 같은 의미.)

O4. 우리가 입는 옷들에 따라서 사람들은 우리를 다르게 대접한다.

연구 · treat 대우하다
· 위 1번 문장과 같은 구조로도 영작 가능하다 : People treat us differently depending on what we are wearing. 이때 clothes 대신에 what 이하를 넣는다.

O5. 만약 당신이 무언가 우아한 것을 입고 있다면, 당신은 품위 있고 중요하다고 느낄 것이다

연구 · 지각 동사 feel 뒤에는 형용사가 온다. 따라서 importantly를 쓰면 안 됨.
· elegant 우아한
· distinguished 품위있는

O6. 더구나, 한 사람의 정체성은 그가 입는 옷과 밀접하게 관련이 있다.

연구 · furthermore 더구나, 게다가 (besides, in addition, moreover도 괜찮다.)
· A is linked to B : A는 B와 연계되어 있다, 관련이 있다, 심지어는 'A는 B에 영향을 주다'까지도 표현할 수 있다. 유사 표현을 정리하자면, A is related to B / A is tied to B / A is connected with B/ 아니면 A affects or influences B.

07.

만약 사람들이 같은 옷을 입는다면, 그들은 매일 무엇을 입어야
하는지 걱정할 필요가 없을 것이다.

연구 • 이번엔 what 뒤에 절 대신 to+동사원형을 써 영작해보자.
what+to 동사원형 : '~해야 할 지'의 의미를 갖는다.
e.g. I don't know what to say. 뭐라고 말해야 할 지 모르겠어.
(물론 이 문장을 what+절 구조로 바꿀 수 있다. I don't know what I have to say.)

08.

이런 이유 때문에 많은 사람들이 그들이 감당할 수 없는 명품을
갈망한다.

연구 • 이런 이유 때문에, 이래서, 이렇기 때문에, 다 for this reason으로 표현하면 된다.
• luxury items 명품, 사치품
• afford 감당하다, 돈을 내고 구입할 수 있다 (알아두면 요긴하게 쓸 수 있는 단어이다.)

09.

예를 들어, 만약 당신이 취업 면접에서 최고의 정장을 입는다면,
당신은 아마 자신감을 더 많이 느낄 것이다.

연구 • '예를 들어, 가령'의 표현으로 for instance, for example, say 등 다양하게 알아두면 재산이 된다.
• to go to a job interview해도 ok. 단 go 없이도 의미가 깔끔하게 전달되기 때문에 생략해도 된다.
• you're likely to do something 할 가능성이 있다 (you will probably do something도 좋다.)

• self-assured '자신에 대한 자신감이 있는, 마음이 흔들리지 않는' 등을 표현할 때 쓰면 좋다. 여기서는 you're likely to be more confident in yourself도 가능하다.

10. 대부분의 사람들은 다른 상황에 적합하게 옷을 입으려고 노력한다.

____

____

____

11. 우리가 무엇을 입는가에 따라 사람들이 우리를 판단할 수 있기 때문에, 우리가 옷을 입는 방식은 분명 영향을 준다.

____

____

____

🔵연구 • according to ~에 따라, depending on과 같다고 했다.
• the way A does B : A가 B하는 방식, 방법
• 영향을 주다 : has an impact 대신에 is important, matters 등으로 영작해도 좋다.

12. 요약하면, 스타일은 정체성을 반영하고, 그래서 사람들은 그들이 느끼기에 그들이 누구인가를 표현하는 옷을 선택한다.

____

____

____

🔵연구 • and thus 따라서 (=therefore)
• clothing that they feel it expresses ~ : ~를 표현한다고 느껴지는 옷
• who they are에서와 같이 who, how, where, when 등을 사용해 표현을 쉽게 할 수 있는 경우가 많다

e.g. I don't know how to solve this problem. 이 문제를 어떻게 풀어야 할지 모르겠어.

e.g. We did not set where and when we're going to have the meeting. 그 회의를 어디서, 언제 열지 정하지 않았다.

13. 간단히 말해서, 우리가 입는 것은 우리의 행동에 영향을 끼친다.

Independent Writing
Further Writing Practice 9

9

Time alone Vs. Time with friends

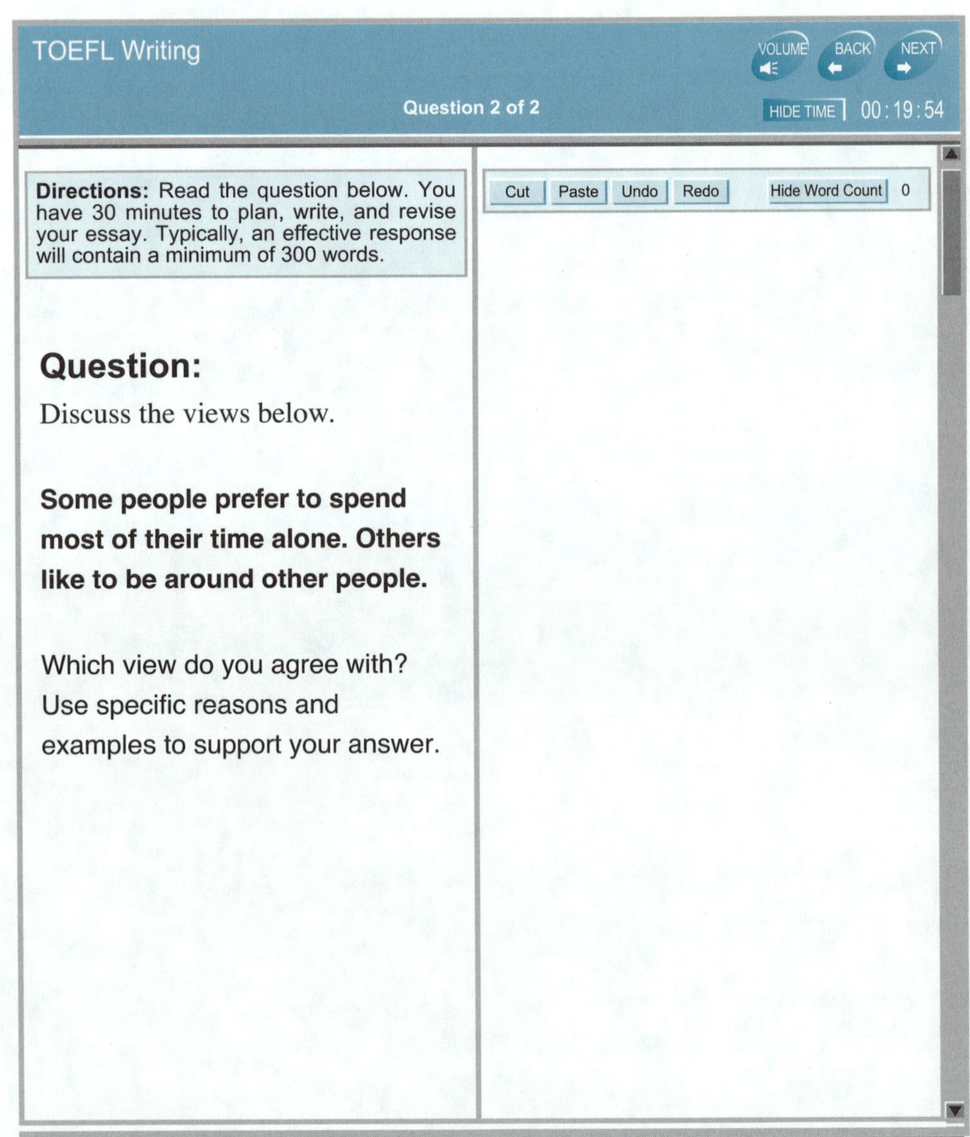

Key Ideas

혼자서

❖ 혼자서 시간을 보내는 것을 즐긴다.

❖ 다른 사람에 맞출 필요가 없이 내가 원하는 걸 할 수 있다.

❖ 다른 사람들의 생각에 영향을 받지 않고 혼자 생각하는 습관을 기를 수 있다.

친구와 함께

❖ 친구들과 시간을 보내면서 서로에게 배우는 것이 많다.

❖ 여가 시간은 혼자보다는 친구들과 보내야 더 즐겁다.

❖ 친구들과 지내면서 사회성을 기를 수 있다.

Vocabulary Brainstorming

- 혼자 있다
    - → be alone, spend time alone or all by oneself
- 외롭다
    - → feel lonely
- 집단적 사고 방식
    - → a group mentality
- 영향을 받다
    - → be influenced by
- 사회적인 사람
    - → a social person
- 충성심
    - → loyalty
- 우정을 쌓다
    - → build a friendship
- 칭찬
    - → compliment
- 기분을 띄워주다
    - → cheer a person up

Time alone

01.

만약 내가 혼자 시간을 보내는 것과 친구와 시간을 보내는 것 중에서 선택을 해야 한다면, 나는 전자를 택하겠다.

____

____

____

연구
- the former 전자, the latter 후자
  (앞에 사용한 단어의 반복을 피하는 좋은 방법이 된다.)
- 선택하다 choose, opt for, go for 등 다양하게 표현해 본다.

02.

내가 혼자 있을 때, 나는 나의 목표들에 관해서 생각하고 그것들을 달성할 전략을 발전시킬 시간을 갖는다.

____

____

____

연구
- think about A : A에 대해 골똘히 생각하다
  think of A : A를 떠올리다, 그냥 A에 대해 생각하다
- achieve goals 목표를 달성하다
  (fulfill, realize, attain one's goals도 같이 알아 두면 표현이 다양해 진다.)

03.

비록 어떤 사람들은 다른 사람들이 주변에 없을 때 그들이 외로움을 느낀다고 말하긴 하지만, 나는 음악을 들을 수 있고 내가 좋아하는 책들을 읽을 수 있기 때문에 혼자 있는 것을 즐긴다.

연구
- be around 곁에 있다, 주변에 있다
- listen 뒤에 꼭 to를 넣어야 한다!

04.

만약 우리의 시간이 모임 안에서 계속 보내지면, 우리는 그 모임의 사고방식을 키워갈 가능성이 있다.

연구
- be likely to+동사원형 : ～할 가능성이 있다
  (가능성이 높을 때 very likely로 표현하면 편하다. 반면에 '～할 가능성이 없다'는 be unlikely to, '그럴 가능성이 희박하다' be very unlikely to로 영작하면 된다.)

05. 내가 혼자 있을 때, 나는 내 친구들의 의견에 영향을 받지 않고 내 자신의 개인적인 가치관을 결정할 수 있다.

⟨연구⟩ • decide to+동사원형 : ~하기로 결정, 결심하다, decide on+명사 : ~에 대해 결정하다
e.g I had a hard time deciding on my major. 전공을 결정하느라 애 먹었다.
• without ~ing : ~하지 않고
(보통 우리는 without을 명사와 같이 쓰는데 동사와 함께 사용하면 긴 문장을 간결하게 정리할 수 있어 좋다.)

06. 다른 사람들과 함께 어울리기를 바라는 것은 당연하지만, 나는 혼자 보낸 시간이 결국에는 더 소중하다고 생각한다.

⟨연구⟩ • it's natural to+동사원형 / it's natural that+절 : ~하는 것은 당연하다, 자연스러운 일이다
(it's not surprising that ~으로도 표현 가능하다.)
• eventually, in the long run 결국에는, 장기적으로

07. 요약하면, 나는 위의 이유 때문에 혼자 있는 것을 선호한다.

Time with friends

01. 비록 내가 혼자 시간을 보내는 것을 즐기긴 하지만, 나는 언제나 가능하면 친구들과 함께 있는 것을 선호한다.

____

____

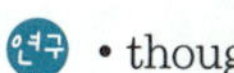

- though는 although와 같은 의미로 '비록 ~할지라도'를 표현할 때 쓰면 된다.
- prefer+~ing/ prefer+ to 동사원형, 둘 다 '~하는 것을 선호한다, 더 좋아한다'로 사용되는데, 'A와 B 중 A를 선호한다'를 표현할 경우엔, I prefer A to B / I prefer A over B 라고 처리해 전치사 to나 over를 추가해야 한다.
  이 표현은 찬성, 반대를 묻는 토플 에세이에 자주 등장하는 단골 문장 구조이다.
- whenever possible 언제나 가능하면

02. 비록 내가 아주 독립적이긴 하지만, 나는 또한 아주 사교적인 사람이다.

____

____

- '매우, 아주 ~하다'를 표현할 때 very에 더해 pretty, highly도 함께 알아 두면 든든하다.

03. 우리는 웃음을 나누는 것은 물론이고 다양한 토픽에 관해 진지한 토론도 한다.

연구 • 자주 쓰게 되는 문장 구조 중 하나인 'not only A but also B : A뿐만 아니라 B도'를 쓸 때는 뒤에 but also를 빠뜨리지 않도록 신경 써야 한다.

04. 영화를 보러 가는 것이든, 아니면 운동을 하는 것이든, 혼자 있는 것 보다는 친구와 함께 있는 것이 항상 더 좋다.

연구 • 일반적으로 whether는 if와 비슷한 의미로 많이 쓰이지만, if와 달리 가능한 상황이 둘일 때만 사용된다. I don't know whether it is good or not. 과 같이 or 뒤의 의미가 짐작 가능한 경우에는 생략하기도 한다. I don't know whether it is good.
• 여기선 whether A or B를 '둘 중 어느 쪽을 하더라도'의 의미로 쓰자.

05. 나는 누구이고 내가 세상 어디에 적합한지를 내가 가장 잘 깨닫게 되는 것은 다른 사람들과의 내 인간관계를 통해서이다.

연구 • who I am, where I fit ~ : 의문사를 사용해 표현하면 편리하고 의미 전달이 잘 된다.

06.

나는 친구들의 충실과 신뢰 때문에 나의 친구들을 소중히 여긴다.

연구
- because+절, because of+명사/명사구
  (다 아는 내용이지만 영작할 땐 자주 틀린다.)

07.

만약 어떤 나쁜 일이 일어나면, 나는 내 친구들이 나를 돕기 위해 거기에 있을 것임을 안다.

연구
- help out 뒤에 붙은 out은 없어도 상관없지만, 있으면 '구해주다, 어려움에서 구해내다'의 의미를 더 살려준다.

08.

결론적으로, 친구들이 없는 인생은 폭이 좁고 만족스럽지 못하다고 나는 믿는다.

연구
- limited 폭이 좁은, 제한된 (not complete, incomplete도 ok.)
- unfulfilling 만족스럽지 못한
  (unsatisfactory, not satisfactory로도 표현 가능하다. 거듭 말하지만, 동의어, 동의표현 정리가 영작 실력 배양의 중요한 기초 작업이다.)

Independent Writing
Further Writing Practice 10

10

Should I read only books on real events?

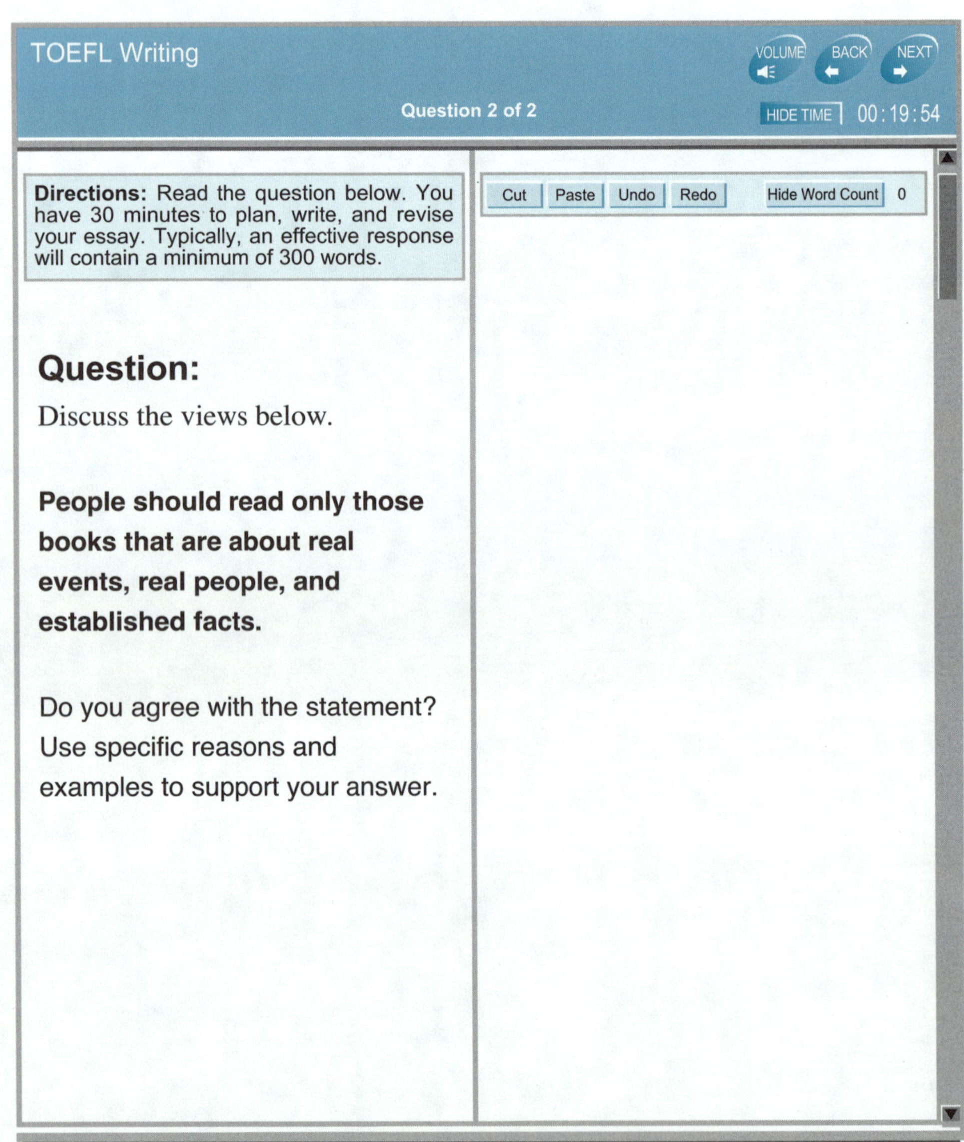

Key Ideas

• **Agree** (Only non-fiction books)

❖ 실제 일어난 일이나 존재한 인물에 대한 책만해도 꽤 많다.

❖ 우리 생활과 직결돼 있기 때문에 더 도움이 된다.

❖ 약간의 소설 책을 곁들이는 건 좋겠지만, 주로 지식을 주는 책을 읽는 것이 더 바람직하다.

• **Disagree** (Both fiction and non-fiction books)

❖ 상상의 날개를 펼 수 있어 소설이나 동화책을 읽는 것은 중요하다.

❖ 동화책에서 중요한 교훈을 얻을 수 있다.

❖ 독서도 일종의 오락인데, 즐길 수 있는 책을 읽을 수 있어야 한다.

Vocabulary Brainstorming

• 창의력을 개발하다 → develop one's creativity

• 세상을 넓혀준다 → open up one's world

• 상상력을 길러 준다 → develop one's imagination

• 다양한 감정들을 경험한다 → experience a wide range of feelings / emotions

• 오래 남는 경험을 얻는다 → get lasting experiences

• 이야기 하기 → storytelling

• 읽을 만하다 → be worth reading

• 오락 → entertainment

• 재미있는 → interesting, enjoyable, entertaining

• 만화책 → comic book

• 소설류 → fiction, fictional books, fictitious works

• 풍부한 정보 → a wealth of information

• 사실과 정보에 바탕을 둔 → based on facts and information

01.

단지 실제 사실인 것들에 대한 책들만이 읽을 가치가 있다는 생각에 동의하기 어렵다.

____

____

____

연구
- it is hard to agree with the idea that ~라는 생각에 동의하기 어렵다.
  I can hardly agree with the idea that으로 처리해도 좋다.
- worth ~ 동명사 or 명사 : ~할 만한 가치가 있는

02.

독서는 일종의 오락이기 때문에, 사람들은 그들이 재미있다고 느끼는 무엇이든 읽도록 격려를 받아야 한다.

____

____

____

연구
- since ~ 하니까, 하기 때문에
- a form of 일종의, 한 형태의
- be encouraged to do A : A를 하라고 격려를 받다, 권장 받다
- whatever+절 : ~하는 거라면 뭐든
  e.g. I am willing to agree with whatever you say. 난 네가 뭐라 하든 간에 동의할 거야.

03.

허구적 이야기들은 우리의 세계를 열어주고 우리가 창의력을 개발하는 데 도움을 준다.

____

____

____

연구
- open up our world 우리 세상을 열다 (widen our horizon도 ok.)

04. 사람이 논픽션 책에서 많은 실질적 정보를 배울 수 있다는 것은 사실이다.

____

____

🔵 **연구** • it is true that ~ : ~한 것은 사실이다
• a great deal of 상당한 양의, 많은(=much, a lot of)

05. 그러나, 세상에 대한 허구적 이야기나 허구 소설을 읽는 것은 사람의 상상력을 개발하는 데 도움을 준다.

____

____

🔵 **연구** • yet 그러나 (=however, still, nevertheless, nonetheless)
• account 이야기, 설명 (=telling, story)

06. 비록 논픽션 책에 풍부한 정보가 있지만, 우리는 허구적 이야기와 소설의 가치를 과소평가해서는 안 된다.

____

____

🔵 **연구** • a wealth of information 풍부한 정보, 많은 정보
• downplay 과소평가하다 (=underestimate, look down upon)

07.

사실, 이야기를 하는 것은 우리가 충만하고 풍부한 삶을 살려면 충족되어져야 하는 인간의 정서적인 필요이다.

연구
- in fact 사실 (=actually)
- meet the need 필요를 충족시키다
  (참고로, meet demand for A : A에 대한 수요를 충족시키다. 이처럼 어울리는 동사와 목적어를 세트 표현으로 정리해 두면 도움이 된다.)

08.

그러나, 당신은 문학, 시, 그리고 드라마에서 발견되는 허구 작품들에서 가치, 도덕, 그리고 희망에 관해 많은 것을 배울 수 있다.

연구
- fictional writings 허구 작품
  (fictional stories/works/novels/accounts 등 다양하게 표현해 보자.)
- morals 도덕
- literature 문학

09.

이들 이야기들이 여러 맥락에서 다양한 감정들을 경험하도록 우리에게 도움을 준다.

연구
- a wide range of 다양한 종류의, 큰 폭의
  e.g. a wide range of choices 넓은 선택의 폭, 다양한 선택
- a variety of 다양한, 여러 개의 (=a number of)

10. 정보화 시대에서는, 당신이 더 많은 지식이 있을수록, 당신은 더 좋다.

연구
• the +비교급, the +비교급 : …하면 할수록 ~하다
• better off 더 좋은, 보다 나은 상황에 있는

11. 많은 이야기를 읽는 아이들이 그들의 상상력을 이용하고 더 넓은 관점에서 세상을 볼 가능성이 더 크다.

연구
• be better able to do A : A를 더 잘 할 수 있다 (better 대신에 more를 써도 ok.)
• see the world from a wider perspective 보다 넓은 관점에서 세상을 보다
(perspective, point of view는 앞에 전치사 from이 들어간다.)

12. 허구적 이야기들이 문화와 전통의 형성에 중요한 역할을 한다.

연구
• play a role in A : A에 한 몫을 하다, 역할을 하다
• crucial 중요한 (important, vital, essential 등과 같이 알아 두자.)
• in the formation 형성에, 형성하는 데 (in forming/shaping으로 처리해도 된다.)

13. 일찍이 아동기부터, 우리는 픽션과 논픽션 모두에 노출되어야 한다.

연구
- as early as ∼ : 일찍 ∼부터
  (반대로 as late as ∼ : 늦게 ∼까지)
- be exposed to A : A에 노출되다

14. 무엇을 읽을지 고르는 것은 사람의 취향과 성향에 따른 개인적인 선택이다.

연구
- 동명사를 주어로 잡는 연습을 많이 해 볼 필요가 있다.
- based on ∼에 근거한, 에 따른
- tastes and tendencies 취향과 성향
  (이 표현 역시 같은 글자로 시작하는 두 단어를 and로 묶은 세트 표현이다.)

15. 비록 전기와 역사 책이 가치가 있지만, 철학과 예술의 세계에 뿌리를 둔 허구 작품들도 똑같이 가치가 있다.

연구
- rooted in ∼에 뿌리를 둔, ∼을 바탕으로 한 (=based on)

16. 사실, 우리는 삶에서 가장 중요한 대부분의 교훈들을 우리의 아동기 이야기들로부터 배운다.

연구 • most of +명사 : 대부분의 ~
(이때 명사가 셀 수 있는 가산명사 일 경우 복수로 써야 한다는 점을 잊지 말자.)

Independent Writing
Further Writing Practice 11

11

A new factory in your neighborhood

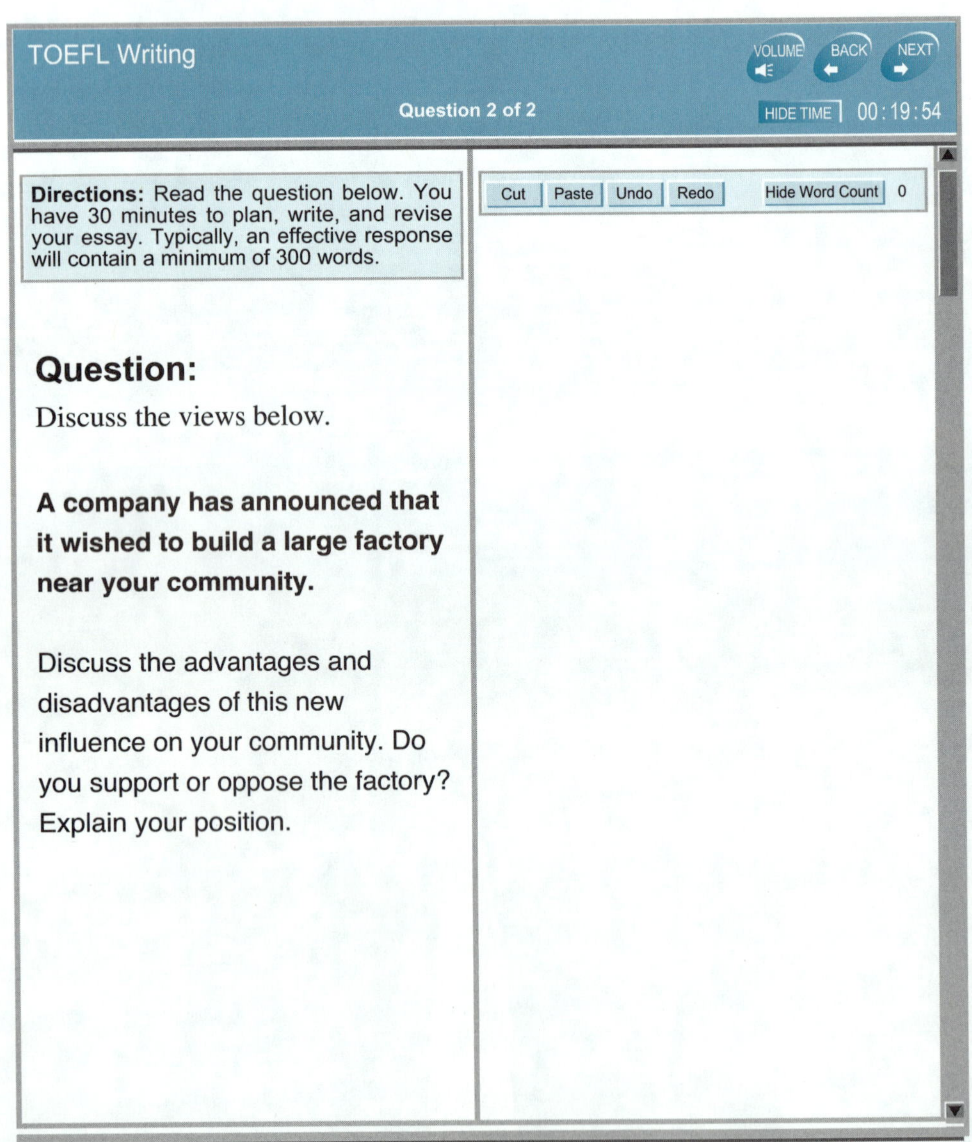

Key Ideas

장점
❉ 신규 고용이 창출된다.
❉ 지역 사회 경제가 살아난다.
❉ 세금을 더 많이 거둘 수 있어 다양한 복지 활동이 가능해 질 것이다.

단점
❖ 공기가 오염될 것이다.
❖ 근로자들의 유입으로 지역사회 인구가 급증해, 교통 체증이 악화될 것이다.
❖ 공장 때문에 환경이 오염되어 전부터 살던 주민들이 동네를 떠나게 될 것이다.

Vocabulary Brainstorming

- 고용을 창출하다
  → create employment or jobs
- 실업
  → unemployment
- 번영
  → prosperity
- 향상된 생활 수준
  → increased standard of living
- 세금 징수
  → tax collection
- 환경오염
  → environmental pollution
- 대기를 오염시키다
  → pollute or contaminate the air
- 수질오염
  → water pollution
- 대기오염
  → air pollution
- 교통체증
  → traffic congestion

01. 대부분의 산업과 공장은 지역사회에 좋은 것과 나쁜 것 모두를 가져다 준다.

연구
- most+복수 명사 : 대부분의 ~들은
- bring A to B : B에게 A를 가져다 주다, 안겨주다 (=give B A or give A to B)

02. 만약 기업이 나의 지역사회에 공장을 짓기로 발표한다면, 나는 아마도 좋은 감정과 나쁜 감정 모두를 갖게 될 것이다.

연구
- **가정법 과거** : if 주어+과거동사, would+동사원형 : ~할 거라고 했다면
  (이때 뒤에 would 대신 will을 쓰는 실수를 종종 하게 되는데, 앞 주절 동사가 과거이기 때문에 would가 와야 한다. *e.g.* If I were you, I would attend the seminar. 만약 내가 너였다면 그 세미나에 참석했을거야.)
- have mixed emotions about A : A에 대해 좋은 감정과 나쁜 감정이 교차한다, 두 가지 감정 다 갖고 있다 (참고로, a mixed blessing 불행과 행운이 동시에 온 반쪽짜리 행운.)

03. 새로운 공장은 종종 많은 새 일자리와 더 큰 번영을 가져다 준다.

연구
- 가져다 주다 (=bring, offer, provide)

04. 공장을 짓는 데에는 장단이 있다.

- there are advantages and disadvantages to ~ing : ~하는 데는 장단이 있다
  (자주 쓰게 되는 표현인 만큼 틀리지 않게 쓸 수 있도록 연습하자.)

05. 새 공장을 짓는 것을 지지하는 결정은 그것의 긍정적인 측면과 부정적인 측면을 비교해 본 뒤에 내려져야 한다.

- the decision to do A : A를 하기로 한 결정 (이렇듯 ~하기 위한 또는 ~하기로 한 결정, 계획 등을 영작할 땐, a plan to do A로 처리해 명사 뒤에 to 동사원형으로 만드는 게 좋다.)
- make a decision 결정을 내리다. (동사와 어울리는 목적어 세트. 참고로 다음 표현도 알아두자. meet the demands, meet the needs)
- weigh both the positive and negative aspects 긍정적인 측면과 부정적인 측면을 다 분석, 비교해 보다 (= analyze, consider)

06. 수반된 위험이 혜택보다 크기 때문에, 나는 지역사회에 공장을 짓는 데 반대한다.

- the risks outweigh the benefits 위험이 혜택보다 많다
  (there are more risks than benefits.)
- 장단, 손해와 이익, 위험과 혜택 등은 토플 에세이 작성시 자주 쓰게 되는 단어들이다. 단단히 정리 해두자.
- advantages and disadvantages 장단

- risks and benefits 손해와 득실, 위험과 혜택
- the bright and dark sides 밝은 측면과 어두운 측면
- the good and bad results 좋은 점과 나쁜 점
- the positive and negative aspects 긍정적인 측면과 부정적인 측면

07. 게다가, 공장은 종종 환경오염을 일으키고, 이것이 지역 사회의 삶의 질을 해칠 수 있다.

____

____

____

 • in addition 게다가, 또한 (=moreover, besides, furthermore)
- create environmental pollution 환경 오염을 일으키다
  (create 대신 cause, trigger를 써도 좋다.)
- harm A : A를 손상시키다 (=damage, ruin)

08. 또 다른 우려는 지역 사회가 갑작스러운 인구증가를 경험할 것이고, 이것이 이어서 심각한 주택 문제를 일으킬 것이다.

____

____

____

 • another concern is that+절 : 또 다른 우려, 문제는 ~이다
  (additional problem is that ~도 같은 뜻.)
- experience a sudden increase in A : A가 갑자기 늘어나는 것을 겪다
  ('~의 상승, 또는 감소'할 땐 전치사 in이 들어간다 : a sharp increase or decrease in export 수출의 급격한 상승, 감소)
- experience 경험하다 (=go through, undergo)
- in turn 이로 인해, 이에 이어서
  (앞의 것이 원인이 되어 다음에는 ~결과로 이어진다는 내용을 영작할 때 in turn은 감칠맛을 더해 준다.)

09. 그 결과, 교통 정체가 악화될 것이다.

연구 • as a result, 그 결과, 결과로 (=consequently)

10. 분명히, 많은 지역사회들이 지역 사람들에게 고용을 제공할 수 있는 새로운 공장을 환영할 것이다.

연구 • certainly 물론 (=of course)

11. 그 공장은 많은 새로운 일자리를 만들 것이고, 새 일자리들이 실업을 줄이고 지역사회에 더 많은 돈을 가져다 줄 것이다.

연구 • create new jobs 신규 고용을 창출하다, 새 일자리를 만들다
(the factory will employ or hire new people로 처리해도 된다.)

12. 늘어난 조세 수입이 지역사회로 하여금 새로운 시설과 서비스를 제공할 수 있게 해 줄 것이다.

연구
- tax revenue 조세 수입, 세입
- enable A to do B : A가 B를 할 수 있게 하다

13. 그것이 환경을 해치지 않는 한, 나는 지역사회 안에 새 공장을 짓는 것을 지지한다.

연구
- as long as+절 : ~하는 한 (조건부나 부분적 찬성이나 반대 입장을 표현할 때 쓸 수 있다.)

14. 간단히 말해서, 새로운 공장을 지지할지 반대할지의 결정은 지역사회의 필요와 바람에 기초해야 한다.

연구
- in short 짧게 말해, 간단하게 말하자면 (=in sum, in a nutshell)
- the needs and wants 필요와 바람

15. 나는 단점이 혜택보다 크다고 느끼기 때문에, 여기에 새 공장을 짓는 계획을 나는 지지할 수 없다.

연구
- drawback 단점, 결점 (=shortcoming, risks)
- the drawbacks are greater than the benefits 단점이 혜택/장점보다 더 크다
  (=the drawbacks outweigh the benefits, there are more drawbacks than benefits)

Independent Writing
Further Writing Practice 12

12

The influence of movies and televisions

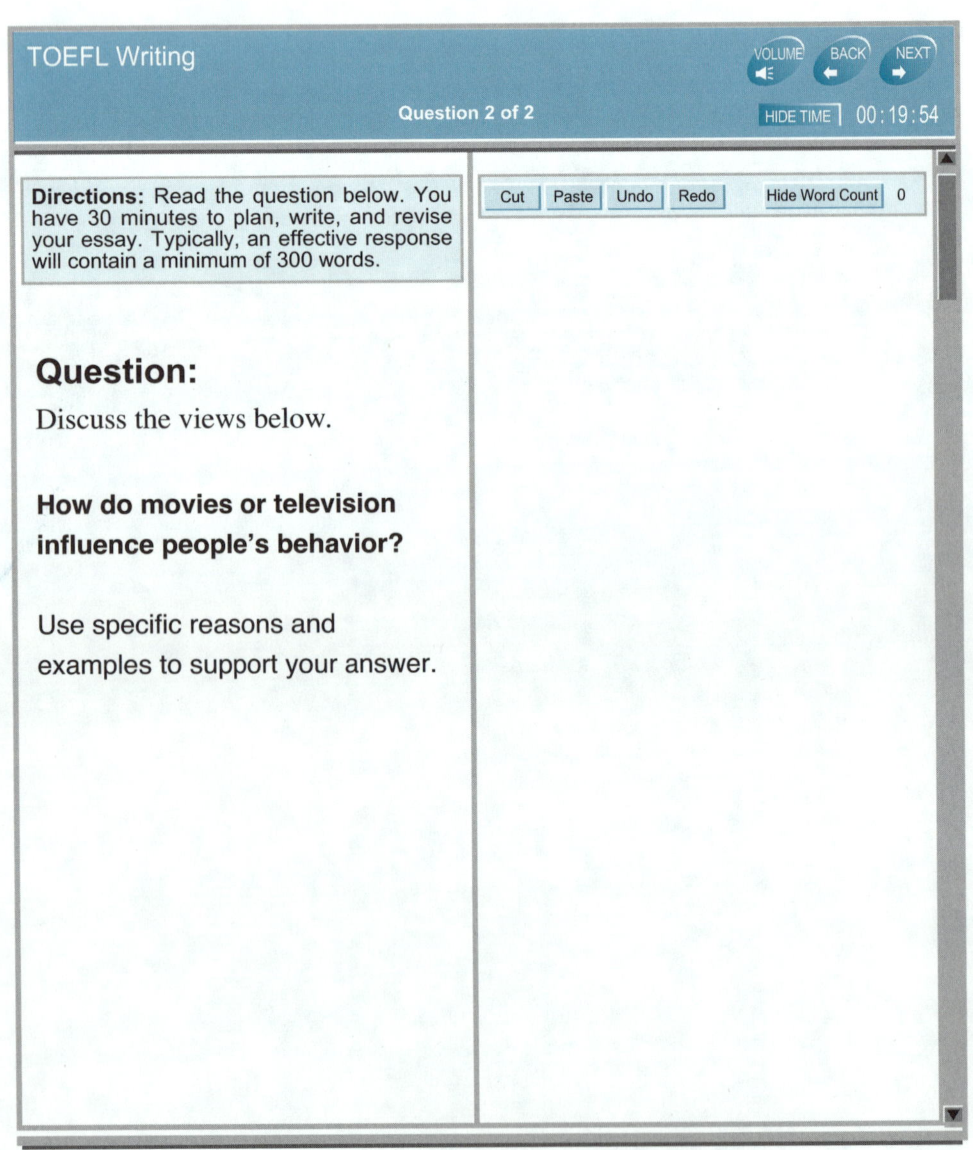

Key Ideas

❖ 긍정적, 부정적 영향을 동시에 준다.

❖ 폭력적, 선정적 내용은 사람들의 행동에 부정적으로 영향을 준다.

❖ 교육적 프로그램은 오히려 많은 내용을 집에 앉아서 배울 수 있는 기회를 제공한다.

❖ 다양한 세계, 문화, 사람들을 접할 수 있어 견문이 넓어진다.

❖ 비판적인 시청자는 유익한 영화나 텔레비전 프로그램을 골라 볼 것이다.

Vocabulary Brainstorming

• 폭력적 행동
  → violent acts

• 선정적
  → sexually improper, lascivious

• 사람의 행동에 영향을 주다
  → influence people's behavior, have some effects on people's actions, affect their behavior and actions.

• 교육적 프로그램
  → educational program

• 오락
  → entertainment

01. 내 생각에는, 텔레비전과 영화는 사람들의 행동에 좋은 쪽과 나쁜 쪽 모두 영향을 준다.

연구
- in my opinion 내 생각에는 (=personally I think)
- influence A : A에게 영향을 주다 (=have some influence on A, affect A)
- in both good and bad ways 좋게도 또 나쁘게도

02. 나는 영화와 텔레비전이 우리의 행동에 좋은 쪽으로 혹은 나쁜 쪽으로 영향을 준다고 믿는다.

연구
- 평서문에서 조동사 do를 써서 강조의 의미를 살리면 좋다.
- for the better or for the worse 좋은 쪽으로 혹은 나쁜 쪽으로

03. 텔레비전은 중요한 교육적인 도구가 될 수 있다.

04.
더구나, 최근 수십 년 동안 영화와 텔레비전은 전 세계 사람들의 태도에 엄청난 영향을 주었다.

____

____

____

연구
- moreover 더군다나, 게다가 (=furthermore, in addition)
- during the last few decades 지난 수십 년 동안
- have enormous/little effect on A : A에 거대한/미미한 영향을 주다
- people all over the world 전세계 사람들(이 표현은 바로 쓸 수 있도록 연습해 두자.)

05.
만약 사람들이 그들이 보는 것을 선택할 때 조심하고 잘 고른다면, 그들은 텔레비전 프로에서 많은 것을 배울 수 있다.

____

____

____

연구
- selective 선별적인, 잘 고르는
- when ~ing : ~할 때
- learn something from A : A에게 ~을 배우다

06
물론, 영화와 텔레비전을 보는 것이 우리에게 또한 좋을 수 있다.

____

____

____

연구
- of course 물론 (=certainly, it is true that~, nobody can deny that ~)

07. 어떤 프로그램들은 다른 인종과 생활 양식에 관해 사람들을 교육하는 데 도움을 준다.

연구 • educate A about B : A에게 B에 대해 가르치다 (teach도 ok. 보통 education, educator, educational까지는 쓰는데 동사 educate는 잘 안 쓰게 된다. 이 기회에 한번 써보자.)

08. 영화를 보는 것은 사람들이 다른 인종과 문화에 대해 가진 편견들을 극복하는 데 도움을 줄 수 있다.

연구 • help A (to) do B : A가 B 하는 것을 돕다
• overcome A : A를 이겨내다, 극복하다 (=overcome a problem, a handicap)

09. 동시에, 많은 폭력적이고 성적으로 부적절한 텔레비전 프로그램과 영화가 있다.

연구 • improper 부적절한, 그릇된 (반대는 proper를 쓴다.)

10. 텔레비전 프로그램들은 종종 우리의 행동에 부정적으로 영향을 준다.

연구
- A influences B in a negative or positive way. : A는 B에게 부정적 또는 긍정적인 영향을 미친다. (=A has a positive effect/influence on B. 또는 A negatively or positively influences/affects B.)

11. 우리가 텔레비전에서 폭력적인 행동을 더 많이 보면 볼수록, 우리는 현실에서 그것들에 대해 점점 덜 민감해지게 된다.

연구
- the+비교문, the+비교문 : ~하면 할수록, 더 ~하다
  (글에 힘을 실어주거나 효과를 주는 데 유용한 문장 구조이다.)
- sensitive to A : A에 민감한
- in reality 실제 현실에서

12. 프로그램들이 폭력이 먹힌다는 것을 알게 되었기 때문에 텔레비전에 지나친 폭력이 있다.

연구
- excessive 지나친 (=too much)
- on television 텔레비전에 (여기서 전치사 on을 기억해 두자.)
- A sells : 'A가 팔린다'고 직역해도 좋고 'A가 먹힌다, 인기 있다'로 의역하면 더 좋다.
  (=A is appealing)

13. 만약 사람들이 텔레비전을 너무 많이 보면, 그들이 자신의 상상력을 쓰기를 중단하기 때문에 사람들은 수동적이 될 것이다.

연구
- stop ~ing : ~하는 것을 중단하다 (참고로, stop to do A : A를 하기 위해 하던 일을 멈추다 *e.g.* He stopped to smoke. 그는 담배를 피우기 위해 멈췄다.)

14. 결론적으로, 프로그램이나 영화에 따라 영향이 긍정적일 수도 혹은 부정적일 수도 있다.

연구
- can be either A or B depending on C : C에 따라 A도 될 수 있고 B도 될 수 있다

15. 다시 말해서, 그들이 당신에게 어떤 영향을 주는가는 당신이 얼마나 많이 보고, 무엇을 보고, 그리고 당신이 본 것에 당신이 어떻게 대응하는지에 달려있다.

연구
- how+절 : 어떻게 ~하는가
  (대신 the degree/level of+명사도 쓸 수 있다. : the degree of influence)
- depend on A : A에 달려 있다 (=be determined by A)
- 평서문에서 how, how much, what을 적절하게 사용해 문장의 길이는 길지만 내용은 쉽게 따라갈 수 있게 한다.

Independent Writing
Further Writing Practice 13

13

A working teenager student

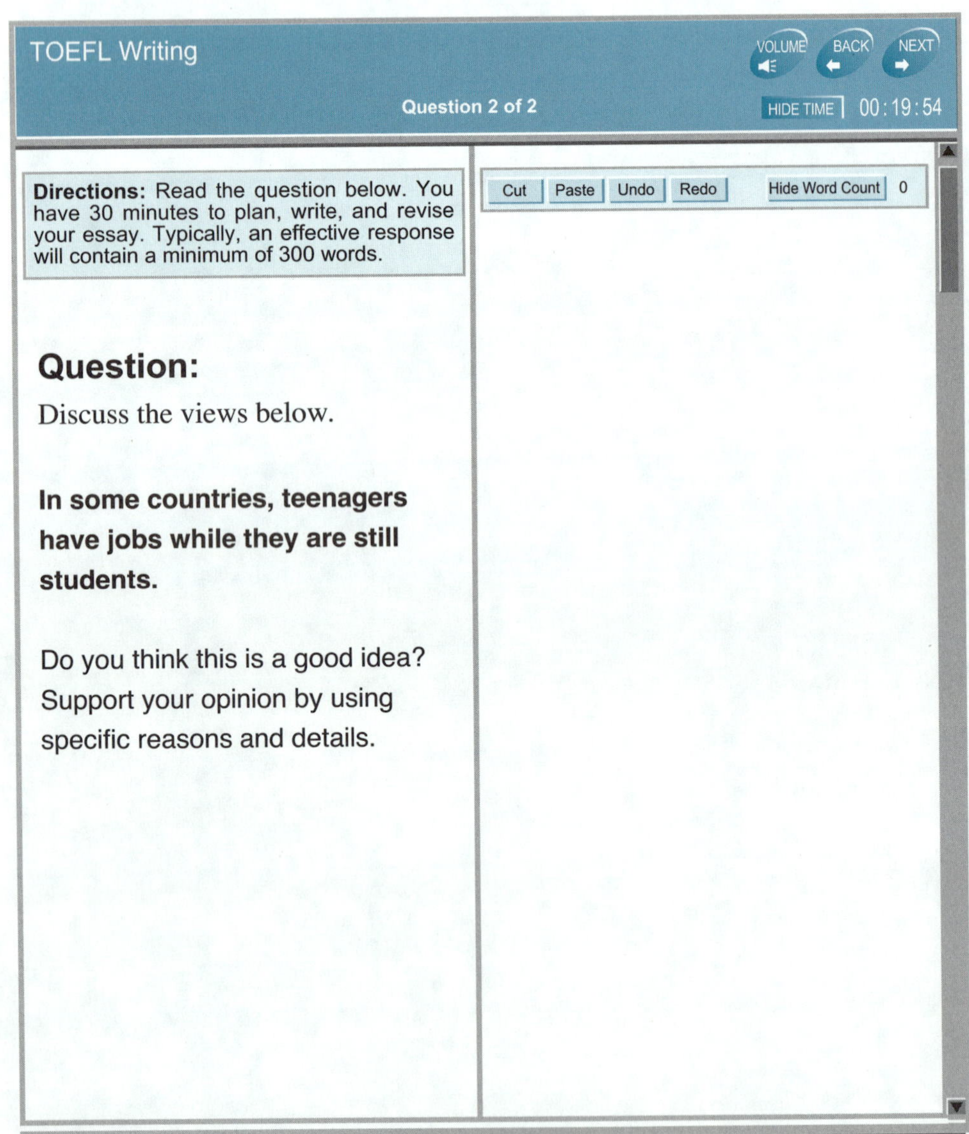

Key Ideas

찬성

❖ 부모님을 이해할 수 있는 계기가 된다.

❖ 책임감과 근면함을 배울 수 있다.

❖ 장래에 취업 시 참고할 수 있는 경험을 얻게 된다.

반대

❖ 고등학교 때까지는 공부에 전념해야 한다.

❖ 순수성이 너무 일찍 상실 된다.

❖ 공부를 뒷전으로 미룰 수 있다.

Vocabulary Brainstorming

- 공부에 방해가 되다 → interfere with one's studies

- 방과 후에 일하다 → work after class

- 성적 → grades

- 일을 하다 → have/hold a job

- 일하는 십대 → a working teen, a teenager holding a job

- 아르바이트 → a part-time job

- 가족의 예산 → family budget

- 일의 세계 → the work world

- 동료 → coworker

- 명령을 따르다 → follow orders

- 자퇴하다 → drop out of school

- 학과 외 활동 → extracurricular activities

Agree

01.
나는 십대들이 학교가 끝난 후 아르바이트 일을 갖도록 허용되어야 한다고 생각한다.

연구 • be allowed to do A : A를 할 수 있도록 허용되다

02.
나는 장점이 단점보다 훨씬 많다고 믿는다.

연구 • '장점이 단점보다 훨씬 많다'는 토플 에세이에 자주 등장하는 표현이다. 쉽게, there are more benefits than drawbacks로 처리해도 되고, outweigh란 단어를 넣어 간결하게 표현할 수 있다. 장점과 단점을 뜻하는 여러 동의어를 꼭 정리해 두어야 한다.
  • 장점 : benefits, advantages, good aspects, bright side, merit
  • 단점 : drawback, disadvantages, bad aspects, dark side, weak point

03.
십대 아이가 학교가 우선이라는 것을 알고 있는 한, 나는 그 아이가 하루에 몇 시간 일을 하도록 허용하는 데 아무 문제가 없다고 본다.

연구 • as long as ～하는 한
  • school comes first 학교가 우선이다, 더 중요하다
    (school is more important로 처리해도 된다.)
  • What is the problem with you?란 기본 표현에서 응용하면 쉽다. problem with something or ～ing : ～에 관련된 문제, ～할 때 생기는 문제
  • let은 have, make와 함께 뒤에 to 없는 동사원형을 받는 사역동사이다. let 대신 allow를 쓰게 되면, allowing her to work a few hours a day로 to를 넣어줘야 한다.

04. 일을 하는 십대들은 그들의 시간을 효율적으로 사용하는 것을 배울 것이다.

연구
• learn to do A : A하는 것을 배우다 (learn how to do A로도 표현 가능하다.)

05. 일을 하면서, 십대들은 돈을 번다는 것이 얼마나 어려운지 깨닫게 될 것이다.

연구
• while ~ing : ~하면서, 하는 동안

06. 적어도, 그들이 그들 부모의 도움을 당연시 하지는 않을 것이다.

연구
• at least 적어도, 최소한
• take something for granted ~을 당연시 하다

07. 그러나, 부모들이 학교가 최우선 순위라는 점을 처음부터 분명히 하는 것이 중요하다.

연구
- however를 문장 맨 앞에 넣어도 되지만, 주어나 보어 뒤에 써도 효과적이다. 물론 이때는 쉼표를 앞뒤로 넣어주어야 한다.
- make it clear 확실히, 명료하게 하다
- the top priority 최우선 순위, 가장 중요한 (=the most important thing)

08. 모든 것들을 고려할 때, 십대 아이는 학교가 파한 뒤 작은 일을 함으로써 얻을 것이 더 많다고 나는 생각한다.

연구
- all things considered 모든 걸 고려해 보면 (=all in all) (마지막 단락의 첫 문장 앞을 이끄는 연결구로 유용하다.)
- after-school 방과 후의, 학교가 파한 뒤

Disagree

01. 십대 아이가 학교를 다니는 동안 일을 한다는 생각을 내가 지지할 수 없는 이유는 많이 있다.

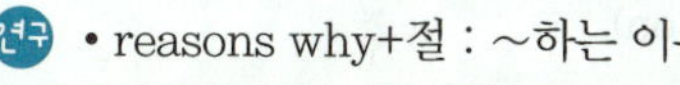

- reasons why+절 : ~하는 이유, reasons for+명사 (명사구)
- There are many reasons for my support for the idea of ~
- while 뒤에 being을 생략해도 된다. 원래대로 while still being a student로 해도 ok.

02. 무엇보다 먼저, 한국에서 고등학교 교과과정은 정규 학생들에게 많은 것을 요구한다.

- first and foremost 우선 가장 중요한 것은 (첫 주장을 펴는 단락의 머리 문장에 사용된다.)
- place heavy demands on ~ : ~에게 많은 것을 요구하다 (쉽게 the high-school curriculum is very demanding to full-time students로 처리해도 좋다.)

03. 어떤 학생들은 방과후에 일을 해서 그들 가족에게 주어진 재정적 부담을 덜어 주고 싶을 수 있다는 점을 나는 이해한다.

- lessen the financial burden 재정적 부담을 줄이다, 완화하다 (=ease, alleviate, lighten)

04. 그러나, 결국에는 오로지 그들의 공부에만 초점을 맞춤으로써 학생들은 혜택을 볼 것이다.

• yet 그러나 (=however, nevertheless, still)
• in the long run 장기적으로 (over the long term, eventually로도 가능하다.)
• focus on 에 초점을 맞추다, 중점을 두다 (=concentrate on)
• solely 단지, 오로지 (=only)

05. 십대 아이에게, 학교가 일 다음으로 두 번째가 될 가능성이 있다.

• is likely to do B : B가 될 가능성이 있다, ~하게 될 것이다
• second to A : A 다음으로 두 번째
  (이때 전치사 to를 기억해 두자. second to none은 누구에게도 두번째가 아닌, 즉, 최고라는 뜻.)

06. 일자리는 돈을 가져오지만 이 시기에 돈이 모든 것은 아니다.

07.

너무 일찍 일의 세계에 들어감으로써, 그들은 대부분 그들의 순수성을 잃어 버릴 것이다.

____

____

____

 • too early 너무 일찍 (=prematurely)
- many of the things처럼 of 뒤가 가산명사일 땐 many
  (그러나 이 예문처럼 of 뒤 명사가) 불가산명사일 경우엔 much를 잘 가려서 써야 한다.

08.

결론적으로, 나는 십대들이 고등학교를 다니는 동안 일자리를 얻는 것은 위에 언급한 이유들 때문에 좋은 생각이 아니라고 생각한다.

____

____

____

 • 'it is not good for A to do B : A가 B하는 것은 좋은 생각이 아니다'란 기본 문장 구조. 확실히 익혀두자.
- while 뒤에 ~ing은 '~하는 동안'이라고 했다.
- for the reasons I stated, mentioned, enumerated above는 토플 에세이 작성시 마지막 단락의 끝 부분에 자주 쓰게 되는 표현인 만큼 실수 없이 쓸 수 있도록 익혀두자.

Independent Writing
Further Writing Practice 14

14

The qualities of a good neighbor

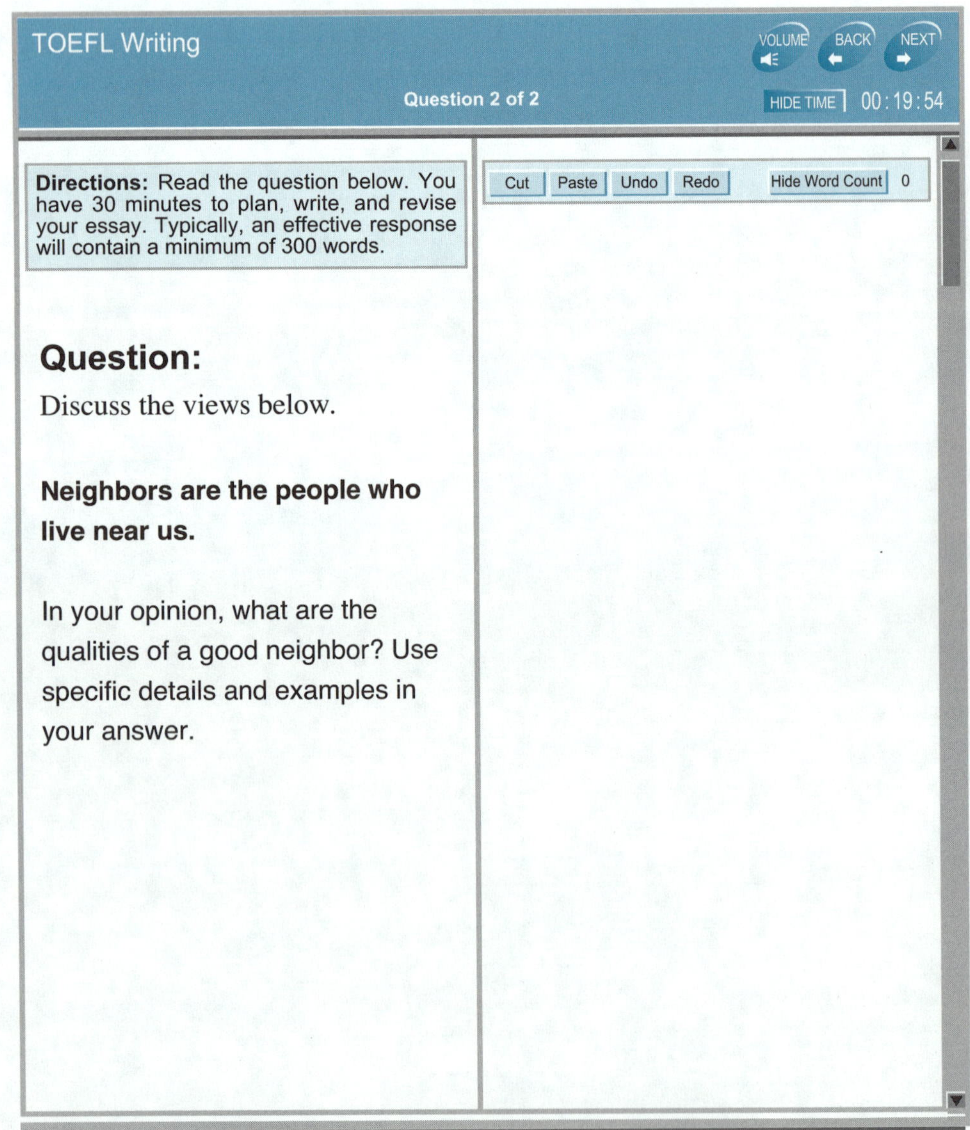

Key Ideas

❖ 이웃의 사생활을 침범해서는 안 된다.

❖ 이웃에게 피해를 줄 만큼 텔레비전이나 오디오를 너무 크게 틀어서는 안 된다.

❖ 이웃을 존중해야 한다.

❖ 만나면 최소한 인사는 해야 한다.

❖ 이웃이 어려울 때 도와줘야 한다.

Vocabulary Brainstorming

• 사생활
  → one's privacy

• 존중하다
  → respect

• 재산
  → property

• 허락을 구하다
  → ask one's permission

• 소음의 정도
  → level of noise

• 인사하다
  → greet, say hello to

01. 대부분의 사람들은 적어도 한 두명 이웃이 있는 지역에서 산다.

연구 • at least 최소한

02. 만약 당신이 좋은 이웃들을 가지고 있다면 자신을 운이 좋다고 생각해라.

연구 • consider yourself lucky if+절 : ～하면 행운인 줄 알아라

03. 존중은 이웃의 가장 중요한 자질이다.

연구 • important quality 중요한 자질

04. 이웃들은 가까이서 함께 생활한다. 따라서 서로의 사생활을 존중하는 것이 필수이다.

연구 • a necessity 필수, 꼭 필요한 것
(여기서 it is necessary to respect each other's privacy로 해도 무리는 없다.)

05. 좋은 이웃은 또한 당신의 재산도 존중한다.

연구 • **존경에 관련된 표현**
- respect someone/something 존중/존경하다
- respect for someone/something ~에 대한 존중/존경 (명사로 쓸 땐 뒤에 전치사 for)
- be respectful of someone/something ~를 존중/존경하다, 존경하는 마음을 갖다
  (형용사로 쓸 땐 전치사 of)

06. 예를 들어, 그는 당신의 공간을 침범할 수 있는 어떤 일을 하기 전에 당신의 허락을 물을 것이다.

연구 • infringe upon/on 침해하다, 침범하다
e.g. They should not infringe on others' privacy.
그들은 다른 이들의 사생활을 침해해서는 안 된다.

07. 이것은 담장을 고치기 전에 그가 당신의 허락을 물을 것이라는 것을 뜻한다.

연구 • 토플 에세이에서 앞 문장 전체를 주어로 받을 때 this를 사용하면 논리적 흐름을 보여 줄 수 있어 좋다. This means that ~ : 이 말은 ~을 뜻한다

08. 이웃이 당신 가족의 일부처럼 될 가능성이 있다.

연구 • there is potential for someone to do something 누가 무엇을 할 가능성이 있다

09. 그들이 휴가로 집에 없는 동안 이웃들은 서로의 집을 돌볼 수 있다.

연구 • take care of someone/something 돌보다
• 여기서의 while은 '~하는 동안'의 의미.
  그러나 While some say A, others say B에서는 while이 '반면에'란 의미를 갖는다.
• be away 집이나 사무실에 없다, 부재 중이다 (be out of town도 사용 가능하다.)

10. 같은 맥락에서, 만약 당신이 시간 외 근무를 해야 할 경우 좋은 이웃은 당신의 자녀들을 돌보아 줄 수 있다.

연구 • in the same vein 같은 맥락에서 (=in the same context, likewise)

11. 좋은 이웃들은 서로의 삶을 보다 쉽게 만드는 데 도움이 된다.

---

12. 이웃들은 또한 세심해야 한다. 자신들의 소음 수준도 의식을 할 정도로.

연구 • conscientious 신중한, 조심 스러운
• be aware of A : A를 의식하고 있다

13. 주변 사람들을 방해하지 않도록 사람들은 자신들이 얼마나 시끄러운
지에 대해서도 신경을 쓸 필요가 있다.

연구 • so that : 그래서 ~하도록 (=so as to)

14. 마주치게 되면 좋은 이웃들은 서로에게 인사한다.

연구 • come in contact 만나다, 마주치다 (=meet)

15. 마지막으로, 이웃들은 우리 삶에서 중요한 사람들로서 역할을 할 수
있다.

연구 • act as+명사 : ~로서의 역할을 수행하다

Independent Writing
Further Writing Practice 15

15

Growing up in the countryside Vs. Growing up in a big city

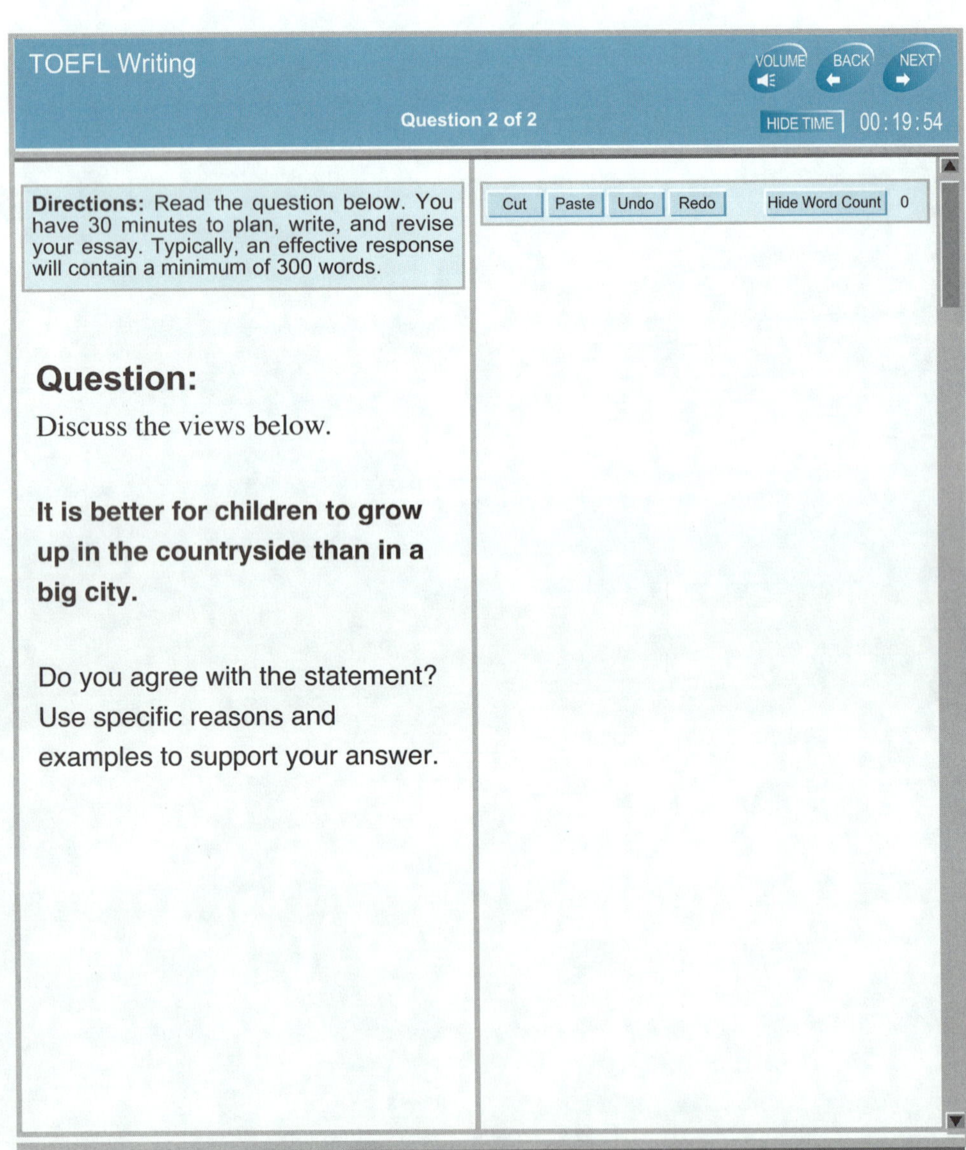

Key Ideas

찬성

※ 자연과 가깝게 자란다.

※ 교통사고와 같은 위험에서 떨어져서 성장한다.

※ 정서 발달이 더 고루 이루어진다.

반대

❖ 문화 생활을 즐길 수 있다.

❖ 다양한 자극을 받으며 자랄 수 있다.

❖ 많은 사람들과 접하면서 자라기 때문에 대인 관계가 원만해진다.

Vocabulary Brainstorming

- 도시 사람
  → city dwellers

- 문화적 경험
  → cultural experience

- 문화 생활
  → cultural activities

- 과외 활동
  → extracurricular activities

- 도심
  → urban center, downtown

- 사람과 교류하다, 접하다
  → interact with people

- 도시생활이 주는 기회
  → the opportunities city life gives you

01. 시골에서 자라는 것은 장점이 있다. 그러나, 내 생각에는, 아이들은 대도시에서 자라는 게 더 좋다.

연구
- it is better for A to do B : A가 B하는 것이 더 좋다, 낫다
  (이 구조는 it is good or bad for A to do B의 변형이다.)
- grow up 자라다 (=be brought up)

02. 시골에서 자란다는 것은 어느 정도의 고립을 의미한다.

연구
- ~ing means A : ~한다는 것은 A를 의미한다, 뜻한다
- a certain amount of : 어느 정도의 ~ (=a certain degree of)

03. 내가 대도시가 더 좋다고 느끼는 한 가지 이유는 아이들이 교류할 사람들이 더 많을 것이기 때문이다.

연구
- one reason+절 : ~하는 한 가지 이유는
- feel+절 : ~라고 느끼다, 생각하다, 여기다 (=think, find, believe)
- interact with A : A와 교류를 하다

04. 시골에서는, 당신이 매일 보는 사람들은 당신과 비슷할 것이다.

 • in the countryside 시골에서는 (=in the country, in the rural areas)
  • the people you meet everyday 매일 만나는 사람들
    (=the people you interact with everyday)
  • tend to+동사원형 : ~하는 경향이 있다, ~할 것이다

05. 도시에서는 시골에서보다 아이들이 이웃과 친구들과 매일 어울리기가 더 쉽다.

• it is easier for A to do B : A가 B를 하는 것이 더 쉽다
    (it is easy, difficult for A to do B의 응용 문장이다.)
  • on a daily basis : 매일, 하루 단위로 on a ~ basis : ~을 기초로 하여, 규칙으로 하여
    on an yearly basis : 매년, 일년 단위로

06. 도시 사람들은 다른 여러 곳 출신이고 많이 이사를 다니는 경향이 있다.

• come from ~에서 오다, 출신이다
  • move around 이사 다니다.

07. 아이들은 대도시에서 자라면서 더 많은 문화적인 경험을 얻을 수 있다.

연구 • gain cultural experiences 문화적 경험을 얻다, 갖게 되다
(enjoy cultural activities로도 처리 가능하다.)

08. 예를 들어, 시골에서 사는 아이는 박물관에 가기가 더 어렵다고 느낄 것이다.

연구 • A finds it difficult or easy to+동사원형 : A는 ~하는 것을 어렵게, 쉽게 느끼다
(여긴다. 알아두면 영작에 도움이 되는 문장 구조이다.)

09. 시골에서는, 영화관도 극장도 혹은 박물관도 없어서, 거기서 자라는 아이들은 이들 문화적 경험에 아주 자주 노출되지는 못할 것이다.

연구 • there are not으로도 가능하지만, 동사는 긍정으로 하고 no를 사용하는 표현 방법도 효과적
이다. 단, 이때 맨 마지막 나열 항목 앞에 and가 아닌 or가 온다는 점 잊지 말자 :
I have no dogs, cats, or rabbits.
• be exposed to A : A에 노출되다, A를 접하다

15. Growing up in the countryside Vs. Growing up in a big city

10.
도시에서 자라는 아이는 많은 흥미로운 곳들을 방문할 수 있는 장점을 가지고 있다.

연구
- A has the advantage of ~ing or 명사 : A는 ~하는 장점을 누린다/가지고 있다
  (참고로, 'the advantage to A : A가 주는 장점, 혜택' 할 땐 전치사 to.)

11.
더구나, 도시에는 아이들이 과외 활동에 참여할 수 있는 기회가 더 많이 있다.

연구
- an opportunity for A to+동사원형 : A가 ~를 할 수 있는 기회
  (chance를 쓰면 ~할 수 있는 가능성.)
- extracurricular activities 과외 활동. *cf.* curricular (학과의)는 curriculum (학과)라는 명사에서 파생된 형용사.

12.
나는 큰 도시에서 자랐고 그것이 내게 제공해 준 모든 기회들을 고맙게 생각한다.

연구
- appreciate 인정하다, 높이 평가하다, 고맙게 생각하다 (=be grateful, thankful for)
- all the+복수 명사 : 모든 ~
- afford 제공하다, 주다 (=offer, provide)

13. 시골 아이들은 도시 중심에서 너무 멀리 떨어져 살기 때문에 이 기회들을 가질 수 없다.

연구 • far away from A : A에서 멀리 떨어진
• urban 도시의 (반대는 rural 시골의)

14. 모든 것을 고려할 때, 도시가 아이들을 현실 세계에 더 잘 대비시켜 주기 때문에 나는 아이들이 도시에서 자라는 것이 더 좋다고 생각한다.

연구 • prepare A for B : A를 B를 위해 준비시키다, 대비시키다

15. 간단히 말해서, 도시가 아이가 자라기에 최고의 장소라는 것이 내 의견이다.

연구 • it is my opinion that+절 : ～하다는 것이 내 의견이다
(=I think, believe that ～)
• be the best place for A to+동사원형 : A가 ～하기에 가장 좋은 곳이다

Independent Writing
Further Writing Practice 16

16

Quick decisions Vs. Slow decisions

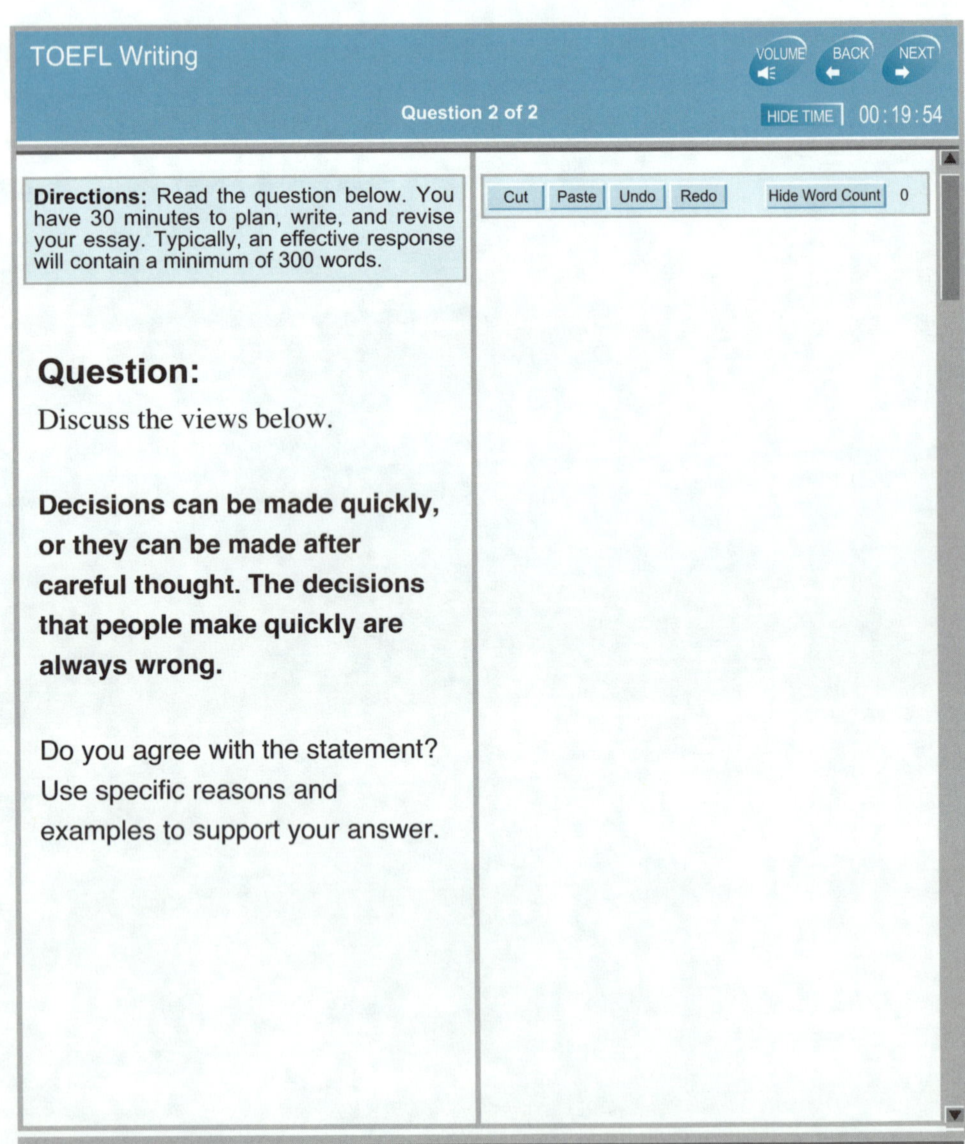

Key Ideas

- **Agree** (Quick decisions are always wrong)

❊ 신중히 여러 요인을 고려할 시간이 없이 내린 결정이기 때문에 우리 인생에 크게 영향을 주는 결정은 꼭 심사숙고한 다음에 내려야 한다.

❊ 성급하게 내린 결정은 반드시 후회하게 되어 있다.

- **Disagree** (Quick decisions are not always wrong)

❖ 어떤 경우에는 직감에 따라 신속하게 결정을 내려야 할 때가 있다.

❖ 의사 결정에 있어서 직감은 중요한 역할을 한다.

❖ 모든 결정을 신중하게 생각한 뒤 내릴 순 없다.

❖ 빠르게 내린 결정도 제대로 된 경우가 많다.

❖ 그다지 중요하지 않은 결정들은 직감에 따라 신속하게 내리는 게 좋다.

Vocabulary Brainstorming

- 빨리 내리는 결정
  - → quick decisions, decisions made quickly

- 직감
  - → intuition

- 고려
  - → consideration

- 제대로 된 결정
  - → right decisions, decisions made correctly

- 요인
  - → factors

Disagree

01. 비록 조심스럽게 생각해서 내린 결정들이 보통은 최선이지만, 때로는 빠른 결정을 내리는 것도 필요하다.

연구
- carefully thought-out 신중하게 생각을 한 (이처럼 하이픈으로 연결해 한 형용사처럼 사용할 수 있다. *e.g.* a carefully-designed plan, a well-planned scheme)
- It is necessary to do A : A를 하는 것이 필수적이다/필요하다
  (알아두어야 할 기본 문장 구조 중 하나다.)

02. 빠른 결정들은 종종 위험하지만, 나는 잘 풀려 나간 여러 신속한 결정들을 내려왔다.

연구
- while ~ : ~한 반면에, 하지만
- risky 위험한, 위험 부담이 따르는
  (이 단어가 떠오르지 않으면 부정문으로 바꾸어 while quick decisions often are not safe 로 돌려서 표현할 수 있는 재치도 있어야 그럴듯한 토플 에세이를 작성할 수 있다.)
- '지금까지 ~해 왔다'를 의미하기 때문에 현재 완료형을 쓰는 것이 맞다.
- work out 잘 풀리다, 돌아가다, 뜻대로 되다 (=function well, yield good results)

03. 때로 사람은 그냥 어떤 것을 보거나 생각하고는 즉시 그것이 바르게 내리는 결정이라는 것을 안다.

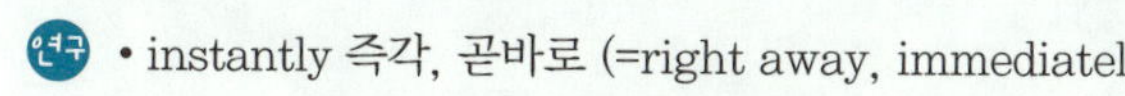

- instantly 즉각, 곧바로 (=right away, immediately)
- make a decision 결정을 내리다
  (동사와 그 동사에 어울리는 목적어를 함께 세트로 알아두면 글쓰기가 훨씬 수월해 진다.)

04. 모든 결정이 내리기 어려운 것은 아니고, 따라서 모든 결정이 똑같은 양의 고려 시간을 필요로 하는 것은 아니다.

- A is difficult, easy to+동사원형 : A는 ~하기 어렵다, 쉽다
  (It is difficult, easy to do A로 처리해도 좋다.)
- thus 따라서, 그렇기 때문에 (=so)
- A requires B : A를 하는 데 B가 필요하다, 요구된다
  (B is necessary or needed to do A로 표현해도 된다.)

05. 비록 어떤 결정들이 지식과 노하우에 바탕을 둔 신중한 고려를 필요로 하지만, 몇몇 나의 최고의 결과들은 빨리 내려진 결정에서 나왔다.

- though 비록 (=although, while it is true that)
- expertise 전문적 지식
- make decisions라는 기본 구조를 응용하자. decisions made quickly 빠르게 내려진 결정
  (=quickly-made decisions)

06. 더구나, 어떤 사람들은 다른 이들보다 그냥 더 잘 결정을 내리는 사람들이고 따라서 바른 결정들을 더 빨리 내릴 수 있다.

연구 • moreover 더군다나, 게다가 (=besides, in addition, furthermore)
　　• decision maker 결정을 내리는 사람, 결정권자
　　(또는 Besides, some people simply can make decisions better than others and ~로 처리해도 된다.)

07. 결론적으로, 나는 모든 빠른 결정들이 잘못이라는 주장에는 동의하지 않는다.

연구 • in conclusion 결론적으로 말해 (=to conclude, to wrap up)

Agree

01. 빠른 결정은 종종 어떤 상황과 관련된 모든 요소들을 고려하지 못한다.

- fail to do A : A를 하지 못하다
- take into account A or take A into account : A를 고려하다, 참고하다 (=consider)
- concerning ~에 관련된 (=related with, involved in)

02. 빠른 결정과는 달리, 신중하게 숙고한 결정은 경험과 전문지식에 의해 대개 뒷받침된다.

- unlike A : A와 달리
- deliberate 심사숙고 하다, 심의하다
- be backed by A : A에 의해 뒷받침 되다, A의 지탱, 후원을 받다 (=supported by)
- experience and expertise 경험과 전문지식
  (change and challenge, slow and steady처럼 가능하다면 같은 알파벳으로 시작하는 두 단어로 짝을 만들면 표현이 완성도가 있어 보인다.)

03. 만약에 어떤 사람이 자기 인생 진로에 엄청나게 영향을 줄 수 있는 결정을 심각한 고려 없이 내린다면, 그 사람은 나중에 그것을 분명히 후회할 것이다.

🔵연구 • person은 성별의 구분이 안 되기 때문에 뒤에서 이를 받을 때 his or her, he or she처럼 양
   쪽을 다 언급하는 게 politically correct하다.
   • influence A : A에 영향을 주다 (=have some influence on A)
   • the course of one's life : 인생의 진로, 방향
   • surely 분명히, 반드시 (=certainly, be bound to, definitely, undoubtedly)

04. 즉흥적인 결정은 그 결정의 결과에 영향을 줄 수 있는 중요한 요소들을 종종 간과한다.

____

____

🔵연구 • on-the-spot decisions 즉흥적 결정, 그 자리에서 내리는 결정
     (=decisions made on the spot, quickly-made decisions)
   • neglect 간과하다, 무시하다, 고려하지 않다
   • affcct 영향을 주다 (=influence)
   • outcome 결과 (=result, consequence)

05. 그것이 바로 중요한 결정을 내리기 전에, 가능하다면, 시간을 좀 갖는 게 언제나 바람직한 이유이다.

____

____

🔵연구 • that is why+절 : 그것이 바로 ~하는 이유이다
     (=that is the reason why+절, that is the reason for+~ing or 명사)
   • advisable 충고할만한, 바람직한 (=recommendable, desirable)
   • if possible 가능하다면 (=if the circumstances allow)
   • take some time 시간을 좀 갖다

06. 판단에서 실수를 피하려면, 결정을 내리는 것은 항상 조심스럽고 신중한 생각에 기초해야 한다.

연구
- errors 실수, 잘못 (=mistakes) 여기서는 to avoid misjudgment로 처리해도 간결해 진다.
- decision-making 의사결정, 결정 내리기
- cautious and careful도 experience and expertise와 같은 표현 방법이다. 동일 글자로 시작하는 두 단어의 짝.

07. 결정을 내리기 전에 보낸 일 분이 나중에 많은 시간과 어려움을 절약해 줄 수 있다.

연구
- save time 시간을 절약하다, 아껴주다

08. 간단히 말해서, 비록 어떤 사람들이 빠르게 좋은 결정들을 내릴 수 있다 해도, 나는 개인적으로는 결정을 내리기 전에 신중한 고려를 위해 약간의 시간을 두는 것을 선호한다.

연구
- in short 간단히 말하자면 (=in a nutshell, in sum, in summary)
- be able to+동사원형 : ~할 수 있다 be unable to+동사원형 : ~할 수 없다
- personally 개인적으로
- allow some time for A : A를 위한 시간을 두다, 내다 (=take some time for A)

Independent Writing
Further Writing Practice 17

17

Life-time employment

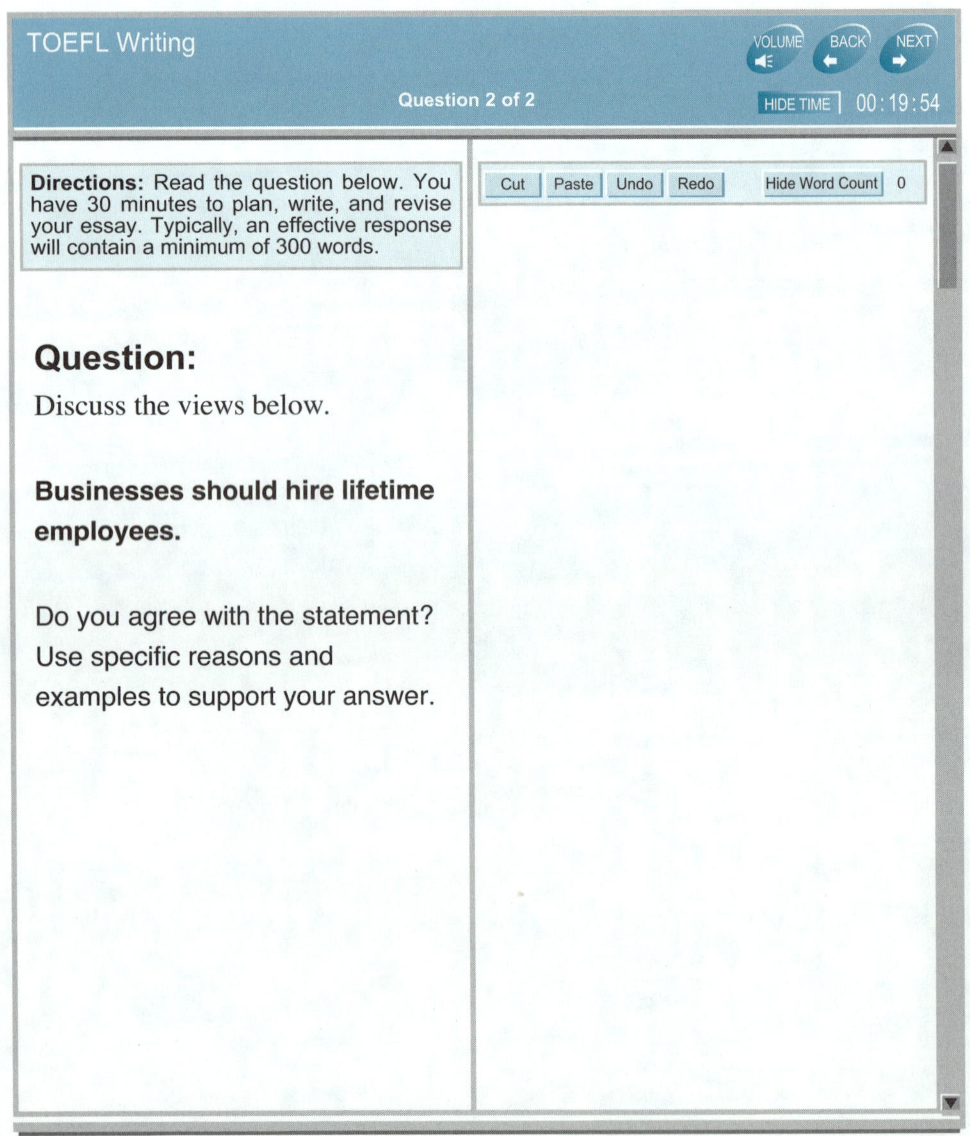

Key Ideas

반대

❊ 시대가 변하면서 기업은 새로운 기술을 지닌 노동자들이 필요하다.

❊ 평생 고용이 보장되면 나태해지는 노동자들이 생긴다.

❊ 새로운 직장을 찾아갈 수 있는 선택의 기회를 노동자들에게 주어야 한다.

찬 성

❖ 경험이 쌓인 노동자들이 기업 활동에 매우 중요하다.

❖ 신규 직원을 채용해 훈련할 필요가 없어진다.

❖ 평생을 한 기업을 위해 일하면 그 기업에 대한 충성심이 생긴다.

Vocabulary Brainstorming

- 고용하다
    → hire, employ
- 평생 고용하다
    → hire someone for lifetime
- 해고하다
    → fire
- 퇴직하다, 퇴직
    → retire, retirement
- 직원, 피고용인
    → employee, worker
- 숙련공
    → experienced/skilled worker
- 경쟁
    → competition
- 훈련
    → training

- 기업
    → company, business, firm
- 직장
    → workplace
- 이익을 내다
    → make profits
- 안정적인 임금
    → stable wages
- 임금 삭감
    → pay cut
- 완전 고용
    → full employment
- 평생 고용 계약
    → lifetime contract

Disagree

01. 나에게는, 오늘날의 노동인력을 지배하는 요소들은 업무 수행과 변화할 수 있는 능력이다.

연구
- governing 지배하는, 통제하는, 크게 영향을 주는 (=controlling)
- workforce 노동인력

02. 회사에 대한 충성은 직원을 채용하는 데 있어 더 이상 주요 고려 사항이 아니다.

연구
- no longer 더 이상 아니다 (부정+any longer)
- a consideration in ~ing : ~하는 데 있어 고려 사항

03. 오늘날 경쟁이 아주 치열하다. 노동자들은 성공적으로 과업을 수행할 수 있는 능력을 바탕으로 채용된다.

연구
- nowadays 요즘엔 (=these days, today)
- steep 가파른, steep competition 치열한 경쟁
- perform 수행하다 (참고로 performer 공연자 performance 공연, 실적)

04. 만약 직원들이 평생동안 고용된다면, 새로운 생각을 가진 젊고 활기
찬 인력이 회사에 들어오는 것은 더 어려워 질 것이다.

(연구) • become less possible for A to do B : A가 B할 가능성이 줄다, 즉 더 어려워지다
(get more difficult for A to do B, A will have a harder time doing B도 가능하다.)

05. 만약 기업들이 평생 계약을 제공하면 좋겠지만, 이는 오늘날의 세계
경제에서 아주 비현실적인 것이다.

(연구) • global economy 세계화 된 경제, 세계 경제 *cf.* global market 세계 시장
• is simply impractical 아주 비현실적이다 (여기서 simply는 very와 같다.)

06. 우리는 신선한 관점을 지닌 새로운 노동자가 필요하다.

(연구) • point of view 관점 (=perspective)

07. 평생 계약은 과거의 것이다.

____

____

____

(연구) • a thing of the past 과거의 것, 옛날에나 볼 수 있었던 것, 옛말이다
• 'lifetime contracts became history' 평생 고용 계약은 이제 옛말이 되었다, 역사 속으로 사라졌다

08. 그들이 평생 직장을 확보했다는 것을 알게 되면 직원들의 근무 윤리가 저하될 수 있다.

____

____

____

(연구) • work ethic 근무윤리
• in the knowledge that ~ : ~를 알게 되면
(이 문장은 가정법으로 처리해도 좋다 : An employee may lose some work ethic, if he knows that ~)

09. 기업들은 구식 기술을 가진 직원들을 유지하기보다는 새 직원들을 불러 옮으로써 신기술에 적응할 필요가 있다.

____

____

____

(연구) • rather than ~ing : ~하는 대신에, ~하기보다는
• outdated 낡은, 구식의 (반대는 updated, up-to-date 최신의)

10. 숙련된 노동자들은 한 회사에 대한 헌신보다는 이동의 자유를 선호하는 경향이 있다.

연구 • prefer A over B / prefer A to B : B보다 A를 선호하다
• commitment to A : A에 대한 헌신, 책임감

Agree

01. 기업들이 직원들을 평생동안 고용해야 한다는 생각에 나는 동의한다.

연구 • I agree with the idea that+절 : ~라는 생각에 나는 동의한다
(공식처럼 알아 두는 게 좋다. 같은 의미로 I support the idea that+절, I agree with the statement that+절도 함께 알아 두길….)

02. 어떤 기업 문화에서는, 노동자들이 젊은 나이에 채용이 되고 그들이 퇴직할 때까지 고용된다.

연구 • hire, employ 고용하다
cf. employment 고용 fire 해고하다 retire 은퇴하다 retirement 은퇴

03.

그런 생각에 기초해 볼 때, 나는 회사가 경험이 있는 노동자의 가치를 간과하는 것이 어리석다고 생각한다.

____

____

____

🔵 • based on such idea 그런 생각에 기초해 볼 때, 그런 생각을 감안해
    (=in light of this, because of that, that is the reason why)
  • overlook A : A를 간과하다

04.

계속적인 직업 훈련에 대한 필요가 줄어들게 되기 때문에 직원들을 계속 일하도록 하는 것이 회사에게 시간과 돈을 절약해 줄 수 있다.

____

____

____

🔵 • keep someone on the job 계속 일자리에 머물게 하다, 일하게 하다
  • save someone time/money 누구에게 시간/돈이 덜 들게 하다, 절약해 주다
  • as는 여러 가지 의미로 사용되는데, 여기서는 because의 의미로 써보자.

05.

한 회사에서 오랜 시간 동안 일한 직원은 자신들의 고용주에게 아주 충성스러운 경향이 있다.

____

____

____

🔵 • tend to 동사원형 : ～하는 경향이 있다
    (너무 단정적으로 표현하기보다는 '～하는 경향이 있다'는 식으로 하는 게 더 부드럽다. 또 다른 예로, this is the best way보다는 this is one of the best ways가 더 부드럽다.)
  • loyal to A : A에게 충성스러운, 뒤에 따라 붙는 전치사 to까지 챙겨야 한다.

06. 따라서, 만약 회사가 어려운 시기를 겪고 있다면 이들 노동자들은 일시적인 급여 삭감을 더 기꺼이 견뎌낼 것이다.

연구
- endure 참다, 견디다 (=put up with, bear)
- pay cuts 급여 삭감
- undergo something : ~를 겪다, 경험하다 (=experience, go through)

07. 마찬가지로, 기업들은 자신들이 속한 지역사회에 기여해야 하는 도덕적 의무를 가지고 있다.

연구
- in the same way 마찬가지로 (=likewise)
- contribute to 기여하다 / belong to 속하다.
  이때 뒤에 오는 전치사 to 잊지 말아야 한다.

08. 전반적으로, 평생 고용은 고용주와 직원 양자에게 혜택을 준다.

Independent Writing
Further Writing Practice 18

18
Vacation Vs. A car

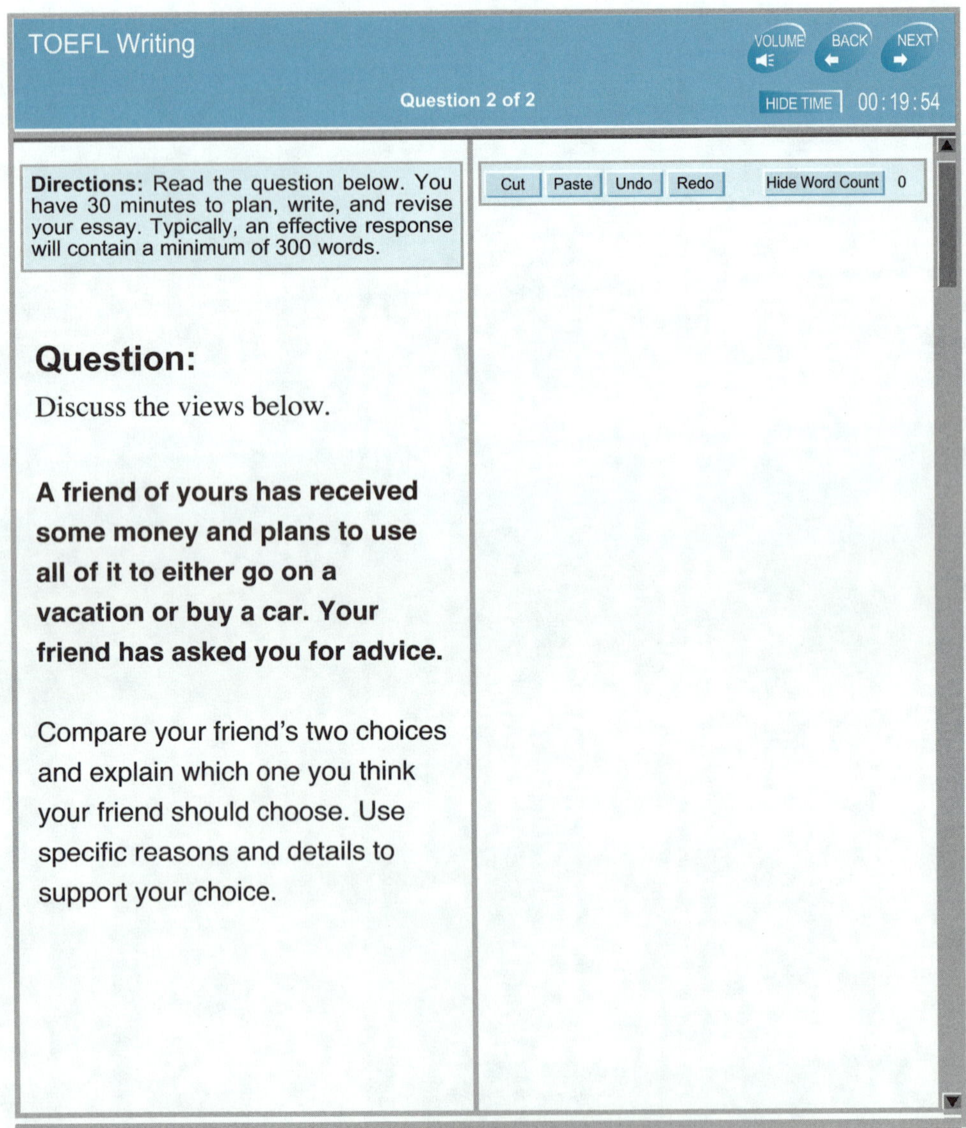

Key Ideas

• Buy a car

❖ 더 오랫동안 즐거움을 느낄 수 있다.

❖ 여행을 더 편하게 갈 수 있다.

❖ 대중 교통에 의존하지 않아도 된다.

• Go on vacation

❖ 마음이 풍성해 진다.

❖ 일상의 스트레스를 해소할 수 있어 재충전의 기회가 된다.

❖ 저축한 돈으로 가기는 힘들지만 그냥 생긴 돈으로는 여행을 가기가 심리적으로 덜 부담이 된다.

❖ 외국 여행을 갈 경우 안목이 넓어져 하는 일에 도움이 된다.

Vocabulary Brainstorming

- 추억
  - → memories
- 대중 교통
  - → public transportation
- 부담
  - → burden, liability
- 보험
  - → insurance
- 수리
  - → repair
- 연료
  - → fuel
- 주차비
  - → parking fee
- 휴식
  - → relaxation
- 떠나다
  - → take time away from
- 보다 좋은 투자
  - → a better investment

Go on a vacation

01. 돈에 관한 결정들은 항상 어려운데, 사람이 큰 액수를 쓰고 싶어 할 때는 특히 그렇다.

연구
- money decision 돈에 대한 결정
  (decision on money or decisions about how to spend money로 풀어 써도 좋다.)
- especially 특히 (=in particular)

02. 만약 내 친구가 그런 결정에 직면한다면, 나는 그가 휴가를 가야 한다고 권할 것이다.

연구
- be faced with A : A에 직면하다, A라는 문제에 봉착하다
- recommend 뒤에는 should+동사원형 또는 should를 생략하고 동사원형이 온다.
  그래서 3인칭 단수 주어 he 뒤에 goes가 아닌 동사원형 go가 온다.

03. 물론, 휴가는 우리에게 오래 남는 추억을 줄 것이다.

연구
- of course로 시작한 다음 지금까지 주장한 내용과 다소 배치되는 사항을 지나치듯이 추가할 수 있다.

04.

투자가 아주 일시적인 것이기 때문에, 휴가에 돈을 쓰는 것은 비현실적이라고 어떤 사람들이 말할 수 있다.

연구
- investment 투자
- temporary 일시적

05.

학교나 직장에서 시간을 내는 것이 활력을 찾고 마음의 평화를 회복하는 데 도움이 된다.

연구
- take time away from A : A에서 벗어나 시간을 갖다/내다
  cf. The work will take too much time away from your studies.
  그 일은 공부할 시간을 너무 많이 빼앗을 거야.
- rejuvenate ~에 활력을 불어넣다, 젊게 하다

06.

휴가의 즉각적인 혜택들에는 기분전환과 스트레스 해소가 포함된다.

연구
- immediate benefits of A : A의 즉각적인 혜택 (=short-term benefits)
- relaxation 한숨 돌림, 기분 전환

07. 휴가는 친숙한 모든 것에서 벗어날 수 있는, 그리고 세상을 새로운 시각에서 볼 수 있는 기회이다.

* escape from 벗어나다 (=leave behind)
* all that is familiar 친숙한 모든 것 (routine '일상'이란 표현을 써도 좋다.)

08. 그러므로, 나는 새 자동차에 투자하는 것보다는 휴가를 가는 것을 추천할 것이다.

* therefore, 따라서, 그래서 (=in light of this, so)
* recommend that+절 : ~하는 것을 추천하다
* recommend+명사 : ~을 권하다, 추천하다
* rather than ~ing or 명사 : ~하는 것보다는

Buy a car

01. 먼저, 자동차는 휴가보다 더 오래 지속될 것이라는 점이 분명하다.

연구 • there is no doubt that+절 : ~는 의심의 여지가 없다, 확실하다
  (certainly를 넣어 문장 구조를 잡아도 된다. First, a car will certainly last longer ~.)
• last 지속되다, 견디다 (뒤에는 전치사 없이 바로 기간을 쓰면 된다.
  e.g. The party usually last two hours. 그 파티는 주로 두 시간 계속된다.)

02. 자동차를 운전하는 것은 아주 즐거울 수 있다.

연구 • be enjoyable 즐거운 것이다, 즐길 수 있는 것이다
  (be something you can enjoy로 풀어서 써도 된다.)

03. 자가용 자동차의 장점들은 아주 많다.

연구 • private car 자가용

04. 무엇보다 먼저, 대중 교통에 의존하지 않아도 되는 편리함이 있다.

연구
- first and foremost 무엇보다 먼저
  (토플 에세이에서 첫번째 이유를 드는 도입부에 쓰면 좋다.)
- the convenience of ~ : ~의 편리함, 참고로, 반대는 the inconvenience of ~

05. 사람은 자동차를 소유하는 것이 보험 비용, 유지, 연료비, 그리고 주차요금을 포함한다는 것을 고려할 필요가 있다.

연구
- '일반적으로 누구나'를 뜻할 땐 one으로 처리하면 편리하다.
- consider 고려하다 (=take into account)
- fuel costs 연료비

06. 자동차는 사람을 거의 어느 곳에나 데려갈 수 있고, 따라서 다른 이들에게 의존할 필요가 덜하다.

연구
- virtually 거의 (=almost, practically)
- and thus 따라서, 그렇기 때문에 (=therefore, so)

07. 자동차는 무거운 물건들을 운송하는 것을 포함해서 더 많은 용도를 갖고 있다.

연구
- many+복수명사+including A, B, and C : A, B, C를 포함한 여러 가지
  (대상을 열거할 땐 including이나 such as를 쓰면 편리하다.)
- objects 물건들

08. 따라서, 유용성과 편리함을 모두 고려하면, 자동차를 사는 것이 더 좋은 투자일 것이다.

연구
- Thus 따라서, 이렇기 때문에 (=in light of this, therefore)
- take into account ~을 고려하다 (take into consideration도 같은 의미.)
- usefulness 유용성

Independent Writing
Further Writing Practice 19

19

Borrowing money from a friend

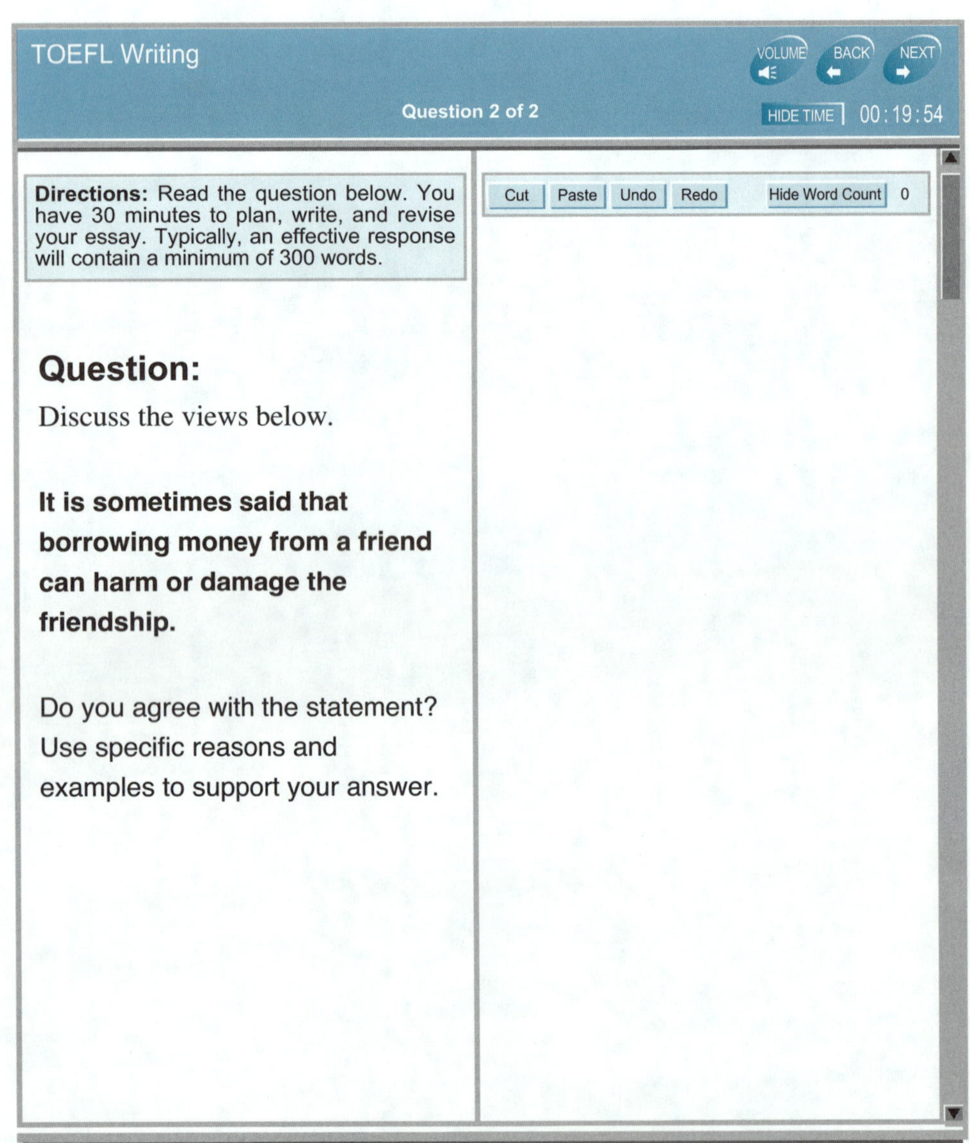

Key Ideas

찬성

❖ 친구와는 돈 거래를 가급적 피해야 한다.

❖ 우정에 금이 갈 수 있다.

❖ 돈을 다시 갚지 못하면 서로의 감정뿐 아니라 우정도 망가진다.

❖ 돈은 은행에서 빌리는 게 친구와의 관계를 유지하는 방법이다.

반대

❖ 필요할 때 도와 주는 것이 친구다.

❖ 돈을 제 때 갚으면 친구와의 신뢰도 재확인 되는 등 우정이 더 돈독해 질 수 있다.

❖ 다른 사람보다 친구에게 속 사정을 털어놓기가 더 쉽기 때문에 친구에게 돈을 빌리는 것이 더 좋다. 이를 통해 두 사람의 관계가 더 가까워 질 수 있다.

Vocabulary Brainstorming

- 감정을 상하다
  - → hurt feelings
- 돈이 필요하다
  - → be short of cash/money
- 우정을 상하게 하다
  - → damage the friendship
- 우정을 망가뜨리다
  - → ruin/destroy the friendship
- 돈을 친구에게 빌리다
  - → borrow money from a friend
- 우정이 위험하게 되다
  - → risk friendship
- 돈을 갚다
  - → pay back a loan, repay the borrowed money

01. 나는 친구로부터 돈을 빌리는 것이 우정을 해치고 다치게 한다는 점에 동의한다.

---

02. 가까운 사이가 돈거래가 개입되면서 망가질 수 있다.

연구
- ruin a relationship 사이/관계를 망가뜨리다
- come into play 개입하다, 끼어들다

03. 돈을 빌리는 것은 우정의 본질적인 성질을 손상시킬 수 있다.

연구
- undermine (자기도 모르게 서서히) 해치다, 손상시키다 (=damage, hurt)
- essential 본질적인, 필수적인, 핵심적인 (=necessary, basic, core)

04. 그것이 우정에 분노와 어색함을 유발시킬 수 있다.

연구 • cause a feeling 어떤 감정을 유발하다, 불러일으키다
(이때 cause는 긍정적, 부정적 감정을 다 받을 수 있다. 그러나 '부정적 감정을 일으키다'를 영작할 땐 trigger란 동사를 써도 좋다 : It can trigger resentment and anger.)

05. 만약 내가 친구에게서 돈을 빌린다면, 그 친구는 나에게 영향력을 갖게 될 것이다.

연구 • 가정법 문장의 전형적 구조이다. 즉, if가 이끄는 절은 현재, 뒷절은 미래시제.

06. 당신이 빌린 돈을 언제 갚을 수 있을 것인가라는 문제도 또한 있다.

연구 • the question of ~ 라는 문제 (the problem of 해도 문제 없다.)

07. 친구가 돈을 다시 갚을 시한을 정하는 것은 어색할 것이다.

연구 • set a deadline for something : ~에 대한 시한, 날짜를 정하다, 설정하다
(참고로, '목표를 정하다'도 set a goal.)

08. 이들 모든 문제들이 불쾌한 감정들을 초래할 수 있고 우정을 심하게 해칠 수 있다.

🔵연구 • result in 결과를 초래하다 (참고로, result from 은 ~에서 비롯되다)

09. 마지막으로, 나는 그것이 우리의 신뢰를 무너뜨릴 수 있기 때문에 친구로부터 돈을 빌리고 싶지는 않을 것이다.

🔵연구 • lastly 마지막으로 (last도 가능함.)
 • destroy one's trust 신뢰를 무너뜨리다 (=ruin/harm/damage one's trust)
 (참고로, 반대는 enhance/strengthen/improve/deepen one's trust 신뢰를 강화하다, 두텁게 하다)

10. 간단히 말해서, 친구에게서 돈을 빌리는 것은 좋은 생각이 아니다.

---

11. 대개, 우정이 위험에 처할 수 있을 것이다.

연구
- more often than not 자주, 대개
- be at risk 위험에 처하다 (뒷부분은 you can lose your friendship으로 처리해도 된다.)

12. 우선, 좋은 우정은 단단한 신뢰의 토대 위에서 만들어진다.

연구

13. 어려울 때 우리는 도움을 얻기 위해 친구에게 자주 의지한다.

연구
- in times of need 어려울 때, 도움이 필요할 때
  (when을 넣어 when we need a hand or help로 처리할 수 있다.)
- turn to A for B : A에게서 B를 구하다, B를 얻기 위해 A에게 의지하다
  ('누군가에 의지하다'는 turn to, depend on, rely on, resort to, count on 등으로 영작 가능
  하다.)

14. 빌린 돈을 제때에 갚는 것은 원칙의 문제이다.

____

____

____

연구
- on time 제때, 정확한 시간에 (참고로 in time은 시간 안에 충분히 일찍.)
- a matter of : ~의 문제이다

15. 빌려 주는 경우에, 사람은 자신이 감당할 수 있는 손실 이상의 돈을 절대 빌려 주지 말아야 한다.

____

____

____

연구
- in the case of ~ : ~의 경우에는
- afford to do something : ~하는 것을 감당하다

16. 당신이 돈이 필요할 때, 돈을 은행에서 빌려라 : 이것이 당신의 우정을 구해 줄 것이다.

____

____

____

Independent Writing
Further Writing Practice 20

20

Smoking in public places

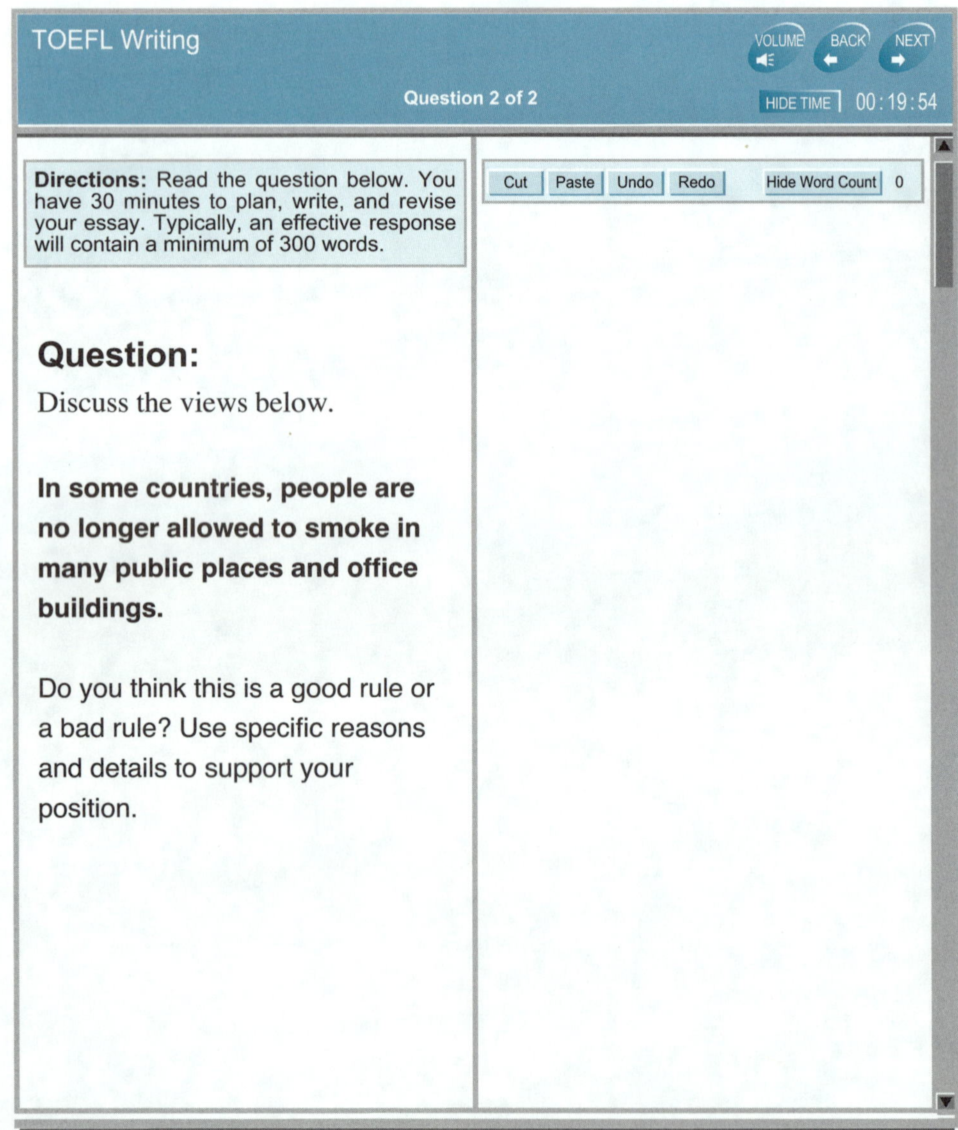

Key Ideas

It's a good rule

❈ 간접 흡연을 막을 수 있다.

❈ 흡연자 본인의 건강에도 도움이 된다.

❈ 흡연자가 다른 사람들의 건강을 해칠 권리가 없다.

Vocabulary Brainstorming

- 흡연 금지
    → ban on smoking, banning smoking
- 흡연자의 건강을 개선하다
    → improve the smoker's health
- 간접 흡연
    → second-hand smoking, passive smoking
- 해로운 공기를 마시다
    → breathe harmful air
- 흡연을 말리다, 하지 않게 하다
    → discourage smoking
- 금연 규칙, 법
    → non-smoking rule, non-smoking laws
- 암을 유발하다
    → cause cancer
- 담배 냄새
    → the smell of cigarettes

01. 공공장소와 사무실 건물에서 흡연을 금지시키는 것이 여러 가지 이유에서 좋은 생각이라고 나는 강하게 믿는다.

연구
- I strongly believe that ~ : 나는 ~라고 강하게 믿는다
  ('강하게 반대하다, 찬성하다 strongly agree or disagree with ~'도 같이 알아 두자.)
- it is a good/bad idea to+동사원형 : ~하는 것은 좋은/나쁜 생각이다
- for a number of reasons 여러 가지 이유에서 (토플 에세이에서 자주 쓸법한 표현이다.)

02. 무엇보다 먼저, 이 법은 간접흡연에 의해 발생하는 피해를 막아 줄 수 있다.

연구
- prevent 예방하다 (참고로, prevent A from ~ing : A가 ~하는 것을 막다, 못 하게 하다)
- second-hand smoking 간접 흡연 *cf.* second-hand 손을 거친, 중고의 second-hand book store 헌책방 (반면 firsthand는 형용사로는 direct의 의미, 부사로는 personally의 의미로 많이 쓰인다. firsthand experience 직접 경험)

03. 최근 연구는 간접흡연이 암을 유발한다는 것을 보여주었다.

연구
- recent research has indicated/demonstrated/showed that ~ : 최근 연구는 ~라는 사실을 보여주었다
- research는 복수로 쓸 수 없다. 대신, studies는 복수가 가능하다
- lately, studies have revealed that ~ : 최근 들어 조사, 연구는 ~라는 사실을 밝혀 주었다
  (이런 표현들을 써서 자신의 입장을 뒷받침하면 효과적이다.)

04.
그들이 해로운 공기를 마시지 않아도 되기 때문에 이 조치가 분명히 비흡연자들을 즐겁게 할 것이다.

연구
- certainly 분명, 확실히 (=definitely, surely, undoubtedly)
- please A : A를 즐겁게 하다, 만족시키다
- non-smokers 비흡연자

05.
예를 들어 캘리포니아와 뉴욕 같은 미국의 일부 주들은 식당이나 카페 같은 공공장소에서 흡연을 이미 금지시켰다.

연구
- As, such as B, C, and D : B, C, D와 같은 A들은
  (이때 such as 대신 including을 써도 된다.)

06.
이것이 흡연이 수반하는 위험에 대한 사람들의 인식을 높여 줄 것이다.

연구
- increase the awareness of A : A에 대한 인식을 높이다 (좀처럼 쉽게 안 떠오르는 표현인 만큼 잘 익혀 두는 게 좋다. enhance, improve 같은 동사를 넣어도 된다.)
- A entailed in B : B에 수반되는 A (A involved in B도 같은 뜻.)

07. 많은 사람들이 폐암을 비롯한 흡연 관련 질환으로 이미 목숨을 잃었다.

____

____

____

🔵 연구 • A-related B : A에 관련된 B (=B partly caused by A)

08. 만약 이 법이 실행된다면, 그들이 소비하는 담배 수량을 줄이도록 도와줌으로써 흡연자들의 건강을 개선시켜 줄 것이다.

____

____

____

🔵 연구 • 가정문이다 : if+과거, 주어+would/should/could/might+동사원형
• cut down on A : A를 줄이다(주로 수량)
• consume 소비하다

09. 그들이 담배를 피울 기회가 더 적을 것이기 때문에, 그들은 담배를 더 적게 피울 것이다.

____

____

____

🔵 연구 • have more or less opportunity to+동사원형 : ～할 기회가 더 많다 또는 적다

10. 그 법이 젊은이들에게 흡연에 따르는 위험을 보여줄 것이기 때문에 그 법은 젊은이들이 흡연을 시작하지 않도록 유도할 것이다.

____

____

____

- discourage /dissuade A from ~ing : A가 ~하는 것을 말리다, 못하도록 유도하다
  (반대는 encourage A to+동사원형)

11. 흡연은 선택이지만 다른 사람의 건강이 걸려 있기 때문에, 그 선택은 신중히 고려해서 해야 한다.

____

____

____

- A is at stake : A가 문제가 되다, 걸려 있다
- 뒷부분은 one should carefully consider the matter before making the decision으로 풀어 써도 된다.

12. 단지 그들이 끊기를 원치 않기 때문에 다른 사람들이 흡연의 부정적인 결과로 피해를 입도록 강요할 권리는 아무도 없다.

____

____

____

- have the right to+동사원형 : ~할 수 있는 권리가 있다
- force A to+동사원형 : A에게 ~하라고 강요하다, A에게 강제로 ~하게 하다
- the negative/positive consequences of A : A의 긍정적인/부정적인 결과

13. 사무실 건물안의 금연에 대해서는, 모든 노동자들이 자기 고용 장소
에서 안전하고 건강할 권리를 가지고 있다고 나는 믿는다.

연구
- as to A : A에 대해서는 (=concerning A)
- every worker has ~ : every 뒤엔 언제나 단수 명사인데, 종종 '모두 다'라는 의미를 생각하
다가 복수명사를 쓰는 실수를 하게 된다.

14. 모든 것을 고려할 때, 공공장소와 사무실 건물에서 금연은 좋은 법인
것이 명백하다.

연구
- it is crystal clear that ~ : ~하다는 것은 명백한, 자명한, 의심의 여지가 없는 일이다

15. 더구나, 나는 이 법이 우리 나라에서 가능한 빨리 시행되기를 바란다.

연구
- what is more 더욱이 (=more importantly)
- wish A +과거 동사 : A가 ~하길 바란다
(이때 동사를 과거시제로 써야 한다는 점을 잊지 말자.)
- implement a law 법을 시행하다 (동사와 목적어가 어울리는 세트 표현.)
- as soon as possible 가능한 빨리
(친구에게 쓰는 가벼운 이메일에는 줄여서 ASAP라 써도 된다 : let me know about it
ASAP. 그 일에 대해 가능한 빨리 알려줘.)

LNB PRESS

TOTAL ENGLISH

해설집

TOTAL iBT TOEFL®

Writing

Total Note-taking System
동영상강좌 + 별책부록 무료제공
세계 최초 저작권 등록

이을기 · 채미영 박사 공저

LNB PRESS

LNBPRESS.com

이 을 기

- 서울대 졸업
- 외대 동시 통역 대학원 한영과
- Boston University Law School 수학
- (전)포항제철 사장 전담 통역
- (전)서울 외대 통역대학원 영어과 강사
- (현)대치동 TOTAL ENGLISH 대표
- 저서　토플 기초공사 Listening
　　　　토플 기초공사 Writing
　　　　Total iBT 토플 Reading
　　　　Total iBT 토플 Listening
　　　　Total iBT 토플 Speaking
　　　　Total iBT 토플 Writing
　　　　Total iBT 토플 Vocabulary

채 미 영

- 서울대 졸업
- 외대 동시 통역 대학원 한영과
- Boston University 교육학 박사 과정 수학
  (Bilingual Education 전공)
- Walden University 영어 교육학 박사
  (박사 논문: A content-based ESL instructional method for
  Korean students)
- (전)서울 외대 통역대학원 영어과 강사
- (현)대치동 TOTAL ENGLISH 원장
- 저서　토플 기초공사 Listening
　　　　토플 기초공사 Writing
　　　　Total iBT 토플 Reading
　　　　Total iBT 토플 Listening
　　　　Total iBT 토플 Speaking
　　　　Total iBT 토플 Writing
　　　　Total iBT 토플 Vocabulary

추천의 말

보스턴 칼리지 린치 교육대학원
마리아 브리스크 박사

Congratulation
Message

This book skillfully combines both the author's theoretical knowledge of English as a Foreign Language Education and practical expertise of an experienced EFL teacher. The systematic approach to test preparation found in this book should be extremely helpful to EFL learners preparing to take the new generation of iBT TOEFL test.

Maria Estela Brisk Ph.D Professor
Lynch School of Education Boston College

Writing Answers

Writing Answers

Diagnostic Test

Task 1

에어로빅 체조

Reading Translation

에어로빅 체조의 장점들은 잘 알려져 있다. 여성잡지들은 하나같이 에어로빅의 장점을 극찬하고, 의사, 개인코치, 다이어트 프로그램들도 이를 뒷받침한다. 에어로빅이 건강과 체력을 증진시킨다는 사실은 잘 기록되어 있으며, 문명사회에서 에어로빅이 좋다는 것을 모르는 사람은 거의 없을 것이다.

에어로빅 체조는 몸의 가장 중요한 근육인 심장을 자극하여 더 튼튼해지게 하며 효율성을 높인다. 하지만, 에어로빅을 하면 심장뿐만 아니라 몸 전체가 좋아진다. 하버드 학생들의 건강 연구 결과에 따르면, 운동을 하면 평균수명이 연장되는 것으로 나타났다. 규칙적인 운동을 하는 사람들은 감기나 독감에 걸릴 확률이 낮고, 면역시스템 또한 더 강하다. 심장병, 고혈압, 뇌졸중, 당뇨병, 그리고 일부 암에 걸릴 위험도 운동하는 사람들에게 더 적다. 또 체중부하운동을 하면 뼈가 튼튼해져 골다공증에 걸릴 확률이 낮아진다.

에어로빅 체조는 다른 운동에 비해 열량 소모량이 많기 때문에, 체중감량이나 체중유지에도 좋다. 에어로빅을 하는 사람들은 더 많이 먹으면서도 몸무게를 줄일 수 있으며, 열량소모 효과는 운동이 끝난 후에도 계속된다. 이렇듯 에어로빅은 신체적 건강을 증진시킬 뿐 아니라, 정신적 건강에도 도움이 된다. 에어로빅 체조를 하면 인체의 자연적 진통제인 엔도르핀이 분비돼 스트레스, 우울증, 그리고 불안감을 완화시켜 준다. 엔도르핀은 운동하는 사람들이 흔히 기대하는 "좋은 기분"을 느낄 수 있게 해 준다. 에어로빅을 하러 체육관에 갈 시간이나 돈이 없는 사람들도 있겠지만, 이런 사람들은 에어로빅 체조를 생활화하는 방법도 있다. 에어로빅 댄스나 걷기, 자전거타기 등 다른 에어로빅 운동은 집에서도 할 수 있다.

Listening Script

Professor

I'll bet most of you do aerobic exercise every week, don't you? So I'm sure you're all aware of the benefits of aerobic exercise. But did you know that too much exercise can be just as bad as overeating? As a matter of fact, too much exercise can become a very serious health concern.

So how can you tell that you're overexercising? Here are some warning signs to take note of. First of all, you'll find yourself feeling exhausted instead of refreshed and energized. Don't push yourself until you're exhausted. You might also notice a loss of appetite or frequent headaches. If you notice muscle soreness, loss of coordination, or recurrent illness, cut back on the exercise. And … pay attention to your heartbeat. If there's an abnormal increase in your heart rate in the morning, you are exercising too much. Overexercise can even cause depression and gastrointestinal disturbances.

Here's the best way to approach your exercise program. Start out small and increase your daily exercise very gradually. If you notice any of the signs of overexercise, cut back to the level you were at before noticing the symptoms. Watch for muscle injuries, and if you have those, cut back. And … don't allow your exercise program to rule your life. If you miss a day, don't obsess about it; just get back on track the following day. Exercise is a total lifestyle choice, and one day more or less won't make a difference. Don't make your exercise program the basis of your self-esteem, and don't put it ahead of taking good care of yourself. Above all, keep in mind that keeping a healthy balance between your exercise program, your diet, your rest, and all the other aspects of your life is really the key thing. So be realistic and keep it fun.

Listening Translation

교수

여러분은 매주 에어로빅 체조를 하지요? 따라서 에어로빅의 장점에 대해서는 모두 잘 알고 있으리라 믿는다. 하지만 지나친 운동은 과식만큼이나 나쁘다는 것을 알고 있었나요? 사실, 운동을 너무 많이 하면 건강에 심각한 문제를 야기할 수 있다.

그렇다면 우리가 운동을 과하게 하고 있는지 어떻게 알 수 있을까? 몇 가지 주의해야 할 증상에 대해 말해 보겠다. 무엇보다도 먼저, 운동을 해도 가뿐하거나 힘이 나지 않고, 오히려 피로감만 느껴질 것이다. 지칠 때까지 무리해서 운동을 하지 말아라. 이외에도 식욕이 떨어지거나 잦은 두통이 올 수도 있다. 만약 근육통과 움직임이 둔해진다고 느끼거나 병에 자주 걸리게 되면 운동량을 줄여 보도록 해라. 그리고 … 심장박동에 주의를 기울여라. 만일 오전에 심장박동수가 비정상적으로 늘어나면, 이는 운동이 과하다는 징후이다. 지나친 운동은 우울증과 위장병까지도 유발할 수 있다.

운동생활을 가장 효과적으로 할 수 있는 방법은 다음과 같다. 처음에는 조금씩만 운동하다가, 운동량을 단계적으로 늘려가라. 과다운동의 증상을 발견하게 된다면, 그러한 증상이 나타나기 이전 수준으로 운동량을 줄여라. 근육이 다치지 않도록 조심하고, 만약 근육이 손상되었다면 운동량을 줄여라. 그리고 … 운동으로 인해 여러분의 생활이 지장을 받지 않도록 해라. 하루 운동을 못했다고 해서 괴로워하지 말고, 그 다음 날부터 다시 시작해라. 운동은 평생동안 하는 생활의 선택이다. 이틀 정도 운동을 하지 않아도 큰일 나지 않는다. 운동량을 여러분의 자존심으로 삼지 말고, 자신을 잘 보살피는 것보다 운동을 더 우선순위에 두지 말아라. 무엇보다, 운동, 식생활, 휴식, 그리고 다른 생활을 균형 있게 관리하는 것이 가장 중요하다는 사실을 명심해라. 현실적으로, 그리고 즐겁게 운동해라.

Answer

There are many benefits to aerobic exercise, including a stronger heart and a healthier immune system. It also helps with weight loss and weight maintenance as well as reducing stress. On the other hand, however, it is possible to overdo aerobic exercise, and that can create dangerous health problems. Not only can it make you exhausted, but it can produce muscle soreness, lead to recurrent illness, and reduce your performance. Even depression and gastrointestinal problems can be related to too much exercise.

If you notice that your morning heart rate is abnormally fast, you are exercising too much. It's important to keep in mind that in order to obtain the benefits of aerobic exercise, you have to maintain a healthy balance and not overdo it. Otherwise, you lose much of the benefit and end up with problems besides. So if you start noticing problems, you should reduce the amount of exercise until the exercise routine makes you feel good without excessive fatigue and does not generate problems. Above all, do not obsess about your exercise program or feel guilty if you can't exercise on a particular day. Since an exercise program is a long-term commitment, a day missed here or there doesn't mean much; it's the overall persistence over a long period of time that will give you the results you want.

Answer Translation

에어로빅 체조는 심장을 튼튼하게 해 주고 면역시스템을 강화하는 등 많은 장점을 가지고 있다. 또 스트레스 해소뿐만 아니라 체중감량과 몸매유지에도 도움이 된다. 하지만 다른 한편으로는, 운동을 과다하게 하여 건강을 훼손할 수도 있다. 과다운동은 피로를 유발할 수도 있을 뿐만 아니라, 근육통, 잦은 병, 그리고 효율성 저하를 낳을 수도 있다. 심지어 우울증과 위장병까지도 과다운동의 결과로 발생할 수 있다.

만일 오전 심장박동이 비정상적으로 빠르다는 것을 느낀다면, 이는 당신이 운동을 지나치게 많이 한다는 뜻이다. 에어로빅 체조의 혜택을 누리기 위해서는 적절한 균형을 유지하고 과다한 운동을 피해야 한다는 사실을 명심해야 한다. 그렇지 않으면, 에어로빅의 혜택은 받지 못하고 오히려 문제만 생길 수 있다. 따라서, 만약 문제가 있다는 것을 알게 된다면, 운동으로 인해 피곤함을 느끼는 것이 아니라 기분이 좋아지는 수준까지 운동량을 줄여야 한다. 무엇보다, 운동으로 스스로를 혹사시키지도 말고, 하루 운동하지 못했다고 해서 죄책감을 느끼지도 말아라. 운동은 꾸준한 의지가 필요한 것이므로, 하루이틀 못 해도 큰 영향을 미치지는 않는다. 끈기를 갖고 오랜 기간에 걸쳐 해야만, 당신이 원하는 결과를 얻을 수 있다.

Task 2

강의 방식

Key Ideas

• 교사 위주의 수업 방식:
—교사가 수업 내용을 더 가장 잘 안다.
—수업 시간을 더 효율적으로 사용할 수 있다.
—학생은 외우기만 하면 된다.

• 학생이 참여하는 수업 방식:
—정보화 시대에는 비판적 사고가 필요하다.
—교사의 일방적인 수업은 수동적인 학생을 만든다.
—토론과 발표를 통해 능동적인 학습을 유도해야 한다.

Vocabulary Brainstorming

대화: dialogue, conversation, exchange of ideas
교육: education, schooling
산업화: industrialization
수동적 학습: passive learning
일방적 지도: unilateral teaching
교사 위주의 수업: teacher-directed class
외우다: memorize
필기를 하다: take notes in class
정보화 시대: the Information Era
쌍방향 교육: interactive / two-way learning
능동적 학습: active learning
비판적, 창의적 사고: critical, creative mind / thinking
양성하다: foster
토론: discussion
발표: presentation

Basic Sentence Writing Practice

1. 교사 주도의 수업은 가장 시간 효율적인 지도 방법이다.

> **연구** 교사 주도의 teacher-centered, teacher-directed
> 가장 …하다: 최상급을 사용
> 시간 효율적인: time-efficient

2. 그 어느 누구도 교사만큼 그 수업 내용을 잘 알지 못한다.

> **연구** 부정문을 이용한 최상급 표현이다. Nobody… better than … 으로 처리. 또는 The teacher is the one who … best 도 같은 의미.

3. 학생들은 학우의 발표를 들음으로써 혼란스러워 할 것이다.

> **연구** 혼란스러워 하다 get confused. 이때 confusing 과 confused의 차이에 유의. '혼란스럽게 만드는'은 confusing, '혼란스러워 하는'은 confused. 함으로써 by ~ing

4. 만약 교사가 모든 말을 다 하면, 학생들은 그저 수업 시간에 듣는 내용을 외우기만 하면 된다.

> **연구** 모든 말을 다 하다 do all the talking
> 외우다 memorize

5. 이러한 일방적 교육 방식의 주요 단점 중 하나는 그것이 수동적인 학습자를 만든다는 것이다.

> (연구) 단점 shortcoming, disadvantage, drawback
> 일방적 unilateral
> 수동적 학습자 passive learner

6. 창의적이고 비판적인 사고를 길러 주기 위해, 학생들이 수업 시간에 능동적인 역할을 할 수 있도록 해야 한다.

> (연구) … 하기 위해 to + 부정사
> 기르다, 양성하다 to foster
> 창의적인 creative   비판적인 critical
> 할 수 있도록 해야 한다 should be allowed + to 부정사
> 능동적 역할을 하다 take an active part, play an active role

7. 우리가 대화에 참여할 때, 우리는 논리적인 주장을 제시하기 위해 우리의 생각을 날카롭게 하는 것을 배운다.

> (연구) …에 참여하다 be involved in, be engaged in, participate, take part in
> 날카롭게 하다 sharpen up
> 논리적 주장 a logical argument

8. 보다 능동적인 학습 방식을 설계하기 위해 소크라테스와 공자 같은 위대한 교사들이 사용한 양방향 교육 방식을 고려해야 한다.

> (연구) 소크라테스 Socrates   공자 Confucious
> 양방향 two-way, interactive
> 학습 방식 learning format

Basic Sentence

1. The teacher-directed class is the most time-efficient teaching method.
2. Nobody knows the content of a class better than the teacher.
3. Students would get confused by listening to their classmates' presentations.
4. If the teacher does all the talking, the students just have to memorize what they hear in class.
5. One of the main drawbacks of this unilateral teaching method is that it creates passive learners.
6. To foster creative and critical minds, students should be allowed to take an active part in class.
7. When we are engaged in a conversation, we learn to sharpen up our ideas to present a logical argument.
8. The two-way educational methods used by great teachers like Socrates and Confucious should be considered to design a more active learning format.

Sample Essay

The most primitive format of education was based on dialogues between a teacher and his students. The exchange of ideas between Socrates and his followers is a good case in point. With industrialization, however, school became a training center for propective workers in factories. Teacher-directed class became the norm because it was considered the most time-efficient way to foster passive workers. Now in the Information Era, such a passive learning method cannot meet the intellectual requirements of the modern, complex society.

Most of us are used to teacher-directed class format. While the teacher does all the talking, we have to just take notes and do the assigned homework. A high test score served as reliable proof that we digested well what we had learned in class. One of the main drawbacks of this unilateral teaching method is that it creates passive learners. Since the basic task of a student is to just memorize what's being told, he or she does not use his critical thinking. Regurgitating what one heard in class is not evidence of his or her intelligence. Today's society needs people who can think critically and creatively. To foster creative, critical minds, students should be allowed to take an active part in class.

Both Confucious and Socrates, the two major scholars of the East and the West, are known to have taught their students through dialogues. That means they did not do all the talking. Instead, they let their students participate in the learning by exchanging ideas. When one is engaged in a conversation, he learns to sharpen up his ideas to present a logical argument. In modern schools, I think students can learn to arrange their ideas in a more logical manner through presentations or discussions in class.

I remember I once had to do a group presentation in a social studies class. First, we gathered as much information on the topic as possible. This part did not take up much energy or time. What was very time-consuming was deciding how to present the topic. It was very perplexing in the beginning. We did not know how to arrange all the information we collected. Fortunately, after much discussion, we found a good focus on which to base our presentatoin. From that experience, I learned that knowing details of a topic is not enough. Facts can be easily retrieved from diverse sources including the Internet. What really matters is how logically we arrange the facts we have collected. I would not have learned this if I had not had an opportunity to take an active role in class.

In the Information Era, critical and creative thinking is more important than ever. Given this, I believe interactive learning, in which students actively participate in class, should be encouraged. Presentations and discussions are good ways to make students get involved in the learning process. The two-way educational methods used by such great teachers as Socrates and Confucious should be considered to design a more active learning format.

Essay Translation

가장 원시적인 형태의 교육은 교사와 학생간의 대화를 위주로 이루어졌다. 소크라테스와 그의 추종자들 사이의 의견교환이 좋은 사례이다. 하지만 산업화로 인해 학교는 공장에서 일하게 될 노동자들을 훈련하는 곳이 되었다. 교사위주의 수업이 수동적인 노동자 양성을 위해 가장 시간 효율적인 방법이라고 여겨졌기 때문에, 이러한 방식의 수업이 주를 이루게 되었다. 오늘날의 정보시대에서는 그러한 수동적 학습 방법은 복잡한 현대사회의 지적 요구수준을 충족시키지 못한다.

우리의 대부분은 교사위주의 수업 형태에 익숙해 있다. 교사 혼자서 말을 하는 동안 우리는 그저 필기를 하고, 숙제를 해야 한다. 높은 시험점수는 우리가 수업시간에 배운 내용을 잘 이해했다는 믿을 만한 증거였다. 이러한 일방적 교습 방식의 주요 단점 중 하나는 학생을 수동적으로 만든다는 것이다. 학생은 그저 듣는 것을 외우기만 하면 되기 때문에, 비판적인 사고를 하지 못한다. 수업시간에 들은 내용을 그대로 되뇌는 것으로 그 학생의 지능을 알 수는 없다. 오늘날의 사회는 비판적 그리고 창의적 사고를 가진 사람들을 필요로 하고 있다. 창의적이고 비판적인 사고를 기르기 위해서는 학생들이 수업에 적극 참여할 수 있도록 해야 한다.

각각 동양과 서양의 주요 학자인 공자와 소크라테스는 대화를 통해 학생을 가르쳤던 것으로 알려졌다. 이는 그들만이 말을 하지는 않았다는 뜻이다. 그 대신, 의견을 주고받음으로써 학생들이 학습과정에 참여할 수 있도록 해주었다. 대화를 하는 사람은 논리적인 주장을 발표하기 위해 좀 더 예리하게 생각하게 된다. 나는 현대 학교에서는 학생들이 수업시간에 발표와 토론을 함으로써 자신의 생각을 좀 더 논리적으로 정리할 수 있다고 생각한다.

한번은 사회학 수업시간에 그룹 발표를 해야 했었다. 먼저 우리는 발표 주제에 대한 정보를 최대한 많이 모았다. 이 부분은 그다지 많이 힘들거나 시간이 오래 걸리지 않았다. 시간이 정말 많이 걸린 부분은 그 주제를 어떻게 발표할지 결정하는 일이었다. 처음에는 정말 어떻게 해야 할지 몰랐다. 우리는 그 동안 모은 정보를 어떻게 정리해야 할 지 몰랐다. 다행히도 오랜 토론 끝에, 어떤 관점에서 주제를 발표해야 할지 알아냈다. 그 때의 경험을 통해 나는 한 주제를 자세하게 아는 것으로는 충분하지 않다는 것을 배웠다. 정보는 인터넷을 포함해 다양한 출처에서 쉽게 찾을 수 있다. 정말 중요한 것은 그렇게 찾은 정보를 얼마나 논리 정연하게 정리하느냐이다. 만일 수업에 적극적으로 참여할 기회가 없었다면 이러한 사실을 알지 못했을 것이다.

정보시대에는 비판적, 창의적 사고가 그 어느 때보다 중요하다. 이 점을 감안할 때, 나는 학생들이 수업에 적극 참여하는 쌍방향 교육이 장려되어야 한다고 생각한다. 발표와 토론은 학생이 학습과정에 참여할 수 있도록 하는 좋은 방법들이다. 보다 역동적인 학습방법을 만들기 위해서는 과거 소크라테스 및 공자와 같은 학자들이 사용했던 양방향 교육 방법이 고려되어야 한다.

Writing Answers

Integrated Writing

1 지구온난화

Reading Translation

지구의 미래가 당면한 가장 심각한 위협 중 하나는 온실효과라고도 알려진 지구온난화이다. 과학자들은 지구의 기온이 갈수록 조금씩 상승한다는 것과, 이 같은 온난화가 전 세계적으로 파괴적인 효과를 낳을 수 있다는 사실을 발견하였다. 약간의 기온상승에 따른 변화들이 벌써부터 분명하게 나타나고 있다. 예를 들어, 알프스 산맥의 식물들을 연구한 결과, 추운 지역에서 자라는 식물들이 기온상승으로 인해 더 높고 추운 곳으로 이동하고 있는 것으로 나타났다.

하지만, 지구온난화가 전 세계에 미치는 영향은 이보다 더 클 것으로 예상된다. 극지방의 만년설이 녹아 전 세계의 해수면이 올라 가면서 저지대의 침수사태가 발생할 수 있다. 허리케인과 열대성 태풍의 강도가 심해져, 이에 따른 피해가 늘어날 수도 있다. 또한, 더욱 광범위한 해안침식이 일어나고, 해수면 상승으로 습지가 사라지게 될 것이다. 1992년에 유엔이 발표한 보고서에 따르면, 만약 이산화탄소 및 기타 다른 온실가스의 배출량이 현 수준으로 증가한다면, 방글라데시와 네덜란드의 해안평원은 2100년경에 물에 잠기게 되고, 몰디브 섬들은 완전히 사라지게 될 것이다. 해수면이 2피트만 올라가도 이 규모의 피해가 발생할 것이다.

지구온난화의 원인은 다양하다. 그 중 하나는 산림의 파괴이다. 나무들은 대기로부터 이산화탄소를 제거해 주는 가장 중요한 자연적 장치인데, 매일 5천5백 에이커 가량의 숲이 파괴되면서 전 세계적으로 이산화탄소 농도가 연 0.4%씩 증가해 수백만 년 만에 최고치를 기록하고 있다. 인구증가도 지구온난화에 영향을 미친다. 지구온난화를 완화하기 위해 우리 모두가 할 수 있는 일이 몇 가지 있다. 전력소비를 줄이고, 집의 남쪽에 나무를 심고, 에너지 효율적인 자동온도조절장치를 설치하는 것 등이다.

Listening Translation

교수

자, 여러분, 오늘은 아주 "뜨거운" 주제 … 지구온난화에 대해 배울 차례이다. 여러분도 나처럼 언론을 통해 이 주제에 대해 끊임없이 듣고 있을 것이다. 그러니 지구온난화가 정치적으로 가장 중대한 문제 중 하나라는 사실도 알 것이다. 사람들은 대기의 이산화탄소가 늘어나기 때문에 ─ 이는 기술발달과 산림파괴에 따른 결과이다 ─ 지구온난화 현상이 발생하고, 이는 우리의 환경에 파괴적인 결과를 낳을 것이라고 주장한다. 하지만, 실상을 들여다 보면, 지구온난화는 수백만 명의 사람들이 진실로 받아들인 하나의 허구에 불과하다.

대기의 이산화탄소 배출량이 증가하고 있는 것은 사실이지만, 이산화탄소의 증가량은 인간이 석탄, 석유, 천연가스를 태워 발생시키는 이산화탄소 양과 일치하지 않는다. 그러니까 … 이는 인간의 활동과 전혀 상관이 없을 수도 있다는 말이다. 그저 환경의 자연스러운 현상 … 아마 태양에너지의 변동에 따른 현상일 수도 있다. 그리고 이산화탄소 증가율은 사실 미미한 수준이다.
지구온난화를 막을 수 있는 다른 요소들도 있다. 예를 들어, 열대 우림과 초원지대를 태울 때 생기는 연기는 기온을 끌어내리는 효과를 가진다. 이 같은 효과는 불에서 나오는 온실가스의 온난화 효과와 맞먹는다.

사실, 현재 과학자들은 지구온난화의 가설이 더 이상 유효하지 않다고 말하고 있다. 이들은 지난 50년 간의 기온을 정확하게 측정함으로써, 이러한 사실을 검증할 수 있었다. 이 측정 결과는 우려할 만한 지구온난화는 일어나지 않는다는 것을 분명하게 보여 준다. 그리고 … 앞으로도 그러할 가능성은 거의 없다. 재앙적인 기온 상승은 그동안 과학자들이 집계한 통계자료와 맞아떨어지지 않는다. 그러니까, 다음에 누군가가 지구온난화 문제를 언급한다면, 여러분은 두 단어로 대답할 수 있다: "허위 경고"라고

Answer

Global warming has been presented as a major threat to our environment, and even our lives. Some claim that the earth is heating up quickly due to greenhouse gases generated by the use of coal, oil, and electricity, and that the effects will be catastrophic. The ice caps will melt, and the sea level will rise, causing flooding, erosion, and more violent storms.

However, scientists have been unable to verify the global warming hypothesis in 50 years of careful data-gathering. They have measured the earth's temperature precisely for the past 50 years. But they find no evidence of the type of major catastrophic global warming that has been claimed will occur. Instead, they find that although the earth is warming slightly, there is no indication that it will warm up enough to cause all of the major impacts claimed by global warming theorists. They also discovered that our use of coal, oil, and electricity really has nothing to do with the slight warming that is taking place. It is more likely related to fluctuations in the sun's energy instead. One of the observations of global warming theorists is true. That is that there is a higher level of carbon dioxide in the atmosphere than there used to be. However, the rise is probably caused by other environmental factors and not by anything that people are doing.

Answer Translation

지구온난화는 우리 환경, 그리고 심지어 우리의 생명에 대한 가장 큰 위협 중 하나로 대두되었다. 혹자는 지구의 온도가 빠르게 상승하는 이유가 석탄, 석유, 그리고 전기의 사용으로 인한 온실가스 때문이며, 이는 재앙적인 결과를 낳을 것이라고 주장한다. 만년설이 녹고, 해수면이 상승하여, 침수, 침식, 그리고 더 강력한 태풍 등이 야기될 것이라고 주장한다.

하지만, 과학자들은 조심스럽게 자료를 수집해온 지난 50년 동안 지구온난화 가설을 입증하지 못했다. 이들은 지난 50년간 지구의 온도를 정확하게 측정하였다. 하지만 일부에서 주장하는 것처럼 재앙적인 지구온난화가 발생할 것이라는 그 어떠한 증거도 찾지 못했다. 과학자들은, 비록 지구가 따뜻해지고 있는 것은 사실이지만, 지구온난화 이론가들이 주장하는 것처럼 대대적인 타격을 미칠 정도의 기온상승은 일어나지 않을 것으로 보인다고 말한다. 과학자들은 또한 석탄, 석유, 그리고 전기의 사용이 현재 진행되고 있는 미미한 기온상승과도 아무런 상관이 없다는 사실을 알게 되었다. 그보다는 태양에너지의 변동과 관련이 있을 가능성이 더 높다. 지구온난화 이론가들이 주장하는 것 중 한 가지는 사실이다. 예전보다 대기의 이산화탄소 농도가 높아졌다는 것이다. 하지만, 이 같은 이산화탄소의 증가는 인간의 활동으로 인한 것이 아니라, 다른 환경적 요소에 따른 결과인 것으로 보인다.

2 세계화

Reading Translation

세계화는 국가 간의 경계선을 없애 교역과 투자의 자유로운 이동을 구현하기 위한 노력이다. 세계화의 목적은 국제경제를 통합하는 것이다. 세계화로 인해, 국가 사이의 불평등이 많이 해소되었다. 저개발국가들은 해외 자본을 유치할 수 있고 국제수출시장에 진입할 수 있다. 그리고 선진 기술을 배울 수 있다. 보호받는 국내 생산업체들의 독점체제가 무너지고, 저개발국가 국민들의 생활수준이 향상된다. 이 같은 향상은 빠른 성장을 가능케 해, 빈곤이 완화되고 더 높은 생활수준이 실현된다.

세계화의 특징 중 하나는 전문화이다. 전문화는 각 나라나 지역이 가장 잘 재배할 수 있는 농산물을 재배하고, 가장 잘 만들 수 있는 제품을 생산할 수 있도록 해 준다. 예를 들어, 만약 중국이 쌀 재배에 완벽한 기후 때문에 다른 나라들보다 더 효율적으로 쌀을 재배할 수 있고, 오리건주는 중국과 같은 이유로 다른 어느 지역보다 목재를 더 잘 생산할 수 있다면, 중국과 오리건주는 서로 쌀과 목재를 무역할 수 있다. 이 같은 교역활동의 결과로, 양측 모두 예전보다 더 많은 쌀과 목재를 확보할 수 있기 때문에, 양측 모두 번영한다.

우간다 농민들은 생존농업으로 연명하며 굶주림에 허덕이곤 했다. 그러다가 유럽에 수출할 꽃을 재배하기 시작하면서, 그렇게 하면 더 많은 돈을 벌 수 있다는 사실을 알게 되었다. 그 돈으로 자신들이 생존농업을 통해 생산할 수 있는 것보다 훨씬 더 많은 식량을 구입할 수 있었다. 이것은 세계화의 혜택을 보여 주는 일례이다. 빈곤국가들은 자신들이 들어갈 수 있는 틈새시장을 찾아 발전할 수 있는 기회를 얻는다. 궁극적으로 세계화는 빈곤을 퇴치하고, 모든 이들에게 공평한 국제환경을 조성할 수 있을 것이다.

Listening Translation

교수

오늘은 세계화의 역기능에 대해 말하겠다. 우리는 흔히 세계화가 세계 빈곤 문제에 대한 해결책이라고 생각한다. 물론 세계화가 빈곤을 완화할 수 있는 잠재력을 갖고 있기는 하지만, 많은 문제점들도 수반한다.

세계화로 인해 희생되는 것 중 하나는 국가 간의 차이이다. 모든 이들은 경쟁에서 이기기 위해 선진국에서 하는 것이라면 무엇이든 따라한다. 따라서 여러 지역에서 전통적으로 내려져 온 관행은 사라지게 된다. 다양성이 없어지는 것이다. 모든 것이 "똑같아진다"고 할 수 있다. 모든 것이 똑같아져서, 어느 국가나 지역의 특산물만이 갖고 있던 특징들이 사라지게 된다.

개발도상국의 소규모 농장주들에 대해서도 생각해 볼 필요가 있다. 이 농부에게는 시장에 내놓을 준비가 다 된 쌀 수확물이 있다고 가정해 보자. 그런데 이 농부는 세계의 큰 국가들과 경쟁하고 있다는 사실을 잊으면 안 된다 … 갑자기 세계 곳곳에서 쌀 가격이 내려 가면, 이 농부는 자신의 수확물을 팔 수 없게 된다. 만약 그가 큰 나라의 대규모 농장주라면, 다른 걸 재배할 수도 있을 것이다. 하지만 이 작은 농장주는 그렇게 할 수가 없다. 그렇게 할 만한 자원을 가지고 있지 않기 때문이다. 따라서 그는 경제적 파탄을 겪게 된다. 자 … 이것은 세계화의 심각한 역기능이다. 약한 자가 강한 자와 겨뤄야 하는데, 약한 자는 당연히 매우 불리한 조건에 처해 있는 것이다.

세계화는 국가 경제를 파괴하고 국내 생산업자들을 파산으로 이끌 수 있다. 세계화된 경제에서 성공할 수 있는 기회는 무한대이지만, 실패할 가능성 또한 그렇다. 개발도상국들은 경쟁에서 살아 남고, 세계시장에서 경쟁하는 과정에서 경제적인 파탄을 맞지 않기 위해서는 훈련과 조언을 필요로 한다. 우리는 세계화에 문을 활짝 열기 전에, 견제와 균형이 제대로 이루어지고 있는지 확인해 봐야 한다.

Answer

There are a lot of arguments for and against globalization. On the one hand, globalization removes trade and economic barriers around the world, enabling smaller nations to compete successfully with larger ones. In that sense, globalization could eventually bring every nation into its own prosperous niche and wipe out poverty worldwide.

On the other hand, there are a lot of unresolved problems with globalization, too. Local producers everywhere could go out of business because they are unable to compete with the lower prices on exports coming in from other nations. When global pricing forces them out of the market with their current crop, they have no time to turn around and produce a different crop. They are simply not equipped to compete with larger, technologically advanced nations. And as the local producers go out, diversity and the regional character go with them. Everything becomes just like whatever the biggest nations are producing.

For globalization to work, it must be integrated with protections for local growers and initiatives to train and mentor developing nations. The opportunities in globalization are unlimited, and with mentoring assistance, smaller nations could take advantage of those opportunities without risking everything. With those safeguards in place, globalization could improve the global economy and promote better trade around the world.

Answer Translation

세계화에 대해서는 찬성하는 주장도 반대하는 주장도 많다. 한편으로, 세계화는 전 세계의 무역장벽과 경제장벽을 무너뜨려, 작은 국가들이 큰 국가들과 성공적으로 경쟁할 수 있게 해 준다. 그런 면에서, 세계화는 궁극적으로 모든 나라들이 번영하고 빈곤을 퇴치하는 데 기여할 것이다.

또 다른 한편으로는, 세계화와 관련된 미결 문제들도 많이 있다. 국내 생산업자들은 다른 나라의 저가 수입품 때문에 제대로 경쟁할 수 없어 파산할 수도 있다. 국제가격 하락으로 자신들이 재배하는 것을 시장에 내놓을 수 없게 되면, 이들은 다른 농작물을 재배할 시간이 없다. 더 크고, 최첨단 기술로 무장한 국가들과 경쟁할 준비가 되어 있지 않은 것이다. 그리고 국내생산업자들이 사라지면, 다양성과 지역적인 특성 또한 사라지게 된다. 모든 것이 그저 강대국이 만드는 것과 똑같아진다.

세계화가 효과적으로 진행되기 위해서는, 국내 농민들에 대한 보호와 개발도상국들에 대한 훈련 프로그램이 함께 이루어져야 한다. 세계화로부터 얻을 수 있는 기회는 무제한적이기 때문에, 개발도상국들도 적절한 교육이 담긴 지원만 받을 수 있다면 그 기회들을 잡을 수 있을 것이다. 이러한 보호장치만 있다면, 세계화는 세계경제를 활성화시키고 세계교역을 증진시킬 수 있을 것이다.

3 홈스쿨링

Reading Translation

홈스쿨링은 학부모와 아이들에게 큰 호응을 얻고 있는 새로운 교육 스타일이다. 홈스쿨링을 받은 아이들은 최대한의 개별적인 교습을 받으며 그들만의 학습 속도에 맞게 공부할 수 있다. 쉬운 부분은 빨리 넘어갈 수 있어 지루하지 않고, 어려운 부분은 천천히 공부할 수 있어 혼동과 불완전한 이해를 막을 수 있다. 학생들은 불공평한 교사들, 학교친구들의 괴롭힘, 나쁜 영향을 미치는 아이들, 혹은 부모가 못마땅해 하는 도덕적·종교적 신념을 피할 수 있다.

비록 홈스쿨링을 반대하는 사람들은 홈스쿨링을 받은 학생들이 사회에 대한 적응능력이 부족하다고 지적하지만, 그동안의 경험은 이 같은 주장을 뒷받침하지 못한다. 홈스쿨링을 받은 아이들은 그 어떠한 사회적 장애도 보이지 않는다. 오히려, 공립학교에 다니는 아이들보다 사회성이 좋고, 학우들의 압력도 덜 받게 된다.

자신의 아이들을 자택에서 공부시키는 부모들은 홈스쿨링을 성공적으로 하기 위해서는 몇 가지 주의할 사항이 있다고 말한다. 첫째, 대체로 공립학교제도는 홈스쿨링에 찬성하지 않는다고 경고한다. 어떤 제도는 홈스쿨링지원프로그램을 제공하지만, 대부분은 학생들의 교육을 통제하기 위한 또 다른 방법에 지나지 않는다. 학부모들은 이 같은 프로그램에 등록하지 말라고 경고한다. 만약 등록하면, 아이들이 무엇을 배울지에 대한 결정권을 학교에서 갖게 된다. 둘째, 이들 부모들은 단지 교실환경을 모방하기 위해 홈스쿨링을 시킬 것이 아니라, 학습환경을 자유롭게 관리할 수 있는 점을 적극 활용해야 한다고 말한다.

홈스쿨링을 비판하는 사람들도 있기는 하지만, 실제로 경험해 본 사람들은 하나같이 홈스쿨링의 장점을 극찬한다. 홈스쿨링이 공립학교보다 더 나은 학습환경을 제공할 뿐만 아니라, 부모들은 종종 저소득층 학군의 무관심한 교사들보다 아이들을 더 잘 가르친다. 미국, 일본 등 전 세계의 많은 국가에서 홈스쿨링은 성공을 거두었다.

Listening Translation

교수

요즘 들어 홈스쿨링이 큰 인기를 끌고 있는 만큼, 홈스쿨링이 여러 가지 교육문제에 대한 완벽한 해결책이 될 수 없는 이유 몇 가지를 살펴 보는 것이 좋을 것 같다. 첫째, 가정에서 교육받는 아이들은 외부세계로부터 격리되고, 그 결과 사회생활을 하는 데 어려움을 겪는다. 이 아이들은 자신들의 부모형제 하고만 상호작용하는 것을 배운다. 그리도 또 … 공립학교에서나 가능한 다양한 신념과 배경에 노출되어 있지 않다.

교습 훈련의 문제도 있다. 학교 교사들은 정부가 정한 기준에 부합해야 하고, 가르치기 위해서는 그에 필요한 자격증을 취득해야 한다. 하지만 부모들은 각 주제에 대한 학문적인 지식이 부족할 뿐만 아니라 교습 훈련도 받지 않은 사람들이다. 부모들은 학생들에게 자신들이 잘 아는 분야에 대해서만 가르칠 가능성이 있는데, 그렇게 되면 … 아이가 잘 하는 것과 잘 하지 못하는 것 사이의 격차가 더 벌어질 수 있다.

부모들은 또한 아이를 가르치는 일과, 기타 다른 일상적인 일을 균형 있게 잘 해나가지 못할 수도 있다. 가정 내에서 체계가 잘 잡히지 않았다면, 학습환경도 영향을 받을 수밖에 없다. 아이들의 학습에 필요한 자료에도 한계가 있을 수밖에 없다. 집에는 화학실험실이나 외국어 공부에 필요한 시청각 교실이 없다. 뿐만 아니라 부모들은 견학, 전문교사, 그리고 매일매일 필요한 학습자료 등을 아이에게 제공해 줄 만한 경제력이 부족할 수도 있다. 그리고 연극동아리, 밴드, 팀 스포츠와 같은 과외활동도 불가능하다. 비록 홈스쿨링에는 장점이 많다고들 하지만, 부모들은 이 대안을 신중하게 고려하여, 아이들에게 정말 포괄적이고 균형 잡힌 교육을 제공해 줄 수 있을지를 결정해야 한다.

Answer

There are many arguments both for and against home schooling. On the plus side, home-schooled children get individual attention and can work at their own pace. The negative aspects of public education, such as inappropriate subject matter and exposure to bad influences, are eliminated. Home-schooled children also seem to be very well socialized, contrary to public opinion. However, there are drawbacks, too. Parents cannot possibly provide all of the educational resources in their own homes that are available in public schools — science labs, language labs, and textbooks, for example. Many critics say that children suffer from the lack of diversity they would find in public school. And it is hard for parents to provide all the educational opportunities and equipment that schools can provide, such as specialized tutors and field trips.

Then there are some parents who are just not structured or trained enough to be teachers. Parents may restrict themselves mainly to only the subjects they can do well in themselves. In spite of all these drawbacks, however, home-schooled students generally seem to do extremely well. With the many positive and negative aspects of home schooling, parents should choose carefully when it comes to deciding whether to home school or not. Above all, they should carefully evaluate their own abilities as teachers and their capacity to provide adequate educational resources before making their final decision.

Answer Translation

홈스쿨링을 찬성하는 주장도 반대하는 주장도 많다. 장점을 먼저 보자면, 홈스쿨링을 받은 아이들은 개별적인 교육을 받고 자신에게 맞는 속도로 공부할 수 있다. 부적절한 주제와 악영향에의 노출 등 공공교육의 부정적인 측면이 사라진다. 홈스쿨링을 받은 아이들은 또한 일반적인 인식과는 달리 매우 사회적이다. 하지만, 단점도 많다. 부모들은 공립학교가 제공하는 모든 교육자원을 제공해 줄 수 없다. 과학실험실, 어학시청각실, 교재 등이 그 예이다. 많은 비판가들은 아이들이 공공교육을 통해 얻을 수 있는 다양한 경험을 하지 못한다고 주장한다. 또한 부모들은 전문교사와 견학 등 학교가 제공하는 모든 교육기회와 시설을 제공해 줄 수 없다.

이외에도 아이들을 가르칠 만큼 체계적이거나 훈련을 받지 않은 부모들도 있다. 부모들은 자신이 잘 할 수 있는 과목만을 가르칠 수도 있다. 하지만 이러한 단점들이 있음에도 불구하고, 홈스쿨링을 받은 아이들은 대체로 아주 잘 해내고 있는 것 같다. 이렇듯 홈스쿨링에는 긍정적인 측면과 부정적인 측면이 모두 있는 만큼, 부모들은 홈스쿨링을 할지 안 할지를 신중하게 결정해야 한다. 무엇보다, 부모들은 자신들이 갖고 있는 교사로서의 자질과 적절한 교육 제공에 필요한 자신의 능력을 진지하게 평가한 후에 최종 결정을 내려야 할 것이다.

4 비타민 요법

Reading Translation

오늘날 많은 사람들은 건강한 식생활을 하려고 많은 노력을 하는데, 대부분의 의사들은 비타민 요법의 장점에 대해 그다지 높게 평가하지 않고 있는 듯 하다. 하지만 영양을 중요하게 생각하는 많은 내과의사들은 음식에 함유된 것 이상의 비타민과 미네랄을 섭취해 영양을 보충하는 것이 바람직하다고 믿는다. 이러한 영양보충은 전반적인 건강상태와 웰빙을 향상시킬 뿐만 아니라 특정 질병을 치료하는 데도 도움이 된다. 일례로, 투석환자들이나 간경변으로 시력문제를 앓는 알코올중독자들, 그리고 기타 아연결핍증 환자들에게는 아연을 처방해 준다. 이와 마찬가지로, 철결핍성 빈혈에는 철분을, 심한 여드름에는 비타민 A를 처방한다.

비타민 요법의 가장 저명한 선구자 중 하나인 노벨 수상자 라이너스 폴링 박사는 고용량 — 하루 권장량(RDA)을 훨씬 넘는 양 — 의 특정 비타민과 미네랄을 섭취하라고 충고한다. 폴링 박사는 괴혈병과 같은 비타민 결핍성 질환을 예방하기 위해서는 하루 권장량으로 충분하지만, 최상의 건강을 유지하는 데는 턱없이 부족하며, 우리의 몸이 건강해지고 또 그 건강을 유지하기 위해서는 하루 권장량보다 상당히 많은 양의 비타민이 필요하다고 주장했다.

폴링 박사는 비타민 C가 감기를 치료하고 다수의 흔한 질병을 예방, 혹은 치료하는 데 어떠한 역할을 하는지에 초점을 맞추어 연구하였다. 폴링 박사는 대부분의 포유동물은 그들의 몸이 필요로 하는 비타민 C를 체내에서 생산하지만, 인간에게는 이러한 능력이 없다고 지적했다. 따라서, 인간은 음식과 영양보조식품 등을 통해 필요한 양의 비타민 C를 섭취해야 한다.

임산부 등 일부 경우에는 고용량의 비타민을 삼가야 하고, 소비자들은 영양보충요법에 너무 많은 기대를 걸지 않도록 조심해야 한다. 하지만 대체로는, 폴링 박사가 권장한 고용량의 비타민이 우리의 몸을 최상의 건강 상태로 유지하는 데

필요하다고 여겨진다.

Listening Translation

교수

여러분들은 대부분 코를 훌쩍대면 언제나 고용량의 비타민을 섭취하는 습관이 있는 것으로 안다. 그리고 감기가 걸려 비타민 C를 먹으면, 어느 정도 상태가 좋아지는 것을 느꼈을 것이다. 하지만 모든 의사들이 메가비타민요법에 찬성하는 것은 아니라는 점을 알아야 한다. 대부분의 의사들은, 음 … 물론 우리 모두 어느 정도의 비타민은 필요하지만, 잘 먹고 균형잡힌 식생활을 하는 한, 우리가 섭취하는 음식으로부터 필요한 양의 비타민을 얻을 수 있다고 믿는다. 그리고 모든 비타민과 미량영양소를 충분히 섭취하고 싶다면, 법정 일일 권장량을 모두 충족하는 종합비타민제를 먹으면 된다고 한다.

많은 의사들은 메가비타민 요법을 못마땅하게 생각한다. 이들은 비타민 요법이 다발성 경화증과 같은 심각한 증상을 향상시키거나 치료한다는 과학적 증거가 없다고 주장한다. 게다가, 비타민의 과다 섭취는 심각한 부작용을 낳을 수도 있다. 예를 들어, 비타민 A를 너무 많이 섭취하면, 두통이나 다른 증상들을 일으킬 수 있다. 한편 비타민 B6의 과다섭취는 다발성 경화증이 일으키는 것과 비슷한 신경손상을 유발할 수 있다. 비타민 D의 과다섭취는 간에 손상을 입힐 수 있다.

이렇듯 … 음 … 질병치료를 위해 고용량의 비타민을 섭취하는 것은 바람직하지 않다. 어떤 증상이든 메가비타민으로 치료하려 하기 전에, 주치의와 상담하는 것이 안전하다.

Answer

Many people take large quantities of vitamins to stay healthy. According to scientist Linus Pauling, the established RDAs for vitamins are not enough to maintain good health. However, it is also true that megadoses of vitamins can be dangerous. They can cause serious side effects. For example, too much vitamin A can raise the pressure inside the skull. Furthermore, although it is true that vitamin C seems to prevent the common cold, there is no scientific proof that vitamins can help serious conditions like multiple sclerosis

Megavitamin therapy is, in fact, discouraged by many doctors. They claim that people should get needed nutrients from their food instead of taking megadoses of vitamins. They even point out that megadoses of some vitamins can trigger diseases. Too much vitamin B6 is thought to be related to multiple sclerosis, while excessive vitamin D can cause liver damage.

Given this, it is probably advisable to avoid megadoses of vitamins. Just eating a healthful, balanced diet is better. It is safe to take an all-purpose multivitamin that meets the RDA requirements. However, people wanting to remedy a specific health condition or enhance their health should consult their physician instead of just taking more vitamins.

Answer Translation

많은 사람들은 건강을 유지하기 위해 많은 양의 비타민을 섭취한다. 라이너스 폴링 박사에 따르면, 비타민 하루 권장량은 최상의 건강을 유지하는 데 충분하지 않다. 하지만, 고용량의 비타민이 위험할 수 있다는 것도 사실이다. 이는 심각한 부작용을 일으킬 수 있다. 예를 들어, 비타민 A를 너무 많이 섭취하면, 뇌에 대한 부담이 가중될 수 있다. 또한, 비타민 C가 감기예방에 효과적이기는 하지만, 다발성 경화증과 같이 심각한 증상에 비타민이 효과적이라는 과학적인 증거는 없다.

사실 많은 의사들은 메가비타민요법을 못마땅하게 생각한다. 이들은 필요한 양의 비타민을 음식에서 얻어야지, 고용량의 비타민 섭취를 통해 얻어서는 안 된다고 한다. 이들은 심지어 일부 비타민의 고용량 섭취는 질병을 유발할 수 있다고 지적한다. 비타민 B6의 과다섭취는 다발성 경화증과 관련이 있는 것으로 알려졌으며, 비타민 D의 과다섭취는 간에 손상을 입힐 수 있다.

이러한 점들을 고려해 볼 때, 고용량의 비타민을 피하는 것이 바람직해 보인다. 그저 건강하고 균형잡인 식생활을 하는 것이 낫다. 그리고 비타민 하루 권장량을 충족시키는 종합비타민제를 먹는 것이 안전하다. 또한, 특정 건강문제를 치료하거나, 전반적인 건강을 향상시키고자 하는 사람들은 무턱대고 비타민을 섭취할 것이 아니라, 담당 내과의사와 상담하는 것이 좋다.

5 TV 시청

Reading Translation

TV 시청이 아이들에게 미칠 수 있는 부정적인 영향에 대해 우리는 이제서야 조금씩 알아가고 있다. 그동안 우리는 TV가 그저 수동적인 경험에 불과하다는 것만 알았다. 시청자는 거의 생각하거나 움직이지 않고, 단지 텔레비전 앞에 앉아 화면을 본다. 또한 우리는 텔레비전 방송내용의 대부분이 아이들에게 부적절하다는 사실도 알게 되었다. 심지어 만화까지도 폭력적이거나, 우리가 의도적으로는 절대로 허용하지 않을 개념들을 아이들에게 소개한다.

하지만, 최근 들어서야 TV 시청이 독서동기를 잃게 함으로써 아이의 학습능력을 저해할 수 있다는 사실이 밝혀졌다. 어떤 프로그램을 보든지 간에, 아이는 TV시청을 하는 동안 무언가에 매료된다. 부모들은 아이들이 넋을 잃고 TV를 본다고 말한다. 마리 윈씨는 저서 "마약을 켜다 (Plug-In Drug)"에서 "우리는 아이가 텔레비전을 볼 때 능동적이거나 정신을 바짝 차리고 있는 것과는 거리가 멀다는 것을 알 수 있다."고 말한다. 윈씨는 텔레비전 시청과 아이의 독서 및 학습능력 저하 사이에는 분명한 상관관계가 있다고 주장한다. 독서를 할 때 아이는 내용을 잘 이해하기 위해 머리 속에서 장면들을 그려 보며 상상력을 발휘해야 한다. 이런 점에서, 텔레비전 시청은 그런 모든 노력을 불필요하게 만드는 수단인 것이다. 텔레비전을 많이 보는 아이들은 비시각적 경험에 대한 적응능력이 떨어질 수밖에 없다.

가장 확실한 증거는 *Pediatrics Journal* 에 상세하게 게재된 연구결과이다. 바로 텔레비전을 한 시간 볼 때마다 아이가 주의력결핍장애를 겪을 확률이 10%씩 올라간다는 것이다. 디미트리 크리스타키스 박사에 따르면, "유아 2-3세까지는 뇌의 발달이 매우 빠르게 진행된다. 그 시기에 뇌세포 사이의 연결고리가 정말 왕성하게 생겨난다. 텔레비전은 아동의 발달단계의 뇌에 필요이상의 자극을 주는 것이다". 특히 어린

이용 TV 프로그램은 아이들의 흥미를 유지시키기 위해 화면을 빠르게 바꾸기 때문에, 뇌에 대한 자극효과가 가중된다.

Listening Translation

요즈음 부모들은 아이들과 상호작용할 수 있는 방법을 몰라 쩔쩔맨다. 아이들은 한쪽 방에서 텔레비전만 보고, 부모는 다른 방에서 장부를 정리하거나 저녁식사를 준비한다. 때로는 음 … 아이들과 통합 방법이 전혀 없어 보인다. 하지만 가족이 텔레비전을 함께 본다면, 서로 더 가까워질 수도 있고 함께 더 많은 시간을 보낼 수도 있을 것이다.

물론 모든 텔레비전 프로그램이 볼만하지는 않다는 것을 나도 안다. 하지만 이러한 점이 바로 아이들과 함께 텔레비전을 봄으로써 가질 수 있는 장점이다. 부모가 아이들에게 무엇을 봐야 할지를 결정할 수 있도록 도와줄 수 있기 때문이다. 그리고 ─ 이건 여러분도 생각지 못했을 텐데 ─ 그렇게 함으로써 아이들이 실제로 보는 프로그램의 내용을 알 수도 있다. 이렇듯 아이들과 함께 텔레비전을 보면서, 부모들은 아이들이 무엇을 보는지 감시할 수 있고, 또 방송내용을 잘 이해할 수 있도록 도와줄 수 있다.

아이들과 함께 텔레비전을 보는 것의 또 다른 장점은, 아이들을 꼭 껴안아줄 수 있는 좋은 기회가 주어진다는 것이다. 나이와 상관없이, 아마도 아이는 학교에서 힘든 하루를 보냈을 것이다. 유치원에서도 친구들을 괴롭히는 아이들은 있게 마련이고, 또 무서운 선생님이나 왕따 현상 등 아이의 자신감과 편안함을 앗아가는 여러 가지 경험들이 있을 수 있다. 아이가 소파에 누워 부모에게 바짝 다가붙을 때, 아이는 자신감을 회복할 뿐만 아니라 사랑받고 있다는 느낌을 받는다. 한편 부모에게는 아이와 진정으로 하나가 되어 자신의 사랑을 전달할 수 있는 기회가 될 수 있다.

이외에도 텔레비전은 아이가 부모에게 직접 말하기 불편한 것들을 간접적으로 전달할 수 있는 방법을 제공한다. 예를 들어, 학교의 쉬는 시간에 더 큰 아이들이 당신의 아이를 괴

롭히고, 아무한테도 말하지 말라고 협박했을 수도 있다. 만약 TV 프로그램에서 이와 비슷한 상황에 처한 아이가 나온다면, 이 아이에 대해 어떻게 생각 하냐고 당신의 아이에게 살짝 물어볼 수도 있을 것이다.

Answer

TV is an excellent way to spend quality time with your children. You can cuddle with them on the couch while you watch TV and bond with them. It also allows you to see what your children watch and discuss it with them. Although there is inappropriate content in some TV shows, since you're controlling what they watch, you can screen out any content that you do not approve of.

Although children can be mesmerized by television, if you are with them talking to them about it, this will not happen. You can engage the child in conversation and keep him actively thinking and chatting so that he does not become totally absorbed in watching TV but can interact, think, and make comments.

Studies show that watching TV can induce attention deficit disorder, but these are merely saying that children learn to become impatient because TV provides such immediate stimulation. They are not accustomed to waiting for stimulation to arise naturally from staying focused on a story they are reading. Talking to your child and asking questions while you watch TV with him combats this by stimulating thought.

Keeping your child company and talking with him while he watches can eliminate most negative impacts of TV watching. And you'll have the added pleasure of developing a strong bond with your child at the same time.

Answer Translation

텔레비전 시청은 아이들과 오붓한 시간을 보낼 수 있는 좋은 방법이다. 소파에 앉아 TV를 보는 동안 아이들을 껴안아 주면서, 그들과 하나가 될 수 있다. 또한 아이들이 어떤 프로그램을 보는지 알 수 있고, 그 프로그램에 대해 아이들과 이야기할 수도 있다. 일부 프로그램의 내용은 부적절하기도 하지만, 아이들이 보는 것을 당신이 컨트롤하기 때문에, 못마땅한 내용이 있다면 이를 당신이 직접 배제할 수 있다.

아이들은 보통 넋을 잃고 텔레비전을 보지만, 부모가 아이들에게 이야기를 건네며 TV를 함께 본다면, 그런 일은 없을 것이다. 부모가 아이와 대화하고, 계속해서 말이나 생각을 하게 만든다면, 아이는 텔레비전에 푹 빠지는 대신 부모와 상호작용하고, 생각하고, 자신의 의견을 말할 것이다.

연구결과에 따르면, TV 시청은 주의력결핍장애를 유발할 수 있다. 이는 TV가 즉각적인 자극을 주기 때문에, 아이들이 갈수록 조급해진다는 것을 의미한다. 책을 읽을 때에는, 그 이야기에 집중하면서 자연스럽게 자극이 생기지만, 텔레비전을 보는 아이들은 그러한 자극을 기다리지 못한다는 것이다. 아이들과 함께 텔레비전을 보면서, 아이들에게 말을 걸고 이런저런 질문을 던지면, 아이가 생각을 하게 돼 이 같은 문제가 해소될 수 있다.

아이가 텔레비전을 볼 때, 부모가 함께 보면서 말을 걸어 주면, TV 시청의 부정적인 영향을 거의 모두 없앨 수 있다. 게다가 아이와의 관계를 돈독히 하는 즐거움을 동시에 얻을 수 있다.

6 유기농 식품

Reading Translation

오늘날의 대규모 농업에는 인체에 매우 해로운 살충제가 광범위하게 사용된다. 살충제는 암 등의 심각한 질병을 유발할 수 있기 때문에, 정부는 살충제의 화학물질 함유량 기준을 정해두었다. 하지만 조사 결과에 따르면, 대부분의 식품이 정부의 허용기준보다 더 많은 양의 살충제를 함유하고 있는 것으로 나타났다. 뿐만 아니라, 여러 살충제의 혼합으로 인한 독성이 인체에 미칠 수 있는 장기적인 영향은 아직 밝혀지지 않았다. 식품에 함유된 유독화학물질도 모자라, 식수에도 다량의 살충제와 질산염이 함유돼 있다. 식수의 독성농도를 줄이는 데 드는 비용은 납세자가 부담해야 한다.

이 같은 독성 문제에 대한 한 가지 해결방법은 바로 유기농 식품이다. 유기농업의 경우에는, 농약이 전혀 사용되지 않는다. 수확량을 늘리기 위해, 농약 대신 자연적인 방법이 사용된다. 즉, 화학비료 대신 유기질 비료를 사용하고, 토양의 질을 유지하기 위해 화학비료에 의존하는 대신 윤작을 사용하고, 환경을 파괴하는 대신 보호하는 것이다. 유기농업은, 비료생산에 사용되는 화석연료 등 재생불가능 자원에 대한 의존성을 낮추는 등 여러 혜택을 가져다 준다.

연구결과에 따르면, 유기농장은 일반농장에 비해 다섯 배의 식물을, 44% 더 많은 들판 새를, 1.6배 더 많은 절지동물(새들의 먹이가 되는 벌레들)의 서생을 가능케 하는 반면, 훨씬 더 적은 양의 해충을 유발한다. 오염되지 않은 식품이 제공하는 안전과 건강혜택 이외에도, 유기농업은 생물다양성의 증가와 환경보호의 혜택을 선사한다. 다른 보존방식의 비용이 높다는 점과, 기존농업방식의 실제 비용과 유기농업의 혜택 등을 모두 감안해 볼 때, 유기농업은 소비자의 위험을 줄이는 비용효과적인 농업방식이라고 할 수 있다.

Listening Translation

유기농업의 혜택에 대해서는 누구나 들어 봤을 것이다. 그리고 불필요한 유독화학물질을 먹고 싶어하는 사람은 없을 것이다. 하지만 … 유기농업을 지나치게 신뢰해서도 안 된다. 무엇보다 지난 50년 간 이룩한 과학기술의 발전을 과연 모두 내던져 버려야 하는지 한번 생각해 봐야 한다. 그러한 … 음 … 발전의 덕택으로 우리는 똑같은 시간 안에 훨씬 더 많은 양을 생산할 수 있는 반면, 유기농업의 수확량은 훨씬 더 낮은 수준이다. 사실상 유기농업은 굶주림에 허덕이는 이 세상의 많은 사람들을 죽음으로 몰아 넣을 수 있다. 이들이 먹어야 하는 음식을 충분히 빨리 생산해내지 못하기 때문이다.

유기농업이라도 이를 제대로 하지 않을 경우에 문제를 야기할 수 있다는 점 또한 알아야 한다. 유독화학물질을 사용하지 않는 것이 환경에 좋기는 하지만, 거름이나 기타 유기질 비료의 남용은 질소오염을 낳을 수 있다. 뿐만 아니라 유기농 식품의 가격은 기존의 농업방식으로 생산된 식품에 비해 두 배 정도 더 높다. 때문에 대부분의 소비자들은 유기농 식품을 살 수 없다. 이렇듯 소비자의 부담이 클 뿐만 아니라, 높은 가격으로 낮은 수확량을 언제나 만회할 수 있는 게 아니기 때문에 농민들이 부담해야 하는 비용도 훨씬 더 높다. 이외에도 시간 상의 문제가 있다. 한때 기존농업에 사용됐던 땅을 유기농업용 땅으로 바꾸는 데는 몇 년이 걸린다. 나는 이 문제에 대해 우리가 좀더 장기적인 안목을 갖고, 유기농법의 혜택을 누리기 위해 이 모든 것을 희생해야 하는지를 결정해야 한다고 생각한다.

Answer

There are a lot of arguments in favor of organic farming in today's world. The chemicals used for conventional farming are extremely hazardous to humans and can cause cancer and other serious diseases, for one thing. Those toxic chemicals also find their way into the environment, where they can harm the environment and the wildlife. However, organic farming is not necessarily the perfect answer to those problems, either.

Organic farming represents a move backward to the farming methods of 50 years ago, before farmers understood how to produce bigger, better crops. And without using pesticides, farmers cannot get the same yields. So organic farming means smaller yields and higher cost to the farmer as well as higher prices to the consumer. Furthermore, with the lower yields, farmers cannot produce enough food to feed the world's hungry masses before they starve to death. And even organic farming methods can pollute the environment if not used correctly; nitrogenous pollution from too much manure is just as damaging to the environment as toxic chemicals are.

While the benefits of organic farming for consumer health and environmental protection are excellent, we cannot lose sight of the benefits of conventional farming. Perhaps it would be best to combine the best of both methods to lower toxicities while maintaining production as much as possible.

Answer Translation

오늘날 유기농업에 찬성하는 주장이 많다. 먼저, 기존농업방식에 사용되는 화학물질은 인체에 극도로 위험하고, 암 등 심각한 질병을 유발할 수 있다. 이러한 유독화학물질은 환경에도 영향을 미쳐, 환경 및 야생생물에 피해를 끼칠 수 있다. 하지만 유기농업이 이 같은 문제들에 대한 완벽한 해결방법이라고도 할 수 없다.

유기농업은 50년 전, 농부들이 어떻게 하면 더 좋은 농작물을 더 많이 생산할 수 있을지 모를 때 사용되었던 농업방식으로 되돌아가는 것을 의미한다. 또 살충제를 사용하지 않고서는, 농부들은 똑같은 수확량을 생산하지 못한다. 따라서 유기농업은 농부들에게 있어 더 적은 수확량과 더 많은 비용을 의미할 뿐만 아니라, 소비자들은 더 높은 가격을 부담해야 한다. 게다가, 수확량이 줄어들면 농민들은 이 세상의 굶주리는 많은 사람들을 먹일 식량을 충분히 생산하지 못하게 돼 이들을 죽음에 이르게 할 것이다. 또한 유기농업조차도 제대로 이루어지지 않으면 환경을 오염시킬 수 있다. 유기질 비료의 남용으로 인한 질산오염은 유독화학물질만큼이나 환경에 해롭다.

소비자의 건강과 환경에 대한 유기농업의 혜택이 큰 것은 사실이지만, 기존농업방식의 혜택 또한 잊어서는 안 된다. 두 농업방식의 장점을 한데 모아 독성농도를 낮추면서 최대한의 생산량을 유지하는 것이 최선의 방법일 것이다.

7 일광 노출

Reading Translation

과다한 일광욕이 해로울 수 있다는 연구결과에도 불구하고, 많은 사람들은 여전히 구릿빛 선텐을 신분의 상징으로 여기고 있다. 햇빛은 두 종류의 자외선 — 자외선A(UVA)와 자외선B(UVB) — 를 방출하는데, 후자는 피부를 손상시킬 뿐만 아니라 시력장애, 알레르기, 그리고 면역체계의 저하를 유발한다. UVB는 화상, 조기노화, 그리고 피부암을 유발하는 것으로도 알려졌다. 불행히도 피부가 햇빛에 그을리는 과정은 피부가 화상을 입거나 손상을 입는 과정과 다르지 않다. 과다한 일광욕에 따른 피부의 손상효과는 누적되고 돌이킬 수 없기 때문이다.

피부암은 가볍게 볼 만한 질병이 아니다. 미국에서 매년 피부암 진단을 받는 백만 명의 환자 중 7천3백은 목숨을 잃는다. 일광노출시간이 더 길고 그 정도도 더 심한 태양지대에 사는 사람들은 타 지역에 사는 사람들보다 암에 걸리는 확률이 2.5배 더 높다. 백인은 피부를 보호해 줄 자연적인 차단장치가 없기 때문에 피부암으로 인한 사망률이 더 높다. 피부암 사망자의 76%는 흑생종으로 인해 목숨을 잃는다. 흑생종이란 검은 점과 흡사한 어두운 색의 반점이 특징인 피부암의 일종이다.

피부암에 걸리지 않더라도, 일광욕을 좋아하는 사람들은 조기노화 현상을 겪게 될 위험이 있다. 피부가 햇빛에 장시간 노출되다 보면 탄력을 잃어 주름이 생길 뿐 아니라, 반점이 생기거나 피부색이 변색된다. 알레르기도 또 하나의 골칫거리인데, 이것은 특정 질환이나 약물로 인해 더 심해질 수 있다.

그리고 마지막으로, 햇빛에 장시간 노출되면 일사병으로도 사망할 수 있다. 인체가 과다열을 견딜 수 있는 능력은 제한되어 있고, 여러 가지 요소들로 인해 이 같은 내성이 약해질 수 있다. 때문에, 일광욕을 할 때에는 물을 충분히 마시고, 얼굴을 덮고, 몸의 상태가 나빠지기 시작하면 서둘러 햇빛을 피하는 것이 중요하다.

Listening Translation

교수

우리의 건강을 증진시키는 가장 효과적인 물질 중 하나가 우리 모두에게 무료로 공급된다. 바로 햇빛이다. 햇빛의 장점은 오래 전에 알려졌고, 의사들은 종종 특정 질환을 앓는 환자들에게 기후가 좀더 온후한 지역에서 살 것을 권장한다.

자, 음 … 햇빛의 가장 기본적인 장점 중 하나는 적외선이다. 태양열은 신경통, 관절염 음 … 축농증 등 많은 병을 치료하는데 사용된다. 또한 햇빛은 건강하고 자연적인 윤활유를 생성해, 피부를 매끄럽게 해 주고 보호해 준다. 또 대부분의 식품이 햇빛을 받아 자라므로, 햇빛이 없다면 우리가 먹을 만한 것도 그리 많지 않을 것이다.

태양의 자외선은 박테리아와 바이러스 등 해로운 미생물을 죽이기도 한다. 사실 … 자외선은 공기와 물체 표면에 있는 진균류, 곰팡이, 진드기 등 우리가 원하지 않는 많은 것들을 죽일 수 있다. 햇빛의 힘은 너무 강력해서, 북향 창문에 반사된 햇빛이라 할지라도 창문턱과 바닥의 먼지 속에 들어 있는 박테리아를 박멸할 수 있다. 자외선의 95% 정도가 이미 창유리에 의해 여과됐어도 말이다. 자외선은 피부의 세균을 직접 죽여, 기저귀로 인한 발진, 무좀, 여드름 등의 피부병을 치료해 준다.

또한 우리가 섭취하는 비타민 D의 대부분은 햇빛으로부터 오는 것이다. 비타민 D는 체내 콜레스테롤 수치를 낮추고 우리의 몸이 칼슘을 제대로 처리할 수 있도록 도와 준다. 이러한 효과를 얻으려면, 피부의 최소 6인치 정도를 매일 한 시간씩 직사광에 노출시켜 인체가 필요로 하는 양의 비타민 D를 받아야 한다.

마지막으로, 햇빛은 대부분의 신체활동을 조절하는 데 도움이 된다. 수면, 호르몬수치, 갑상선기능, 그리고 혈당수치를 향상시킨다. 심지어 혈액산소를 증가시키기도 한다.

Answer

People today are sternly warned to avoid overexposure to the sun, since it has been linked to skin cancer. However, they are overlooking the many health benefits of sunlight for the skin and the entire body. The warmth of the sun, for instance, lubricates the skin by drawing out the skin's natural oils. And the ultraviolet rays in sunlight kill germs and other disease-causing organisms. Sunlight is used to treat various skin diseases like athlete's foot and acne. If the skin is exposed to sunlight for an hour per day, it will manufacture the day's requirement of vitamin D.

The UVB rays of the sun promote premature aging and skin cancer, but on the other hand, the sun does much to promote health as well. Sunlight kills molds, viruses, fungi, and dust mites — all of which can create serious disease. Even filtered sunlight coming in a window, for example, will kill bacteria in the dust on the windowsill, almost immediately

In addition to these benefits, sunlight has been found to regulate many body processes. Sleep, hormones, and blood sugar all respond to sunlight. Sunlight even increases the oxygen in the blood. Therefore, although it is wise to take precautions when in the sun to protect against sunburn and sunstroke, it makes sense to permit judicious sun exposure. Sunlight is a benefit provided by nature that people would do well to use.

Answer Translation

오늘날 사람들은 햇빛에 대한 과다노출을 피한다. 지나친 일광욕이 피부암을 유발할 수 있기 때문이다. 하지만 이들은 햇빛이 피부, 그리고 몸 전체에 많은 혜택을 가져다 준다는 사실을 잊고 있다. 일례로, 햇빛이 선사하는 따뜻함은 피부의 자연적인 윤활유를 생성시켜 피부를 매끄럽게 해 준다. 그리고 햇빛의 자외선은 병균 등 질병을 유발하는 미생물을 박멸한다. 햇빛은 무좀과 여드름 등 여러 가지의 피부병을 치료하는 데도 사용된다. 만일 피부가 하루에 한 시간씩 햇빛에 노출된다면, 인체가 하루에 필요로 하는 양의 비타민 D가 만들어질 것이다.

태양의 자외선B는 조기노화와 피부암을 촉진시키기는 하지만, 햇빛은 건강증진에 큰 도움을 주기도 한다. 햇빛은 심각한 질병을 유발할 수 있는 곰팡이, 바이러스, 진균류, 그리고 진드기 등을 죽인다. 심지어 창문을 통해 여과되어 들어 오는 햇빛은, 예를들어, 창문턱에 앉아 있는 먼지의 박테리아를 거의 즉각적으로 죽인다. 이러한 장점 외에도, 햇빛은 많은 신체활동을 조절해 준다는 사실이 밝혀졌다. 수면, 호르몬, 그리고 혈당은 모두 햇빛에 의해 향상된다. 햇빛은 심지어 혈액산소를 증가시키기도 한다. 따라서 물론 일광욕을 할 때에는 화상이나 일사병 등에 대한 예방조치를 취하는 것이 좋지만, 햇빛에 적당히 노출하는 것도 필요하다. 햇빛은 자연이 제공하는 혜택이므로, 사람들은 이를 마음껏 누려야 한다.

8 수분 섭취

Reading Translation

모든 생물체를 구성하는 주요 물질은 물이다. 사실상 물은 산소에 이어 두 번째로 생명에 가장 필요한 요소이다. 인체의 3분의 2가 물로 구성되어 있다. 우리의 뇌는 거의 85%가 물이며, 조직도 70% 정도가 물이다. 인간의 신체작용을 위해서는 물이 필요하다. 물은 거의 모든 종류의 물질을 용해시키고 운반할 수 있는 만능 용매이다. 물은 소화액, 혈액, 소변, 임파액, 그리고 땀 등 모든 체액의 기본을 이룬다. 인체는 물을 이용해 산소와 영양소를 세포로 운반하고, 독소와 노폐물을 체외로 배설시킨다. 노폐물이 제거되면 폐, 신장, 간장에 대한 부담이 줄어든다. 물은 체온을 조절해 주고 심지어 기관의 윤활제 역할까지 한다. 수분을 많이 섭취하면, 피부가 건강해지고 체중감량에도 도움이 된다.

수분을 섭취하는 것은 너무나도 중요해서, 필요한 만큼의 물을 마시지 않을 경우 목숨을 잃을 수도 있다. 사람은 음식을 먹지 않고는 두 달 이상도 살 수 있지만, 물을 마시지 않고는 일 주일 이상을 살 수 없다. 만일 우리의 몸에 물이 부족하다면, 갈증과 탈수 현상이 일어날 것이다. 적절한 수분량을 유지하기 위해서는, 음료수나 음식에 함유된 수분의 형태로 매일 약 1 1/2쿼트 — 컵으로 여섯 잔 — 의 물을 마셔야 한다. 많은 전문가들은 하루에 최소한 여덟 잔의 물을 마셔야 수화작용의 혜택을 온전히 누릴 수 있다고 권장한다.

적절한 수분 섭취의 효과는 확실하게 나타난다. 물을 지나치게 안 마시던 사람이 충분한 수분 섭취를 하게 되면, 자신의 몸에 큰 변화가 발생하는 것을 느낄 것이다. 컨디션도 훨씬 좋아지고, 힘도 나며, 피부색도 훨씬 밝아지는 것을 느끼게 될 것이다. 물을 마시는 것은 우리의 건강을 위해 축배를 드는 것이다.

Listening Translation

매일 적어도 여덟 잔의 물을 마셔야 한다는 것은 우리 모두가 이미 알고 있는 사실이다. 하지만 다트머스 의과대학의 헤인즈 발틴 박사는 이 같은 원칙을 뒷받침할 만한 과학적인 증거가 없다고 한다. 발틴 박사는 신장 전문의이며, 신장과 수분균형에 대해 두 권의 책을 저술하였다. 그는 전통적인 8-8 방식(매일 8온스의 물을 여덟 번 마시는 것)이 사람들의 강박관념에 불과하며, 반드시 지켜야 하는 것은 아니라고 생각한다.

발틴 박사는 건강한 성인의 인체는 적절한 수분균형을 이룰 수 있다고 믿는다. 그는 어디든 물병을 들고 다니는 사람들을 보면서, 그렇게 할 필요까지는 없다고 생각한다. 그는 우리의 몸이 많은 양의 물을 필요로 하지는 않는다고 말한다. 그리고 카페인음료는 일일 수분섭취량에서 제외시켜야 한다는 말은 허튼소리라고 말한다.

음 … 하지만 이것이 모든 사람들에게 해당하는 것은 아니다. 발틴 박사는 온화한 기후환경에 살고 대체로 정적인 생활을 하는 건강한 성인에게만 적용된다고 말한다. 그가 8-8 방식을 무시하기는 하지만, 신장결석과 같은 몇몇 질병을 예방하거나 치료하기 위해 충분한 수분 섭취가 좋다는 점은 인정한다. 또한 힘든 육체적 활동을 하거나, 장거리 비행기 여행을 하거나, 더운 날씨에 노출될 경우에는, 더 많은 양의 물을 마셔야 할 것이라고 한다. 하지만 이러한 경우를 제외하고는, 대부분의 사람들이 물을 충분히 마시고 있다고 생각한다.

발틴 박사는 과다한 수분 섭취는 오히려 건강에 해로울 수 있다고 생각한다. 물을 너무 많이 마셔서 신장이 분비를 못하게 되면, "수분중독"에 걸릴 수 있고 … 이는 정신착란, 심지어 죽음으로 이어질 수도 있다. 과다 수분 섭취의 또 다른 단점은 물에 함유된 오염물질을 마시게 되고 소변을 자주 보게 된다는 것인데 이는 불편할 뿐만 아니라 당혹스러운 일이 아닐 수 없다.

Answer

Although most experts agree that everyone should drink at least eight eight-ounce glasses of water per day (the 8 x 8 rule), at least one expert disagrees. Dr. Heinz Valtin believes that the average person really needs less than that and argues that the 8 x 8 rule is overkill. He maintains that only people with kidney stones or who are exercising heavily or living where the weather is hot need that much water. Not only that, he believes that too much water can be dangerous, or even fatal. He cites examples of water intoxication and the effects of water that has been polluted.

On the other hand, the traditional wisdom is that drinking eight glasses of water a day is health-giving. Since most of the body consists of water, and many body processes use water, it is thought that water is necessary for the body to function properly and maintain good health. The body cannot survive for more than a week without water. The old rule that says that caffeinated drinks do not count toward the daily total amount of water needed can be ignored, though. Valtin counts water from such drinks along with plain water and the water that is contained in foods eaten. Since either too much or too little water can cause serious problems, maintaining a balanced water intake is best.

Answer Translation

대부분의 전문가들은 사람이 하루에 적어도 8온스의 물을 여덟 번 마셔야 한다(8×8 방식)는 점에 동의하지만, 적어도 한 명은 그렇지 않다. 헤인즈 발틴 박사는 보통 사람의 경우, 그보다 더 적은 양의 물을 필요로 하고, 8×8 원칙은 지나치다고 주장한다. 그는 신장결석이 있거나, 운동을 많이 하거나, 더운 곳에 사는 사람들만이 그만큼의 물을 마셔야 한다고 주장한다. 또한 그는 물을 너무 많이 마시는 것은 오히려 건강에 해롭거나 치명적일 수 있다고 믿는다. 이러한 주장을 뒷받침하기 위해 그는 수분중독과 오염된 물의 섭취를 예로 든다.

한편, 일반통념은 매일 여덟 잔의 물을 마시는 것이 건강에 좋다는 것이다. 인체의 대부분이 물로 구성되어 있고, 많은 인체작용에도 물이 필요하기 때문에, 몸이 제대로 작동하고 건강을 유지하기 위해서는 물이 필요하다고 우리는 믿어 왔다. 우리의 몸은 물을 마시지 않고 일 주일 이상을 살아 남지 못한다. 하지만 카페인음료를 일일 수분섭취량에 포함하지 말아야 한다는 원칙은 무시해도 된다. 발틴 박사는 이 같은 음료에 담긴 물을, 생수, 그리고 음식에 들어 있는 수분과 함께 일일 수분섭취량에 포함시킨다. 물을 너무 많이 마셔도, 또 너무 적게 마셔도 심각한 문제가 발생할 수 있으므로, 적당한 수분섭취가 가장 좋은 방법이다.

Writing Answers

Indpendent Writing

1 대학교육

Basic Sentence

1. I think that all students should have the chance to enter a university.
2. My belief is based on the fact that the college entrance examination process is not fair.
3. The entrance exam does not measure how well a student will study his or her major.
4. Some students realize the importance of education after graduating from high school.
5. Entering a college is not the only option available to high school graduates.
6. They have to assess their talents and tendencies before choosing what to do after graduation.
7. University is an academic place where only academically talented ones can perform well
8. Tough college entrance examinations and high grade point average requirements are important parts of the screening process.

Sample Essay

After graduating from high school, one is faced with many choices. Some decide to continue studying, while others enter the world of work. It is true that in our society people regard going to university a much better choice than holding a job right after finishing high school. However, I believe higher education is only for those students who are good at and enjoy studying for the following set of reasons.

Firstly, entering a college is not the only option available to high school graduates. There are many career choices awaiting them when they finish secondary education. Some may decide to start working for a company, others may pursue their dreams which are not related to academic studying. One of my friends, for instance, wanted to be a singer and complained throughout high school that she did not have enough time to practice singing. She went to a pop music institute right after graduation and is now working as a singer for a musical band. Higher education is a good choice but not the only one for high school students. They have to assess their talents and tendencies before choosing what to do after graduation.

After all, university is an academic place that offers higher education. Not everyone can perform well in college. Only those who are academically minded and talented can enjoy the benefits of higher education. If a student did not do well in middle and high school, he is very unlikely to do well in universtiy. In a sense, secondary education is a preparatory course for higher education. Without good preparation, university education will be just a waste of time and money. This is one of the most important reasons why I believe that higher education should be available only to good students.

Lastly, if universities are open to all students without any screening process, the level of higher education will drop dramatically. Tough college entrance examinations and high grade point average requirements are important parts of the screening process. Without them, it would be difficult for universities to choose good candidates. I deplore the present reality in which all high school students have to spend too many hours studying to meet the college admission requirements. However, I believe a strict screening process is very important to maintain the quality of higher education.

My position on this statement is primarily based on the belief that college is basically an academic place where only academically talented ones can perform well. A university degree is important, but it is not the only tool to be successful in life. Those who are not good at studying may pursue other careers where they can realize their full potential. Higher education is a good choice, but not the best or the only one for every student.

Sample Essay Translation

고등학교를 졸업한 학생들은 많은 선택 앞에 놓이게 된다. 어떤 학생들은 공부의 길을 선택하는가 하면, 또 어떤 학생들은 사회생활을 시작한다. 우리 사회에서는 고등학교를 졸업하자마자 직장생활을 시작하는 것보다 대학에 진학하는 것이 훨씬 더 현명한 선택으로 여겨진다. 하지만 나는 다음의 이유로 공부를 잘 하고 또 좋아하는 학생들만이 고등교육을 받아야 한다고 생각한다.

첫째, 대학 진학만이 고등학교 졸업생들에게 있어 유일한 선택이 아니다. 고등학교를 마치고 할 수 있는 일이 많다. 회사에 취직할 수도 있고, 공부와는 별개의 꿈을 추구할 수도 있다. 예를 들어, 내 친구 한 명은 가수가 되고 싶어했는데, 고등학교생활 내내 노래연습을 할 시간이 부족하다고 불평했었다. 그 친구는 졸업하자마자 음악학원을 찾아 갔고 지금은 한 음악밴드의 보컬로 활동하고 있다. 대학교육을 받는 것도 좋지만, 그것이 고등학교 졸업생의 유일한 선택은 아니다. 그들은 졸업 후 진로를 선택하기에 앞서 자신의 재능과 취향을 파악해야 한다.

대학이란 고등교육을 제공하는 교육기관이다. 모든 사람들이 대학생활을 잘 해낼 수 있는 것은 아니다. 지적 호기심과 재능이 있는 사람만이 고등교육의 혜택을 누릴 수 있다. 중고등학교 시절에 공부를 잘 하지 못했던 학생들은 대학에서도 그러할 가능성이 크다. 어떻게 보면 고등학교는 대학생활을 준비하는 예비과정이라고 할 수 있다. 준비가 잘 되어 있지 않은 학생에게 대학교육은 단지 시간과 돈의 낭비일 수 있다. 이것이 바로 내가 대학에는 공부를 잘 하는 학생만이 가야 한다고 믿는 가장 중요한 이유 중 하나이다.

마지막으로, 만약 대학이 걸러내는 과정 없이 모든 학생을 받는다면, 고등교육의 질이 현저히 떨어질 것이다. 어려운 대학 입학 시험과 높은 학점을 요구하는 것은 걸러내는 과정의 중요한 부분이다. 이러한 과정이 없다면, 대학이 좋은 학생들을 선발하기가 힘들 것이다. 나는 모든 고등학생들이 대학입학조건을 갖추기 위해 엄청난 시간을 쏟아 부어야 하는 현실이 안타깝다. 하지만 엄격하게 학생들을 걸러내는 과정이 대학교육의 수준을 유지하기 위해서는 매우 중요하다고 믿는다.

내가 이와 같은 입장을 취하는 것은 대학이 기본적으로 공부에 소질이 있는 학생들만이 잘 해낼 수 있는 교육기관이라고 믿기 때문이다. 물론 대학 졸업장은 중요하지만, 인생에서 성공하기 위해 필요한 유일한 도구는 아니다. 공부에 소질이 없는 학생들은 자신의 잠재력을 십분 발휘할 수 있는 다른 직업을 추구하면 된다. 대학교육은 좋은 선택이지만, 모든 학생들에게 있어 가장 좋은 선택도 유일한 선택도 아니다.

2 대중 매체

Basic Sentence

1. Famous people's rights to privacy should be respected.
2. Celebrities should be able to keep their public and private lives separate.
3. Their work put them in the spotlight.
4. Television cameras often follow every move of famous stars.
5. Too much media attention can endanger the lives of famous people.
6. The broadcasters should stick to public information.
7. The media needs to respect the privacy of celebrities and public figures.
8. It seems that the media digs up these facts without thoughtful consideration.
9. The media can unjustly damage the careers of public figures by exposing details of their private lives.
10. When the media spends time scrutinizing a person's personal life, it takes time away from other important issues.

Sample Essay

It is true that the names of renowned actresses on the front page of a newspaper are more eye-catching than any economic or political news. Taking full advantage of such tendency, the media reports every move of public figures and celebrities. This often infringes upon their privacy, and can even damage their public careers. Then, one may wonder whether the media has such authority to expose someone's personal life to the public. I disagree that the mass media can report the personal lives of famous people for the following set of reasons.

First, although public figures and celebrities have chosen careers that attract media attention, they are still entitled to have their private lives. Therefore, the media should respect their rights to privacy by only reporting the public aspect of the celebrities' actions. Then, the famous people can keep their public and private lives separate. After all, the judgement of public figures should be based on what they do professionally, not on the irrelevant gossip of their private lives.

Another reason why I disagree with the statement is that the mass media can be classified as a form of commercial activities. They report news in exchange for money. Paparazzi are a good case in point. They relentlessly follow stars with their camera to get bits of their candid personal lives. Then they sell the photos for hundreds of dollars. To a different degree, the mass media also profits by digging up the private sides of public figures' lives.

Lastly, when the media spends time investigating a person's private life, it takes time away from other important issues. I do not want to hear about the extramarrital affairs of an actress. Rather, I want to know what's happening in the real world. There are numerous important political, economic, and social developments that should be focused on. The main function of the mass media is to report meaningful news that matters to the general public's lives.

Although I admit that the gossip about famous people's lives attract my attention, I disagree that the mass media has the rights to invade their privacy. They have rights to privacy just like any other citizen, and the media should respect it. Taking profits by violating a person's privacy is just immoral. Besides, there are many other important news items that should be covered by the media.

Sample Essay Translation

신문의 1면을 장식하는 유명한 여배우들의 이름이 그 어떤 경제 혹은 정치관련 기사보다 사람들의 눈길을 끄는 것은 사실이다. 이러한 사실을 파악한 언론은 공인과 연예인의 일거수일투족을 보도한다. 이로 인해 연예인들은 종종 사생활을 침해 당하고 심지어 그들의 활동하는데 있어 피해를 입을 수도 있다. 그렇다면 과연 언론이 다른 사람의 사생활을 대중에게 공개할 권한이 있는지 물어보지 않을 수 없다. 나는 다음과 같은 이유로 대중매체가 유명인들의 사생활을 보도해도 된다는 데 동의하지 않는다.

첫째, 비록 공인이나 연예인들이 언론의 관심을 끄는 직업을 선택하긴 했지만, 그래도 사생활을 보호 받을 권리는 있다. 따라서 언론은 그들의 사생활을 존중하여 그들의 언행 중 공적인 측면만을 보도해야 한다. 그래야 비로소 유명인들은 자신의 공적인 생활과 사적인 생활을 각각 영위할 수 있다. 공인에 대한 평가는 그들의 활동을 기반으로 내려져야지 활동과는 상관없는 사생활 관련 가십을 기반으로 내려져서는 안 된다.

언론이 유명인들의 사생활을 보도해도 된다는 데에 동의하지 않는 또 다른 이유는 대중매체가 일종의 상업활동으로 분류될 수 있기 때문이다. 언론매체는 돈을 받고 소식을 전한다. 파파라치가 대표적인 사례이다. 그들은 유명연예인들의 사생활을 알아내기 위해 카메라를 들고 그들을 끈질기게 따라다닌다. 그리고는 수백 달러를 받고 사진을 판다. 정도의 차이는 있겠지만, 언론매체 또한 유명인의 생활 중 사적인 측면을 캐냄으로써 이익을 낸다.

마지막으로, 언론이 누군가의 사생활을 알아내기 위해 시간을 보낸다면, 그만큼 중대한 사안을 취재할 시간을 뺏기는 것이다. 나는 여배우의 혼외정사에 대해 듣고 싶지 않다. 그보다는 세상에서 어떠한 일들이 벌어지고 있는지에 대해 알고 싶다. 언론이 좀더 신경 써서 보도해야 할 중요한 정치, 경제, 사회 뉴스거리가 많다. 대중매체의 주요 역할은 일반 국민의 삶에 있어 의미 있는 소식을 전달하는 것이다.

물론 나도 유명인들의 사생활에 관한 가십에 관심이 있다. 하지만 언론이 그들의 사생활을 침해할 권리가 있다고는 생각하지 않는다. 유명인들도 다른 시민과 마찬가지로 사생활을 보호받을 권리가 있고, 언론은 이 권리를 존중해야 한다. 한 사람의 사생활을 침해함으로써 이익을 얻는 것은 도덕적으로도 옳지 않다. 게다가 언론이 취재해야 할 다른 중요한 뉴스들이 많다.

3 20세기의 가장 두드러진 변화

Basic Sentence

1. The 20th century has witnessed many changes both on technological and social fronts.
2. The advent of the Internet, in particular, has greatly contributed to improving the quality of our life.
3. Most people would agree that computers and the Internet were two of the most outstanding developments of this century.
4. This global network opened an interactive communication channel.
5. Thanks to the Internet, we can chat with people from around the world without even leaving our desks.
6. This real time two-way communication is one of the great benefits of the Internet.
7. Today's cellular phones are equipped with sophisticated functions.
8. With a cell phone, you can log onto to the Internet wherever you are and whenever you want.

Sample essay

The 20th century has witnessed many changes both on technological and social fronts. If I had to choose one change that should be remembered, I would definitely opt for the dramatic development in telecommunication. The advent of the Internet and cellular phones, in particular, has significantly contributed to improving the quality of our lives. Thanks to these two innovations, we can lead our social and business lives beyond limitations of time and geographical distances.

Most people would agree that computers and the Internet were two of the most outstanding developments of this century. Computers alone brought out meaningful changes to our lives. Producing and keeping records of information became much easier than when we had to resort only to typewriters. The contribution of the computers, however, has increased dramatically as they became linked to each other through a worldwide web, known as the Internet. This global network opened an interactive communication channel, thus connecting people beyond national boundaries. Thanks to the Internet, we can chat with people from around the world without even leaving our desks. The exchange of information and opinions became much smoother and swifter. Something that has happened on the other side of the globe is known to us almost instantly. We not only passively get the news but also actively participate by providing real time feedbacks on the event. This instant two-way communication is one of the great benefits of the Internet.

Another breakthrough in telecommunication is the development of cellular phones. Computers are not the only terminal through which one can access the Internet. Today's cellular phones are equipped with functions to transmit text and audio-visual materials through the Internet. In countries like Korea, the use of cell phones is so widespread that this new gadget has already become an essential part of one's life. This portable terminal allows people not only talk to each other but also to instantly retrieve information from the Internet. One no longer has to look for a payphone to call someone or a PC room to log onto the Internet. The cell phones provide all these functions wherever you are and whenever you want.

In conclusion, although there have been many important changes in the 20th century, I believe the advancement in telecommunications, represented mostly by the development of the Internet and cellular phones, is the most noteworthy change. The Internet almost eliminated the geographical limitations in pursuing effective social and business lives. Cellular phones also greatly contributed to saving our time and efforts by opening an instant channel for communication and information exchanges. Thanks to these innovations, we can lead much more comfortable and time-efficient lives.

Sample Essay Translation

20세기에는 기술적 그리고 사회적으로 많은 변화가 있었다. 만약 기억해야 할 변화 하나를 골라야 한다면, 나는 정보통신의 놀라운 발달을 선택할 것이다. 특히 인터넷과 핸드폰의 출현은 우리의 삶의 질을 향상시키는 데 상당한 기여를 했다. 이 두 가지 혁신 덕분에, 우리는 시간과 공간의 구애를 받지 않고 사회 및 경제활동을 할 수 있게 되었다.

대부분의 사람들은 컴퓨터와 인터넷이 금세기의 가장 뛰어난 기술발달이라는 데 동의할 것이다. 컴퓨터만 해도 우리의 삶에 의미 있는 변화를 가져다 주었다. 정보를 작성하고 기록하는 작업이 우리가 타자기에만 의존해야 했던 시절에 비해 훨씬 더 수월해졌다. 하지만 컴퓨터의 기여도는 컴퓨터가 인터넷이라고 알려진 월드와이드웹을 통해 서로 연결되면서 더욱 높아졌다. 이 글로벌 통신망으로 인해 쌍방향 커뮤니케이션 채널이 열리게 되어 각 국가의 사람들이 서로 연결되었다. 인터넷 덕분에, 우리는 우리의 책상에 앉아 전 세계 사람들과 채팅을 할 수 있다. 정보와 의견을 교환하는 일이 훨씬

더 원활하고 신속해졌다. 우리는 지구 반대편에서 일어나는 사건을 거의 즉시 알 수 있다. 이제 우리는 수동적으로 뉴스를 전달 받을 뿐만 아니라 그 사건에 대한 의견을 실시간으로 제공함으로써 적극적으로 참여하기도 한다. 이러한 즉각적인 양방향 커뮤니케이션이 인터넷이 제공하는 가장 큰 혜택 중 하나이다.

정보통신기술 발달에 있어 또 한 가지 특이할 만한 점은 바로 핸드폰의 개발이다. 컴퓨터만이 우리가 인터넷에 접속할 수 있는 유일한 단말기가 아니다. 오늘날의 핸드폰에는 인터넷을 통해 문자 및 음성-영상 메시지를 전송할 수 있는 기능이 탑재되어 있다. 한국 등의 나라에서는 핸드폰 보급률이 너무 높아서, 이 기기는 이미 필수품이 되어버렸다. 이 휴대용 단말기는 사람들이 서로 통화할 수 있게 해 줄 뿐만 아니라 인터넷에서 정보를 찾을 수 있게도 해 준다. 이제는 누군가에게 전화하기 위해 공중전화기를 찾거나 인터넷에 접속하기 위해 PC방을 찾을 필요가 없다. 핸드폰이 이 모든 기능을 우리가 원하는 장소와 시간에 제공하기 때문이다.

결론적으로 20세기에 중요한 변화가 많이 발생하긴 했지만, 나는 인터넷과 핸드폰의 개발로 대표되는 정보통신의 발달이 가장 두드러진 변화라고 생각한다. 인터넷으로 인해 우리가 사회, 경제활동을 하는 데 따르는 지리적 제약이 거의 다 사라졌다. 핸드폰 또한 즉각적인 커뮤니케이션 채널을 엶으로써 우리가 시간을 절약하는 데 큰 기여를 했다. 이러한 혁신 덕분에, 우리는 훨씬 더 편하고 시간 효율적인 생활을 할 수 있게 되었다.

4 기술 발전과 학습

Basic Sentence

1. Computer technology has greatly improved the way we get information.
2. Through the Internet, students can gather information with a click of the mouse.
3. It is certainly more convenient to sit at home and do research using your computer.
4. Students now have a wealth of information available to them through the Internet.
5. They have access to library databases around the globe.
6. Students nowadays can benefit from distance learning.
7. Computer technology has only further distracted students from learning.
8. Most students use computers and the Internet to play games and chat with friends.
9. The computer has become another source of entertainment.
10. In many cases computer technology hinders the student's true learning.

Sample Essay

The 20th century has brought about many technological developments in every aspect of our lives. Sophisticated machines have made our work much easier than before. This is also the case with our learning activities. Thanks to the invention of computers, in particular, we can learn new information much quicker and easier. Although some people may disagree with this, I personally think that computer technology has significantly contributed to our learning in both its quantity and quality for the following reasons.

Firstly, the Internet and the World Wide Web have opened every major library and database to students around the world. In the past, we had to resort only to local libraries to look for needed information. But now the Internet, which is open 24 hours a day and seven days a week, has given us access to resources beyond the geographical and time limitations. This unlimited, easy access allows students to get more information and learn it more quickly.

Another beauty of computer technology is that it has created an interactive learning environment. Unlike books, where the learners only passively receive the information, the computer and the Internet make it possible for learners to exchange opinions not only with the author of the book but also with other readers. This "dialogue" is, in fact, the most effective form of acquiring knowledge. The massive exchanges of e-mails between college students and professors testify such effectiveness.

Lastly, the computer technology diversified the types of information that students can use to learn. While books give us only written messages, the computer and its related equipment are offering audio-visual materials as well. In foreign language education, for example, audio materials play an important role in providing accurate pronunciation. Nowadays, with the help of the Internet websites based on audio-visual materials, many students are learning English-as-a-foreign-language more quickly and easily than before.

In sum, technology, especially computer-related technology, has made our lives more convenient than ever. Despite its unintended drawbacks, I believe that the computer and the Internet are making learning easier and quicker. As long as we are aware of the problems and willing to solve them, I think we have a lot to gain from this ever-developing technology.

Sample Essay Translation

20세기에는 우리 삶의 모든 측면에서 수많은 기술발달이 이루어졌다. 최첨단 기계로 인해 우리는 예전보다 훨씬 더 수월하게 일을 할 수 있게 되었다. 우리의 학습 활동도 마찬가지다. 특히 컴퓨터의 발명 덕분에 우리는 훨씬 더 빠르고 쉽게 새로운 정보를 접할 수 있다. 물론 동감하지 않는 사람도 있겠지만, 나는 다음과 같은 이유로 과학기술이 학습의 양과 질 모든 면에 있어 상당한 역할을 했다고 생각한다.

첫째, 인터넷과 월드와이드웹(www)으로 인해 주요 도서관과 데이터베이스가 전 세계 학생들에게 공개되었다. 과거에는 필요한 정보를 찾기 위해서는 지역 도서관을 찾는 길밖에 없었다. 하지만 이제는 언제든지 접근 가능한 인터넷 덕분에 시간과 공간에 구애받지 않고 모든 정보를 활용할 수 있게 되었다. 이러한 무제한적이며 쉬운 접근성은 학생들이 더 많은 정보를 얻고 이를 더 빨리 배울 수 있도록 해준다.

컴퓨터 기술의 또 다른 장점은 쌍방향 학습 환경을 제공한다는 것이다. 학습자들이 정보를 수동적으로만 받아들여야 하는 책과는 달리, 컴퓨터와 인터넷은 학습자들이 책의 저자뿐만 아니라 다른 독자들과도 의견을 교환할 수 있도록 해 주었다. 이 같은 대화가 사실상 가장 효과적인 형태의 학습방법이다. 대학생들과 교수들이 방대한 양의 이메일을 주고받는다는 사실이 바로 이러한 학습효과를 입증한다.

마지막으로 컴퓨터 기술로 인해 학생들이 학습에 활용하는 정보의 종류가 다양해졌다. 책은 우리에게 문자로 된 정보만을 제공하는 반면, 컴퓨터와 관련 기기들은 오디오-영상 자료까지 제공한다. 특히 외국어 교육에 있어 오디오 자료는 정확한 발음을 들려 주는 등 매우 중요한 역할을 한다. 오늘날 오디오-영상 자료를 기반으로 한 인터넷 웹싸이트의 도움으로 많은 학생들이 영어를 예전보다 더 빠르고 쉽게 배우고 있다.

요컨대 기술, 특히 컴퓨터관련 기술로 인해 우리의 생활은 그 어느 때보다 더 편리해졌다. 비록 의도하지 않은 단점도 있긴 하지만, 나는 컴퓨터와 인터넷이 학습과정을 더 쉽고 빠르게 만들어주고 있다고 믿는다. 컴퓨터 기술이 갖고 있는 문제점들을 인식하고 이를 해결하려는 의지가 있는 한, 나는 끊임없이 발달되는 이 기술로부터 많은 것을 얻을 수 있다고 생각한다.

5 친구의 수

Basic Sentence

1. We all need friends, both in times of trouble and in times of happiness.
2. By surrounding oneself with many friends, he or she can get diverse experiences.
3. I want to have a lot of friends around me, so I can learn new things from different people.
4. Outgoing people tend to prefer being with a large group of people.
5. With one or two friends, one can establish a more solid, deeper relationship.
6. You can share your personal problems and get some psychological comfort.
7. Another benefit of such a deep relationship is that one can save time in deciding what to do with friends.
8. An individual's personality and preferences definitely influence the number of friends she wants to be with.

Sample Essay

Some people prefer to be around a large number of friends, while others want to be with only one or two close friends. It is difficult to say which is a better way of spending time because the choice depends on one's personality and preferences. As for me, though at times I like being with many people, I prefer a smaller group.

Spending time with a large number of friends can be a lot of fun and helpful. To some people, more company equals more fun. Since you are with many different kinds of people, you can learn new things from them. This way you can catch up on more varieties of social issues. The diverse experiences that you can get from your large pool of acquaintances may enrich your relationship. Usually outgoing people tend to prefer this type of friendship. They find diverse experience more important than deeper relationships with one or two friends.

Surrounding oneself with just a couple of friends, on the other hand, has its own advantages as well. First of all, one can establish a more solid, deeper friendship. Though having a bunch of friends around may be entertaining, it does not create a setting for private, intimate conversations. With one or two friends, you can share your personal problems and get some psychological comfort. Although some people may say that such a small circle of friends may be boring, I prefer to have quality time with my friends. Shy, quiet people often prefer this kind of friendship.

Another benefit of such deep relationship is that one can save time in deciding what to do with friends. In a large group, it usually takes much more time and trouble to reach an agreement on what to do together. Different people mean different opinions and tastes. With just one or two friends, however, the decision can be made more easily and quickly. It's certainly much easier to go places, for example, with only a couple of friends. The trip would be much more enjoyable and time-efficient.

An individual's personality and preferences definitely influence the type of group in which he or she wants to be. Though there may be some exceptions, usually outgoing people prefer to be around a large number of people, while quiet ones spend time with a couple of friends. Given the quality time I can have with a small circle of close friends, I personally prefer the latter type of friendship. I value the in-depth conversation with a close friend much more than the excitement of being in a large group.

Sample Essay Translation

어떤 사람은 많은 친구들과 함께 있는 것을 좋아하는 반면, 또 어떤 사람은 친한 친구 한 두 명하고만 있기를 원한다. 각각의 선택은 개인의 성격과 취향에 따라 다르기 때문에 둘 중 어느 것이 시간을 보내는 데 더 좋은 방법인지 말하기는 어렵다. 하지만 내 경우에는, 비록 가끔은 많은 사람들과 있고 싶기도 하지만, 몇 명하고만 있는 것을 더 좋아한다.

많은 친구들과 시간을 보내는 것은 재미도 있고 유익할 수도 있다. 어떤 사람은 함께 있는 친구가 많을수록 더 재미있어 한다. 다양한 종류의 사람들과 함께 있으면 그들에게서 새로운 점을 배울 수 있다. 그렇게 함으로써 여러 가지 사회 이슈를 접할 수 있다. 많은 사람들을 앞으로 해서 얻을 수 있는 다양한 경험들은 우리의 대인관계를 풍요롭게 할 수 있다. 보통 외향적인 사람들이 이러한 유형의 우정을 더 좋아한다. 그들은 다양한 경험이 한두 명의 친구와 깊이 사귀는 것보다 더 중요하다고 생각한다.

한편, 한두 명의 친구하고만 사귀는 것도 나름대로의 장점이 있다. 첫째, 보다 탄탄하고 깊은 우정을 맺을 수 있다. 많은 친구들을 사귀는 것이 재미있을지는 몰라도, 개인적이고 친밀한 대화를 할 수 있는 분위기는 조성되지 않는다. 한두 명의 친구와는 우리의 개인적인 고민을 털어놓고 또 그들로부터 정신적 위안을 받을 수 있다. 소수의 친구를 사귀면 지루할 것이라고 말하는 사람들도 있지만, 나는 나의 친구들과 의미 있는 시간을 보내고 싶다. 내성적이고 조용한 사람들은 보통 이러한 유형의 우정을 선호한다.

이런 깊은 관계의 또 다른 혜택은 친구들과 무엇을 할지 결정하는 시간을 절약할 수 있다는 점이다. 사람 수가 많으면, 함께 무엇을 할지에 대한 의견을 일치하는 것이 보통 어렵고 또 시간도 많이 걸린다. 사람이 많다는 것은 그만큼 각기 다른 의견과 취향이 많다는 것을 의미한다. 하지만 친구가 한 두 명밖에 없다면, 더 쉽고 더 빨리 결정할 수 있다. 예를 들어, 친구가 몇 명밖에 없으면, 어딘가에 가는 것이 훨씬 더 쉬워진다. 그 여행은 훨씬 더 즐겁고 시간효율적일 것이다.

한 사람의 성격과 취향은 그 사람이 어떤 환경을 좋아하는지에 분명히 영향을 미친다. 비록 예외가 있을 수는 있지만, 보통 외향적인 사람들은 많은 수의 사람들과 있기를 좋아하는 반면, 조용한 사람들은 한두 명의 친구들과 시간을 보내고 싶어한다. 한두 명의 친한 친구들과 의미있는 시간을 보낼 수 있다는 점을 고려할 때, 개인적으로 나는 두 번째 유형의 우정을 선호한다. 나는 친한 친구와의 깊이 있는 대화가 많은 친구들과 재미있게 보내는 것보다 더 소중하다고 생각한다.

6 직업 선택에 있어 돈의 중요성

Basic Sentence

1. Money is an important means of survival.
2. In most cases, one's career choice is made based on the pay.
3. The amount of money one can get from work plays the most crucial role in choosing a profession.
4. No matter how wonderful a job may be, we cannot hold it for a long time without a decent pay.
5. I strongly disagree that the most important factor in choosing a job is the money we earn.
6. We often tend to think that higher-paying jobs are more rewarding that lower-paying ones.
7. One's tastes and tendendies should be serioulsy considered when choosing a creer.
8. If we think only about the pay, it will be hard for us to hold the job for a long time.

Sample Essay

Holding a job is an important part of our lives. Some people start working right after finishing high school, while others after graduating from university. Regardless of the educational level, we all have to choose a career when we step into the adult life. The pay one can get from a job definitely plays a crucial role in the choice, but I disagree that it is the most important aspect of a job.

First of all, money is one of the many aspects that we have to consider but not the single most important one. One of my teachers, for example, once told us that he was reluctant to get into the teaching profession because of the low pay. In terms of money, it was much more profitable for him to become an office worker than a high school teacher. Now after 20 years of teaching, he says that he was wise enough to consider aspects other than the pay. Although he might have made some more money, he can't imagine himself working stuck in an office for his entire life. He is very happy with his career choice.

The wage is just one kind of reward we get from work. We often tend to think that higher-paying jobs are better and more rewarding than lower-paying ones. But that's not always the case. Sense of satisfaction, achievement, and worthiness are other forms of reward that we can get from a job. I love teaching and have no doubt that I'll become a teacher when I have to choose a career. As my high school teacher said, this profession is not the most attractive one in terms of pay. However, I know I will get greater satisfaction and happiness by doing something that I consider meaningful not only for me but also for society.

Lastly, a career-choice should be made based on our tastes and tendencies, since we spend most of our time working. If we spend only a small fraction of our time and effort on work, our preference will not matter much. But the truth is that many of us have to spend most of our time at a workplace. Therefore, it is important for us to consider what we can do and would like to do best. If we consider only the pay of a job, it will be hard for us to bear the work for a long time. If I hold a profession that I can do best while enjoying it, I will be able to withstand the hardship involved in the work.

In sum, I clearly disagree with the statement that money is the most important aspect of a job. Money is one of the many critical factors to consider when choosing a profession but not the single most important one. Sense of satisfaction and worthiness are also meaningful reward we get from a job. Besides, our competence and preference should be considered when making a career choice as well.

Sample Essay Translation

직장에 다니는 것은 우리 삶의 중요한 부분이다. 어떤 사람들은 고등학교를 졸업하자마자 일을 하기 시작하고, 또 어떤 사람들은 대학을 졸업한 후에 일을 하기 시작한다. 학력과 상관없이 우리 모두는 현실세계에 발을 딛는 순간 직업을 선택해야 하는 문제에 당면한다. 직업 선택에 있어 봉급의 수준이 결정적인 역할을 하긴 하지만, 나는 그것이 직업의 가장 중요한 요인이라고 생각하지는 않는다.

무엇보다 돈이란 우리가 고려해야 할 많은 사항 중 하나이지만 그 중 가장 중요한 것은 아니다. 일례로, 우리 선생님 중 한 분께서는 낮은 봉급 때문에 교사가 되기를 꺼려했었다고 언젠가 말씀하셨다. 금전적인 측면만 본다면, 고등학교 선생보다는 회사원이 되는 것이 훨씬 더 나았다. 하지만 교편을 잡은 지 20년이 지난 지금 그 선생님께서는 돈 이외의 요소들을 감안하기를 참 잘했던 것 같다고 말씀하신다. 회사원이 되었더라면 물론 돈은 더 벌 수 있었겠지만, 자신이 평생을 사무실에 틀어박혀 일하는 모습을 상상할 수 없다는 말씀이시다. 그는 자신이 선택한 직업에 매우 만족해하셨다.

월급은 우리가 일을 통해 얻는 많은 보상 중 한 가지에 불과하다. 우리는 종종 월급을 적게 주는 직장보다 월급을 많이 주는 직장이 더 좋고 더 보람 있다고 생각한다. 하지만 항상 그런 것만은 아니다. 만족감, 성취감, 보람 등도 우리가 일을 통해 얻을 수 있는 것들이다. 나는 가르치는 일이 좋고, 앞으로 직업을 선택해야 할 때 교사가 될 것이라고 자신 있게 말할 수 있다. 우리 고등학교 선생님이 말씀하신 것처럼, 이 직업은 봉급을 생각하면 가장 매력적인 직업은 아니다. 하지만 나는 나뿐만 아니라 사회를 위해서도 의미 있다고 생각하는 일을 할 때 보다 많은 만족과 행복을 느낄 것이라는 점을 알고 있다.

마지막으로 우리가 대부분의 시간을 일하면서 보내기 때문에 직업은 개인의 취향과 성향을 고려하여 선택해야 한다. 만약 우리가 일을 하는 데 쓰는 시간과 노력의 양이 얼마 안 된다면, 우리가 그 일을 좋아하느냐 마느냐는 그다지 중요하지 않을 것이다. 하지만 우리가 깨어 있는 시간의 대부분을 직장에서 보내는 게 현실이다. 따라서 우리가 무엇을 가장 잘 하는지, 그리고 어떤 일이 하고 싶은지를 고려해야 한다. 만일 월급수준만 보고 직업을 선택한다면, 그 직장에서 오랫동안 견디기가 힘들 것이다. 반대로 내가 가장 즐기고 또 가장 잘 할 수 있는 직업을 갖는다면, 일에 따르는 어려움을 잘 견뎌낼 수 있을 것이다.

요컨대, 나는 직장생활에 있어 돈이 가장 중요한 요소라는 주장에 동의하지 않는다. 돈은 직업을 선택할 때 감안해야 할 많은 사항 중 하나이긴 하지만, 그 중 가장 중요한 것은 아니다. 성취감과 보람 등도 우리가 일을 통해 얻을 수 있는 의미 있는 보상이다. 또한 직업을 선택할 때에는 각자의 능력과 취향도 고려해야 한다.

7 광고의 유익성

Basic Sentence

1. These days we are bombarded with constant commercials.
2. The whole point of advertising is to encourage us to buy things we don't need.
3. We spend a lot of money trying to keep up with our neighbors.
4. Advertising is a necessary evil that forces us to live a lifestyle beyond our budget.
5. Advertising is the best way to tell people about a new product that can improve their lives.
6. Today's consumers are smart enough to tell whether a commercial is a false ad or not.
7. Companies should always keep in mind that today's consumers cannot be fooled by useless advertising.
8. The majority of ads inform us about new products and services that could improve the quality of our lives.

Sample Essay

Compared to the past, these days we are surrounded by constant commercials coming from different media. Television, radio, newspapers, and the Internet are all full of advertisements promoting new products and services. You may want to run away from all these messages trying to sell you things. But the truth is that they actually make our complicated modern lives easier. Without the help of the information we get from the ads, it would be much more difficult and confusing for us to decide what to buy. Therefore, I personally think that in general commercials play a positive role in improving our lives.

First, advertising is the best way to tell us about new products that can enhance our lives. Everyday tons of new products and services hit the market. Some of them can make our lives more comfortable and convenient. Yet, since there are so many new things being released at the same time that it is difficult for ordinary consumers to tell the difference among them. Advertising helps us discern which product and service will really improve the quality of our lives. Recently, I saw an advertisement for an air purifier on a cable channel. The ad was very detailed and showed me all the benefits of having the air purifier in an apartment. I bought the product and am happy with my purchase. Thanks to the clean air coming from the purifier, I have had headaches less frequently.

Successful advertising does not always mean successful products. Today's consumers are smart enough to tell whether a commercial is a false ad or not. Businesses cannot sell the products simply by posting a fancy advertisement. They have to provide quality products that match the message of their advertising. Otherwise, they will lose their consumers' trust. If the air purifier had not been as good as the advertisement claimed, I would have returned the product and never bought that company's product again. However, since I liked the quality of the air purifier, I know that the company is trustworthy. This consumer's trust is one of the keys to success in the business world. Companies and advertisers should always keep in mind that today's consumers cannot be fooled by useless, ungrounded advertising.

It is true that some advertisements may try to sell us things that we really do not need. However, the majority of them inform us about new products and services that could improve the quality of our lives. As long as we have an eye to tell which ones are false ads, I think we can get some handy information about things that can be useful to us. Besides, such marketing policies as free refund service make our decision based on advertisement much easier than before. If you don't like what you've purchased, you can just return it. Since companies are aware of this, they are very unlikely to promote false ads.

Sample Essay Translation

과거와 달리 오늘날 우리는 각종 언론매체를 통해 끊임없이 쏟아져 나오는 광고들로 둘러싸여 있다. TV, 라디오, 신문, 그리고 인터넷은 새로운 상품과 서비스를 선전하는 광고들로 가득 차있다. 당신은 물건을 팔려고 하는 이러한 메시지로부터 도망치고 싶어 할지 모른다. 하지만 사실 이러한 광고들은 복잡한 현대생활을 더 수월하게 만들어 준다. 광고가 제공하는 정보의 도움이 없다면, 무엇을 살지를 결정하는 일이 훨씬 더 어렵고 힘들 것이다. 따라서 개인적으로 나는 광고들이 대체로 우리의 삶을 향상시키는 데 긍정적인 역할을 한다고 생각한다.

첫째, 광고는 우리의 생활을 향상시킬 수 있는 새로운 상품에 대해 알 수 있는 최선의 수단이다. 매일같이 수많은 신제품과 서비스가 시장에 나온다. 어떤 것들은 우리의 생활을 더 편안하고 편리하게 만들 수 있다. 하지만 동시에 출시되는 상품들이 너무나도 많기 때문에 일반 소비자들이 이 모든 상품들의 차이를 알 수 있기란 쉽지 않다. 광고는 실제로 우리의 삶의 수준을 끌어올릴 수 있는 상품과 서비스가 어떤 것들인지 구분할 수 있도록 도와 준다. 최근에 나는 케이블 TV에서 공기청정기 광고를 하나 보았다. 광고는 매우 상세했고 아파트에서의 공기청정기 사용이 어떤 장점을 갖고 있는지 보여 주었다. 나는 그 제품을 샀고 내 결정에 매우 만족해한다. 청정기에서 나오는 깨끗한 공기 덕분에, 나는 예전만큼 자주 두통을 앓지 않게 되었다.

광고가 성공적이라고 해서 제품 또한 성공적인 것은 아니다. 오늘날의 소비자들은 똑똑해서 허위광고와 그렇지 않은 것을 구별할 줄 안다. 기업은 멋진 광고만 내보내서는 제품을 팔 수 없다. 광고의 내용에 걸맞은 고품질 제품을 제공해야 한다. 만약 내가 산 공기청정기가 광고가 주장했던 것만큼 좋지 않았다면, 나는 제품을 반품하고 다시는 그 회사의 제품을 사지 않았을 것이다. 하지만 공기청정기의 품질이 마음에 들었기 때문에, 나는 그 회사가 믿을 만한 회사라는 것을 안다. 이러한 소비자 신뢰가 기업 성공의 가장 중요한 요소 중 하나이다. 기업과 광고주는 쓸모없고 근거 없는 광고로 오늘날의 소비자들을 기만할 수 없다는 사실을 항상 기억해야 한다.

물론 우리가 정말 필요하지 않은 물건을 팔려고 하는 광고도 있을 수 있다. 하지만 다수의 광고는 우리의 삶의 질을 향상시킬 수 있는 새로운 제품과 서비스에 대해 알려 준다. 나는 우리가 허위광고를 식별할 줄 아는 눈이 있는 한, 광고에서 우리에게 필요할 수 있는 물건에 대한 유용한 정보를 얻을 수 있다고 생각한다. 게다가, 무료 환불 서비스와 같은 시장 메커니즘은 우리가 광고를 보고 결정을 내리는 일을 예전보다 더 쉽게 만들어 준다. 만일 구매한 물건이 마음에 들지 않는다면, 그저 반품하면 그만이다. 회사들도 이러한 점을 알고 있기 때문에, 허위광고를 할 가능성이 거의 없다.

8 외국어 습득

Basic Sentence

1. Children can benefit from studying foreign languages at an early age.
2. here is no good reason to start foreign-language instruction the moment a child begins school.
3. Trying to learn two different languages at once may be too difficult for a child.
4. The child may become confused, and end up learning neither language well.
5. There are both advantages and disadvantages to beginning foreign language education at an early age.
6. Nowadays, English as a foreign language is in great demand.
7. Early foreign-language education faciliates acquisition of the language.
8. A child can learn many foreign languages at once without hampering acquisition of his native language.
9. Study after study support such facts.
10. It is beneficial for children to learn about another country through foreign language study because it can broaden their horizon.

Sample Essay

In general, people agree that at least one foreign language, especially English, is necessary to be successful in today's society. However, they do not show such a solid consensus as to when to start learning English. Some argue that the sooner we start learning it, the better off we will be. Others, however, oppose English language learning at an early age saying that it will hamper their native language acquisition. I, personally, believe that early foreign language education is beneficial for the following reasons.

First of all, a young child can learn a foreign language much easier and quicker than an adult. They do not take it as something that they have to analyze and memorize. Rather, they approach the language the way they do their mother tongue. They learn it naturally without being bothered by complicated grammar rules. Some linguists scanned the brains of a child and an adult while they were speaking a foreign language. To our surprise, they were found to be using different parts of their brain for the same activity. The adult used the section of the brain that specializes in analysis, while the child used the part that is utilized for one's native language processing.

Those who oppose early foreign language learning often argue that it will damage a child's first language acquisition. However, study after study has shown that a child can learn many languages at the same time as long as the "one-person one-language" principle is respected. When the consistency is maintained, a child can learn up to nine languages at once without losing his or her native language. Although nine is too many, I believe one foreign language won't disturb the child's first language development.

Lastly, early exposure to a foreign language will help a child to have a broader perspective. We live in a globalized world, where the social and economic exchanges across national boundaries have become a part of our lives. By learning a foreing language from an early age, a child can learn about different cultures and lifestyles as well. This will help him develop a more cosmopolitan view. Besides, by learning others' language and culture, one can understand and appreciate one's own language and culture better.

In conclusion, given the above benefits, I agree with the statement that children should start learning a foreign language as soon as they start school. I even believe that they should be exposed to a foreign language much earlier than that. Not only is the acquisition of the language easier at an early age, but it also provides the child with a wider world perspective.

Sample Essay Translation

대체로 사람들은 오늘날 사회에서 성공하기 위해서는 최소한 하나의 외국어, 특히 영어는 필수적이라는 데 동감한다. 하지만 영어를 배우기 시작해야 하는 시점에 대해서는 그만큼 탄탄한 공감대를 형성하지 못하고 있다. 어떤 사람들은 영어를 일찍 배울수록 더 유리할 것이라고 주장한다. 하지만 다른 사람들은 모국어 습득에 걸림돌로 작용한다며 조기 영어 학습에 반대한다. 나는 다음의 이유로 조기 외국어 교육이 필요하다고 생각한다.

무엇보다 어린 아이는 어른에 비해 훨씬 더 쉽고 빨리 외국어를 배울 수 있다. 아이들은 외국어를 분석하고 암기해야 하는 것으로 인식하지 않고 모국어를 습득하는 것과 똑같은 방법으로 외국어를 배운다. 복잡한 문법에 구애 받지 않고 자연스럽게 배우는 것이다. 몇몇 언어학자들이 외국어를 하는 아이와 어른의 뇌를 검사해 봤더니, 놀랍게도 외국어로

똑같은 활동을 하면서도 아이와 어른이 각각 뇌의 다른 부위를 사용하고 있다는 사실이 발견되었다. 어른은 뇌에서 분석을 담당하는 부분을 사용하는 반면 아이는 모국어 처리를 담당하는 부분을 사용하고 있었던 것이다.

조기 외국어 교육에 반대하는 사람들은 이것이 모국어 습득을 저해한다고 주장한다. 하지만 수많은 연구 결과, "1인 1언어" 원칙이 지켜지는 한 아이들은 동시에 여러 언어를 배울 수 있다는 사실이 드러났다. 이러한 일관성이 유지된다면, 아이들은 모국어를 잃지 않으면서 한꺼번에 최고 아홉 개의 외국어를 배울 수 있다. 아홉 개는 좀 많은 감이 없지 않지만, 한 개의 외국어를 배운다고 모국어 습득에 방해가 되지는 않을 것이라고 생각한다.

마지막으로, 일찍이 외국어에 노출된 아이들이 좀더 폭넓은 사고의 틀을 갖게 된다. 오늘날 우리는 국가 간 사회 및 경제 교류가 삶의 일부가 되어버린 세계화 시대에 살고 있다. 아이들은 어린 나이에 외국어를 배움으로써 다양한 문화와 생활양식에 대해서도 배울 수 있다. 이는 아이가 보다 넓은 시야를 가질 수 있도록 도울 것이다. 게다가 다른 나라의 언어와 문화를 배움으로써 자국의 언어와 문화 또한 더 잘 이해하고 더 소중하게 생각하게 된다.

위와 같은 혜택을 감안할 때, 나는 아이들이 학교에 들어가자마자 외국어를 배우기 시작해야 한다는 주장에 동의한다. 나는 심지어 그보다 더 이른 시기에 외국어에 노출되어야 한다고 믿는다. 어린 나이에 외국어를 공부하는 아이는 그만큼 더 쉽게 배울 수 있을 뿐만 아니라 더 넓은 세계관을 갖게 된다.

Writing Answers

Actual Test

Task 1

수력전기

Reading Translation

수력전기는 가장 좋은 에너지원 중 하나이다. 깨끗하고, 재생가능하고, 믿을 만하며 환경정책목표에도 부합한다. 수력전기는 떨어지는 물을 이용해 운동에너지를 전기로 변환한다. 가파른 경사지를 따라 흘러 내리는 강물은 수전 생산에 적합하다. 강 맨 꼭대기는 댐으로 막혀 있고, 계곡은 물로 차서 큰 저수지, 혹은 호수를 형성한다. 댐 상층부의 수문을 열어 물이 터널을 따라 터빈으로 흘러 들어가게 한다. 물은 터빈을 움직이는 동력이 되고, 터빈은 발전기를 돌린다. 발전기에서는 전기가 생산된다. 한편 이 전기는 케이블을 통해 목적지로 운반된다. 또, 햇빛으로 바다와 호수의 물이 증발하면서 구름이 형성되고, 이 구름은 비가 되어 산 위에 떨어져 댐에 물을 공급해 준다.

수력전기는 대단히 효율적이다. 터빈을 돌리기 위해 열을 필요로 하지도, 방출하지도 않기 때문이다. 그렇기 때문에 수력전기는 매우 저렴하다. 소비자가격은 1kwh 당 3센트 정도인데, 가격이 이렇게 저렴할 수 있는 이유는 수력발전시설 가동비가 비교적 적게 들기 때문이다. 물은 절대 고갈되지 않는 연료이므로, 수력전기는 재생가능하고 지속가능하다. 수력전기를 생산하기 위해서는 최소한의 시설만이 필요하다. 댐과 관련 시설물만 건설된 후에는, 이를 운영할 관리자만 있으면 된다. 댐은 홍수를 훌륭하게 억제할 수 있고, 흘러 내리는 물의 비율도 조정할 수 있다. 전기는 끊임없이 생산될 수 있고, 풍력, 태양력, 혹은 파력 전기보다 훨씬 더 믿을 만하다.

수력전기는 방사선이나 오염물질을 배출하지 않기 때문에, 환경에 미치는 영향 또한 미미하다. 수력발전은 운영비가 저렴할 뿐만 아니라 관광 및 휴양 활동을 증가시키기 때문에, 수력전기는 훌륭한 에너지원이다.

Listening Script

Professor

Now, hydroelectricity ··· as I'm sure you know ··· is widely used in the United States for generating electric power. Unfortunately, though, there have been some ··· uncalculated andunpredicted drawbacks of this type of electricity. For one thing, the initial cost of building a dam is extremely high — hundreds of millions of dollars — and the length of time to complete one is also prohibitive.

However, one of the biggest drawbacks is the negative impact that a dam has on wildlife. I can see by your faces that you've heard that a dam doesn't harm the environment. Well ··· that's only true if you're talking about radiation or pollution. In fact, the creation of the reservoir floods the surrounding land and destroys the habitats of the animals that live there. And it doesn't just affect the animals, either. People who live in the area must be uprooted from their homes to find housing elsewhere, usually at greater cost. In the end, the impact of a dam can destroy forests, reduce biodiversity, and disrupt fisheries.

Salmon are one of the victims of dam-building. They have to swim upstream to spawn, but when they try to do that, they're stopped by the manmade dam built right in the middle of their river. In some cases, fish "ladders" have been built to help the salmon "climb" the series of dams to get to their spawning grounds. But where that has not happened, salmon are stuck ··· unable to reproduce.

And … as if all that weren't enough … it's recently been discovered that hydroelectric plants emit greenhouse gases that can lead to global warming. These gases are similar to those given off by thermal power plants. These gases come from the decomposition of the biomass in the reservoirs and from biomass flowing in from the river's catchment area.

Listening Translation

교수

자, 수력전기란 … 여러분도 알겠지만 … 미국에서 전력을 생산하기 위해 흔히 사용되고 있다. 하지만 안타깝게도, 수력전기와 관련된 몇 가지 예측하지 못했던 단점들이 발견되었다. 첫째, 댐 건설에 드는 초기비용이 수억 달러에 달해 지나치게 높은 수준이다. 또한 준공기간도 엄청나게 길다.

하지만, 가장 큰 단점 중 하나는 댐이 야생생물에 미치는 부정적인 영향이다. 여러분의 표정을 보니, 댐이 환경을 해치지 않는다고 들었던 것 같은데 … 그건 방사선이나 오염물질이 방출되지 않는다는 선에서만 사실이다. 사실, 저수지를 만들면 그 주변지역이 침수되고 그 곳에 사는 동물들의 서식지가 파괴된다. 또 동물들에게만 영향을 미치는 것도 아니다. 그 지역 주민들은 자신들의 집을 떠나 다른 데에서 살 곳을 찾아야 한다. 보통 더 많은 비용을 지불하고 말이다. 결국에는, 댐의 영향으로 산림이 파괴되고, 생물다양성이 줄어들고, 어장이 파괴된다.
댐 건설로 인한 희생자 중 하나가 연어이다. 연어들은 산란기가 되면 물 위로 헤엄쳐 가야 하는데, 강 한 가운데에 건설된 인공 댐 때문에 그렇게 하지 못한다. 어떤 경우에는, 연어들이 산란지에 도달하도록 일련의 댐을 "올라가게" 하기 위해 "어제"를 만들기도 했다. 하지만 그렇지 않은 경우에는, 연어들은 오도가도 못해 번식할 수 없게 된다.

그리고 … 그것도 모자라 … 최근에는 수력발전소가 지구온난화를 야기하는 온실가스를 배출한다는 사실이 발견되었다. 이 가스는 열 발전소에서 방출되는 것과 비슷하다. 이 가스들은 저수지 안의 바이오매스와 강의 집수 지역으로부터 흘러 들어오는 바이오매스가 분해되면서 생기는 것이다.

Answer

Hydroelectric power has many things to recommend it. It is cheap power, once you get past the initial cost of building a dam. It's clean power; it doesn't generate any radiation or pollution. It's a low-maintenance type of power, requiring only a few supervisory people on hand to keep it going. And it's both a reliable and a renewable energy source. It even increases tourism, which brings money into the area where it is located. These factors make it far better than nuclear or other forms of power. However, there are some unfortunate drawbacks to hydroelectric power as well. When the dam is built, the flooding of the area destroys wildlife habitats and displaces the people who live there.

Dams pose a problem for salmon, too. Salmon have to swim upstream to spawn, and with dams in the way, the salmon cannot get to their spawning grounds. The only way around the problem is to build special fish "ladders" that enable the salmon to make their way up the dam in steps so they can reach their spawning grounds.

Recently, it has been found that there is an additional drawback to hydroelectric dams. They give off greenhouse gases. This is due to the decomposition of biomass in the reservoirs, and it is a serious problem because it contributes to global warming.

Answer Translation

수력전기는 많은 장점을 가지고 있다. 댐 건설에 드는 초기 비용만 치르고 나면, 매우 저렴한 전력이다. 이는 방사선이나 오염물질을 많이 배출하지 않는 깨끗한 전력이다. 관리가 수월하여 수전발전기를 가동할 관리인 몇 명만 있으면 된다. 그리고, 수전은 믿을 만하고 재생가능한 에너지원이다. 하지만, 안타깝게도 수력전기에는 몇 가지 단점들도 있다. 댐을 건설하면, 주변지역이 침수되어 야생생물의 서식지가 파괴되고 그 곳 주민들은 이재민 신세가 된다.

댐은 연어들에게도 문제가 된다. 연어들은 알을 낳기 위해 물 위로 올라 가야 하는데, 댐이 길을 가로막고 있어 연어들이 산란지에 도달할 수 없다. 이 문제를 해결하기 위한 유일한 방법은 특수 "어제"를 만들어 연어들이 계단을 올라 물 위로 헤엄쳐 갈 수 있게 만들어 주는 것이다.

최근에는 수력전기의 또 다른 단점이 발견되었다. 수력전기는 온실가스를 배출한다. 이는 저수지에 있는 바이오매스가 분해되면서 일어나는 현상이며, 지구온난화를 유발하기 때문에 심각한 문제가 되고 있다.

Task 2

새 공휴일 제정

Key Ides

—의미 있는 사건이어야 한다.

—인터넷 발명일을 새 공휴일로 정하겠다.

—그 날 사람들은 게시판에 인테넷에 대한 의견을 주고 받는다.

Vocabulary Brainstorming

기념하다 commemorate, honor

역사적 인물 historial figure

공휴일을 만들다 create a holiday

인터넷 the Internet, the worldwide web, the Net

발명하다 invent, create

혁명적으로 바꾸다 revolutionize

의사 소통하다 communicate

의사소통 통로 communication channel

실시간의 real time

정보 공유 sharing information

전세계 사람들 people across the world

온라인 on-line, virtual

메시지를 올리다 post messages

Basic Sentence Writing Practice

1. 대부분의 공휴일들이 역사적 인물이나 사건을 기념하는 것은 사실이다.

 …라는 점은 사실이다 It is true that + 절
기념하다 commemorate, honor, celebrate
역사적 인물 historial figure, person

2. 만약 새 공휴일을 만들 수 있는 권한이 내게 주어진다면, 나는 인터넷 날을 선택할 것이다.

 … 할 권한이 주어진다면 If I were given the authority + to 부정사
공휴일을 만들다 create a holiday / designate a holiday

3. 우선, 인터넷은 사람들이 서로 의사 소통하는 방식을 혁명적으로 바꾸었다.

 혁명적으로 바꾸다 revolutionize, dramatically change / transform
의사 소통하다 communicate
서로 each other, one another

4. 그러나 각 방법은 각각의 단점들을 갖고 있다.

 '그러나' however : 문장 중간에 쉼표 사이에 however를 넣어도 좋다.
각각의 its respective
단점 drawback, shortcoming, diadvanta problem

5. 인터넷은 이 모든 문제를 해결하고 하나의 효과적인 의사
소통 통로로 떠올랐다.

> (연구) 문제를 해결하다 solve / address / straighten
> out / deal with / correct a problem
> …로 떠오르다 emerge as
> 의사소통 통로 communication channel

6. 사람들은 그들이 관심이 있는 거의 모든 것에 대한 즉각적
인 피드백을 받을 수 있다.

> (연구) 즉각적인 피드백 instant feedback
> 거의 almost, practically, basically
> …에 관심있다 be interested in

7. 실시간 정보 공유는 이 발명의 중요한 혜택 중 하나이다.

> (연구) 실시간의 real time
> 정보 공유 sharing of information, information
> sharing도 okay!
> 중요한 important, vital, essential, critical,
> primary
> 혜택 중 하나 one of the benefits of …

8. 전세계 사람들이 정부가 만든 공식 온라인 게시판에 메시
지를 올릴 수 있을 것이다.

> (연구) 전세계 사람들 people across the world, people
> around the world
> 메시지를 올리다 post messages
> 온라인 게시판 on-line / virtual bulletin board

Basic Sentence

1. It is true that most holidays commemorate an important historical figure or event.
2. If I were given the authority to create a new holiday, I would choose "Internet Day".
3. First of all, the Internet revolutionized the way people communicate with each other.
4. Each method has, however, its respective shortcomings.
5. The Internet solved all these problems and emerged as an effective communication channel.
6. People can get instant feedback on basically everything they are interested in.
7. The real time sharing of information is one of the essential benefits of this invention.
8. People across the world could post messages on an official on-line bulletin board made by the government.

Sample Essay

It is true that most holidays commemorate an important historical figure or event. August 15th, for example, honors the day Korea gained its independence from Japanese Colonial rule. Americans also celebrate the same event on its Independence Day, July 4th. This similarity between the two countries far away apart validates the fact that holidays generally are designated based on a meaningful event or person. If I were given the authority to create a new holiday, I would choose the day on which the Internet was first used. I believe the significance of the Internet is as large as any other historical events.

First of all, the Internet revolutionized the way people communicate with each other. Before its invention, people relied on phones, mails, and direct contacts to exchange opinions. Each has, however, its respective shortcomings. Mail, for example, is too slow to deliver the message, while the phone is too expensive to exchange lengthy conversations. Personal contacts, on the other hand, are limited by time and space constraints. One has to be there to communicate with someone. This is something you cannot do if you have to talk to a large number of people. The Internet solved all these problems and emerged as an effective communication channel. It's fast, inexpensive, and free from time and space limitations. One can talk to a person or a large group of people on the other side of the globe instantly without leaving his desk. The Internet not only overcame the disadvantages of previous communication tools but also added the additional advantages of comfort and convenience.

Thanks to this innovative communication channel, people can get instant feedback or share their opinions on basically everything they are interested in. The real time sharing of information is one of the essential benefits of this invention. The speed and the convenience of the worldwise web even changed people's minds and attitudes on many aspects of life. They tend to take on a more active role and participate more in social events. The accessibility made such involvement much easier.

On the new Internet holiday, I would like people to go to huge on-line bulletin boards prepared by the government. There they could post their opinions about the significance and the future course of the computer use, in general, and the Internet, in particular. They might explain how e-mails and web sites became an integral part of their everyday life. The government could give awards to the best stories based on their originality. This holiday event will hopefully make people recognize the value of this precious communication tool. At the same time, new, meaningful suggestions as to the future course of the Internet could be gathered directly from its ordinary users.

The Internet still holds some problems to overcome such as spam e-mails and mistreatment of private information. Nevertheless, it has dramatically transformed the way we exchange information. Given its social, historical values, I believe the Internet holiday will be as meaningful as any other holidays. The constructive opinions posted on the official bulletin board on that day will also contribute to further development of this innovative technology. Who knows? In the future, we may really have a holiday called "Internet Day".

Essay Translation

대부분의 공휴일이 중요한 역사적 인물이나 사건을 기념하는 것은 사실이다. 예를 들어, 8월 15일은 한국이 일본의 식민 지배로부터 해방된 날을 기념한다. 미국인들도 7월 4일에 독립기념일 행사를 갖는다. 멀리 떨어져 있는 이 두 나라 사이의 이러한 공통점은 공휴일이 대체로 의미있는 사건이나 인물을 중심으로 제정된다는 사실을 입증해 준다. 만약에 나에게 새로운 공휴일을 제정할 수 있는 권한이 주어진다면, 나는 인터넷이 최초로 사용된 날을 선택할 것이다. 나는 인터넷이 다른 역사적 사건만큼이나 중요하다고 믿기 때문이다.

먼저 인터넷은 사람들이 서로와 의사 소통하는 방식을 송두리째 바꾸어 놓았다. 인터넷이 발명되기 이전에는 사람들은 편지, 전화, 직접만남 등을 통해 서로 의견을 주고받았다. 하지만 이러한 방법은 각각 나름대로의 문제점을 안고 있다. 예를 들어, 편지는 메시지를 전달하는 데 너무 오랜 시간이 걸리며, 전화는 오랜 통화를 하기엔 너무 돈이 많이 든다. 한편, 직접만남은 시간과 공간의 제약을 받는다. 누군가와 대화하기 위해서는 직접 그 곳에 있어야 하기 때문이다. 많은 사람들과 이야기해야 할 경우에는 사실상 불가능한 방법이다. 인터넷은 이러한 모든 문제를 해결하면서 효과적인 커뮤니케이션 수단으로 부상하였다. 인터넷은 빠르고, 저렴하고, 시간과 공간의 제약을 받지 않는다. 인터넷 사용을 통해, 우리는 우리의 책상을 떠나지 않고도 지구 반대편에 있는 사람들과 실시간으로 대화를 나눌 수 있다. 인터넷은 기존 커뮤니케이션 수단의 단점을 극복했을 뿐만 아니라 편안함과 편리성이라는 새로운 장점을 가져다 주었다.

이 혁신적인 커뮤니케이션 수단 덕분에, 사람들은 사실상 거의 모든 관심분야에 대해 서로 의견을 교환할 수 있게 되었다. 실시간 정보 공유는 인터넷 발명에 따르는 가장 큰 혜택 중 하나이다. 월드와이드웹의 속도와 편리성은 삶에 대한 사람들의 생각과 태도까지도 바꾸어 놓았다. 사람들은 사회 활동에 보다 적극적인 역할과 참여를 하게 되었다. 바로 접근성(accessibility)으로 인해 이렇게 사회에 참여하는 게 훨씬 더 쉬워졌기 때문이다.

새롭게 제정되는 인터넷 날에는, 사람들이 정부가 준비한 대형 온라인 게시판을 찾았으면 한다. 거기서 넓게는 컴퓨터 사용, 그리고 좁게는 인터넷의 중요성과 앞으로 나아갈 방향에 대한 자신들의 의견을 올릴 수 있을 것이다. 또는 이메일과 웹싸이트가 어떻게 우리의 삶의 일부가 되었는지에 대해 설명할 수도 있다. 정부는 독창성을 기준으로 최고의 글을 쓴 사람에게 상을 줄 수 있다. 인터넷의 날이라는 공휴일을 계기로 사람들이 이 소중한 커뮤니케이션 수단의 가치를 재평가하게 될지도 모른다. 동시에 인터넷이 앞으로 나아갈 방향에 대한 참신하고 의미있는 건의사항을 일반 사용자들로부터 직접 받을 수 있는 기회가 될 것이다.

인터넷은 여전히 스팸 메일과 개인정보 도용 등 해결해야 할 문제점을 안고 있다. 그럼에도 불구하고 인터넷은 우리가 정보를 교환하는 방법을 대대적으로 변화시켰다. 인터넷의 사회적 역사적 가치를 감안할 때, 나는 인터넷의 날이 그 어떤 공휴일만큼이나 의미 있을 것이라고 확신한다. 그 날 공동게시판에 올라오게 될 건설적인 의견들은 이 혁신적인 기술이 더더욱 발전되는데 기여할 것이다. 실제로 미래에 인터넷의 날이라 불리는 공휴일이 생길지 누가 아는가.

Independent Writing
Further Writing Practice
Answers

1. Do you want to live in a big city or in a small town?

(어떤 이들은 작은 타운에 살기를 선호하고 다른 이들은 대도시에 살고 싶어한다. 여러분은 어떤 곳에 살고 싶은가요? 구체적인 이유와 내용을 들어 여러분의 대답을 뒷받침하시오.)

모범답안

1. Since I have lived in both a small town and a big city, I have experienced the good and bad sides of the two places.

2. Personally, I prefer to live in a big city rather than a small town.

3. Having lived in a big city for ten years, I can' t imagine myself living in a small town.

4. In a big city, you can do many things day or night.

5. I grew accustomed to the variety of entertainments available in big cities.

6. In a big city, you can live without a car because public transportation is very convenient.

7. Since supermarkets are open 24 hours, you can go shopping at your convenience.

8. Another good thing about living in a city is the variety of cultural activities available.

9. People in the city can live in the same apartment building for twenty years and never get to know their neighbors.

10. All in all, big cities offer more opportunities and excitement than small towns.

2. Eating at restaurants Vs. Eating at home

(어떤 사람들은 외식을 선호한다. 다른 사람들은 집에서 음식을 마련해 먹는 것을 선호한다. 당신은 어떤 쪽이 좋습니까? 당신이 선호하는 쪽을 설명하고 당신의 대답을 뒷받침 해 줄 예들을 제공하시오.)

모범답안

Eating at home

1. I prefer to eat at home for the several reasons mentioned below.

2. Overall, it is less expensive to eat at home than to eat out.

3. While restaurants may save you time, they certainly do not save you money.

4. Even a fast food lunch costs more than a lunch made at home.

5. Cooking food at home provides more control over the specific ingredients.

6. At home, portion size can be controlled so as to prevent overeating.

7. In fact, eating food at home saves more time than eating out; considering the time spent driving to a restaurant, parking, waiting for service, and driving home.

8. I usually get sick when I eat fast food too often.

9. I like to eat fresh foods, but fast food restaurants usually pre-cook their food.

10. While I enjoy eating at nice restaurants, I wouldn't be able to afford to do so everyday.

11. Cooking at home is both less expensive and healthier than eating out.

Eating out

1. Some people enjoy eating out regularly.

2. For me, going to a restaurant is the best option for many reasons.

3. Those with very busy jobs outside the home do not have time to cook.

4. They like the convenience of eating out.

5. Though I enjoy cooking, I eat at restaurants as often as possible.

6. Many people think that eating out is expensive, which is not necessarily true.

7. Some restaurants have low prices and thus, are very affordable.

8. There is another benefit to eating at a food stand or a restaurant.

9. When eating out, the food is prepared and delivered to the table without your lifting a finger.

10. At restaurants, there is no worry about the clean up after the meal.

11. Eating at restaurants takes up much less time than cooking food at home.

12. If I could afford to, I would eat out every day.

13. In conclusion, I prefer eating out because it saves time and is very convenient.

3. The effects of human activities on the Earth

(어떤 사람들은 지구가 인간 활동으로 인해 상처받고 있다고 믿는다. 다른 이들은 인간 활동이 지구를 더 살기 좋은 곳으로 만든다고 느낀다. 여러분의 의견은 무엇인가요? 구체적인 이유와 예를 들어 여러분의 대답을 뒷받침하시오.)

모범답안

1. From the human perspective, the Earth is a much more convenient place to live in than it was in the past.

2. From the environmental point of view, however, the Earth has become polluted through human activities.

3. Rivers and streams, for example, have been contaminated by unchecked factory emissions.

4. In large cities, environmental concerns include air and water pollution.

5. Companies and communities dump waste into their water sources.

6. Another problem is that we are depleting our natural resources very rapidly.

7. One way to stop environmental pollution is by boycotting products from companies that cause environmental damage.

8. We can make the Earth a better place to live by pursing environmentally friendly alternatives.

9. Air pollution caused by cars is one of the gravest problems facing large cities.

10. In Seoul, for instance, there are campaigns that encourage the use of public transportation and carpools.

11. There should be more effective ways of getting rid of the garbage we produce than just burying it in landfills.

12. Companies should develop new alternative clean energy.

13. As consumers, we have to buy energy-saving products.

14. It is true that the overall quality of human life has improved immensely over the past few decades.

15. Still, there is a long way to go before human beings are able to solve such environmental problems as industrial waste and harmful chemicals.

4. Why do we now live longer than before?

(일반적으로, 이제 사람들은 더 오래 산다. 여러분의 에세이에서 구체적인 이유와 내용을 들어 이 장수 현상의 원인에 대해 논하시오.)

모범답안

1. I think there are several reasons why people are living longer now.

2. Two of the main reasons for longevity are improved health care and better nutrition, which are available to everyone.

3. Education, health care, and workplace safety all have played major roles in increasing longevity.

4. Although not everyone can get the best health care, everyone can get basic health care and advice.

5. When a person is informed about how to take care of her health, she often lives a longer, happier life.

6. The major factor extending our life span today can be attributed to the advancements made in medical science.

7. Long ago, since health care was not available to everyone, many people resorted to folk remedies.

8. The truth is that when better medicine and health care are available, the number of people who die at an early age gets reduced.

9. Today, doctors know more about what causes diseases and how to cure them.

10. Having access to quality health care can greatly affect longevity.

11. Now we have antibiotics and other medicines to help to cure infections.

12. Balanced nutrition has also greatly contributed to extending our life spans.

13. People try to eat low-fat foods and more vegetables and fruits, which are now available year-round.

14. Low-fat diets and foods with less salt have also contributed to extending peoples' lives.

15. In summary, thanks to increased health education, improved health care, and balanced nutrition, people can live much longer than before.

5. Friends different from you Vs. Friends similar to you

(어떤 사람들은 자기와는 다른 사람을 친구로 사귀고 다른 이들은 자기와 비슷한 사람을 친구로 사귄다. 여러분과 다른 친구를 사귀는 장점을 여러분과 비슷한 친구를 사귀는 장점과 비교하시오. 당신은 어떤 사람을 친구로 사귀고 싶습니까?)

모범답안

1. Being friends with people who are similar to or different from you has both advantages and disadvantages.

2. As for me, I like to make friends with people who are different from me.

3. For one thing, they often bring a new point of view to our lives.

4. You can also enjoy the various experiences that come from not having much in common with your friends.

5. On the other hand, friends who are different from us help us to try new things and to have new experiences.

6. People who have friends with different tastes tend to appreciate differences of opinion.

7. Someone who is different from you generally won' t have the same reaction to a given situation as you.

8. It can be interesting and informative to share our opinions and tastes with people who differ greatly from us.

9. On the other hand, it can be difficult to maintain friendships that do not have common interests.

10. First, friends with common interests tend not to argue about what to do because they usually enjoy doing the same thing.

11. And since they are similar, they likely have much in common with one another.

12. Besides, it is enjoyable to spend time with those who see life from the same vantage point as we do.

13. Moreover, having similar tastes helps to deepen the level of trust and friendship possible between two people.

14. Since they most likely think alike, friends with similar tastes will seldom have any personality conflicts.

15. All things considered, I think it is preferable to have friends who are similar to me.

16. In my case, I find it rewarding to have both kinds of friends : those who are different from as well as those who are similar to me.

17. Finally, having many friends who are different from me enables me to share my views on life with people who have different perspectives.

6. Stress management

(사람들은 여러 다른 방식으로 스트레스와 현대 생활의 어려움에서 벗어난다. 어떤 이들은 독서나 운동을 하고, 다른 이들은 정원 가꾸는 일을 한다. 여러분은 스트레스를 줄이는 최선책이 무엇이라고 생각합니까? 구체적인 내용과 예를 들어 답하시오.)

모범답안

1. Stress is a major enemy of one' s health.

2. There tends to be a high level of stress in modern life.

3. People all over the world are becoming busier and busier.

4. As a result, one' s daily routine can be the cause of a great amount of stress.

5. The first step in eliminating stress is to identify the cause.

6. People can reduce stress in their lives by maintaining a healthy lifestyle.

7. Exercising and meditating are the best ways to lower one' s stress level.

8. Exercises such as walking give one the opportunity to get close to the nature.

9. Work-related stress is easier to combat than other types of stress.

10. Other times, I run on a treadmill for half an hour.

11. A good night' s sleep is another effective method in reducing stress.

12. Work-related stress can be lessened by taking a break from work for a while.

13. For some people, a positive attitude means looking for the good rather than the bad in situations and life experiences.

14. For others, stress stemming from relationships is considered to be the most difficult type of stress to relieve.

15. In conclusion, stress is a part of life, but one can reduce it by maintaining psychological and physical health.

7. Studying alone or with a group?

(일부 학생들은 혼자서 공부하길 좋아하고 다른 일부는 그룹으로 공부하길 좋아한다. 여러분은 어떤 공부 방식을 좋아 하는지 구체적인 이유와 예를 들어 여러분의 입장을 설명하시오.)

모범답안

1. Some people like to study alone, while others like to study in a group.

2. As for me, I prefer to study with a group of other students.

3. I have realized that studying alone is more effective for me.

4. Personally, I believe that both methods have advantages and disadvantages.

5. As for me, when I study by myself at home I get distracted very easily.

6. I make very little progress when I study alone at home because I take breaks whenever I want.

7. One advantage to studying in a group is that you can compare your notes with others' .

8. You can also learn others' perspectives on the topic through group discussions.

9. Once we decide when and where to study, we can easily concentrate on our study without getting distracted.

10. Of course, it doesn' t help if you are in a group that does not take studying seriously.

11. In addition, when studying together, you can find out what other people think.

12. Finally, there is nothing I enjoy more than talking with my friends about an intellectual topic.

13. In short, it has taken me many years to finally realize that I study better in a group.

14. In sum, since there are many different ways of studying, it is important for each person to find the method that fits him or her best.

15. In conclusion, whether you study alone or in a group depends a lot on your study habits and on your personality.

8. Do clothes influence our behaviors?

(다음 주장에 동의하나요, 아니면 반대하나요? 사람들은 다른 옷을 입으면 다르게 행동한다. 여러분은 다른 옷을 입는 것이 사람들의 행동 방식에 영향을 준다고 생각합니까? 구체적인 예를 들어 당신의 대답을 뒷받침하시오.)

모범답안

1. People behave differently depending on what they are wearing.

2. I agree that clothes affect behavior.

3. The clothes we wear affect our attitudes as well as our self-perception.

4. People treat us differently depending on the clothes we wear.

5. If you are wearing something elegant, you're likely to feel distinguished and important.

6. Furthermore, a person's identity is closely linked to the clothing that they wear.

7. If people wore the same clothes, they would not have to worry about what to wear everyday.

8. For this reason many people desire luxury items that they cannot afford.

9. For instance, if you wear your best suit to a job interview, you're likely to feel more self-assured.

10. Most people try to dress appropriately to different occasions.

11. Since people may judge us according to what we are wearing, the way we dress certainly has an impact.

12. In summary, style reflects identity, and thus people chose clothing that they feel it expresses who they are.

13. In short, what we wear affects our behavior.

9. Time alone Vs. Time with friends

(어떤 이들은 대부분의 자기 시간을 혼자서 보내는 것을 선호한다. 다른 이들은 다른 사람들 주변에 있고 싶어 한다. 여러분은 시간을 혼자서 보내길 좋아하나요, 아니면 다른 사람과 보내길 좋아하나요? 구체적인 예를 들어 여러분의 답변을 뒷받침하시오.)

모범답안

Time alone

1. If I had to choose between spending time alone and spending time with friends, I' d opt for the former.

2. When I am alone, I have time to both think about my goals and develop strategies to achieve them.

3. Although some people say that they feel lonely when there aren' t others around, I enjoy being alone because I can listen to the music and read the books that I love.

4. If our time is constantly spent in a group, we are likely to develop the group' s mentality.

5. When I am alone, I can decide on my own personal values without being influenced by the opinions of my friends.

6. It' s natural to desire the company of others, but I think that time spent by oneself is more valuable in the long run.

7. In sum, I prefer being alone because of the above reasons.

Time with friends

1. Though I enjoy spending time alone, I prefer to be with friends whenever possible.

2. Although I am pretty independent, I am also a highly social person.

3. We not only share laughs but also have serious discussions on diverse topics.

4. Whether it' s going to the movies or playing sports, it' s always better to be with friends than to be alone.

5. It is through my relationships with others that I best realize who I am and where I fit in the world.

6. I value my friends because of their loyalty and reliability.

7. If anything bad ever happens, I know my friends will be there to help me out.

8. In conclusion, I believe that life without friends is both limited and unfulfilling.

10. Should I read only books on real events?

(다음 주장에 동의하나요 아니면 반대하나요? 사람들은 실제 사건, 실제 인물, 확실한 사실에 관한 책들만 읽어야 한다. 구체적인 이유와 내용을 들어 여러분의 의견을 뒷받침하시오.)

모범답안

1. It is hard to agree with the idea that only books about real, factual things are worth reading.

2. Since reading is a form of entertainment, people should be encouraged to read whatever they find enjoyable.

3. Fictional stories open up our world and help us develop our creativity.

4. It is true that one can learn a great deal of practical information from non-fiction books.

5. Yet, reading fictional accounts of the world or fictional novels helps to develop one's imagination.

6. Although there is a wealth of information in non-fiction books, we should not downplay the value of fictional stories and novels.

7. In fact, storytelling is an emotional need of human beings that must be met if we are to have full, rich lives.

8. However, you can learn much about values, morals, and hopes from the fictional writings found in literature, poetry, and drama.

9. These stories help us experience a wide range of emotions in a variety of contexts.

10. In the Information era, the more knowledge you have, the better off you are.

11. Children who read many stories are more likely to use their imaginations and see the world from a wider perspective.

12. Fictional stories play a crucial role in the formation of culture and tradition.

13. As early as childhood, we should be exposed to both fiction and non-fiction.

14. Choosing what to read is a personal choice based on one's tastes and tendencies.

15. Although biographies and history books are valuable, fictional writings rooted in the world of philosophy and arts can be equally valuable.

16. In fact, we learn most of life's most important lessons from our childhood stories.

11. A new factory in your neighborhood

(한 기업이 여러분의 지역사회 부근에 큰 공장을 하나 짓는다고 발표했습니다. 여러분 공동체가 받을 새로운 영향의 장단에 대해 논하시오. 여러분은 공장 설립을 찬성하나요 반대하나요? 여러분의 입장을 설명하시오.)

모범답안

1. Most industries and factories bring both good and bad things to a community.

2. If a company announced that it would build a factory in my community, I would likely have mixed emotions.

3. A new factory often brings many new jobs and increased prosperity.

4. There are advantages and disadvantages to building a factory.

5. The decision to support the building of a new factory in your community must be made after weighing both its positive and negative aspects.

6. I oppose the plan to build a factory in my community because the risks involved outweigh the benefits.

7. In addition, factories often create environmental pollution, and this can harm a community's quality of life.

8. Another concern is that the community will experience a sudden increase in population, which, in turn, will cause a severe housing shortage.

9. As a result, the traffic congestion will worsen.

10. Certainly, many communities would welcome a new factory that can offer employment to their people.

11. The factory will create many new jobs, which will decrease unemployment and bring more money into the community.

12. The increased tax revenue will enable the community to offer new facilities and services.

13. As long as it does not harm the environment, I support the building of a new factory in my community.

14. In short, the decision to support or oppose a new factory must be based on the needs and wants of the community.

15. Since I feel the drawbacks are greater than the benefits, I cannot support a plan to build a new factory here.

12. The influence of movies and televisions

(영화나 텔레비전은 사람의 행동에 어떻게 영향을 줄까요? 구체적인 이유와 예를 들어 여러분의 대답을 뒷받침 하시오.)

모범답안

1. In my opinion, television and movies influence people's actions in both good and bad ways.

2. I believe that movies and television do influence our behavior, for the better or for the worse.

3. Television can be an important educational tool.

4. Moreover, during the last few decades movies and television have had an enormous effect on the attitudes of people all over the world.

5. If people are careful and selective when choosing what they watch, they can learn a lot from TV programs.

6. Of course, watching movies and television can also be good for us.

7. Some programs help to educate people about different races and lifestyles.

8. Seeing movies can help people overcome prejudices they have about different races and cultures.

9. At the same time, there are many violent and sexually improper TV programs and movies.

10. TV programs often influences our behavior in negative ways.

11. The more violent acts we witness on television, the less sensitive we become to them in reality.

12. There is excessive violence in movies and on television because programs have found that violence sells.

13. If people watch too much TV, they will become passive because they stop using their own imagination.

14. In conclusion, the influences can be either positive or negative depending on the program or movie.

15. In other words, how they affect you depends on how much you watch, what you watch, and how you respond to what you watch.

13. A working teenager student

(어떤 나라에서는, 십대들이 학교를 다니면서 일을 한다. 여러분이 이것이 좋다고 생각하나요? 구체적인 이유와 내용을 들어 여러분의 의견을 뒷받침하시오.)

모범답안

Agree

1. I think teenagers should be allowed to have a part-time job after school.

2. I believe the benefits far outweigh the drawbacks.

3. As long as a teen knows that school comes first, I find no problem with letting her work a few hours a day.

4. Working teens will learn to use their time efficiently.

5. While working, teenagers will come to realize how hard it is to earn money

6. At least, they will not take their parents' support for granted.

7. It is crucial, however, that parents make it clear from the beginning that school is the top priority.

8. All things considered, I think a teenager has more to gain by having a small after-school job.

Disagree

1. There are many reasons why I do not support the idea of a teenager working while still a student.

2. First and foremost, the high-school curriculum in Korea places heavy demands on full-time students.

5. For a teenager, school is likely to come second to work.

6. Jobs bring money but money is not everything at this age.

7. By entering the work world too early, they will lose much of their innocence.

8. In conclusion, I do not think it is a good idea for teenagers to have jobs while attending high school for the reasons I stated above.

14. The qualities of a good neighbor

(이웃들은 우리 근처에 사는 사람들이다. 당신 생각에는 무엇이 좋은 이웃의 자질들인가요? 구체적인 내용과 예를 당신의 대답에 사용하시오.)

모범답안

1. Most people live in areas where they have at least one or two neighbors.

2. Consider yourself lucky if you have good neighbors.

3. Respect is the most important quality of a neighbor.

4. Neighbors live close together, thus respect for each other's privacy is a necessity.

5. A good neighbor will also be respectful of your property.

6. For example, he or she will ask your permission before doing anything that may infringe upon your space.

7. This means that before fixing a fence he or she will ask your permission.

8. There is potential for a neighbor to become like a part of your family.

9. Neighbors can take care of each other's houses while they are away on vacation.

10. In the same vein, a good neighbor will take care of your children if you have to work overtime.

11. Good neighbors help to make each other's lives easier.

12. Neighbors should also be conscientious; being aware of their noise levels.

13. People need to be careful about how loud they are so that they don't disturb the people around them.

14. Good neighbors greet each other when they come in contact.

15. Lastly, neighbors can act as important people in our lives.

15. Growing up in the countryside Vs. Growing up in a big city

(아이들은 대도시 보다는 시골에서 자라는 것이 좋다. 이 주장에 대한 여러분의 찬성이나 반대 입장을 구체적인 이유와 예를 들어 논술하시오.)

모범답안

1. Growing up in the countryside has benefits, but in my opinion it is better for children to grow up in a big city.

2. Growing up in the country means a certain amount of isolation.

3. One reason I feel big cities are better is that children will have more people to interact with.

4. In the countryside, the people you meet everyday tend to be just like you.

5. It is easier in a city for children to socialize on a daily basis with neighbors and friends than in the country.

6. City dwellers tend to come from many different places and to move around a lot.

7. Children can gain more cultural experiences growing up in a big city.

8. For example, a child who lives in the countryside may find it more difficult to go to a museum.

9. In the countryside, there are no cinemas, theaters, or museums, so children who grow up there won't be exposed to these cultural experiences very often.

10. A child growing up in the city has the advantage of being able to visit many interesting places.

11. Moreover, there are more opportunities for children to participate in extracurricular activities in a city.

12. I grew up in a big city and appreciate all the opportunities it afforded me.

13. Children from the country do not have these opportunities because they live so far away from urban centers.

14. All in all, I think it is better for children to grow up in a city because it prepares them better for the real world.

15. In short, it is my opinion that a city is the best place for a child to grow up.

16. Quick decisions Vs. Slow decisions

(신속하게 결정을 내릴 수도 있고 조심스럽게 생각해 보고 결정을 내릴 수도 있다. 빨리 내린 결정은 항상 잘못된다는 주장에 여러분은 동의하나요, 아니면 반대하나요? 당신의 입장을 근거와 예를 들어 뒷받침하시오.)

모범답안

Disagree

1. Although carefully thought-out decisions are usually best, sometimes it is necessary to make quick decisions.

2. While quick decisions are often risky, I have made many quick decisions that worked out very well.

3. Sometimes one simply sees or thinks of something and instantly knows that it is the right decision to make.

4. Not all decisions are difficult to make, thus, not all require the same amount of time for consideration.

5. Though some decisions require careful consideration based on knowledge and expertise, some of my best results have come from quickly-made decisions.

6. Moreover, some people are just better decision makers than others and therefore can make the right decisions faster.

7. In conclusion, I do not agree with the statement that all quick decisions are wrong.

Agree

1. A quick decision often fails to take into account all the factors concerning a situation.

2. Unlike a fast decision, a carefully deliberated decision is usually backed by experience and expertise.

3. If a person makes a decision that will greatly influence the course of his or her life without serious consideration, he or she will surely regret it later.

4. On-the-spot decisions often neglect important factors that may affect the outcome of the decision.

5. That is why it is always advisable, if possible, to take some time before making an important decision.

6. To avoid errors in judgment, decision-making should always be based on cautious and careful thinking.

7. A minute spent thinking before making a decision may save much time and difficulty later.

8. In short, although some people are able to make good decisions quickly, I personally prefer to allow some time for careful consideration before making a decision.

17. Life-time employment

(기업들은 평생직 직원들을 채용해야 한다. 당신은 이에 찬성합니까, 아니면 반대합니까? 구체적인 논증과 예를 사용해 당신의 대답을 뒷받침하시오.)

모범답안

Disagree

1. To me, the factors governing today's workforce are job performance and ability to change.

2. Loyalty to the company is no longer a major consideration in hiring an employee.

3. Nowadays competition is very steep. Workers are hired based on their ability to successfully perform a task.

4. If employees are hired for lifetime, it will become less possible for young and dynamic workers with new ideas to join the company.

5. While it would be wonderful if businesses offered lifetime contracts, in today's global economy this is simply impractical.

6. We need new workers with a fresh point of view.

7. Lifetime contracts are a thing of the past.

8. Employee' work ethic may decrease in the knowledge that they have secured a lifetime job.

9. Companies need to adjust to new technology by bringing in new employees, rather than keeping those employees with outdated skills.

10. Skilled workers tend to prefer freedom of movement over commitment to a single company.

Agree

1. I agree with the idea that businesses should hire employees for their entire lives.

2. In some business cultures, workers are hired at a young age and employed until they retire.

3. Based on such idea, I think it is foolish for a company to overlook the value of an experienced worker.

4. Keeping employees on the job can save a company time and money as there will be less need for continual job training.

5. Employees that have worked with one company for a long time tend to be very loyal to their employers.

6. Therefore, these workers are more willing to endure temporary pay cuts if the company is undergoing hard times.

7. In the same way, companies have a moral obligation to contribute to the communities that they belong to.

8. Overall, lifetime employment benefits both employers and employees.

18. Vacation Vs. A car

(여러분 친구 중 하나가 돈을 약간 받고 휴가를 가거나 자동차를 구입하는 데 그 돈을 모두 사용할 계획이다. 그 친구가 여러분에게 조언을 구했다. 친구가 계획하는 2가지를 비교하고 여러분이 생각하기에 그 친구는 어떤 선택을 해야 하는지를 설명하시오. 구체적인 이유와 내용을 들어 여러분의 선택을 뒷받침하시오.)

모범답안

Go on a vacation

1. Money decisions are always difficult, especially when one wants to spend a large sum.

2. If my friend is faced with such a decision, I would recommend that he go on a vacation.

3. Of course, a vacation would give us lasting memories.

4. Some might say that it is impractical to spend money on a vacation, as the investment is so temporary.

5. Taking time away from school or work helps to rejuvenate and restore peace of mind.

6. The immediate benefits of a vacation include relaxation and relief from stress.

7. A vacation is an opportunity to escape from all that is familiar and to see the world from a new perspective.

8. Therefore, I would recommend going on a vacation rather than investing in a new car.

Buy a car

1. First, there is no doubt that a car will last longer than a vacation.

2. Driving a car can be very enjoyable.

3. The advantages of a private car are quite substantial.

4. First and foremost, there is the convenience of not having to depend on public transportation.

5. One needs to consider that owning a car includes insurance costs, maintenance, fuel costs, and parking fees.

6. A car can take one virtually anywhere, and thus there is less need to depend on others.

7. A car has many more uses including the transportation of heavier objects.

8. Thus, taking into account both usefulness and convenience, buying a car would be a better investment.

19. Borrowing money from a friend

(친구에게서 돈을 빌리는 것이 때로는 우정을 해치고 다치게 할 수 있다고들 말한다. 여러분도 동의하나
요? 구체적인 예와 이유를 들어 이에 대한 여러분의 찬성이나 반대 입장을 설명하시오.)

모범답안

1. I agree that borrowing money from a friend can harm or damage the friendship.

2. Close relationships can be ruined with the exchange of money coming into play.

3. Borrowing money can undermine the essential qualities of friendship.

4. It can cause resentment and awkwardness in the friendship.

5. If I borrow money from a friend, he or she will have power over me.

6. There is also the question of when you'll be able to pay back the loan.

7. It would be awkward if a friend would set a deadline for repayment.

8. All these issues can result in harsh feelings and severely harm the friendship.

9. Lastly, I wouldn't want to borrow money from a friend because it might destroy our
   trust.

10. In short, borrowing money from a friend is not a good idea.

11. More often than not, the friendship would be at risk.

12. Firstly, a good relationship is built upon a solid foundation of trust.

13. In times of need we often turn to our friends for help.

14. Paying back a loan on time is a matter of principle.

15. In the case of lending, one should never lend more money than one can afford to
    lose.

16. When you need money, borrow it from a bank : this may save your friendships.

20. Smoking in public places

(일부 국가에서는, 많은 공공장소나 사무실 건물에서 흡연이 금지되어 있다. 이러한 규칙이 좋은 것인지 나쁜 것인지 구체적인 이유와 내용을 들어 여러분의 입장을 설명하시오.)

모범답안

1. I strongly believe that it is a good idea to ban smoking in public places and office buildings for a number of reasons.

2. First of all, this law can prevent the damage caused by second-hand smoking.

3. Recent research has indicated that second-hand smoking causes cancer.

4. This measure will certainly please non-smokers because they do not have to breathe harmful air.

5. Some states in the U.S., such as California and New York, already ban smoking in public places including restaurants and cafes.

6. This will increase people's awareness of the risks entailed in smoking.

7. Many people have already died from smoking-related diseases including lung cancer.

8. If this law were implemented, it would improve smokers' health by helping them cut down on the number of cigarettes they consume.

9. Since they will have less opportunity to smoke, they will smoke fewer cigarettes.

10. The law will discourage young people from starting to smoke because it will show them the dangers that accompany smoking.

11. Smoking is a choice, but since other people's health is at stake, the choice should be made with careful consideration.

12. No one has the right to force others to suffer the negative consequences of smoking just because they do not want to quit.

13. As to the ban on smoking in office buildings, I believe that every worker has the right to be safe and healthy in his or her place of employment.

14. All in all, it is crystal clear that banning smoking in public places and office buildings is a good law.

15. What is more, I wish this law were implemented in our country as soon as possible.

iBT 토플 해결사
TOTAL iBT 토플 5총사!

- iBT토플 해결의 열쇠인 TOTAL Note-taking System 별책 무료 제공
- 실전 시험 10 Set에 달하는 다량의 문제 수록
- iBT 100점 돌파를 위한 고난이도 문제 엄선
- 영어 교육학 박사와 동시 통역사가 만든 전문 iBT 준비서

Total Reading

- 실전 수준의 고난도 지문 엄선
- 실전 시험 환경과 동일한 교재 구성
- 실전 RC 주제와 가장 근접한 지문

Total Listening

- 세계 최초로 전체 Script에 모범 Note-taking 수록
- 실전 시험 그대로 영국과 호주식 발음 녹음 추가

Total Speaking

- Model Speaking 답안은 물론 기본 말하기 문형까지 제공
- 통합형 문제를 위한 모범 Note-taking 수록

Total Writing

- 기본 문장 연습에서 완성된 Essay까지 단계별 학습
- 통합형 문제를 위한 모범 Note-taking 수록
- 여러 학생들이 고득점을 받은 검증된 Writing formula

Total Vocabulary

- 무한궤도 자동 암기 시스템으로 학습 효과 배가
- 예문 중심 구성으로 독해력까지 향상
- 문맥상의 의미 습득을 통한 iBT 토플형 어휘 학습

Note-taking Book
특별부록 제공

ISBN 89-91999-06-9

정가 18,000원

■ Listening Tape 별매 / ■ Speaking Tape 별매